365 DEVOTIONS

MOMENTS WITH YOU

DAILY CONNECTIONS FOR COUPLES

DENNIS & BARBARA RAINEY

WITH LAWRENCE KIMBROUGH

Regal

From Gospel Light
Ventura, California, U.S.A.

Published by Regal Books
From Gospel Light
Ventura, California, U.S.A.
Printed in the U.S.A.

Published in association with the literary agency of Wolgemuth & Associates, Inc.

Library of Congress Cataloging-in-Publication Data
Rainey, Dennis, 1948-
   Moments with you : 365 all-new devotions for couples / Dennis and Barbara Rainey.
      p. cm.
   ISBN 978-0-8307-4384-1 (hard cover)
   1.   Spouses—Prayers and devotions. 2.   Marriage—Religious aspects—Christianity. 3. Devotional calendars. I. Rainey, Barbara. II. Title.
   BV4596.M3R3555 2007
   242'.644—dc22
                                                                        2007015499

1   2   3   4   5   6   7   8   9   10   /   10   09   08   07

Rights for publishing this book outside the U.S.A. or in non-English languages are administered by Gospel Light Worldwide, an international not-for-profit ministry. For additional information, please visit www.glww.org, email info@glww.org, or write to Gospel Light Worldwide, 1957 Eastman Avenue, Ventura, CA 93003, U.S.A.

This book is dedicated to Randy and Kay Creech.

Thanks for your friendship,
for caring about godly families
and for "giving God all the glory!"

ACKNOWLEDGMENTS

Barbara and I have been surrounded by many top-notch people in our 31 years of leading FamilyLife. And although our names will be the ones that appear on the cover of this book, there is no question in our minds that a project of this magnitude would never have been accomplished without an "A+ Team." There's no way the word "thanks" captures our gratefulness and appreciation for each of you who helped. But here goes . . .

Lawrence Kimbrough and Dave Boehi: You two were masterful in researching, writing, editing and grabbing some very rough content and helping to craft it into a manuscript that really works.

Mary Larmoyeux: Thank you for how you researched, wrote and edited, and helped with a host of administrative details.

Rienk Ayers: What an eye and gift you have for editing and clarifying content. I'm glad this is one of your hobbies! You are a great partner and friend, in more ways than one!

Michele English: Your knowledge of where to find content and your researching, becoming a super sleuth at times, tracking legions of administrative details . . . and helping to serve our staff and constituents while we worked on this . . . is "heaven class."

Janet Logan and Todd Nagel: You all finish out a great team that is the best! Thanks for all you are and all that you do that helps build godly marriages and families.

Bill Eyster: Thanks for your leadership and friendship. You know that this book would *never* have been written if you hadn't answered the call and sacrificed much to help "Every Home, become a Godly Home." Thanks for still being "giddy."

Paula Dumas: You continue to amaze both of us! Thanks for basing your life and gifts on "The Kingdom Assignment" that He has for you. We are grateful God has given us the privilege of working together. We are glad you don't drive a Porsche!

Robert and Andrew Wolgemuth: We appreciate your hearts and professionalism. You have been a huge encouragement to us to keep writing.

Tammy Meyers: Thanks for your faithfulness, loyalty and commitment to excellence. You do what counts where it matters.

And Kim Bangs: You and the team at Regal knocked it out of the park! I'm grateful for your hearts, vision and execution.

INTRODUCTION

The longer we are married, the more we realize that a marriage needs constant nourishment—we need to spend time together working on our relationship. That's why we've created this new devotional—to encourage you to draw closer together. We promise you that as you spend "moments" reading, thinking, talking, and praying together, you *will* grow closer to God and one another.

You can expect that *Moments with You* will prompt a lot of conversation between you and your spouse over the things that *really* matter—the real issues of life, marriage and family. One of you could read the opening Scripture aloud, and then pass the book to the other to read the primary text. The discussion question gives you the opportunity to grapple and interact together with the biblical truths in each devotion—and you can't answer them with a grunt, or a yes or no! We've designed them to help you truly connect with one another—heart to heart.

Each devotion ends with a closing prayer, and we hope this simple exercise will turn into a regular part of your marriage. We believe if couples faithfully prayed together on a daily basis, they could decrease their chances of ever divorcing by 99.9 percent. Why? Because God intends for marriage to be a spiritual relationship consisting of *three*—not just a man and a woman, but the two of them and their God relating spiritually and remaining committed to each other for a lifetime. Wouldn't it be natural for God, the One who initiated the relationship, to want a couple to bring their troubles, worries, and praises to Him on a regular, daily basis?

We suggest that you find a consistent time to complete these daily devotions—a time when you won't be interrupted by the phone, the television, or the needs of family or friends. This may be early in the morning . . . or just before you go to sleep at night. If you will commit to doing this consistently, we're confident you will be pleased with what it does to your relationship.

One final feature of each devotional is the "Connect" link at the bottom. Each Internet link will lead you to additional resources—suggested articles, books, radio programs, and more—on that day's topic. We've selected some of the finest resources from leading marriage and family experts to give you greater understanding and help.

As we wrote in our first devotional, *Moments Together for Couples*, spending this time together "will be the best investment you could make." We guarantee it!

DENNIS & BARBARA RAINEY

MOMENTS
WITH YOU

FAMILY

God created man in His own image, in the image of God He created him;
male and female He created them.

GENESIS 1:27

I believe there is nothing more powerful on Earth than family. It is the single most influential force for good (or for evil) in all human existence.

From birth, it marks you. Your family crafts your conscience and shapes your soul. At home you learn life's lessons and begin the art of practicing them. At home you learn to love and to do what's right. More than merely giving you a street address, your home and family imprint you with a spiritual and sexual identity shaped by the two people who gave you life. Truly, nothing compares to the strength of being tightly wrapped in the protective fiber of family. It's who you are. It's where you belong.

And if all goes well—as it should—it is your family that surrounds you when you start life's journey, when you face life's hardest trials, when you go through the valleys and when you die. More than anyone else, the members of your family are the ones who are there for you, caring for you and mourning the loss of you when you're gone.

This should come as no surprise, because God created the family. At the very dawn of time, "God created man in His own image, . . . male and female He created them." Of all the ways He could have chosen to inaugurate His creation, He chose to start with family. In fact, the Bible begins with a marriage in Genesis and ends with a marriage in Revelation. Marriage and family have always been central to what God is doing on planet Earth.

I believe family is still of utmost importance to our heavenly Father. It holds the key to our health, our success as a society, and our future. And I believe it is worth whatever effort is required to nurture, encourage and support it.

Why not celebrate the family God has given you today?

DISCUSS

In what ways past and present has God blessed your life through your family?

PRAY

Thank God for the gift of your family, regardless of its inadequacies and failures.

I NEED YOU

The eye cannot say to the hand, "I have no need of you."
1 CORINTHIANS 12:21

I still remember the first time I told my mom and dad, "I love you." Being a typically ungrateful, unexpressive teenager, I found looking my parents in the eye and saying those three little words excruciating.

I also remember the first time I told Barbara I loved her. My heart was jumping wildly. Adrenaline was the only thing flowing faster than the beads of sweat on my forehead. I wasn't sure either one of us would survive the experience!

Those are hard words to say to someone for the first time, aren't they? Telling another person "I love you" represents risk and vulnerability. Yet there are three other words that are often even harder to express: "I need you."

"I *need* you."

Oh, at one time they flowed fairly easily from your lips. Think back to those early days of romance and intrigue. She made you laugh. He made you feel secure and stable. She brought warmth into a room. His sensitivity made you feel valued and important.

Yes, saying "I need you" came effortlessly at first. But sometime after your wedding day, the thief of familiarity can steal that sense of need. You go your own way. You think you know best. You figure you can do fine by yourself.

Isn't it interesting that in Genesis 2:18-25, Adam had to be *told* he had a need? God said, "It is not good for man to be alone" (verse 18). And even after that authoritative statement, Adam still had to name a few million creatures before he realized that none of them were what he needed. His need was for *someone*. He needed *her*.

Don't wait to be told what you already know to be true. You need her. You need him. Say it frequently and specifically.

DISCUSS

What keeps you from easily and openly admitting how much you need your spouse? Turn to your spouse and say, "I need you." Then share why and how you need him or her.

PRAY

Ask God to give you a true perspective on your own limitations—your own dependence on Him and on each other.

Get Connected for More Information
http://www.familylife.com/moments/communication

NEED BY EXAMPLE

Two are better than one because they have a good return for their labor.
ECCLESIASTES 4:9

I shared with you yesterday about three little words that aren't always so easy to say: "I need you." But sometimes, all it takes to get those words flowing again is just a reminder of how many ways you truly do depend upon each other.

You need your spouse for:

- *Honesty*—Who else knows you so well and can give you such an honest perspective on things when you need it most?
- *Variety*—How black-and-white and one-dimensional would your life be without someone to add color and texture to it?
- *Encouragement*—Who still believes in you when others don't—including yourself? Who helps you remember your uniqueness and significance?
- *Togetherness*—Who else can multiply your joys, divide your sorrows and add to your experience with God by sharing it together?
- *Counterbalance*—When you're going too fast, who helps you put on the brakes? When you're afraid to take a risk, who encourages you to go for it?
- *Understanding*—When you don't want to talk, who can draw you out? Who else can force you to be real and authentic with your emotions?
- *Parenting*—How could you raise your children without someone to temper your weaknesses, complement your blind spots and help reinforce your positions?
- *Romance*—Who else can share your most intimate secrets, see you at your most vulnerable, yet allow you to express yourself without shame, with pure joy in return?
- *Companionship*—Who is the difference between doing things single-handedly and doing them together, as a couple?

You really do need each other. And God knew what He was doing when He gave you to one another.

DISCUSS
Make your own list of the ways you need each other, or prioritize the top five from the list above. Then be sure to share your list with each other.

PRAY
Thank God for giving you someone to experience life with—someone you need probably more than you know.

Get Connected for More Information
http://www.familylife.com/moments/communication

TAMING THE DRAGON

Therefore encourage one another and build up one another,
just as you also are doing.
1 THESSALONIANS 5:11

It can lie. It can gossip. It can slander. It can also murmur and complain. It can manipulate and flatter. It can tear down. It can paint itself in nice words, even while cutting someone to ribbons.

My friend Joe Stowell calls it "the dragon in our dentures." Our tongue. It can truly be deadly.

On the other hand, when that "dragon" is under the power of the Holy Spirit, when we are daily training it to be submitted to Christ's control and available for His use and purposes, He can transform it into an instrument that delivers encouragement.

I remember being in church one Sunday morning when I spotted a prominent local oncologist walking by. I'd been hearing about some special things he'd been doing with his cancer patients—some unique ways he was allowing God to minister through him in the course of practicing his profession. So I caught his attention and said, "Hey, I just wanted you to know I really appreciate what you're doing. Do you realize what an incredible minister for Christ you are? You're making quite a difference in our community."

It was like I'd hit him with a stun gun. A dazed expression flashed across his face. And after a moment's pause, he looked at me and said, "Really?"

I said, almost laughing now, "Well, yeah. The things I've been hearing about the work you do are really inspiring. We could use a lot more Christ followers like you."

He shook my hand and smiled. "You don't know how much I needed to hear that this morning. Thank you."

I was reminded again how often people just need a nod of encouragement in their journey, no matter how confident he or she may appear to be.

Shared a good word with someone lately?

DISCUSS

Think about some things you've been noticing in others that are really worth praising. Slay the dragon and encourage them.

PRAY

Ask God to make you and your words build up, not tear down.

Get Connected for More Information
http://www.familylife.com/moments/communication

STOP AND LISTEN

Everyone must be quick to hear, slow to speak and slow to anger.
JAMES 1:19

A group of carpenters building an icehouse in the north country of Canada was taking a lunch break when a boy came upon them and heard their conversation. One was bemoaning a watch he had lost at some point in the morning's work. Though he'd looked for it for a couple of hours, he hadn't been able to find it.

"Would you mind if I went into the ice house and looked?" the boy asked. "Yeah, sure," the men laughed, certain he'd never find anything in a dark room with no electricity. Within 30 seconds, the boy emerged holding the watch in his hand. The carpenters couldn't believe it! "How did you find it?"

"It was simple," the boy said. "I just stopped in the middle of the room, stood still and listened for ticking."

Many of us (especially us men) are rightly accused of not listening very well. We rarely stop and take time to focus our attention—to really hear—what our spouse is trying to tell us. Instead, we quickly say things like, "That's dumb, honey. You shouldn't feel that way. You're blowing this all out of proportion." Those are statements that come from not really seeking to listen and understand where our wife or husband is coming from.

During serious conversations or conflicts, you need to stop and listen, ask questions or paraphrase what your spouse is saying in order to understand what he or she really means. Asking a good question can often be like an emotional crowbar to dislodge how somebody really feels.

Listening is another way of saying, "You're important to me, and I love you."

DISCUSS
The person who says, "You're not listening to me," is usually right. How often are these words spoken between you? What is one habit you can change to become a better listener?

PRAY
Thank God for always being there to listen to us, no matter how illogical or reactionary we may sometimes be. Ask for His counsel in how to be more like Him. And pray for yourself that you will be a better listener to your partner.

Get Connected for More Information
http://www.familylife.com/moments/communication

THE POWER OF WORDS

Let no unwholesome word proceed from your mouth,
but only such a word as is good for edification.
EPHESIANS 4:29

Kids today take "keyboarding" rather than typing, but when I was young, we learned to type on actual typewriters. In high school I struggled in my typing class, but I made a great discovery: If I could type 60 words a minute, even with 15 errors, I would get an A in speed and an F in accuracy. Round those together, and that would give me a C for the class. I could live with that.

But my gray-haired typing teacher, Mrs. Whittington, didn't like my logic. Or my behavior. And one day in front of the whole class—exasperated with me over something I'd done—she pointed her very boney finger at me and said, "Dennis Rainey, you will never amount to anything."

I'm sure before the day was out, she forgot her comment. But I *never* forgot it. And when I graduated from college, I drove over to her house and rang her doorbell. When she came to the door, I said (kindly), "Hi, Mrs. Whittington, I'm Dennis Rainey. I wanted you to know that I just graduated from college and am getting ready to go into full-time Christian ministry."

In other words, "I'm going to amount to something, in spite of what you said." I'm sure she wondered why in the world I came to her house to tell her that!

Now, should I have done that? Probably not. But words can hurt. They go deep and leave a mark, for good or for bad.

That's why Paul instructed us to use our words for *edification*—to build up, to strengthen, to lighten the load of another, to give someone the heart to match the need of the moment. He wasn't talking about flattery, or false praise, but about speaking words of support and encouragement.

Because when we're not building each other up, we're probably tearing each other down.

DISCUSS
Share an example of something encouraging your spouse said to you once that you've never forgotten. Talk about how that made you feel.

PRAY
Pray that your hearts will be filled with grace and that grace-filled words will follow.

WE ARE THE CHAMPIONS

The heart of the wise instructs his mouth and adds persuasiveness to his lips.
PROVERBS 16:23

I told you yesterday about a schoolteacher whose exasperated words left a permanent mark on my young spirit. How true it is that our words—especially those spoken in anger or under pressure—have the power to wound deeply and linger long in our memories.

But I also remember the words of another teacher—my sixth-grade basketball coach—who planted some positive thoughts in my mind. Funny, I don't even remember his name, but I'll never forget how he started each day's practice. He would walk into the gym and shout, "What's the good word, guys?" We would stop our warm-ups and roar back in unison, "State champs 1966!"

Remember that we were only 12 years old. But he already had us looking forward 6 years down the road when we'd be seniors in high school, trying to win a state basketball championship. Even during breaks between drills, when we stopped for a breather and waited for his next instructions, he'd ask, "What's the good word, guys?"

"State champs 1966!"

I wish I could report that we won the state title in 1966. Unfortunately, we lost in the first round. But we did become much better players than anyone thought we would—all because of a sixth-grade coach who had a vision and who planted a goal in the minds of young basketball hopefuls who couldn't dribble their way out of a wet paper bag.

In the same way, the words you speak to your spouse and children have a deep and lasting effect. Your tongue can be either a verbal ice pick that chips away self-esteem, or a paintbrush that adds splashes of vibrant color to it by your affirmation and encouragement. What'll it be?

DISCUSS
When are the times you're most likely to say hurtful, damaging things? How could you prevent that? What kinds of words could take their place?

PRAY
Pray that the Holy Spirit, who lives in you, will be the guardian of your lips and give you the courage to plant encouragement in the hearts of others.

 Get Connected for More Information
http://www.familylife.com/moments/communication

WHY GOD COMES FIRST

*When I pondered to understand this, it was troublesome in my sight
until I came into the sanctuary of God.*
PSALM 73:16-17

If you were asked to name three things that pose the gravest general threats to the health of today's marriages—and to your marriage in particular—what would be on your list? When Barbara and I were asked the same question recently, here are the three we gravitated toward:

Threat number one is not really knowing who God is. In his book *The Knowledge of the Holy,* A. W. Tozer wrote, "The low view of God entertained almost universally among Christians is the cause of a hundred lesser evils among us." When we fail to attribute to God the majesty of His supreme position over us and all creation, we weaken our need to stay accountable to Him in our behaviors and attitudes toward each other. We also lower the healthy self-esteem that's derived from measuring our value in the light of His love and grace. Tozer summed it up, "The most important thing you think is what you think about God."

Threat number two is selfishness. This shows itself in numerous degrees, from not wanting to help fold socks . . . to not caring what our schedules are doing to our families . . . to outright adultery. But in reality, this second threat breeds on the first one. Lives that are being constantly molded and characterized by a fear of the Lord will move toward humility and self-denial rather than living to satisfy self.

Threat number three is lack of biblical skills in resolving conflict. Conflict happens in marriage. It is simply unavoidable. But many people are not fully aware of the wealth of scriptural truth on this subject. Just following the admonition of a verse like Ephesians 4:32—being "kind to one another, tender-hearted, forgiving each other, just as God in Christ has forgiven you"—will change your life.

DISCUSS
Which of these three threats strike the closest to where you are right now? What commitments should you make to each other to counteract them?

PRAY
Ask that you may see God in greater grandeur and glory with each passing day and that the resulting glow would enlighten and enliven your marriage.

Get Connected for More Information
http://www.familylife.com/moments/relationshipwithgod

HOLES IN THE WALL

Watch the path of your feet and all your ways will be established.
PROVERBS 4:26

The Great Wall of China is one of the great wonders of the world, a true master-piece of engineering. It's the only man-made structure that can be seen from outer space. Five to six horses could trot side by side on top of it. I've walked along it myself, and it is awesome to see this massive structure snake its way through the mountains.

The wall was built, of course, to protect China from invasion. Watchtowers and various battlements dot its construction at frequent intervals. But in the first hundred years after the wall was completed, enemies managed to invade the country three times, breaching the security of this enormous, rock-solid defense. How?

They didn't go over it. They didn't go through it. They didn't need to knock it down. Because while China was building this impenetrable defense system, it was apparently neglecting to build character into its children's lives.

All the invaders had to do was *bribe the gatekeepers*.

I think of that story whenever I hear parents talk of the dreams and goals they have for their children. Many parents today are vitally concerned with the education their kids receive and the skills they develop. They spend hours shuttling them to school and to various extracurricular activities, looking for-ward to the day when they will earn scholarships and enter the working world, establishing themselves in successful and lucrative careers. But none of these accomplishments are worth anything without the character to back them up.

It's our children's CQ, not their IQ—their "character quotient," not their intelligence—that will secure their futures and enable them to stand strong in battle.

DISCUSS

Think of a time when you modeled character to your children—and they got the message! Talk about what you both need to do to develop each of your children's CQ.

PRAY

Ask for the faith to maintain your own integrity—and the opportunities for your children to see it in action.

Get Connected for More Information

AMERICAN DREAMERS

But godliness with contentment is great gain.
1 TIMOTHY 6:6, *NIV*

Whether you know it or not, your marriage is susceptible to the American Dream Syndrome—the notion that you can have it all, that you *deserve* it all. The more stuff you have, the better off you are. Desire to acquire. The slogans, like the wish lists, are practically endless.

Yet contrary to the seductive tune of the American Dream, enough is never enough. Getting more only fuels the urge to get more. So how do you learn to live within that truth without constantly feeling like your lives don't measure up?

You embrace contentment.

Contentment arises from a spirit of gratefulness. It's the courageous choice to thank God for what you have *and* for what you don't have. Even when you don't know where this week's grocery money is coming from. Even when the washer goes on the blink. Even when the kids need braces. Even when your next-door neighbor drives home in a new car or is gone on a fabulous vacation to an exotic location.

The apostle Paul, who wrote the words that appear at the top of this page, knew how it felt to be beaten, shipwrecked and imprisoned. He knew the hardship of being pummeled with rocks and left for dead. But he also knew that God could be trusted. He knew his situation was being monitored by the all-wise awareness of his loving heavenly Father.

Occasionally, we all need to be reminded: Material things will never satisfy the hunger in our hearts. A couple who fails to see this could spend a lifetime chasing the American Dream, only to find it to be a desert mirage, forever just out of reach.

DISCUSS

What are three things you wish you owned? What are three circumstances you wish were different?

PRAY

Bring your needs and shortages before the Lord right now. Leave them there, thank Him for where He has you, and walk on embracing contentment.

Get Connected for More Information
http://www.familylife.com/moments/spiritualgrowth

GREENER EVERY DAY

As you have received Christ Jesus the Lord, so walk in Him, having been firmly rooted and now being built up in Him and established in your faith, just as you were instructed, and overflowing with gratitude.

COLOSSIANS 2:6-7

Not long after I was born in 1948, someone gave my mother a little blue ceramic vase shaped in the form of baby booties. And in that vase was a small philodendron plant. Not that special.

I brought that vase home from my mother's house a few years ago. Its edges were a bit calcified—a crust of minerals had been left after the evaporation of all the water that had been poured into it over the years. But that original green plant was still in there. Still living. Still growing. In fact, when we added some fresh soil and a little plant food into the mix, it began to strengthen again.

Almost 60 years old, and still going strong.

To me, that little plant is an ongoing reminder of what happens when you are continually watered by the Word, when you're repeatedly fed by relationship with our Creator and Sustainer. That plant sits there as old as I am—almost to the day—yet still maintains its health, vitality and potential for growth.

There's life in being what God has called us to be. Life in obedience. Life in ongoing service and witness. Life in being a follower of Jesus Christ, finding our joy in seeking Him for daily direction and purpose.

Spiritual growth is a command from the Scriptures. As our passage for today says, "As you have received Christ Jesus the Lord, so walk in Him, having been firmly rooted and now being built up in Him and established in your faith, just as you were instructed, and overflowing with gratitude." But more than a command, it is God's invitation to life and fulfillment, to become a person who is still growing at every age.

DISCUSS
Think of two or three areas where God has really been growing you lately. Name two or three other areas that could use some watering and feeding.

PRAY
Thank God for continuing to use us as reflections of His life and glory. And thank Him for being at work in us and making this happen.

SMALL WONDER

We have done only that which we ought to have done.
LUKE 17:10

When you think about the great humanitarian efforts achieved by the advance of Christianity over the years, you possibly think of hospitals and rescue missions and hunger relief. But perhaps the power of Christianity is proven best every day in homes and families and marriages like yours—when people who are self-centered by nature put their spouse's needs before their own. It's something He only accomplishes in us when we do the following:

1. *Put Christ first in all things.* When Barbara and I signed the "Title Deed" of our lives over to Christ as a young married couple, we officially gave Him everything that was ours—all rights to our lives, dreams and possessions. Have we ever failed to remember the One who really owns our hopes, dreams and possessions? Sure. But whenever we've been tempted to live for ourselves, we've always been able to look each other in the eye and remember a time when we submitted everything of ours into His keeping and signed that title deed.

2. *Give up all rights and entitlements.* Paul said, "For though I am free from all men, I have made myself a slave to all" (1 Corinthians 9:19). Not a slave to some, but to *all.* And just as a slave relinquishes all rights to personal time and desires, we as Christ's followers are commanded to put others above ourselves. It's the only way to be the kind of wife or husband God intends us to be.

3. *Be selfless in the little things.* Sometimes I don't want to get out of my favorite chair to help Barbara carry in the groceries, sweep the kitchen or clean a toilet bowl. But it's in these minor, everyday moments that we teach our selfish selves who is boss. This is part of what the Bible means when it tells us to "learn to do good" (Isaiah 1:17)—to constantly choose death to self, to always choose sacrificial love until it becomes our first response.

DISCUSS

Who owns your life? Your dreams? Your possessions? Consider formally signing a title deed of your life, and give God 100 percent ownership. There's great freedom that will result from this transaction!

PRAY

Pray that submissiveness to God's will and the needs of others will be your true desire.

Get Connected for More Information
http://www.familylife.com/moments/spiritualgrowth

PIECES OF THE PATTERN

BY BARBARA RAINEY

Make this tabernacle and all its furnishings exactly like the pattern I will show you.
EXODUS 25:9, *NIV*

Back when I used to do a lot more sewing, I enjoyed looking through pattern books. It was fun to select the style I wanted and then cut out the small pieces of tissue paper that indicated what went where and how everything fit together.

But that's just it—all those little shapes that represent the sleeves and the bodice and the front and the back don't mean anything unless they eventually come together to form an article of clothing. Until the parts are applied in the context of the whole, they never achieve the purpose that was intended for them by the dress designer.

Many times in marriage, all we can see are the pieces. We see the romance part. We see the conflict part. We see the housekeeping part. We see the bill-paying part. We see the parenting part. But because we spend so much of our time focusing on the individual parts of our marriage, we don't always see them in the bigger picture our Designer had in mind

But the pattern is there nonetheless, and it's contained in the package of God's Word.

I want you to be encouraged that the pattern for your marriage isn't something you were responsible for creating. It's not based on feelings that can be strong today and much different tomorrow. The biblical pattern and plan for your marriage was created in the mind of almighty God, whose wisdom is unrivaled and whose love for you is beyond all bounds.

If you keep putting the pieces where they belong, His pattern will start to show. His design will take its beautiful shape in the form of your marriage.

DISCUSS

How might one of your current marriage issues fit into the pattern God has designed for you? What is the lesson He is trying to teach you?

PRAY

Whatever part of the whole you're dealing with today, ask the Lord to help you handle it faithfully, according to His Word. Together as a couple, thank God for designing a master plan that incorporates your good with His glory.

FLOUR POWER

The things that you carry are burdensome.
ISAIAH 46:1

A few years ago, I went on my first real diet. My doctor told me that even though I wasn't carrying an enormous amount of weight, a guy at my age with my family history and combination of vital statistics was headed toward an encounter with Type II diabetes. He got my attention.

So I did it. I backed off the desserts, watched the carbs, ramped up the exercise routine and dropped 25 pounds in about 4 months. I felt great.

One day it occurred to me, "No wonder I used to be out of breath after climbing 2 measly flights of steps at the office! When you're carrying a 25-pound sack of flour around your waist, it's bound to wear you down throughout the day."

But this devotion really isn't about dieting. It's about the other "bags" we carry around: Past sexual sin. A history of abuse. An affair. Irrational fears. Old secrets. Hidden sin.

These are the bags we don't want to unpack. Things too dark to expose and admit. The problem is that the longer we carry one of these burdens, the heavier it becomes.

One man I know had been carrying his secret for over a decade. As he confessed it to me, it was clear that he needed to be cleansed from the weight of his immoral indiscretion.

A woman was embittered toward her mother. When she finally forgave her mother, she experienced the very best kind of instant weight loss.

Are you going to keep carrying your baggage? Or are you going to drop the weight by dealing with it, talking about it and beginning to process it together? Venture out courageously to seek the Lord together—as husband and wife—for His help and healing.

It may be the best weight you ever lose.

DISCUSS

I know this is serious. But are you carrying the weight of past sins or experiences that are draining your freedom as a person and as a couple? Talk about it with God and your spouse.

PRAY

Pray for openness; pray for understanding; pray for God to give you forgiveness and peace.

Get Connected for More Information
http://www.familylife.com/moments/marriagerelationship

WOMEN ENCOURAGING WOMEN

BY BARBARA RAINEY

Encourage the young women to love their husbands, to love their children, to be sensible, pure, workers at home.

TITUS 2:4-5

When we had six children at home, I often felt overwhelmed, as if all my efforts in parenting were about to crash around me. In the middle of this busy time, some younger mothers asked if I would meet with them once a month to offer some encouragement and advice about parenting. I remember thinking, *Why would they want to meet with me, with all the mistakes I've made? What would I have to offer them?*

Through that experience, however, I learned the significance of Titus 2:4-5 (above), which instructs older women to be involved in the lives of younger women—passing on their wisdom and experience. Younger wives and mothers need mentoring and encouragement from older women who have walked along the same path—even if they've stumbled a few times along the way.

How do you find an older woman to encourage you and build into your life? I'd begin by looking in your local church. Ask God to help you spot someone who is just ahead of your season of life and can give you advice from her experience. And be sure to look for a mature woman who has established a track record of walking with God. Ask those who know her best if she is this kind of woman.

Take the initiative to ask if you can begin calling her or meeting her for coffee or lunch. Tell her that you will bring the questions; all she needs to do is listen and interact with you. Assure her that she doesn't even need to know all the answers; all you need is her time and her advice.

And by the way, there are likely younger women than you who could benefit from your counsel and encouragement. Perhaps you need to be a mentor, too.

DISCUSS

In what ways do you feel the need to be mentored right now, at this season of your life?

PRAY

Ask God to lead you to someone who can help you in your season of life, or ask Him for someone *you* can help.

Get Connected for More Information

http://www.familylife.com/moments/mentoring

Daily Bread

O how I love Your law! It is my meditation all the day.
PSALM 119:97

We're all familiar with the nutritional listings on food and beverage packages. Most of us are interested in total calories per serving, especially calories coming from good or bad fat, as well as readings on carbohydrates, sugar and sodium. But while these government-regulated fact lists work well for food required by our physical body, what if a similar kind of list were available to help us evaluate the *spiritual* content of the products we consume?

What if every TV program, magazine, book, DVD or CD revealed the "recommended daily allowance" of the spiritual necessities it provided—things like holiness, truth, forgiveness, perseverance, grace, justice and repentance? How many of them, rather than supplying *anything* we need, would be shown to actually deplete us, stripping away whatever spiritual health we already have?

But there is one product—the Bible—that is guaranteed to provide everyone in your family with the perfect blend of spiritual nourishment. Whether packaged in cheap paper or top-grain leather, the Bible comes complete with "everything required for life and godliness" (2 Peter 1:3, *HCSB*).

Although most Christians today express a deep fondness for the Scriptures, they are apparently failing to feast on it. Noted researcher George Barna has reported that fewer than 4 in 10 born-again Christians read the Bible on their own *even once* in a typical week. A similar FamilyLife survey conducted in churches throughout the United States found that two-thirds of couples read or discussed the Bible together but only occasionally.

If you want a spiritually healthy family, you must make sure that each member consumes a healthy diet of the everlasting Word of God. It's the difference between a healthy spiritual life and lifelessness.

DISCUSS
What are the chief threats to keeping the Bible central in your family's life? What are we saying when we let those things take prominence over the Scriptures?

PRAY
Pray for daily consumption of the Word, both in priority and in practice.

Get Connected for More Information
http://www.familylife.com/moments/mediachoices

TAKE YOUR POSITIONS

Love and faithfulness meet together; righteousness and peace kiss each other.
PSALM 85:10, *NIV*

If you're like most married Americans, your relationship likely resembles one of these three positions:

1. *Face to face.* Like typical newlyweds, this couple is cruising down the highway of life in a convertible with the top down. A favorite CD is playing love songs through the speakers while their fingers are intertwined. She rests her head on his shoulder, and he plants an occasional peck on her cheek.
2. *Side by side.* This couple has traded in their convertible for a minivan. With toddlers strapped into car seats, with sippy cups rolling around on juice-stained carpets, their relationship is showing signs of strain. It takes everything they've got sometimes to stand beside one another as they make it through the day.
3. *Back to back.* Like ships passing in the night, this couple now drives his and hers cars. Their house is more hotel than home. Friction, harsh words, verbal jabs, and anxiety have replaced whatever amount of intimacy used to pass between them.

Most likely, you've experienced a little of each of these—perhaps all in the same week! But Barbara and I have discovered that the position that holds the most lifelong promise for a marriage is actually *arm in arm*—walking together at the same pace. In the same direction.

It means mutually figuring out the unique rhythm of your marriage—making the investment to know each other so well that you're able to walk in lockstep together.

If you're *face to face*, enjoy and give it time. If you're *side by side*, keep working at it. Even if you're *back to back*, there's hope. God is in the business of making all things new . . . and putting husbands and wives *arm in arm*.

DISCUSS

Which one of the four positions best describes you right now? Why? How can you better connect arm in arm and grow together as a couple?

PRAY

Pray for warning and protection from anything that could threaten to back you away from each other. Pray also that God will show you how you can better walk arm in arm with your spouse.

 Get Connected for More Information
http://www.familylife.com/moments/marriagerelationship

HAVE A GOOD DAY

Let everyone who is godly pray to You in a time when You may be found.
PSALM 32:6

When our children were little, I would pray with them in the morning and ask God that they would "have a good day." Something about the simplicity of that prayer seemed appropriate for what they were facing.

But when Barbara and I were alone and praying for our children, our petitions were often a bit more involved—especially as they grew older. That's because we knew—as you do—that there's a lot more to life than having a good day.

Frankly, there were many times when we prayed that our kids would have *challenging* days. When we were focusing on certain character qualities and issues in their lives—and wanted their hearts to soften and become more teachable—we didn't always pray for good days. We knew that some lessons could only be taught in the schoolroom of a "horrible, terrible, no good, very bad day."

Anne Arkins, coauthor of *While They Were Sleeping,* says that when she prays for her children, she often says, "Lord, do whatever You have to do in their lives to help them recognize their need for You and to see what You want to accomplish in their lives." This prayer reminds us that God is the owner of life and the true Father of our children. He has given us responsibility over them for a season, but what they really need is to be taught and trained by Him and to grow in relationship with Christ.

It is a great privilege to help our children learn to develop good habits, to make right choices and to walk with the Lord. But sometimes this requires a mom or dad being willing to step back, hold out open hands and ask God to teach them a lesson—even if it means not having a very good day.

DISCUSS
What issues are your children facing right now? What choices are they learning to make? What kind of prayer do they need?

PRAY
Pray together for each of your children by name and by need, trusting that God will draw them closer to Him each day, through each circumstance.

GOING TO THE CHAPEL

I will put the fear of Me in their hearts so that they will not turn away from Me.
JEREMIAH 32:40

Many years ago, I was asked to marry a couple in a state where I wasn't licensed to perform weddings. No big deal—on the Friday I arrived in town, I figured I'd just go down to the county recorder's office and sign the right paperwork.

But I was really tired when I arrived that particular Friday afternoon, and I talked myself into taking 15 minutes to stretch out on the bed and rest my eyes. Fifteen minutes turned into more than two hours. When I woke up it was 4:15—too late to get the license.

At this point I had a choice: call my buddy to see if he knew a licensed minister who could assist me, or just let it go. *Who would ever know?* I was comfortable in my Plan B decision. But that night at the rehearsal, the groom asked me, "Hey, did you get down to the courthouse today and get registered?" I blinked twice and then answered, "Oh yeah, sure."

My, how my conscience ate at me throughout the ceremony. And for months afterward. The Lord tightened the screws on me until I knew I had to confess. I finally worked up the courage to call my friend and met with him. I told him, "Uh, you're not going to like hearing this, but I owe you an apology . . . and you're not legally married."

Sure, he forgave me. Yes, we went down and took care of it. But it taught me a great lesson about the state of my heart and my deep need to fear the Lord. Fearing God is what helps us keep our promises. It's what makes our word good. It's what builds faithfulness into our lives. Fearing the Lord helps us stay true to Him, true to others and true deep down within ourselves.

DISCUSS
When have you suffered from not having a right fear of God? Anything right now that's troubling you?

PRAY
Thank God for being displeased with your faithlessness—and for caring enough to keep pursuing you and calling you toward obedience.

NO MATTER WHAT

BY BARBARA RAINEY

[Love] bears all things, believes all things, hopes all things, endures all things.
1 CORINTHIANS 13:7

It didn't take me long to realize that Dennis was not like my father.

My dad was an all-American "Mr. Fixit." He loved working around the house and the yard—making repairs, painting, tinkering on the car.

Dennis, on the other hand, declared early on in jest that "if you can't fix something with baling wire and duct tape, you should throw it away and get a new one." Working around the house was simply not his thing.

I remember the early days in our marriage. Dennis would be plopped in his easy chair in front of the television, and I would circle him like a vulture, trying to give him a gentle hint of how I felt he could better use his time.

Dennis and I have come a long way since then. He's still not Mr. Fixit, but he tries. And somewhere along the way he developed an enjoyment of gardening so that he could spend time with me.

Meanwhile, I've learned the *importance of loving my husband unconditionally.* I need to receive Dennis as a gift from God. And I need to remember that God is working in his life.

In our first month of marriage, Dennis took the initiative to make a small financial investment, and we lost money. At that point, I faced a choice of my own: Would I accept him, or would I make him feel like a further failure?

I realized God wanted to use this mistake to teach Dennis how to become dependent on Christ and be a better husband. I needed to let Him work in my husband's life.

At times like this, a wife learns that love is not all feelings. This is where you honor your wedding vows and say, "You are the man God gave me and I'm committed to you, no matter what."

DISCUSS

What are the ways you complement one another in your marriage? See how many you can list.

PRAY

Ask God to give each of you a real, unconditional love for each other, the type of love described in 1 Corinthians 13.

Get Connected for More Information

http://www.familylife.com/moments/wives

NOURISHED AND CHERISHED

He who loves his own wife loves himself; for no one ever hated his own flesh,
but nourishes and cherishes it, just as Christ also does the church.
EPHESIANS 5:29

There are two words in today's verse given to husbands as a very specific assignment in loving their wives: "nourish" and "cherish."

The word "nourish" means not only "to feed" but also "to nurture to maturity." We have an assignment to help our wives grow. Stated another way, Barbara is my number one disciple. I must take responsibility for her spiritual growth.

Practically speaking, that means praying with her and for her. When the children were little, it meant finding a way to get her some time to be able to get alone and read the Scriptures. All the time, it means talking about the spiritual lessons you are learning. It means considering what spiritual nutrients she needs to become the woman God created her to be.

The word "cherish" is another great term that means "to warm another," and hence, "to cherish." When you pull a blanket over yourself on a cold night, you don't feel an immediate burst of warmth. It takes time for the coolness to subside.

It's the same way with your wife. Every wife, regardless of the season of life she is in, needs her husband to use words that warm her soul—words of delight, encouragement, affirmation and understanding. She needs the warmth of your relationship to endure the "cold" she may be facing. She needs you to enter her world and say, "I'd rather spend time with you than with anyone else in the world."

I don't have many regrets as I look back over our marriage, but I wish I paid more attention to Barbara's spiritual growth. Having 6 children in 10 years and leading an organization that grew 30 to 40 percent a year during that same period were challenges for both of us.

Husband, "seize the day!" Pay attention now to how you can nourish and cherish your wife.

DISCUSS

Ask your wife to share a few things you can do to nourish and cherish her and to help her grow.

PRAY

Husband, use this time to pray for your wife and her top two or three needs right now. Pray, too, that she will grow.

Get Connected for More Information
http://www.familylife.com/moments/husbands

THE BLAND ILLUSION

I came that they may have life, and have it abundantly.
JOHN 10:10

Bill Bright used to tell the story of a man who carefully saved his money until he was finally able to travel on a beautiful cruise ship. It was all he could do just to save enough to buy his ticket. Thinking he wouldn't have enough money to buy meals in the ship's fine dining room, he decided to take along some cheese and crackers for food.

For several days he sat in his cabin, watching the stewards go by with carts full of luscious lobster, prime rib, fresh fruits and vegetables. Finally, he couldn't stand it any longer. He reached out and grabbed one of the stewards by the arm and begged him for a plate of food. "Please, help me. I'll go to work, I'll scrub the deck. I'll do anything to get something to eat. My cheese and crackers are turning stale, and I'm starving to death."

"But, sir," the steward replied, "don't you know? Your food comes with your ticket."

Many Christians live the way this passenger did on the cruise ship. They are "cheese and crackers" believers, living off rations when they could be dining on steak and baked potatoes. They don't allow the Holy Spirit to take control of their lives and produce the luscious fruit of the Spirit—love, joy, peace, patience, kindness, goodness, faithfulness, gentleness and self-control. Instead they live in spiritual poverty.

I've been a "cheese and crackers" Christian on more than one occasion. I've been satisfied at times with the bare bones of salvation, figuring that is all I should really expect. But my spiritual hunger finally got the best of me, and I surrendered my life to Jesus Christ. Nothing can satisfy like Him.

DISCUSS
How well are you feasting on the abundant life that Jesus Christ came to give you?

PRAY
Pray and surrender your life totally to Jesus Christ as your Lord and Savior.

MONEY TROUBLES

The rich rules over the poor, and the borrower becomes the lender's slave.
PROVERBS 22:7

Larry Burkett once told me that of all the couples who divorce in America, between 85 and 90 percent would say the number one problem in their marriage is money. They are unable to agree on how to handle it, save it, spend it, give it, budget it, account for it and keep from arguing about it. In many cases, it's the heavy debt and the pressure of watching it compound ever higher—with no easy solution for bringing it down—that causes a marriage to fall apart.

A number of years ago, I was mentoring a young married man who admitted he was carrying more than $35,000 worth of high-interest credit-card debt. He asked me what he should do about it. I responded, "The same way you'd eat an elephant—one bite at a time. But in order to keep the elephant from growing, I'd strongly encourage you to set all your cards on a cookie sheet, put them in the oven at 400 degrees for 15 minutes and melt them down."

Easy credit is not just a mammoth monster. It's a marriage eater.

If you're in the beginning years of marriage, you need to have frequent and honest conversations about managing your money and specifically your attitude toward debt as a couple. Learn to deny immediate gratification of your wants, until you can actually afford them. Better yet, learn to resist the desire to accumulate stuff for stuff's sake, even if you *can* afford it.

Discuss your spending tendencies with each other. As a couple, fiercely avoid buying things on credit. Create a budget and hold each other accountable for how you manage what God has entrusted to you (see Psalm 24:1).

The bottom line? Debt kills marriages. How you manage money as a couple will have an impact on your marriage, your family and your legacy.

DISCUSS
What financial example was set before you growing up? How has that affected your attitude toward money? How are you and your spouse similar to one another? Different?

PRAY
Offer it all back to God today, to help you be disciplined in using His money His way.

Get Connected for More Information

WORST DAY OF THE YEAR

I will rejoice in the God of my salvation.
HABAKKUK 3:18

If you woke up feeling especially blah this morning, you're in good company. January 24 is now officially "the most depressing day of the year."

Those are the findings of Dr. Cliff Arnall, an English psychologist who specializes in seasonal disorders at the University of Cardiff in Wales. His formula for analyzing such things includes seven variables—the weather, personal debt, monthly salary and even the amount of time since Christmas, among other things—that determine people's feelings of happiness.

He figures January 24 is when credit-card bills start rolling in, reminding us how we got carried away again with our holiday spending. By now many of our New Year's resolutions have fallen by the wayside or at least been riddled with pockets of compromise.

Maybe he's right. Maybe you really are feeling it today. But what Dr. Arnall may not understand is that our joy and contentment doesn't have to be taken away by the bleak clouds of winter or the long wait until our next vacation. As followers of Christ, a settled sense of well-being and belonging can be ours no matter what our set of circumstances.

Hear again the words of a man who knew what to do with a January 24 kind of feeling: "Though the fig tree should not blossom and there be no fruit on the vines, though the yield of the olive should fail and the fields produce no food, though the flock should be cut off from the fold and there be no cattle in the stalls, yet I will exult in the LORD, I will rejoice in the God of my salvation. The Lord GOD is my strength" (Habakkuk 3:17-19).

God is there with you *every day* of the year.

DISCUSS

Maybe this would be a good time to get a jump on Thanksgiving. Talk about everything there is to rejoice in, make a list of things you are thankful for, even on a day that may be blah.

PRAY

Take turns giving thanks to God. Praise is one of the most important elements of worship and in experiencing God in our lives.

THROUGH A GLASS, DARKLY

Once he has looked at himself and gone away,
he has immediately forgotten what kind of person he was.
JAMES 1:24

"I'm writing this letter to tell you about someone I used to know."

In her letter, the woman described a man she greatly admired as she grew up. She had worked as a babysitter for this man's three sons. She was treated like a member of the family, often going with them on trips and vacations.

This husband and father became her model of the type of man she wanted to marry. "During college, I dreamed of meeting and falling in love with someone like him—smart, generous, fun to be with, committed to helping others, a true godly man. By some miracle, God gave me just what I was looking for."

Now she was dismayed, because this man she had admired was about to walk away from his marriage and his children. "I'm trying to figure out what happened to this person I used to know," she wrote. "I can only hope he realizes that he's about to make the biggest mistake of his life."

As you might guess, she sent this letter to the man she was describing. But it didn't work. He left his family and married another woman, and only while he was on his honeymoon did he stop to reflect on what he had done. And he wept as he realized what had become of this man that had once been so influential in a young girl's life.

Sometimes we lose our way. We forget who we really are. And thank God, He inspires some of the people around us to hold up a mirror and let us see who we've become.

If or when this ever happens to you, promise you'll look carefully at the reflection they offer. It might just save your life.

DISCUSS

What can keep us from stepping into the lives of those we love and speaking the truth to them? Is God leading you to hold up a mirror to someone you care about?

PRAY

Pray for the courage to speak the truth in love, while at the same time having the humility to embrace the truth about yourself.

THE IMPORTANCE OF A DAD

He will restore the hearts of the fathers to their children.
MALACHI 4:6

When I gaze at the family snapshots on my desk, a lump forms in my throat. Where are the grinning little boys proudly holding stringers of fish? When did they grow up to become fathers with their own little boys? Where are the little girls in pigtails? When were they transformed into stunning brides?

Time does not stand still, nor does the life of a family.

But there is one thing that doesn't change: the importance of a dad. A boy needs the heart of his father and the fellowship of men. He needs at least one man who pays attention to him, spends time with him, admires him and teaches him how to become a man himself. A boy needs a role model.

From experience, I can tell you how easy it is for dads to be selfish. When our children were younger, I struggled with placing my children's needs above my own desires. I realized that I had a choice to make every day. If I had gone home from work and retreated into my own world, I would have squandered my responsibility to build into my kids.

It requires perseverance, not perfection, to be the father that your children need. You will not be flawless. But you can learn how to reserve energy so that you don't come home from work so emotionally exhausted that you have nothing left for our kids. You can choose not to bend to selfishness but instead to say yes to investing in the next generation.

When our children were little, it occurred to me one day that I needed to save some energy for home. On a card I wrote, "Save Some for Home." I clipped that card to the shade of my lamp on my desk and for more than a decade, it reminded me of my children's needs for a daddy.

Dads, do you have an extra paper clip?

DISCUSS
On a 1- to 10-point scale (1 being poor and 10 being outstanding), grade yourself as a father. How involved are you in your children's lives emotionally, relationally and spiritually?

PRAY
Pray that you will be there for your children.

WE CAN DO BETTER

*Thus says the LORD of hosts, the God of Israel, "Amend your ways
and your deeds, and I will let you dwell in this place."*
JEREMIAH 7:3

I keep asking questions like:

- Why is the divorce rate *inside* the Church nearly identical to the divorce rate *outside* the Church?
- Why do so many Christian men perform aggressively at work yet remain disengaged and passive at home?
- Why do so many Christians *say* their secular job is their ministry but then show so little fruit for their efforts?
- Why do Christians *talk* about family values while their lifestyles are virtually identical to the average non-Christian?
- Why do so few Christians possess confidence that they are on a divine mission?
- Why do less than 10 percent of all Christians regularly tell others about God's forgiveness through Christ?
- If Jesus really changes lives, why do 50 million Americans claiming to be born again have such a marginal impact on society?

The prophet Jeremiah asked similar questions about the "church" of his day. He observed that many people pursued "emptiness" (Jeremiah 2:5) out of the "stubbornness of their evil heart" (3:17), yet they didn't have the good sense even "to be ashamed" (3:3) about it. "They did not even know how to blush" (6:15). Those deceived, distracted "believers" sat comfortably in the house of God—just as they do in our generation, week after week—listening to the teaching of the Scriptures but refusing to let the truth become a matter of obedience, a manner of life.

Which of these questions do *you* need to deal with?

DISCUSS

Pick one of these questions—or one of your own—and think about what you could do to help your church advance a change of direction.

PRAY

Pray that "judgment" will "begin with the household of God" (1 Peter 4:17)—and that we will pay attention when it does.

Get Connected for More Information

http://www.familylife.com/moments/convictions

DOWN BUT NOT OUT

We are afflicted in every way, but not crushed; perplexed, but not despairing.
2 CORINTHIANS 4:8

Have you been through a period of life when everything looked bleak? When it seemed everything around you was coming unraveled? When you hoped the phone wouldn't ring for fear it would be more bad news?

During seasons like that, I'm often reminded of this story:

Karl, a Norwegian fisherman, had taken his two teenage sons out for a day of fishing. The morning had been beautiful when they started out, but the afternoon turned nasty—in a hurry—catching them too far at sea to beat the incoming storm to shore. The wind-whipped ocean began to work into a frenzy, until he and his sons were battling for their lives. As darkness fell on their frantic efforts, even the steady beacon of the seaside lighthouse was suddenly extinguished by a terrific bolt of lightning. Hope seemed lost.

But things were actually worse than Karl knew. Lightning had also struck his home and the structure quickly erupted into a fireball. So when Karl and his sons finally staggered ashore, exhausted, he was met by his wife with the bad news.

Strangely, Karl seemed unfazed, much to his wife's frustration. As he stroked her tear-lined face with his tough, leathery hands, he said, "Don't you understand, sweetheart? When the lighthouse went out, the glow on the horizon became my compass. The fire that destroyed our house guided us home."

Barbara and I and our family have certainly gone through times when there were "fires" burning. But we've also discovered that during these times, these crises have guided us "home," because they've forced us to hunker down in faith, crying out in absolute dependence upon God. "Lord God, You know what You are doing! We don't know what You are up to, but we trust in You."

DISCUSS

What is an example of a trial you've experienced that turned out to have a good consequence from an eternal perspective?

PRAY

Pray that you will face the fires together and that your faith in Christ will grow stronger as you go through them.

Get Connected for More Information

CAN YOU DISH IT OUT?

And He was saying to them all, "If anyone wishes to come after Me, he must deny himself, and take up his cross daily and follow Me."
LUKE 9:23

Did you know there are four ways for a man to load a dishwasher?

1. The way he's been trained by his mother.
2. The way his wife likes it done.
3. The way he does it at his mother-in-law's house.
4. The way he does it when no one's looking.

Now, is one of these methods right and all the others wrong? Can't a man just cram in as many pots and pans and bowls and plates as possible, in whatever arrangement it takes to get the door closed?

Can any woman prove me wrong on this with absolute certainty?

Sure, the proper dishwasher loading method is not a big marriage deal. But it's an example of those little tastes and preferences we have, those minor points of difference that can often fester into major arguments and problems.

If you are going to keep the little things your spouse does from becoming real irritants and obstacles in your relationship, you need to deny yourself, like Jesus said in today's verse. Rather than insisting that your way is right in matters of minor importance, let some stuff go. Rather than nagging and nitpicking—which is like being nibbled to death by a duck—express your dislikes in ways that don't rankle and threaten and lead to even bigger blowups.

Throughout your marriage, you'll have hundreds, perhaps thousands, of opportunities like these to either die to yourself or rise up in your own defense. Remember that there are a lot worse things in life than rewashing the cereal bowls. And yes, I do know how to load a dishwasher now—since 1972, Barbara has been training me!

DISCUSS
What is something your spouse does that drives you crazy? Can you cover it with grace?

PRAY
Thank the Lord Jesus for setting us an everyday example of patience in His dealings with us.

Get Connected for More Information

ADOPTING GOD'S HEART

Vindicate the weak and fatherless; do justice to the afflicted and destitute.
PSALM 82:3

In his book *Fields of the Fatherless*, C. Thomas Davis writes, "If you searched the Bible from front to back, you'd find many issues close to God's heart. But you'd also notice three groups of people coming up again and again. They appear so many times, in fact, you have to conclude that God mentions them purposely to make sure they are at the top of our priority list."

They are *orphans, widows* and *aliens* (or strangers).

God demonstrated His care and provision for these three groups through His instructions to the Israelite farmers in Deuteronomy 24:19: "When you are harvesting in your field and you overlook a sheaf, do not go back to get it. Leave it for the alien, the fatherless and the widow, so that the LORD your God may bless you in all the work of your hands" (*NIV*).

Similarly, if we want our Christianity to be its purest, we too must actively exercise our concern for the left-out and the abandoned: "Religion that God our Father accepts as pure and faultless is this: to look after orphans and widows in their distress and to keep oneself from being polluted by the world" (James 1:27-28).

Caring for the fatherless is not simply a compassionate act. Adoption is not merely an additional means of growing our families to the desired size. Caring for orphans is about obedience and expressing the heart of God.

Perhaps God is calling you to the redemptive task of adoption, as He has Barbara and me. If not, each of us can be part of supporting, praying for and encouraging those who are in the midst of adoption, those who are seeking to acquire God's heart for the fatherless.

DISCUSS
Discuss how you can express the heart of God in caring for orphans. Also ask yourselves, Is there a reason why adopting a child would not be a possibility?

PRAY
Promise the Father that you will pursue His heart for the fatherless and orphaned, in whatever way He directs you to do so—orphan care, foster care, adoption or mission work.

Get Connected for More Information
http://www.familylife.com/moments/adoption

BOILED OVER

But everyone must be quick to hear, slow to speak and slow to anger;
for the anger of man does not achieve the righteousness of God.
JAMES 1:19-20

I believe anger is one of the most dangerous and least talked about emotions. Anger can destroy marriages. It can devastate families. It can crush young people who grow up in homes where they are treated with disrespect and contempt.

There are many people who seemingly never have a problem with their tempers in public but are more volatile than you'd ever imagine in their own homes and families.

A friend of mine, Dan Allender, is a man who has helped many people sort through deep-seated issues of worth, forgiveness and abuse through his wise counsel, writings and speaking. He is indeed a good, godly man. But he'd be the first to tell you that anger has been a tough nut for him to crack.

One day Dan and his wife, Becky, were lost in downtown Denver, and he was boiling over about the poor directions she had given him. Things got so bad that Becky abruptly left the car and began walking away at a brisk pace.

"Where do you think you're going?" Dan blurted out through the rolled-down window. Becky shot back, "I am not going to sit in the same car with you and give you the right to continue to sin against me." Then she snapped open her cell phone and called Dan's best friend to come pick her up.

Oh, the humility of the moment! You likely have a similar story or two you could tell. We do.

Take another look at the verse for today. If anger is an issue in your marriage, I suggest that you memorize it. And if you've allowed anger at your spouse to spill over into your family, I encourage you to ask for forgiveness from your spouse and your children.

DISCUSS

Anger in your marriage and family—how often is it expressed? What impact does it have on your family? Talk about one step of action you'll take to address this emotion in your lives, marriage and family.

PRAY

Pray, pray, pray for slowness to anger.

DO YOU BELIEVE IN MAGIC?

BY BARBARA RAINEY

My beloved extended his hand through the opening,
and my feelings were aroused for him.
SONG OF SOLOMON 5:4

Most romantic relationships begin with a season we call "new love." This season is characterized by an intense focus on each other, a strong mutual attraction, eager anticipation and enthusiasm for building a life together, and a great freedom to express physical intimacy (hopefully after marriage).

Couples in *new love* are eager to sacrifice time and money to fuel this new experience. It feels so good. Their fears are minimized by the emotion of love, and they will talk for hours about their lives and dreams and hopes. New love is easy, delightful and intense. It is intoxicating and magical.

You're probably thinking, *Yes, I remember those days* . . . But why shouldn't your marriage be regularly infused with the thrills of anticipation and other swept-off-your-feet emotions? Why shouldn't there be times when you feel like kids again, hardly able to keep your hands off each other? Why shouldn't you use the time, money and resources you possess to arrange a romantic getaway?

What would happen if you were to say to your wife, "I have a surprise for you next Tuesday at lunch?" All week long, she'd be wondering about what you had up your sleeve.

Or what if you sent your husband an email at work, telling him you had something special in mind for tonight, wondering if maybe he could get home a little earlier than usual (wink, wink)?

Oswald Chambers, the great devotional author of the early 1900s, said, "Human nature, if it is healthy, demands excitement; and if it does not obtain its thrilling excitement in the right way, it will seek it in the wrong way. God never makes bloodless stoics. He makes passionate saints."

What have you done lately to rekindle the magic?

DISCUSS

Talk about how marriage can rob your relationship of romance.

PRAY

God is the creator of passion, excitement and romance. Ask Him to guide you ever closer to the love of your life.

Get Connected for More Information
http://www.familylife.com/moments/romance

TIME FOR ROMANCE

By Barbara Rainey

I am my beloved's, and his desire is for me.
SONG OF SOLOMON 7:10

So often, a man thinks romancing his wife means buying a certain gift or doing a certain thing or creating a certain situation. And, yes, all of these things can communicate romance to a woman. But romance for us is all about relationship and time, about feeling safe and accepted, about simply being together.

So when I think of a true, romantic memory, I'm taken back to one September when Dennis took a whole day off work—not to clean the garage or go fishing or catch up on some writing, but just to spend it with me and do whatever I wanted to do.

We enjoyed a leisurely breakfast. We worked in the yard for a while, feeling the first cool snatches of fall through our flannel shirts. Then we went inside, cleaned up a little, hopped in the car and just took off. We drove for several hours, stopping where we wanted, doing what we wanted.

And in a sense, it was almost like being on our honeymoon to me. For those few hours, we had no responsibilities. No one else to worry about. We were just out having fun together. On an autumn afternoon, I had Dennis all to myself, away from the everyday demands of work and parenting and pressure. We talked and laughed together all day long. It was absolutely wonderful.

No, it wasn't the typical sweep-me-off-my-feet moment. I didn't feel like I was being carried to the castle to live happily ever after. It was much richer and sweeter and deeper than all of that. It was romance in its purest form, being chosen as my husband's delight, seeing his love for me in the joy he found by spending a day . . . just with me.

DISCUSS

Talk about what romance means to you. See how each of your ideas can come together.

PRAY

Ask God to renew your desire for each other's company and give you sheer delight in spending time together.

Get Connected for More Information
http://www.familylife.com/moments/romance

"WHAT I LIKE BEST"

Rejoice in the wife of your youth.
PROVERBS 5:18

We often forget that romance is far more than an after-hours activity we share in the bedroom. Simple, everyday expressions of affection are just as much a part of marital romance as sexual intimacy is—and they give our children a very real sense that all is right in their world.

I love the way an 11-year-old boy captured this sentiment in an essay titled "What I Like Best About My Home":

> My mother keeps a cookie jar in the kitchen, and we can help ourselves to it if it's not too close to mealtime. Except my dad can have some any time. When he comes home from the office, he helps himself, no matter if it's just before we eat. Then he always slaps my mother on the behind and brags about how great she is and how good she can cook. Then she turns around and they hug. The way they do it, you'd think they just got married or something. It makes me feel good. This is what I like best about my home.

I think our children liked seeing us be affectionate. I'd come home after work and lock lips with Barbara in a kiss that was just a little bit more than a quick smacker, and our children would groan and comment, "Gross!" "Go get a hotel room!" But they always said it with a sheepish grin.

So how about it? Hold hands. Open the car door for her. Kiss her on the neck. Come up from behind him and put your arms around him. Snuggle on the couch while you watch a movie. Let your children catch you in kiss that is *not* a handshake!

And don't forget to say "I love you." Out loud. Right there in the kitchen. This is the best kind of "homeland security."

DISCUSS

Tell each other three little incidental things the other does that always makes you feel good, makes you feel loved. What's your favorite kind of affection?

PRAY

Give thanks to God for the opportunity you have to give your children a healthy picture of what *real* love and romance look like.

Get Connected for More Information
http://www.familylife.com/moments/romance

THE SAME, ONLY DIFFERENT

BY BARBARA RAINEY

Male and female created he them.
GENESIS 1:27, *KJV*

Dennis and I received a cute email about the romantic differences between men and women. It began by asking, "How do you romance a woman?"

Answer: "Wine her, dine her, call her, cuddle with her, surprise her, compliment her hair, shop with her, listen to her talk, buy flowers, hold her hand, write love letters, and be willing to go to the end of the earth and back again for her." I could go along with that.

But when it asked the same question the other way—"How do you romance a man?"—the answer was much more brief and to the point.

Answer: "Arrive naked. Bring food."

Ahhh . . . men.

But in a way, this blending of our romantic differences is similar to how you make a good salad dressing. Oil and vinegar are about as dissimilar as condiments get. The only thing they have in common is that they are liquids. Other than that, they're night and day. Oil is smooth; vinegar is sharp. Oil is thick; vinegar is thin. Left alone in the same bottle, the two will always migrate to opposite ends and remain there forever—unless shaken.

Interestingly, however, even after the bottle has been shaken, the two ingredients retain their unique identities. And yet they complement each other in a savory unity. Together, they serve as a zesty finish to an otherwise bland mix of lettuces.

And so it is in marriage. No matter how many times a husband and wife come together, they always remain unique. He will always think like a man; she, like a woman. And although their innate design will never change, they can better understand each other and move to love one another with compassion, knowing that in so doing, they create a savory blend of romantic intrigue.

DISCUSS
What do you love about your romantic differences? Which ones can drive you crazy?

PRAY
Pray for patient understanding and for new ways of embracing and loving this wonderful person you married.

Get Connected for More Information
http://www.familylife.com/moments/romance

NEED MACHINES

By Barbara Rainey

Over our doors are all choice fruits, both new and old,
which I have saved up for you, my beloved.
SONG OF SOLOMON 7:13

Without question, the biggest deterrent to romance for moms is children. These sweet, precious, innocent little ones given to us by God are also self-centered, untrained, unending "need machines" who can suck the life out of our marriage. They often leave us feeling like the mother who said, "It's ironic. Romance gave us our children, and children ended our romance."

But motherhood can simply be a tempting excuse for giving up sex. Caught up in her day-in-day-out responsibilities, a mother can experience a slow shift in loyalty from husband to children. She thinks the needs of her children, since they are so helpless and formative, are more important than the needs of her husband. After all, he's an adult.

True. And yet one reason why this reasoning is faulty—one reason why it's easy for us to have little sympathy for our husband's sexual needs—is that we as women are able to experience our femaleness simply by nurturing our children. We feel fully alive as women when we're caring for them (that is, when we're not totally exhausted!). We feel a deep, innate sense of well-being and fulfillment; it is an indescribable privilege that brings us profound satisfaction. It's what we were made to do.

But it's only part of being a woman. God didn't create you with the capacity and compulsion to nurture just for the sake of your children. He also meant for you to *nurture life in your husband.* Maintaining this balance is one of the biggest challenges of the parenting years; your children need to see Dad and Mom in love.

Nurturing life in your husband may not be as automatic as it is with your children, but it is no less important. God will help you balance the needs of both husband and children when you depend upon Him.

DISCUSS

What are some practical, creative ways you both could keep romance alive, even when living in a house full of children?

PRAY

Pray for God's wisdom in balancing life's demands.

BASKETBALL GODS

You shall have no other gods before Me.
EXODUS 20:3

Some people thought Karen was the best basketball player to ever come from her state. After leading her high-school team to back-to-back appearances in the championship game—once as a winner—she earned a full-ride scholarship to a major college program and capped off her career with a great run in the NCAA women's tournament.

Drafted by a professional team and offered a startling salary as a rookie, she was set to live her childhood dream. For as long as she could remember, basketball had been the focus of her life. And now it was paying her back. Big time.

But strangely, just as she was reaching the pinnacle of athletic success, she slipped into an unexpected funk. She felt uncharacteristically empty and purposeless. After all her sacrifice, after all her incredible achievements, she couldn't seem to shake free from whatever was oppressing her.

Months passed without her being able to draw up enough energy for a single workout. She gorged herself on junk food, and her weight ballooned. The date to report to her pro team came and went. She was literally losing it.

One afternoon, Karen summoned the strength to pick up a basketball and take a few shots in the gym. Within a mere matter of minutes, discouraged by her lack of precision, she put the ball away for good. The very thing she had once hoped to be her ticket to success had eaten her alive.

Idols can do that, you know. There's nothing wrong with basketball—or business or music or writing or entertainment or decorating—but when something becomes the focus of all your dreams and attention and energy, it becomes an idol in your life. For all intents and purposes, you begin worshiping it instead of God.

Nothing can satisfy us like God. And nothing should replace Him in our affections.

DISCUSS

How many false gods could you name in your life? What are you hoping they'll do for you?

PRAY

Ask God to protect your heart from being deceived and to give you an overwhelming desire to worship Him and Him only.

Get Connected for More Information
http://www.familylife.com/moments/relationshipwithgod

I WISH

The LORD redeems the soul of His servants, and none of those who take refuge in Him will be condemned.

PSALM 34:22

Barbara and I planted a maple tree outside our bedroom window about 10 years ago. I don't know what kind of water supply it tapped into, but this tree has just grown like crazy. It's absolutely magnificent! Around the end of October every year, its leaves turn a brilliant yellow and orange that look almost electric—like it's plugged into a light socket.

One fall afternoon, I was outside in that part of the yard, and I said to myself, *Why didn't we plant more of these trees? Imagine how gorgeous our place would look up here with a few more scattered around?* But we didn't. And I can't go back 10 years and do things differently.

Regretting to plant a tree is one thing. Regrets in life are quite another.

I don't have to ask if you've ever felt that way. You may look back over your life and think, *Why didn't I save my purity for marriage? Why haven't I been more consistent in my parenting decisions? Why have I let myself get so busy and distracted from important things? Why didn't I put a stop to this one particular sin years ago instead of letting it linger and defeat me my whole life? Why didn't I obey God when He made it so clear what He wanted me to do? Why didn't I do what He said? Why didn't I surrender my life to Jesus Christ sooner?*

The truth is, all of us wish we'd have done some things differently. We all live with a measure of regret and disappointment. The only difference is whether we let ourselves moan for the past or be thankful for where we are . . . and decide to make choices today that will result in a life of no regrets later.

DISCUSS

Think back over a few of your greatest regrets. What have you learned from these that you can apply today?

PRAY

Thank God that He is a God who forgives even our greatest regrets and gives us faith, hope and courage for the future.

ONE OF A KIND

We are . . . created in Christ Jesus for good works,
which God prepared beforehand so that we would walk in them.
EPHESIANS 2:10

At the Opryland Hotel in Nashville, they give you a map to find your room—and believe me, you need it! The place is so big that the glass ceiling in the atrium is the size of six football fields.

The hotel's exotic plant collection, which takes 20 full-time gardeners to maintain, includes an Asian banana tree . . . right in the heart of Tennessee! This unusual tree grows only one crop of bananas its entire life. Then the team of gardeners cuts it down and plants another.

How interesting that God in His wisdom would create a tree designed to serve just one short-term purpose. Unlike trees that bear fruit annually, the Asian banana tree has a unique calling.

Your family also has a unique calling. You have been set apart by God to fulfill your own purpose. There are certain values and priorities that define who you are—certain goals you've been created to achieve. These guide the way you spend your time, money and energy.

Can you articulate God's purpose for your marriage and family? One of His purposes for Barbara and me has been to equip marriages and families with God's blueprints. In addition, Barbara and I have found that some of His purposes change as we move through the different seasons of a family. When we had children at home, it was clear that one of our purposes was to train them to know God and equip them to obey Him in life.

God *does* have a unique purpose for each of you as individuals and for the two of you as a couple. I encourage you to talk and pray about these purposes together.

DISCUSS
Looking back over the direction of your lives, taking note of your convictions and those things that you are passionate about, what do you think are a couple of God's purposes for you as a couple?

PRAY
Pray for wisdom, unity of spirit and the tenacity to stay true to your calling, no matter what other families act like or expect.

Get Connected for More Information
http://www.familylife.com/moments/spiritualgrowth

YOU DA MAN

Fathers, do not provoke your children to anger,
but bring them up in the discipline and instruction of the Lord.
EPHESIANS 6:4

After speaking at a Promise Keepers event in Houston, I was met by a television crew offstage. The interviewer baited me by mentioning a group of women picketing the event and what they perceived as men being encouraged to take advantage of women.

In reality, the demonstration was pretty minor—a couple dozen women outside the Astrodome while 40,000 men stood inside worshiping the Lord. Still, I looked the camera in its little glass eye and said, "You know, it baffles me how any woman could criticize an organization that's calling men to be responsible fathers and husbands."

I added, as an example, "Up front, just to the left of where I was speaking a moment ago, there were more than 30 prisoners dressed in white. They had been given a day's pass so that they could come to the entire session today. If you went up to interview them right now, you would find that most of these incarcerated men never had a daddy in their lives."

Now I was on a roll. "They didn't have a man in their homes to shape their character, to love them, to cry with them, to be there for them. In fact, many of them have never even seen or met their father. And that's the primary reason why they ended up doing the things that led them into trouble and ultimately into jail."

As I said then—and still believe today—I can't see why calling men back to their primary responsibilities of serving and loving their wives and children would strike anyone as a bad thing. Truth is, we need all the encouragement we can get to be the men our wives and children need us to be.

DISCUSS
Husbands, talk to your wife about the challenges facing you as a husband and father. Discuss one simple step you could take in your marriage or family to lead spiritually.

PRAY
Wives, pray for your husband that God will give him faith, strength and courage to lead your family spiritually and be the man God has called him to be.

KEEP GOING

Whoever does not carry his own cross and come after Me cannot be My disciple.
LUKE 14:27

We don't talk a lot about cross carrying. That's more the fine print of being a follower of Christ—the part we don't generally go around advertising to those we're hoping to draw into Christian faith. But as I understand Jesus' words in Luke 14:27, you and I cannot truly follow Him unless we are carrying a cross.

The cross is not just a popular piece of jewelry but also a unique Christian symbol that represents suffering and sacrifice. So it is with the cross He has asked you to carry. Your cross will undoubtedly extract pain and a price.

Cross carrying is not a one-time decision. No, we must choose daily to pick up our cross, again, and follow Him. We are to *continue carrying it over the long haul.*

Do you know what your cross is? Think with me for a moment. When the Savior asks you, "Pick up your cross and follow Me," what exactly is it that He is asking you to carry?

Is your cross:

- A chronic health issue—physical or emotional?
- Giving up fame, prestige and popularity?
- Giving up material wealth, financial security and living a lifestyle that you've become accustomed to?
- The loss of a dream—infertility, a past divorce, infidelity or the betrayal of a friend?

The bottom line? Cross carrying represents death. Death to the easy way—the world's way. Death to desires. Death to self.

Cross carrying demands focus on Christ (see Hebrews 12:1-3), coming after Christ with faith (see Hebrews 11:6), and perseverance.

Keep carrying your cross—through the balance of the work week, through the long months of a family crisis, through the hard-fought seasons of moral struggle.

Keep carrying your cross.

DISCUSS

What does carrying your cross mean to you right now? What cross has God called you to carry right now as you follow Him?

PRAY

Pray that you won't rebel against what God is asking of you but that you'll submit willingly to His claim on your life and pick up your cross and follow Christ.

Get Connected for More Information
http://www.familylife.com/moments/suffering

LEARNING TO LET GO

Is it not from the mouth of the Most High that both calamities and good things come?
LAMENTATIONS 3:38, *NIV*

Few of us are comfortable with death. That's understandable. Humankind, originally, wasn't designed by God to die. Death is the unnatural ripping of the soul from the body.

And yet as our journey unfolds, nearly all of us will one day be confronted with the impending death of someone dear to us. Just thinking about it feels repulsive. To those who refuse to accept anything but sweetness and light in their relationship with God, a verse like the one above doesn't seem to belong in the Bible.

Paradoxically, in His wisdom, God allowed death to become a part of life. But by denying it, by constantly exhorting terminally ill loved ones to be more positive in their thinking, there is a point where instead of helping them, we merely deny them our company on this journey at a time when they need it the most.

To approach death as though God could never have a part in it creates a major dilemma for the seriously ill. To imply that death means God is no longer in charge threatens a person's freedom to experience His peace and comfort at life's end. To never understand that "it is better to go to a house of mourning than to go to a house of feasting" (Ecclesiastes 7:2) shows how little we understand about the promises waiting to be fulfilled for the Christian on the other side of life.

As my mom drew near to death, she kept asking me, "What do I need to do?" I said, "Mom, you don't really have anything left to do. Feel free to go home, to go on to heaven. It's okay." I was giving her permission to walk into the arms of her Savior, freeing her to embrace death.

Hard words? You bet. But God remains in control. Even in death, God is good . . . all the time.

DISCUSS
Discuss your thoughts, fears and questions about death.

PRAY
Pray for a godly perspective on death. Some day you'll need it.

Get Connected for More Information

ON-THE-JOB TRAINING

Marriage is to be held in honor among all.
HEBREWS 13:4

When a buffet restaurant offered a free Valentine's Day lunch to any couple who's been married for 50 years or more, over 300 people showed up. At a gathering like that, you get a lot more than a good time and good food; you also learn some good advice on what it takes to make a marriage last:

- "If I want anything fairly expensive, I'll talk it over with him, and he'll do the same with me."
- "When you go to bed, always kiss good-night. We always kiss good-bye when we leave each other."
- "I'm the boss. I make sure that everything she wants gets done."
- "Treat each other with kindness, love and respect. Just work it out together. Don't fuss. We stay mad an hour or two, but that's it . . . and it's fun to make up."
- "Look at things in different ways and concentrate on the 'good' in your relationship. I always say, 'This too shall pass,' and it usually does."
- "You do a lot of counting to 10 . . . or 20, if necessary."
- "We were always taught, 'Till death do you part.' Divorce was never discussed in our house."
- "When he was young, he was high-tempered, so I usually didn't say much. But when you don't say anything, you don't have to take anything back."
- "When we said 'I do,' we didn't say it was just for tomorrow. You've got to tie the knot where it can't be untied."

Spoken like real pros.

DISCUSS
Regardless of how long you've been married, what would you say are the secrets of your commitment to each other?

PRAY
Ask God for many years together . . . and for all the daily requirements of life-long love.

BRINGING IT HOME

*Husbands, love your wives, just as Christ also loved the church
and gave Himself up for her.*
EPHESIANS 5:25

On Valentine's Day 2005, Arkansas Governor Mike Huckabee and his wife, Janet, restated and renewed their wedding vows along with 4,000 other couples gathered in Little Rock's Alltel Arena. I had the privilege of performing the ceremony, which included husbands and wives of all ages and backgrounds, celebrating the lifelong commitment of covenant marriage.

One of the most touching stories of the night, however, happened not in the crowded arena, but in a nearby home where a couple was listening to the proceedings on the radio.

At one point, the husband became so moved by the significance of the moment that tears began to well in his eyes. Soon they were streaming down his face. His little son, surprised by what he was seeing, crawled into his father's lap and asked, "What's wrong? Why are you crying?" No explanation seemed to satisfy the young boy's curiosity, so he kept asking his father, "Why are you crying, Daddy?"

Finally, the man pulled his son up close and whispered something into his ear. The boy then crawled down quickly and ran to his mom, who was sitting across the room. He took her by the hand, looked into her eyes and explained, "Daddy said he's crying because he loves you so much."

We have a generation of children today who desperately need to look into the eyes of Mom and Dad and see two people deeply in love with each other, committed to one another for life and honoring God in their relationship. If God has blessed your life with children, make sure your children know and see your love regularly. Make the marriage they see in you the same type of relationship they'll want one day for themselves.

DISCUSS
If your children were asked to describe your relationship, what would they say? Why not ask them.

PRAY
Pray that your children see real love between two real people for a lifetime.

VALENTINE'S DAY MASSACRE

You have not remembered the days of your youth
but have enraged Me by all these things.
EZEKIEL 16:43

It arrives so fresh off the heels of Thanksgiving and Christmas, it's easy to overlook. You've just barely gotten used to writing the new year on your bank checks. For all practical purposes, it's simply the typical weekday between February 13 and February 15.

But this is not a day for practical purposes.

This is Valentine's Day. And Sam forgot it.

Sam's wife had a card addressed to him, hidden in her top dresser drawer. Her gift to him was under her dresses in the closet. She waited for him to make the first move, to end this little dodge of his. There he was, sitting down to watch television at 7:30 at night as if he might be camped out there till bedtime . . . as if he'd actually forgotten what day this is!

Finally, at 10 P.M., when Sam had stumbled upstairs to brush his teeth, he found his wife sitting bolt upright in bed. Somehow the temperature felt noticeably cooler in that room than in the other parts of the house.

"What's the matter? What'd I do?" He did a super-quick scan of his usual offences. Everything checked out.

"Tomorrow morning," she said through clenched teeth, "I expect to find a gift in the driveway that goes from zero to two hundred in less than six seconds. *And it had better be there!*"

With that, she snatched her pillow and blanket and trudged off, presumably to the downstairs sofa, leaving Sam standing there looking very unmanly, totally exposed as a Valentine forgetter. But his pride wasn't about to be threatened so easily.

The next morning his wife found a gift box in the driveway. She tore it open and looked inside.

It was a bathroom scale.

Sam has been missing since Friday.

DISCUSS

What *is* the kind of gift you like to receive on Valentine's Day?

PRAY

Pray that you both will be sensitive to one another's needs for romance and love on the other 364 days of the year.

Get Connected for More Information
http://www.familylife.com/moments/romance

VALENTINE'S YEAR

Be exhilarated always with her love.
PROVERBS 5:19

"I really thought romance was something you did on special occasions like Valentine's Day and your anniversary. But you know, I think my wife might want romance a little more often."

You think?

Valentine's Day came and went yesterday. All over the country, beautiful cards were opened, heart-shaped candy boxes exchanged hands, and flower vases sprouted up on tabletops and nightstands. Last night, lingerie was worn and thrown on the floor where it belongs. And somewhere in the back of your mind, you might have given yourself some pats on the back for points scored. Money in the marriage bank. "Okay, that's done."

Actually, though, Valentine's Day should function as a small reminder of the kind of romance we should be cultivating 365 days a year. It should help us see that the reason why Valentine's Day brings out the best in us—romantically speaking—is because it's something we mark on the calendar. We plan for it. We go to the store a week in advance to avoid that sick feeling of choosing from the picked-over cards left on February 13.

What if you were that thoughtful and deliberate *every* time you made plans to romance your spouse? What if you regularly flipped through the Sunday ads, seeing if there was something you could give her that would bring out a smile? What if you gave yourself the assignment of pulling off a surprise Valentine's Day in the summer or the fall or a week from Wednesday or a month after her birthday—not to give expensive gifts, but just to pick some ordinary days to do some out-of-the-ordinary things?

I hope your Valentine's Day was fun. But wouldn't it be a lot more fun if this became your Valentine's Year?

DISCUSS

What if you took turns doing romantic things for one another for the next 30 days? Share what would be fun and romantic to you. Set a minimum of each of you doing three to five things in the coming month.

PRAY

Thank God for His gift to you and for the love of your life—and for keeping your love life with each other from growing stale.

Get Connected for More Information
http://www.familylife.com/moments/romance

UP CLOSE AND PERSONAL

Each individual among you also is to love his own wife even as himself.
EPHESIANS 5:33

Someone has said, "Love is blind, but marriage is a real eye-opener."

How true. You start marriage from a distance. Your honeymoon view is soft and fuzzy, filtered through a fine mist of warm feelings. Goose bumps. Everything appears to be perfectly put together. But the closer you get to one another, the more flaws you see.

If you were looking at me from across the room, there are some things you couldn't tell about me from that vantage point. You wouldn't be able to see that a childhood case of chicken pox left a noticeable scar on my forehead. You wouldn't notice the little nick I got right above my eyebrow from sledding into a fence when I was five years old.

Marriage is much like that, isn't it? The longer you are together, the more things you learn about this man or woman—this person you once kissed at a candlelit altar—that are not very pleasant, not too pretty. Marriage truly is the process of two selfish people learning to love one another in the midst of their imperfections.

For some, that's where divorce is born . . . if not actual legal divorce, then emotional divorce. But for you, it can be where love and commitment grow, as you draw closer and closer without rejecting the other or fearing rejection yourself.

That's what Jesus did when He saw you. Love motivated Him to move toward people who were unlovable. And in the ongoing experience of marriage, He gives you the opportunity to embody His kind of love each day, getting up close and personal, forgiving, persevering, growing in Christ by refusing to grow apart. In marriage, life is lived in very close proximity. You need Christ to love your spouse through you, despite your spouse's flaws, disappointments and weaknesses.

DISCUSS

Admit two unlovable traits you know about yourself. Then thank your spouse for loving you anyway—for being patient as you fight to overcome them.

PRAY

Lift your prayers of confession before the Lord right now. Then thank Him for His long-suffering and for giving you someone to exemplify love right before your eyes.

Get Connected for More Information
http://www.familylife.com/moments/conflict

A DOSE OF TRUTH

*But speaking the truth in love, we are to grow up in all aspects
into Him who is the head, even Christ.*
EPHESIANS 4:15

I remember when Barbara and I were concerned with the way our teenage son was handling money. Every time we brought up the subject, he became angry.

One evening, I invited our son to go jogging. As we ran, I talked about how he was handling money. When anger began to surface once again, we stopped running and I put my arm around him and said, "You know what? As long as I'm your parent, God has called me to work in your life to develop your character in conformity to the Scripture and to encourage you to become a Christlike person. And right now, I'm called to help you deal with this issue. I just want you to know that your mom and I are together on this subject. We've talked about this. We believe you've got a problem with how you're handling money."

I hugged him again and said, "I don't want to whack you up the side of the head with this. I want to appeal to you and to the Holy Spirit that God has put within your heart for you to yield to God and learn what needs to happen in your life so that you become conformed to the image of Christ."

We started jogging again. After our run, I suggested that we get a glass of lemonade and finish our conversation. To my amazement, my son smiled and said, "You know, Dad, I think I'd like to have that glass of lemonade with you."

It's important to speak the truth in love to our children, but we need to do it with love and compassion. That gives us the ability to appeal to them so that they ultimately learn to yield their wills to Jesus Christ.

DISCUSS
On what issues do your children need a dose of truth in love right now?

PRAY
Ask God to give you the right combination of exhortation and love in order to speak to the hearts of your children.

PAST PROBLEMS

My mother's sons were angry with me; they made me caretaker of the vineyards.
SONG OF SOLOMON 1:6

Song of Solomon is filled with wonderful insights on love and marriage. Many of them have been well taught through sermons and conferences and Bible studies. But some of the deepest lessons lie between the lines, where you see what's really going on in this ancient yet timeless relationship between Solomon and his bride.

Solomon's young bride did not arrive as a woman already refined and elegant—fit for a king. Instead, the Scriptures indicate that she had a humble, impoverished upbringing. Rather than having the milky complexion of a highborn maiden, her skin was dark and weathered from physical, outside work (as seen in today's verse).

As a result, she brought some needs from her past into her relationship with Solomon. And, men, your wife probably did too.

Yet rather than rejecting her because of her past problems and background, Solomon provided his wife with a love that cast out fear. He gave her the security of knowing that he accepted her just the way she was. When he referred to his Shulammite bride as "my darling" (1:15), he used a term that carried connotations of a shepherd—one who fiercely cares for, guards and tends to his charge.

Men, we need Solomon's kind of passion for rescuing and protecting our wife's heart and accepting whatever difficulties from her family upbringing and past may still be troublesome for her. Give her the freedom to struggle with her past without her feeling demeaned or pressured. That freedom comes when she experiences your consistent, committed love to her.

DISCUSS
Talk about some of the past family issues that sometimes still surface in your mind and cause you difficulty. What do you each need the other to know about how these affect you?

PRAY
Ask God to help you forgive each other for failing to be as understanding as you should about the heartaches of the past. Husband, pray too that God would enable you to love your wife with the kind of love that casts out all fear.

QUIVERING

Like arrows in the hand of a warrior, so are the children of one's youth.
PSALM 127:4

The last three verses of Psalm 127 are some of the most precious in the Bible when it comes to thinking about our children. Barbara and I have certainly had a "quiver" full with our six (see verse 5). But part of the reward God talks about in this passage comes with responsibility—the responsibility to launch our children into adulthood at the appropriate time.

If you've done any archery or bow hunting, you know that the moment you make your release, two things happen: (1) the arrow whips off the bow, and (2) you experience "string slap" as the bowstring smacks against your forearm. Man, it can hurt—the same way the flight of your grown children can ache in your heart.

But there is purpose to this pain. There is a reason for this release.

I'm reminded of what Jim Elliot wrote to his parents after informing them that he was being called by God to the jungles of Ecuador as a missionary. Like any parents, Jim's folks wished for him safety and security, a steady income beneath his feet and a roof over his head. But he said to them:

> Remember how the Psalmist described children? He said they were a heritage from the Lord, that every man should be happy who had his quiver full of them. And what is a quiver full of but arrows? And what are arrows for but to shoot? So with the strong arms of prayer, draw the bowstring back and let the arrows fly—all of them, straight at the enemy's hosts!

No, it's not an easy process. You could wish these years didn't have to come so soon. But by releasing your children purposefully into adulthood—with a biblical sense of mission—you place them under the care of the Holy Spirit, helping them learn to be independently dependent upon Him, becoming the young men and women He wants them to be.

DISCUSS
What do you see as your children's purpose? What are you preparing them for?

PRAY
Trust God's ability to give you what you need, when you need it.

Get Connected for More Information
http://www.familylife.com/moments/releasing

LIFE IN THE FAST-FOOD LANE

BY BARBARA RAINEY

Remember the sabbath day, to keep it holy.
EXODUS 20:8

When Truett Cathy opened his Dwarf House restaurant in the Atlanta suburb of Hapeville, Georgia, in 1946, he made a decision never to deal with money on the Lord's Day. The Dwarf House was always closed on Sundays.

Perhaps this policy didn't seem extremely revolutionary to his post-World War II American patrons. But that small restaurant was the first franchise for Chick-fil-A®—and by the organization's sixtieth anniversary, it had multiplied into over 1,200 restaurant locations. As Chick-fil-A continues to grow, it also continues to close its operations on Sunday, traditionally one of the biggest days for food service.

Being closed on Sunday is a reflection of Truett's purpose statement for his company. It's an investment in the spiritual lives of his employees and a witness to both the watching world and the restaurant industry. He still refers to his closed-on-Sunday policy as "the best business decision I ever made." In fact, Chick-fil-A restaurants often generate more money in six days than other comparable restaurants do in seven.

Being closed on Sunday is also a reflection of one of *my* core values: Sabbath rest. I believe that when we yield control of our lives to the Father—when we reserve our Sundays to turn from our activity to rest and to abide more fully in Him—we receive strength for daily living throughout the coming week and live under the blessing of God.

The Sabbath is God's invitation to draw near to Him, to rest in Him, and to linger by His still waters. It's how He helps detoxify you from the pressures of life. It's how He restores your soul.

Perhaps it's even how He makes Chick-fil-A sandwiches taste so good on Monday.

DISCUSS
How does your family practice Sabbath rest? How could you make God-honoring relaxation more of a deliberate effort?

PRAY
Ask the Lord to show you the value of keeping His Sabbath.

Get Connected for More Information
http://www.familylife.com/moments/stress

ARE YOU WORTHY OF IMITATING?

His delight is in the law of the LORD, and in His law he meditates day and night.
PSALM 1:2

I was talking with a businessman recently who is involved in a Bible study with about a half-dozen men. These guys are all "well oiled," financially speaking. But as I listened to him describe these men, I wondered what kind of Christianity they were modeling to their children.

As parents, we need to think about the priorities we are teaching our children by our words and our actions. Ask yourself, *If I could pass on my relationship with God to my kids, would they be satisfied with what they receive? If my children could never experience anything more than what I have today, would they be given enough to chart themselves successfully through life? Would they experience God? Would they know enough of Christ to long for more—a deeper and deeper fellowship with Jesus Christ?*

One thing we often say in our conferences and on radio is that your children will listen to what you say, and they will do what you tell them, but they will become who you *are*. If your daily experience with Christ is less than you want your children to possess, they probably won't ever have it either.

Your model should be the man in Psalm 1—the one whose "delight" is in spending time with God and His Word (verse 2). The one who "meditates" on the things of God through the ins and outs of the day. The one who keeps him- or herself "firmly planted" by those "streams of water" (verse 3).

Only then will you be the model your children need to emulate.

DISCUSS
Share honestly those things that are distracting you right now from your relationship with Christ. How are you showing your children the reality of truly walking with Jesus Christ?

PRAY
Perhaps you should consider using this prayer time separate from one another and consider surrendering your will to His will. Ask Him to make you worthy of being imitated.

Get Connected for More Information

PEER PROBLEMS

He who walks with wise men will be wise, but the companion of fools will suffer harm.
PROVERBS 13:20

Barbara and I often prayed that the Lord would supply healthy friends to come alongside our kids at school and at church—friends who could be good, steady influences on them. But we also learned four critical unvarnished observations about peers:

1. *Don't assume your children's peers have the same values as your family.* Even if they go to the same church and youth group. Even if they seem to be *like* your children in most respects, don't automatically consider them good friends for your kids to be around. Exercise discernment.
2. *Don't assume your children's peers are good choosers of friends themselves.* Just because a boy or girl comes from a good home, you don't know the kind of friends *they* have. You don't know who's likely to be hanging around at their house when your children are there.
3. *Don't believe everything your children's peers say.* Trust me, even good teens can be deceitful. Our children had friends who lied right to our faces. They lied behind our backs. They were "good" kids by most standards, but they needed to be held accountable and checked up on.
4. *Don't assume your children's peers will speak the truth to your children.* More than any of the other three items in this list, this one snuck up and bit us. Our daughters had friends who were from great families but who literally tried to undermine what Barbara and I were attempting to teach.

It takes energy, foresight and thick skin to monitor your children's friendships. But whatever the cost in tension, embarrassment and involvement, it's a bargain compared to the bill some friends can run up in your children's lives.

I'm not encouraging you to give in to fear and raise loners. I'm not telling you that your kids are too good to be around others. I'm just saying that friends bear watching. Getting to know them well is a good investment of your time.

DISCUSS
What do you really know about your children's friends? How could you find out more?

PRAY
Earnestly ask God to bring godly friends into your children's lives.

Get Connected for More Information
http://www.familylife.com/moments/peerpressure

SHORT END OF THE STICK

Hope deferred makes the heart sick, but desire fulfilled is a tree of life.
PROVERBS 13:12

We all come into marriage with a full yardstick of expectations—what love looks like, what our roles will be, what we'll do on weekends, where we'll go for Christmas. But over the years, that yardstick starts getting snapped off an inch or two at a time, until we're left holding something a whole lot shorter than what we brought with us.

This leads to what I call the Unmet Expectation Syndrome. And every time it happens, the natural reaction is to go from disappointment to hurt to anger and finally to punishment—making your spouse pay for not living up to your expectations.

Here are four better ways to deal with these unmet expectations:

1. *Love and forgive.* Because you vowed before God to remain committed to each other, you must both own up to your failures and responsibilities. Your marriage will never outgrow its need for massive doses of forgiveness.
2. *Communicate and seek to understand each other.* Expectations must be managed, and the best way to do that is to keep the communication lines open. Clarify your needs and expectations. Don't leave each other guessing.
3. *Develop God's perspective.* Your spouse will never be able to meet the needs in your life that can only be met by God alone. Let Him be your sufficiency.
4. *Don't throw away the yardstick.* Don't give up on your dreams. Even though expectations sometimes tend to be out of step with reality, God doesn't want you to live with just a few inches of the yardstick. Keep high hopes and expectations in your marriage, work toward them in a healthy way, and give thanks to God as He fulfills your true and deepest desires . . . both through Him and through each other.

DISCUSS
Share one or two examples of expectations you brought into marriage—and how your spouse has exceeded them.

PRAY
Pray for clear enough vision to see what each other truly needs and desires, and for the will to meet the ones you can with joy and selflessness.

Get Connected for More Information
http://www.familylife.com/moments/marriagerelationship

ALL-OUT PARENTING

*The goal of our instruction is love from a pure heart
and a good conscience and a sincere faith.*
1 TIMOTHY 1:5

I suppose I'm hopelessly tied to my upbringing in the '60s and '70s, when there were a lot of radical movements in America. Today I find myself calling for radical parents who hold radical beliefs, who have radical purpose and who are committed to raising a radical generation that follows Jesus Christ wholeheartedly.

I'm challenging parents to embrace things like the following:

- *Radical selflessness*—It's time for every Christian parent to prayerfully ask, *Am I dying to self so that I can be the parent God wants me to be in raising the next generation?*
- *Radical objectives*—Far too many parents are more concerned with their children's IQ than their CQ—their character quotient. I'm convinced that the primary reason children depart from the faith of their parents is that many dads and moms don't have this as their objective: to raise children who have a godly desire to love others and to live holy lives.
- *Radical modeling*—Children are like tiny radar units. They lock on. They track. They observe. And they imitate. You cannot lie and then demand the truth from your kids. You cannot cheat and then discipline a cheater.
- *Radical involvement*—This means getting down on the floor, hugging them, reading to them, affirming them. It also means initiating discussions with them about some of life's most challenging subjects—human sexuality, modesty, temptations, relating to the opposite sex.
- *Radical expectations*—Are you praying that your kids will grow up to become mature soldiers for Christ, godly men and women equipped for a Kingdom assignment? Are you challenging them with the Great Commandment (see Matthew 22:36-39) and the Great Commission (see Matthew 28:19-20)?

If you're going to raise children who live radically for Christ, you need a radical way of thinking, living and believing.

DISCUSS

On a 1- to 10-point scale (1 being poor and 10 being outstanding), rate yourselves as parents in each of the areas above. Discuss where you are winning and what you need to do to win.

PRAY

Ask God to make you radical parents and radical followers of Christ.

Get Connected for More Information
http://www.familylife.com/moments/biblicalparenting

HOPE REBORN

He will surely be gracious to you at the sound of your cry.
ISAIAH 30:19

My mother, Dalcie Rainey, died just before sunrise on a Sunday morning after a gallant two-year battle with Alzheimer's. She was buried that Tuesday. Then Barbara and I, after lingering behind to visit with family for a day, left early on Thursday and drove to Nashville, arriving just in time for the birth of our third grandchild.

The scene outside the birthing room was thick with drama as Barbara and the other wannabe grandmother stood with their ears cupped shamelessly to the door, straining to hear what was happening on the other side. "It's a boy? A girl?" Nurses paced in and out as both women—like two White House reporters—peppered them for any shred of information.

Finally, at 4:43 P.M., one of the happiest sounds in the world trickled under the door—a newborn baby's cry. Our son Samuel soon inched into the hallway, his grin as wide as the Mississippi River we'd crossed a few hours before. The two grannies accosted him, demanding to know the sex of the baby. And though he tried to remain mysterious—"Stephanie hasn't even held him yet . . ."—notice the classic slip. Both grannies seized on the newfound data, and Samuel Peterson Rainey II was celebrated into the world by a burst of hallway cheers.

As I wrote in an email to family and friends later that evening, trying to capture what I was feeling: "What a contrast of emotions—from the grave to the cradle. I'm grateful to God for how this week concluded. It was a great reminder that there is life after death."

We don't always see these extremes in such close proximity. But the truth remains that in God's economy, life follows death. Hope follows loss. Whatever you've endured, God has heard "the sound of your cry." Await new life.

DISCUSS
What is the truth about God that would enable you to change your attitude and believe God for a dream reborn, for pain to be replaced with promise?

PRAY
Pray that you will believe the truth about God and experience hope, even when you can't yet see it.

GET REAL

When you are praying, do not use meaningless repetition as the Gentiles do.
MATTHEW 6:7

Tommy was a National Guard Reservist called into action during the Gulf War. On the last Sunday before his actual deployment, the church he attended had a special time of prayer, sending him off with their promise of support and encouragement.

As you can imagine, the prayers for Tommy's safety were thick with theology and high-sounding words (as churchy prayers often are): "Sovereign God of the universe, we trust that You will protect this young man on his mission, O Lord, and that You will keep him within the shelter of Your wings." All very sincere, I'm sure, but quite flowery and unoriginal.

Then a little eight-year-old voice piped up from the back, "Dear Jesus, don't let Tommy get killed, okay? That's all. Okay. Amen." The sanctuary fell silent, as everyone suddenly knew that the prayers they had encrusted in adult euphemisms had really been grown-up attempts to say this one thing: "Don't let Tommy get killed, okay?" It took a child to express what adults couldn't.

When Robbie Castleman, author of *Parenting in the Pew*, told me that story, it reminded me of something I'd heard my friend Andre Kole, one of the top illusionists in the world, say: "The hardest people in all the world to fool with your tricks are children." That's because children aren't as complex as adults in trying to figure something out. They just see it for what it is. They're not filtering the solution through so many possibilities.

The next time you pray with your spouse or with a child, get real. Get real simple. Be real honest. Get real with God. With total reverence for God, tell Him what you'd really like to tell Him.

I believe God breaks out in a big grin when we get real with Him.

DISCUSS
How are your prayers duplicates of what you've heard others pray? Do you feel comfortable enough with God to be honest with Him? What is one thing you'd like to get real with God about in prayer?

PRAY
Whatever you pray for today, keep it simple. Just talk straight with Him.

BELIEVE IT OR NOT

BY BARBARA RAINEY

Jesus answered them, "I told you, and you do not believe."
JOHN 10:25

We women are awfully fond of admitting that we need our husbands to affirm us and to express their love and appreciation of us through their words and actions. It's important for us to know—especially after children and age have done their demolition work on our bodies and our once-youthful appearance—that we are still desirable and lovely.

But if we want to be able to rest in the security of our husbands' love, we need to do our part as well.

I remember the day, the time, the place and the details of one occasion when Dennis said to me—in the middle of a Saturday afternoon at home—"I love you, Barbara. I think you're wonderful."

I heard what he said. But the first thoughts that rushed through my mind were, *He can't really mean that. I'm worn out by the constant demands of the kids. The house is a mess. I don't have a stitch of make-up on. I can't be all that much fun to be with on most days.* So I said, "I don't know if I believe that or not."

"You don't have to believe me if you don't want to," he answered. "But it's true."

It was like a light bulb clicking on. I don't know why it seemed more sure and certain to me at that moment than any other, but I realized he was right. It was my choice to believe him . . . or not. He couldn't give me the affirmation and love I needed if I wouldn't receive it! I couldn't expect him to affirm and value me if I dismissed his compliments as false.

So rather than listening to my emotions, I chose to believe the truth that he did in fact really love me, and I chose to do my part, which was to receive that love.

DISCUSS
Wives, discuss your need for words of affirmation. Do you believe those words when your husband shares them with you? Why or why not?

PRAY
Wives, ask God to help you be a good receiver of your husband's love.

FUN AND GAMES

A joyful heart is good medicine.
PROVERBS 17:22

Everyone knows about the prestige of the Nobel Prize, an award given to those who make significant political, scientific and literary contributions to the cause of peace and human understanding. (It's named, ironically, for the inventor of TNT. He wanted to be remembered for something constructive rather than destructive.)

But perhaps you've never heard of the Ig Nobel Awards. These prizes are given for achievements that "first make people laugh, and then make them think."

Among recent honorees are those who have studied the following:

- How to stop hiccups
- Why woodpeckers don't get headaches
- Why people dislike the sound of fingernails screeching on a blackboard
- Why dry spaghetti often breaks into more than two pieces when you bend it
- How many photographs a person must take to ensure that nobody in a group photo will have their eyes closed

One of my favorites was the 2006 winner in the "peace" category. He earned his Ig Nobel for inventing an electro-mechanical teenager repellent, a device that makes an annoying noise audible to teenagers but not to adults. (In the interest of fair play, he used the same technology to create cell-phone ring tones that could be heard by teenagers but not by their teachers.)

All this to say: Don't feel like the only way you can cause your children to think and engage with you is through serious teaching. Bring up a wacky topic at the dinner table one night and see where the conversation goes. Get them thinking about making good choices over a game of Twister. Examine the creativity of God by asking them how many different faces they can make.

One of the greatest, most satisfying parts of parenting is learning how to make good use of fun. Laughter is God's lubricant for the soul. Fun reduces friction when a parent wants to get an important truth in his or her child's heart. Learn to laugh. A lot!

DISCUSS

When would be some of the best times to incorporate instructive fun into your family's schedule? Brainstorm something goofy that your kids would love for a family night.

PRAY

Pray that your hearts will be cheerful and fun-loving. There's a lot of life that can really wear you down.

Get Connected for More Information
http://www.familylife.com/moments/familyfun

A PARENT'S TOP FIVE

A righteous man who walks in his integrity—how blessed are his sons after him.
PROVERBS 20:7

Barbara and I have not been perfect parents. But when you have as many children as we do, God gives you a few hundred lessons along the way. And from our years of experience, we've come up with a list of five non-negotiables that all parents need in order to raise a family God's way:

1. *Understand the times.* In past societies, the culture helped reinforce the values that parents were trying to instill in their children. Not today. That's why you need to be surrounded with a few like-minded parents who can support, encourage and counsel one another through the choppy waters of modern life. A great church is where you'll find them.
2. *Have a sacred commitment to each other.* Your kids need to see your vows lived out in every circumstance, in times of both peace and conflict. Make it a priority to resolve disagreements with your spouse, to forgive each other, to remain faithful. These qualities of love build a powerful, profound sense of security in children.
3. *Know what you believe.* You are the textbook your children read. Your deeply held values about life will influence your interactions with your children. As parents, you need to know what your unshakable convictions are.
4. *Remember God's perspective on children.* Never forget that children are a gift from God. Raising your children is a privilege and responsibility He has given to no one else, and they should be raised to know Him and walk with Him.
5. *Strive for the right goal.* More than anything else, your children need to grow to love and fear the Lord. That's more important than ensuring they have a good education, develop different skills or learn how to succeed in today's culture. The fear of the Lord is the beginning of wisdom.

DISCUSS
Which of these purposes strike the deepest chord in you? Which ones need the most work?

PRAY
Pray that your priorities will be shaped by God's Word and will influence your choices for you and your family.

Get Connected for More Information
http://www.familylife.com/moments/biblicalparenting

SINNER ON SITE

If we say that we have no sin, we are deceiving ourselves and the truth is not in us.
1 JOHN 1:8

Part of our job as parents is dealing with the sins of our children. Correcting misbehavior, admonishing them for mistakes in judgment and disciplining them for their own good make up a fairly big wedge on the parenting pie chart.

But I believe it's also important that we never develop the impression that our children are the only ones who ever come up short in the character department. They need to know that the two grown-ups they know best in life confess their sins and need forgiveness, too.

Raising children, perhaps more than any other assignment in life, reveals your true character. The spiritual discipline of admitting your own sin is part of what makes your parenting real and genuine.

I can't count the number of times I made a mistake and needed to ask one of my children for forgiveness. Like the time one of our children stepped on my favorite fly rod. It not only snapped, but so did I. I grabbed the remaining pieces of that rod and began to break them against my bent leg in a fit of anger.

Barbara was stunned. The children scurried and scattered to their bedrooms like bugs. Thirty minutes later, I called a family meeting and apologized for my sin.

I'm not just talking about when your sin is something directed solely at your children—they also need to hear how you deal with things like covetousness or pride or retaliation. If you are honest about your own sins, they won't feel so funny admitting them to you, talking about them and learning how you handle them.

Your children need to know they're living with people who are totally dependent on the mercy and grace of the Lord Jesus Christ. They need parents who are not afraid to admit they fail and need the Savior's forgiveness, just like they do.

DISCUSS
Is there a particular sin that you know you should confess to your children?

PRAY
Pray that you will show your children how to be a true follower of Christ.

Get Connected for More Information
http://www.familylife.com/moments/biblicalparenting

A TOUCH MEANS SO MUCH

BY BARBARA RAINEY

They were bringing children to Him so that He might touch them.
MARK 10:13

One of the biggest needs of your children—no matter what their age—is for physical touch. Regular hugs, kisses and hand holding all say to them, "You are loved."

When your children are little, make sure they have lots of time in your lap to cuddle. Hug them for no reason at all. But also be sure to create special traditions of affection each day, like bedtime kisses and good-morning hugs.

Arriving at home after a day of work or an afternoon of running errands offers another great opportunity to give affectionate touch. When our children were smaller, we turned these greeting times into "The Bear Hug Routine." Dennis would get near Deborah, for instance, and say, "Do you want a baby bear hug, a mama bear hug or a daddy bear hug?" Our children would usually work through all three, amid shrieks of laughter. Even today, they still smile when he asks if they or especially their children want a bear hug. The tradition of affection goes on.

Teenagers and adult children, too, need our loving touch. I remember reaching out to hug Benjamin—his growing frame towering over mine, his emerging beard feeling scratchy on my face. I hugged him quickly, let go and tried to step back, only to be pleasantly surprised when he held on tight. He seemed to be saying, "I may look grown up, I may look like I don't need it, but don't stop. I still love it when you hold me."

Does your relationship with your children have some catching up—some *touching up*—to do?

DISCUSS

Did you come from a hugging family? How did that affect you? How does it affect your parenting? What family member needs a hug from you today?

PRAY

Pray that you will never withhold any expression of love your child really needs.

TUG-OF-WAR (PART ONE)

Let us not lose heart in doing good, for in due time we will reap if we do not grow weary.
GALATIANS 6:9

When you were growing up, did you ever get into a real tug-of-war? You know, the kind with a thick, scratchy rope? Two groups pulling against each other and, in between, a murky mud hole the size of Lake Erie?

There's another tug-of-war taking place today. It's a tug-of-war between a parent and a host of worldly influences.

You've felt the pull. You're getting ready to leave the house, and then you stop cold as you notice how one of your children is dressed. You take a deep breath, utter a silent prayer and say, "Excuse me. You're not wearing *that* to school!"

And so the tug-of-war begins. Your child shoots you a look that would melt steel and replies, "But all of my Christian friends dress like this at school!"

If you waffle (and your child will know this within a millisecond, because kids are equipped with digital sensing devices that let them know that Mom or Dad is caving in), you begin to think, *I'm tired of fighting it. Besides if I pull too hard, who knows what my kids will do . . . they may run away and hate me forever!*

So you let go.

Like so many other parents, you probably are suffering from a new twenty-first-century disease caused by this endless tug-of-war: *moral exhaustion.* Many parents are growing weary of holding on to their moral beliefs, boundaries and commitments, and little by little they loosen their grip.

So today and tomorrow I want to get a megaphone out, come alongside you as a parent, encourage you and remind you of the truth: *"Don't let go of that rope!"*

Get into the Scriptures. Let the truth and prayer together strengthen your grip! Hang on. Dig your heels in. Don't quit!

DISCUSS
Talk about raising children in this culture and feeling morally exhausted. What makes you tired as a parent? Be honest.

PRAY
Ask God to empower you and your spouse, and give you moral courage to raise the next generation.

Get Connected for More Information
http://www.familylife.com/moments/biblicalparenting

TUG-OF-WAR (PART TWO)

What, then, shall we say in response to this? If God is for us, who can be against us?
ROMANS 8:31, *NIV*

Four children had left the nest, and we were down to just two at home. You would think we had the upper hand in this parenting thing. But as we discussed the different strains on our family and the constant tug-of-war between us and the influences of our culture, I looked at Barbara and said, "I think we are wearing down in the battle for our family."

As I mentioned yesterday, it's common for many parents to feel morally exhausted by the cultural forces working against them. May I offer some quick training tips for effective "tug-of-war parenting"?

First, *realize you are not holding the rope alone.* Look at Romans 8:31 above. God is for you. What does it matter who is against you? Feel the strength coming back into your arms and hands? God is holding the rope with you. He promises to give strength to the weary (see Isaiah 41:10).

Second, *understand why you feel weary at times.* Take an inventory of all the forces you are pulling against: curfews, dress, language, limits in dating, language, knowing peers, magazines, music, media, telephones, and other cultural heavyweights. You can't eliminate all your tug-of-war opponents, but you can reduce some.

Third, *recruit some other parents to join you and band together in the tug-of-war.* In other words, look out for somebody else's child and not just your own. This may mean talking with other parents and agreeing to call each other if you observe inappropriate behavior in any of your children. It may mean helping a single-parent mom who's losing her grip with her prodigal child.

As Christians, we are in this tug-of-war together. Grab the rope!

DISCUSS
What can you as a parent do to get some relief from the cultural tug-of-war as you raise your children? Pray for one another? Team up with a small group of parents?

PRAY
Read through Romans 8:28-39. Thank God for loving you, regardless of how well you are doing as a parent.

Get Connected for More Information
http://www.familylife.com/moments/biblicalparenting

HUMOR ME

We do not preach ourselves but Christ Jesus as Lord.
2 CORINTHIANS 4:5

It's always dangerous to make assumptions. I am reminded of the business-woman who found herself with an extra hour of airport down time. She bought a magazine, a coffee and a small package of cookies, preparing to pass the time as best she could in the crowded waiting area.

Absorbed in her reading, she reached over and picked up a cookie to nibble on. To her great surprise, a stranger two seats over reached into the same packet and began eating the second cookie. Stunned, she tried to ignore it. Only after 20 more quiet minutes did she reach in to take the third cookie. The stranger took the fourth. Then he picked up the near-empty package and sarcastically asked, "Would you like the last one?" Infuriated, she marched off in a huff to the airline gate, reached into her bag for her boarding pass . . . and found her unopened package of cookies! Her anger had been based on a wrong assumption.

Some assumptions are much more dangerous than that. It occurs to me, for example, that one of you may never have actually taken the step of faith to surrender your life to Jesus Christ. You may have the wrong assumption that your good works will get you into heaven.

You can change that at this moment. Jesus Christ, who lived a perfect life, died on a cross to pay the divine penalty for your sins and was raised to life to defeat death forever, is as near as your next breath. He offers eternal life to you in His open hands.

If you are not sure you are a follower of Christ, if you've never received His gift of salvation, would you confess your sins to Him right now and, through faith in Him, receive His forgiveness and ask Him to become your Lord and Master?

DISCUSS
Take turns sharing your experience of coming to faith in Christ. Who are some people you know who need the gift of salvation that Christ offers?

PRAY
If you aren't sure where you will spend eternity, pray in faith right now and receive Christ as your Savior and Lord.

IDOLIZING BLUE BELL

Whether, then, you eat or drink or whatever you do, do all to the glory of God.
1 CORINTHIANS 10:31

I think the human race has a problem with addictions. The well-known addictions to drugs, alcohol, sex and pornography have destroyed lives and families for generations. But there are other addictions, even within the Christian community, that are not as evil but are still addictions.

Like food.

Let me illustrate personally. Barbara and I approach food very differently. She eats to live. I love to eat. Food to her is necessary fuel for life. But for me there have been times in my life when I've simply idolized food.

Specifically ice cream.

For years, I felt a day was not complete unless I had enjoyed a mountainous bowl of Blue Bell Vanilla Nut Bean ice cream swimming in chocolate sauce and sprinkled with savory crushed almonds. Honestly, I think I was addicted. And my waistline showed it.

The natural consequence of my addiction forced me to face reality. I became convicted that I was placing way too much importance on ice cream.

I decided that I would use Lent, a 40-day period leading up to Easter that recalls the 40 days Jesus spent in the wilderness, to fast from all desserts. It was fascinating to see how God used this time in my life to create a healthier perspective on food. So much so that for the past three years, I've used this annual season to fast from dessert.

Let me ask you a question: Is there anything that has a grip on your life? Something that has become an addiction and even an idol that has supplanted God in your allegiance? Perhaps it's time to talk about it as a couple and come clean. You and your spouse may need to create some accountability and a lifestyle that will bring about a real life change that honors God.

DISCUSS

Talk about addictions in your family. What are they? How could you use Lent to break their power in your lives?

PRAY

Ask God to help you keep Him at the center of your worship every day and to give you courage to turn away from those things that could ensnare you.

Get Connected for More Information
http://www.familylife.com/moments/spiritualgrowth

SETTING UP HOUSE

A man shall leave his father and his mother, and be joined to his wife.
GENESIS 2:24

On the morning of our oldest daughter's wedding, I sat on a picnic table near our backyard fire pit and wept. This was the very place where we'd shared hundreds of family experiences together over the years, but I knew my relationship with Ashley, who I called "My Princess," was about to change—forever.

Genesis 2:24 instructs newlyweds to "leave" their parents. This doesn't mean cutting off your relationship with them but instead committing to place a higher priority and loyalty on your spouse. This was what Ashley was about to do.

As you think about your parents, here are some healthy boundaries that will enable you to leave, cleave, and protect your marriage:

1. *Never speak disrespectfully about your spouse to your parents.* Early in our marriage, I shared one of Barbara's weaknesses with my mother. I was astounded at how quickly Mom rushed to my side, like a mother hen coming to shelter her wounded chick. My mom never forgot that weakness. As a result, I promised Barbara I would never again discuss negative things about her with my mom.
2. *Be deliberate in the way you plan your holidays.* At some point, it will be time for you to start establishing your own traditions in your own family. And even when those traditions include visiting with parents and in-laws, keep your stay brief.
3. *Don't depend on your parents for finances.* There may be a rare situation where their assistance may be appropriate, but if you depend on them habitually you can play to a weak spot in your parent's lives where they create "emotional IOUs."

And if you're the parent or in-law in this scenario and your children don't build these hedges around their own marriage, be mature and loving enough to build them around yourselves. Encourage your children to leave, cleave and establish their loyalty to one another.

DISCUSS
How well have you done in leaving and cleaving? What still needs some adjustment?

PRAY
Ask God to give you wisdom in how you relate to your parents and, when the time comes, to your adult children.

Get Connected for More Information
http://www.familylife.com/moments/commitment

GO FIGURE

With humility of mind regard one another as more important than yourselves.
PHILIPPIANS 2:3

As a man, I like equations and formulas. Their logic rings true: 2 + 2 = 4. You can always count on that.

But while equations and formulas work when you're trying to figure out how much deck stain to purchase at a home-improvement store, they're not always reliable when it comes to romancing your wife. The same quantity of flowers and love notes that touched her heart so meaningfully a month ago may not have the same effect tonight.

I know. Trust me. I've made this mistake *many* times.

Two plus two doesn't always equal four. Even though I sometimes I wish it did.

This is good, Barbara tells me. Your wife wants you to be a student of her. Part of the intrigue and mystery of marriage is in knowing what communicates love to her at any given time.

Does she need to get out of town for the weekend—or just have a break for an hour? Does she need a full-body massage—or just a foot rub? Would breakfast in bed make her day—or is taking her to lunch on the menu?

Sometimes she likes a planned surprise—perhaps something special you've cooked up for the weekend. Other times, though, she enjoys it when you're impulsive—she's thrilled to know that she just popped into your mind. Sometimes she's in the mood for a soak in the tub. Or she'd like a walk in the snow after dark, hand in hand.

Focus on what *she* enjoys doing. Make *her* feel special. Recognize that she's not a law of physics but rather a puzzle, one that resists being pieced together, solved and framed on the wall. Beware of thinking that passion and romance are as predictable as 2 + 2 + 2 = 6.

We're building a relationship here, not a house addition.

DISCUSS

Husband, ask her, "What's the best thing I can do today to communicate that I love you?"

PRAY

Pray for a heart that doesn't take each other for granted, one that knows how to enjoy *familiarity* without becoming predictable *similarity*.

THE POWER OF A WOMAN

BY BARBARA RAINEY

*I have come out to meet you, to seek your presence earnestly, and I have found you.
I have spread my couch with coverings, with colored linens of Egypt.*
PROVERBS 7:15-16

Few things are more abhorrent to me than seeing women make sexual advances toward married men, either on television or in real life. We should recoil at this kind of behavior. But just because flirtation is often corrupt doesn't mean there's anything wrong with making sexual advances toward *one* married man—the one you're already married to.

I believe we can learn something from the powerful woman described in Proverbs 5-7. Although she is an adulteress and would not typically be seen as a positive role model, perhaps there is a pure use of this power when these tactics are directed toward a woman's own husband. For example:

- *Her lips "drip honey" and are "smoother than oil" (Proverbs 5:3).* There was a time during the dating season when gentle, soothing speech came easily. But now in marriage, it's all too easy to gripe and complain. Words are powerful. Use yours well, and you'll melt him like butter.
- *"She seizes him and kisses him" (Proverbs 7:13).* What would be the look on your man's face if, when you first saw him at the end of a day, you grabbed him around the shoulders and really planted one on him? There's not a man alive who wouldn't wonder what you'd had for lunch that day—and who wouldn't hope you'll have it again tomorrow.
- *She captures him "with her eyelids" (Proverbs 6:25).* We wives can tend to get sloppy with our appearance around the house. That's understandable. But every once in a while, make sure you look good when he comes home. *Really* good. Use your eyes to engage him. "Capture" him with your physical attractiveness.

A wife who understands her allure as a woman is protecting her husband from temptation. She's like a magnet, drawing him home from the seductions of his day.

She's got power. And she knows how to use it.

DISCUSS
Wives, find out from your man what would really make his day.

PRAY
Pray that God will never let Satan, who knows how to twist it, steal the joy of sexual attraction and romance from you.

Get Connected for More Information
http://www.familylife.com/moments/wives

THIS IS THE CHURCH

*They were continually devoting themselves to the apostles' teaching
and to fellowship, to the breaking of bread and to prayer.*
ACTS 2:42

I hope you're already part of a church family—not as a spectator but as a committed, involved participant in a community of followers of Jesus Christ. But if you're not, here are five things you should look for as you consider establishing yourself in a church. If you're already an active member and any of these things are lacking in your congregation, consider what you can do and how you can be praying for these characteristics to blossom there:

1. *Is it anchored in the Scriptures?* Is the Bible clearly taught as the authoritative Word of God? Is the gospel of Jesus Christ the anchor, motivating you to live and proclaim the transforming grace of God in every area of your life?
2. *Does it have a sense of community?* Is there a connectedness between people when the service is over on Sunday morning? Does there seem to be authenticity and honesty in the relationships?
3. *Is it characterized by worship?* Today's culture is incredibly self-centered. You need an interruption in your week to jerk you out of that stream and say, "There's something much bigger than me going on here. Life is not about me; it's about who God is and what He's doing."
4. *Is there opportunity for involvement?* Is this a church where you're encouraged to minister to others? One of the greatest joys of life is to be used by the Lord God Almighty in another human being's life.
5. *Does it build men?* I'm not minimizing ministry to women and children, but a lot of the struggles in our families and culture could become points of victory if men were equipped with a vision for manhood and were living it out.

DISCUSS

Give your church—or the church you are considering—a letter grade in each of these five areas. Compare grades and talk about how you can help your church become more effective.

PRAY

Pray that God will make your church experience one filled with blessing, opportunity and community.

Get Connected for More Information
http://www.familylife.com/moments/church

THANKFUL FOR THE CHANGE

You were continually straying like sheep, but now you have returned to the Shepherd and Guardian of your souls.
1 PETER 2:25

"It almost seems as though our family has moved out of this house and another family has moved in." That's how one couple described the transformation that God brought about in their marriage after they attended one of FamilyLife's Weekend to Remember marriage conferences.

Another woman told how she threatened her abusive husband that she would end their marriage if he didn't go to the conference with her. She had the divorce papers in her pocket, ready to sign. "I am so thankful he chose to go. He cried for the entire weekend as we broke down 20 years worth of brick walls. His entire attitude and outlook have done a one-eighty."

We host more than 150 of these getaways every year in cities all over the United States, helping thousands of couples rediscover what they saw in each other in the first place . . . and more. But it's not just because *we're* there. It's because God is there. Working.

One couple, who admitted that their fighting and bitterness toward each other had only increased in the weeks leading up to the conference, shared how on Saturday night—the date night of the weekend—"we communicated about issues we never even thought to talk about before. We laughed. We cried. In fact, we were so caught up [that] when we looked up at the clock, we realized it was almost 9 P.M. We hadn't even had dinner! We have never been as open and honest with each other."

Maybe you're not the conference-going type. Maybe you prefer the ongoing process of working things out every day. But I promise you, you'd be surprised to see what God can do with one weekend devoted solely to seeking Him and His best for your marriage.

DISCUSS

When was the last time you went away together for a weekend and invested in your marriage? What could be better in *your* marriage with just a little time to stop and think about it?

PRAY

Ask God to show you ways that you can invest in one another and in your marriage on an ongoing basis.

Get Connected for More Information
http://www.familylife.com/moments/conflict

MARGIN FOR ERROR

Many plans are in a man's heart, but the counsel of the LORD will stand.
PROVERBS 19:21

As a particular three-month period of time approached, Barbara and I already knew it would be busier than usual. We had overcommitted and underestimated, which we've had a tendency to do. Everything would need to fall just right if we were to squeeze it all in without anybody suffering.

How was I to know, though, that in the months leading up to this intense season of travel, our family would undergo one of the biggest personal challenges we'd ever faced? How could I have known that Bill Bright, my beloved friend, mentor and boss, would call me up from his death bed, asking me to come to Orlando to meet with him one last time? How could I have known that my mom would fall gravely ill and die—and that four days later our son Samuel's first child would be born?

I couldn't. That's just life. As C. S. Lewis so aptly put it, "We must stop regarding unpleasant or unexpected things as interruptions of real life. The truth is that interruptions *are* real life."

That's why it's essential to build some margin into your schedule—the wiggle room necessary to accommodate immediate needs while allowing for unexpected demands and disruptions.

It means framing your obligations in larger time blocks than they really require, just in case traffic is exceptionally bad or you're delayed leaving the house. It means agreeing on the number of evenings or weekends you will tie up each month with outside activities. It means talking together about possible commitments *before* you say yes, to keep yourselves from living too close to the edge.

You can't prepare for some things, no matter how well you plan. But most schedule shocks can be absorbed by building in a margin, leaving space for surprises.

DISCUSS

Discuss what margins could do for you and your weekly schedule. Talk about what times of the year need margins in your schedule. Decide on a process for protecting one another as you schedule commitments.

PRAY

Pray for wisdom from above in making the courageous choices to get your lives under control—and keep it under control.

Get Connected for More Information
http://www.familylife.com/moments/stress

FOR BETTER, FOR WORSE

Do not merely look out for your own personal interests,
but also for the interests of others.
PHILIPPIANS 2:4

I've been doing daily radio since 1992, and I can recall only one time when I was weeping so hard I couldn't speak. It was the day I interviewed Charlie and Lucy Wedemeyr.

At the age of 30, Charlie began experiencing the early symptoms of ALS, commonly known as Lou Gehrig's disease. A successful high-school football coach, he was given one to three years to live.

Even now as I reflect on our time with them in the studio—with Lucy reading his lips and speaking for him—the emotion is profound. They recalled a day when Charlie, his care becoming more and more demanding on his wife and children, whispered to Lucy, "Maybe it would be better if I just died."

Lucy took a deep breath, asked the Lord for just the right words, and said to Charlie, "We'd rather have you like this than not at all."

Having him "like this" has meant more than two decades of continual life support. It takes Lucy three hours to get him ready each day!

Lucy is a model of what we promised to each other in our wedding vows. In sickness and in health. For better or for worse. Keeping our covenant means more than avoiding divorce—it means we'll be there, living out our love, no matter what.

Don't wait until you get in a dramatic situation where you're facing something like Lucy and Charlie before you cement your promise to care for one another through any circumstance. If you don't prepare for it today by submitting to the Lordship of Jesus Christ over your life and clinging to God's blueprints, you'll be unprepared when—not if—your crisis comes.

DISCUSS

Look each other in the eye right now and recommit yourself to a "for better or for worse" promise. Answer this question: "If what happened to Charlie happened to me, can I count on you?"

PRAY

Thank God for giving you a lifelong marriage partner. Ask Him to help you see each other for the blessing you are—even on days when it's hard.

PAINFUL TRUTHS

BY BARBARA RAINEY

*Therefore the LORD God sent him out from the garden of Eden,
to cultivate the ground from which he was taken.*
GENESIS 3:23

People have often asked about our philosophy of disciplining children. I guarantee we were not flawless in carrying it out, but I do believe the Lord showed us a scriptural pattern of discipline that bore fruit in our family.

I remember a friend asking me on the phone one day what I thought she should do about her little toddler who was throwing food off the high-chair tray. "What you need to do," I said, "is make it painful for her to continue that behavior. That's what God did with Adam and Eve—He gave them pain when they disobeyed."

As I thought more about this, the truth of it came even clearer to me: God gave Adam and Eve two kinds of pain as part of His disciplinary measure: *physical pain* and *emotional pain*.

We know about the pain He gave Eve in childbirth. As this relates to disciplining children, that pain may take the form of spanking (within proper boundaries). But God also placed physical pain on Adam—the pain of hard work in toiling and tending the land. We found that giving our children a difficult work task in response to their disobedience was another biblical form of discipline.

God also gave Adam and Eve emotional pain. He removed them from His presence and from the pleasure of His company. In your family, this may mean sending a young child to his or her room or taking a toy away for a period of time. An older child may be grounded (again, the emotional pain of not being with friends) or given some other restriction.

When these approaches are taken in love, you direct your children toward a path of obedience and restored relationship—just as God does with us.

DISCUSS
When discipline is nothing but immediate reaction to wrongdoing, it loses its sense of purpose. What are some larger goals you have for your children's behavior?

PRAY
Pray that you will have the courage to bring an appropriate amount of pain to bear on your children for disobedience.

Get Connected for More Information
http://www.familylife.com/moments/discipline

THE 80-PERCENT DIFFERENCE

And the wife must see to it that she respects her husband.
EPHESIANS 5:33

I once asked Elisabeth Elliot, who for decades has been one of the most respected women in Christian culture, a very specific question: "If you had a group of wives who had all been married between 10 and 15 years—that difficult stretch when the honeymoon is long gone, when responsibilities are high, when the children are often plentiful and chaotic—what would be the best piece of marriage advice you could give them?"

Her answer, as always, is worth remembering:

> Respect your husband, and don't argue. A wife at that stage of marriage realizes this is not exactly the man she envisioned before the wedding ceremony. This person whom she thought was a prize package has turned out to be a *surprise* package. But the more you can offset the differences in your personalities and the way you respond to each other, the more you can learn to enjoy this man.
>
> My husband once made the statement: "If a woman conceded the fact that her husband was perhaps up to 80 percent of her expectations, she ought to consider herself very lucky." Still, what's she going to do with the other 20 percent?
>
> You can pick away at that 20 percent for the rest of your life, but you're not going to reduce it by very much. One of the secrets of a good marriage is learning to accept with gladness the 80 percent you've got.

Barbara and I have seen that even the best of marriages come with differences of opinion and expectations, with many sources of potential conflict. If we obsess over each other's flaws, they can soon blot out all the other's strengths. Elisabeth is right: Marriage is less about eliminating each other's faults and more about celebrating each other's value.

DISCUSS

Take turns naming three or four things you truly appreciate about one another—the things that made you want to marry each other.

PRAY

As you pray, take turns thanking God for some specific ways that your spouse complements you. And seek His kind of patience and understanding as you deal with your spouse.

Get Connected for More Information
http://www.familylife.com/moments/mediachoices

IS WORSHIP WORTH IT?

Let us not give up meeting together, as some are in the habit of doing,
but let us encourage one another.
HEBREWS 10:25, *NIV*

Ever witnessed anything like this at your house before? After falling under deep conviction during the pastor's sermon entitled "The Family Altar Will Save Your Family," Dad cranks up his courage and announces, "Tonight after dinner, we *will have* family devotions." Later, after finishing his spaghetti, he pushes his plate aside, reaches for the 10-pound family Bible and says, "Everyone please sit up straight and listen carefully. It's time for family worship."

Casting a pleading glance at Mom, he asks, "Honey, would you start us out with a praise chorus?" After a weak song attempt—during which seven-year-old Tom blurts out, "This noise is making my head hurt!"—Dad is already sitting upright and is uptight.

"Okay, now let's read some Scripture. What better place to start than the first three chapters of Genesis?" He then proceeds to read the lengthy selection.

"Does anyone have a comment?" Dad asks. A long silence follows. Tom sticks his face in his water glass and tries to drink through his nose, causing Chrissy, age five, to giggle. "Stop it, you two!" Mom exclaims. "Can't you see Daddy is being spiritual?"

"Dad, I've got a lot of homework," says Chuck, the family teenager. "Can we wrap this up?"

"Well, what about Genesis, everybody? Come on. Any comments?" Dad asks, his voice rising. Feeling desperate, he looks at Mom. She quickly averts her eyes. Finally, Chuck lobs in a conversation starter: "What do you think God was doing before the Bible began?"

"I have no earthly idea," Dad says. "Let's pray."

I'll share some encouraging ideas for family devotions tomorrow, but for now let me say this: *At least this family is trying.* I know family devotions can cause a fair share of stress and self-doubt. But don't let the awkward moments keep you from assembling together.

DISCUSS
Do you have family worship in your home? Why or why not?

PRAY
Ask God to show you how to make family worship fun and interesting for you and your children.

Get Connected for More Information
http://www.familylife.com/moments/familyworship

JUST DO IT

So will My word be which goes forth from My mouth;
it will not return to Me empty.
ISAIAH 55:11

The hypothetical scenario I shared with you yesterday about the frustrations of family worship probably isn't too far from what you've experienced. Just about all of us who have ventured to put the Bible front and center in our homes have had to crawl past situations very similar to that one.

One of the best pieces of advice I could give you about getting started is this: Take the pressure *off*! Don't make this harder than it actually is. Do what works for your family.

At different times in our family's life, we've done different things:

- Barbara led our youngest girls through a children's Bible study in the mid-morning, just working through the book and asking the questions that were written there.
- I took the school-age kids to a local grocery store for a doughnut breakfast once or twice a week, where we'd read a chapter from Proverbs—stopping at any verse that caught our interest enough to talk about it.
- When the youngest four were teens, we started each day with a reading from a devotional that shared stories from history about men and women of faith.
- After dinner on occasion, I might have raised an ethical question of some kind, just to get everyone thinking about how they might handle it. Then I'd read a Scripture that related to our discussion.

There's no formula. No guideline. No perfectly right way. The only real requirement is that you do *something to get your family into the Bible*, even if it feels uncomfortable at first, and plan out what you're going to talk about. You and your children simply need to hear God's Word and interact with it on a regular, daily basis. I promise you, He'll take care of it from there.

DISCUSS
Find a topic that you need to discuss at the dinner table. Schedule it.

PRAY
Ask God for great resources to help you get started.

Get Connected for More Information
http://www.familylife.com/moments/familyworship

EASTER ALREADY?

That I may know Him and the power of His resurrection.
PHILIPPIANS 3:10

As Easter approaches, don't you often wonder why Christmas gets all the good press, while Easter is treated more like a very distant second cousin? After all, it's a commemoration of the greatest news ever proclaimed in history: *Christ is alive and we are forgiven!* Easter arrives with so little fanfare, we almost forget it's coming.

I think there are three main reasons why even Christians neglect the importance of Easter:

1. *It's not interesting to the secular community.* While the entire culture is focused on gift-giving and food-filled festivities at Christmas, Easter doesn't fit as well into our society's love affair with materialism.
2. *It's not connected with many family traditions.* Outside of going to church and having a nice Sunday dinner, few families have Easter memories that pass down from generation to generation. Chances are you don't have a special box containing your Easter reminders. (At FamilyLife we've been pleased to see our Resurrection Eggs help to fill this gap for Christian families. It's simply one idea among many you could try to make your Easter celebration more intentional and meaningful.)
3. *Though we like Advent, we shy away from Lent.* Perhaps many Protestants have the perception that Catholics have the corner on this particular celebration, since it is common during Lent for many Catholics to give up something desirable to commemorate Christ's sacrifice. In some cases, this may be practiced in an overly legalistic way that misses the point altogether, but I think we've recoiled from a great idea—preparing our hearts to celebrate the most precious event of our lives. I think we need to revive this time-honored tradition.

Easter is the crowning point of the Christian's life—the death and resurrection of our Lord and Savior. It's the sole reason for our hope and joy. Make plans now to really celebrate it this year.

DISCUSS
What would you like to do differently and better in your family's Easter celebration? Start now.

PRAY
Pray that you will be able to lead your family toward experiencing the true love, forgiveness and hope that are found in the real story of Easter.

Get Connected for More Information
http://www.familylife.com/moments/holidays

BUT IS IT ENOUGH?

Through His own blood, He entered the holy place once for all,
having obtained eternal redemption.
HEBREWS 9:12

It began as a short, one-night romantic getaway for Martin and Gracia Burnham. It turned into a year-long nightmare when armed Philippine rebels burst into their cabin and took them hostage. These humble, hardworking missionaries, whose hearts had been wedded to their work in the Philippines, now found themselves with a handful of other captives, trudging at gunpoint through the tropical jungles of this island nation.

By the time it was all over, Martin was dead from a stray bullet fired during their rescue. Gracia escaped but was a widow.

There are many amazing accounts of faith recorded in Gracia's autobiography, *In the Presence of My Enemies*, describing the events and emotions of those harrowing 12 months. But one of the most haunting was one she shared with us one day in a radio interview.

As their hostage odyssey neared Easter, Martin and Gracia were told by their captors that a sizable amount of ransom money had appeared in the camp. Gracia's family had collected it, hoping against hope that it would be sufficient to satisfy the terrorists' demands. But in the typical fashion of irrational diplomacy, the leaders of the group called the couple over and made this curt pronouncement: "There is a ransom that's been paid for you, but we've decided it's not enough."

That really struck me, especially with "Easter" and "ransom" being mentioned in such close proximity. How tragic would it be to go through life, not knowing for sure whether Christ's payment—His ransom for us—was enough. What if our lives, instead of being safe and secure in the arms of His forever provision, were still teetering in limbo, subject to the changing whims of an unpredictable, unjust God?

Thankfully, we won't have to worry. His ransom has already been declared complete and acceptable on our behalf.

DISCUSS

Recall for a moment what it was like to be lost, under the penalty of sin and in need of a ransom to be paid by the Savior.

PRAY

Thank Him for the ransom that was paid and a full and totally guaranteed salvation.

Get Connected for More Information
http://www.familylife.com/moments/holidays

ONE MAN'S NUMBER ONE LOVE

Let your fountain be blessed, and rejoice in the wife of your youth.
PROVERBS 5:18

He coached his UCLA Bruins to 10 NCAA basketball titles—including 7 in a row. At one point, his streak of consecutive victories stretched to 88 games, nearly double the amount—even today—of the next coach on the list. Four undefeated seasons. Nineteen conference championships. An overall winning percentage of .813, spanning a career of more than 40 years. Only one losing season in all—his first year in coaching—with the Dayton (Kentucky) High School "Green Devils" in 1934.

And only one wife, for 53 years, until her death on this date in 1985.

But for a man of John Wooden's stature and character, that's not where the numbers end.

According to a *Sports Illustrated* article, Coach Wooden sits down every month on the twenty-first and writes his wife, Nellie, a simple love note. He tells her how much he misses her. He tells her what her life and love always meant to him. He tells her he can't wait to see her again. Then he goes to a stack of other love letters, now numbering in the hundreds, resting on her pillow and tied with a yellow ribbon. He adds the new one to the growing collection and goes to sleep on his side of the bed, drawing the same bedspread over him that once warmed the two of them together.

This is a man who understands that "winning scores and great reputations are meaningless in the eyes of the Lord, because He knows what we really are, and that is all that matters."

So put "devoted husband" above John Wooden's long list of accolades as greatest coach of all time, because that's who he really is.

DISCUSS

How have you seen devoted love lived out in others who've been married for more than 40 or 50 years? In what ways do you plan and promise to show devoted love to each other into your older years?

PRAY

Pray for commitment that goes the distance and for eyes that never grow dim to what God has given you in the gift of your spouse.

Get Connected for More Information
http://www.familylife.com/moments/husbands

I'M HERE FOR YOU

Bear one another's burdens, and thereby fulfill the law of Christ.
GALATIANS 6:2

Barbara and I admit that we've never experienced depression in its rawest, deepest form. Yes, we've had seasons of intense discouragement. We've had our share of valleys, crying out to God in the agony of our souls. We know what it means to suffer. Still, there are ravages and depths of depression we don't know about firsthand.

But if one of you suffers with depression's telltale signs—low self-esteem, severe fatigue and sleeplessness, lack of concentration—we know it affects you both. And the strain of it has the potential to steadily increase the distance you may feel from one another.

So we encourage you today to love your husband or wife in ways that are intensely real, genuine and sacrificial. Instead of taking all of this personally, realize that the emotional darkness your mate is experiencing likely has little or nothing to do with anything you've done or not done. This is simply your chance to listen, to be patient, to go to him or her without accusations or piously offered "overly spiritual" answers.

Rather than urging your mate to "snap out of it!" or flip a switch that allows you to get on with life, this may just be a time to crawl up in bed and hold each other. To pray, offer comfort and read the Scriptures. To remind each other of what's true and eternal and longer lasting than any earthly suffering and hardship.

Do you want to be a hero to your wife? Do you want to be the gleam in your husband's eye? Then be your mate's most faithful encourager. Be his or her rock to lean on when everything seems dark and cold and purposeless. Don't lay blame. Don't become short-tempered. Don't come down hard and make demands.

Just carry the burden . . . "and thereby fulfill the law of Christ."

DISCUSS
Talk about what you need most from each other when you're down or depressed.

PRAY
Ask Christ to shine His own love and comfort and patience and power through you.

Get Connected for More Information
http://www.familylife.com/moments/depression

CHILDREN OF TEARS

Women received back their dead, raised to life again.
HEBREWS 11:35, *NIV*

One thing we painfully learn throughout life, either by direct experience or observation, is that rebellious children can come from any type of home. But even as they run from God and from us, and even in our anguish and frustration, we must hold them before God in prayer, trusting Him to lead them home.

One of the greatest examples of this is Monica, the mother of Saint Augustine. She watched him spend his teenage and young adult years rejecting her Christian faith while outdoing his friends in seeking sinful pleasures.

At one point she persuaded him to meet with an unnamed bishop from North Africa. The bishop refused to speak to Augustine because he considered him as yet unteachable. Even though the meeting proved unsuccessful, the bishop comforted Monica in her distress, saying, "It is impossible that the son of so many tears should perish" (from *Confessions*, St. Augustine).

You may well know the rest of the story: The Lord God dramatically converted Augustine in his Roman garden, urging him to "take and read" the words of the Scriptures that would open his eyes to the wickedness of sin and the promises of Christ. Only the mother of a prodigal can quite understand the joy in Monica's heart when she held her now-grown son in her arms, rescued by God's grace and a mother's prayerful tears. She died nine days later—her purpose in living fulfilled. And Augustine went on to become one of the most influential figures in Church history.

Oh, how the grief that can well up inside of us when we watch a child push God away! Barbara and I have experienced the pain and sorrow that never seem to let up. But we've also found comfort as our concern and tears were routed to God through prayer, knowing that He never stops seeking their restless hearts.

DISCUSS
If you have a child who is breaking your heart, share with one another your concern, disappointment and sorrow.

PRAY
Beg the Lord to redeem His wayward children, by whatever means will get them back. And pray that you will have hearts whose hope is in God.

THE REAL NEED (PART ONE)

A fool does not delight in understanding, but only in revealing his own mind.
PROVERBS 18:2

As I settled into my seat on the small regional jet, I noticed that the man next to me was embroiled in an intense cell-phone conversation. Although he was doing his best to control his anger and keep his voice down, his conversation was unavoidable for me—and all the passengers within two rows of him.

He was talking to his former wife. Listening to him was like watching a sword fight where you can only see one of the competitors. With his blade, he verbally sliced and pierced the woman on the other end of the phone. The conversation ended with a verbal decapitation when he declared, "And *you* are *no longer my wife!*"

He demanded to talk with his daughter, and when she came on the phone, the sword fighter was instantly transformed into a puppy. He began by compassionately asking her questions, but at the end of the conversation he made one last thrust of the sword, saying her mom was a "wimp."

After he hung up the phone, this noble warrior informed me, "Any man can be a father," he said, "but being a parent takes a real commitment. Hard work." I wondered if he was using the same dictionary that I did.

He mentioned that he was living with a woman who was expecting his child. I asked if the baby's birth might lead them to get married, and his response was, "Why spoil a good thing with a piece of paper?"

As I sat there, God reminded me of something: *What is this man's real need?*

As a sinner myself, saved by grace, I recognized that this man's real need was to know God's love and forgiveness. The warrior had certainly made a mess of his life, but there was One who would forgive him and could help him clean it up.

DISCUSS
Who in your life needs to know Jesus Christ as their Lord and Savior?

PRAY
Ask God to help you remember that you, too, are a sinner saved by grace and to help you freely share the hope of the gospel.

THE REAL NEED (PART TWO)

*For all have sinned and fall short of the glory of God, being justified as a gift
by His grace through the redemption which is in Christ Jesus.*
ROMANS 3:23-24

As my flying companion (from the story I began yesterday) and I began to talk,
I asked about his relationship with God. He told me about a near-fatal accident
he had once experienced. After rolling his truck several times, he was pro-
nounced dead at the scene of the accident. A few minutes later, he was resusci-
tated. He said that while he was "dead," he saw a hand come out of the light and
push him back toward his earthly life.

I asked him if he believed God has a reason, or purpose, for his life. When
he nodded yes, I took the next 10 minutes to explain the gospel to him.

You would think that someone who had been through such an experience
would be spiritually receptive to the gospel. He wasn't. Like many, he was
determined to reach heaven on *his* terms, not God's. My new acquaintance
thought that Jesus Christ might be the way for me but not for him.

My conversation that day was a fresh reminder that the real need of people
is to acknowledge their need for the one true God, to admit their sinfulness
and to experience by faith His love and forgiveness. If we don't understand our
own sinfulness and the judgment and penalty it demands, then there seems to
be no need for the Savior.

Jesus Christ died for our sins and was raised so that, if we humble ourselves
and receive Him as our Lord and Savior, we can be forgiven—despite any mess
that we've made of our lives.

No, this man did not make a commitment to Christ. My responsibility
before God was to be faithful to share Jesus Christ and give him the opportunity to surrender to Christ.

I hope he won't forget our conversation. I certainly won't. I'm still praying
for him.

DISCUSS
What is your understanding of your sinfulness? Why do you need the Savior?

PRAY
Spend time praying for people you know, including your children, who need
to understand why they need Christ.

Get Connected for More Information
http://www.familylife.com/moments/helpingothers

INTERNATIONAL FLAVOR

BY BARBARA RAINEY

*Go therefore and make disciples of all the nations, baptizing them
in the name of the Father and the Son and the Holy Spirit.*
MATTHEW 28:19

From early on, Dennis and I let our children know that God had a special mission for their lives. We explained that He had gifted them with abilities, personality and other qualities that were tailor-made to help them accomplish His plan. We also taught them that the Great Commission—found in Matthew 28:19-20—applied not just to grown-ups but also to children.

Granted, there are many local opportunities available to put these principles into practice. Church outreaches. Homeless shelters. Nursing-home visitation. Foster care. But to really cement this calling in an iron-clad, unforgettable way, nothing beats the value of a short-term mission trip. It moves them out of their comfort zones—us, too!—and shows them the real need that others have for Christ.

I remember taking our three youngest daughters on a two-week mission to Russia. We joined a group of 400 men, women and children who gathered in Moscow to minister to the spiritual and physical needs of children there. We went by the busload to schools, orphanages and family centers, distributing boxes of food, medicine, clothing and books.

Our girls were able to hand out Bibles and good-news bracelets everywhere we went. Two of them gave a gospel presentation through an interpreter. Children born and bred in the heart of Arkansas developed a love for people a world away, putting names and faces and hugs and handshakes onto what was once just another dot on a map.

Whatever the risk, whatever the cost, these are eternal investments in the lives of your children, helping them taste both the sacrifice and the joy of being a missionary. They will never forget it.

DISCUSS
If there's an opportunity like this available to you, what would keep you from taking advantage of it?

PRAY
Ask God to give you a heart like His for the world and that if you decide to go, He will provide.

Get Connected for More Information
http://www.familylife.com/moments/spiritualtraining

LURES AND WADERS

Give preference to one another in honor.
ROMANS 12:10

For more than 50 years I have enjoyed fishing. And ever since our honeymoon, when we went fishing together, I've been inviting Barbara to get into the sport with me. Finally she agreed to give it a try on a vacation out West.

I bought her a fly rod and hired a guide to teach her, and finally there we were floating down the majestic Snake River near Jackson Hole, Wyoming. *Finally,* I thought, *she's fishing with me, enjoying the experience.* It was just perfect!

At one point during our float, the guide who was with us began to instruct Barbara in the techniques of fly fishing. Now, one thing you never want to do is stand to the right side of a right-handed fly fisherman; the whipping motion of that line going back and forth can sail wide fairly easily and the fly can snag you. But when I saw the guide had Barbara positioned in the boat to his right, I figured he was the pro and knew what he was doing.

That proved to be a wrong assumption. As he was lofting the fly back and forth the wind began to gust. I thought, *This* really *isn't a good idea for Barbara to be standing to his right.* At that very moment, the guide flung his hook smack-dab in the middle of her forehead. I will never forget that moment. It was a ghastly sight. An imitation Caddisfly on a size 6 hook stuck in my beautiful wife's face! Drops of blood ran down her nose.

It wasn't as bad as it sounds. It didn't even leave a mark. I was reminded of what a great wife God had given me to be willing to get outside her comfort zone and join me in something I enjoy.

When was the last time you stepped outside your comfort zone for your spouse?

And yes, Barbara has been back fly fishing with me since then. But she doesn't stand to my right.

DISCUSS
What would you love for your spouse to try with you just once?

PRAY
Pray that you two will have fun together and be adventuresome.

Get Connected for More Information
http://www.familylife.com/moments/marriagerelationship

WITH FRIENDS LIKE THAT . . .

*It has been granted to you on behalf of Christ not only
to believe on him, but also to suffer for him.*
PHILIPPIANS 1:29, *NIV*

As Bob Lepine, my cohost on *FamilyLife Today*, was leaving for work one morning, he put his arm around his wife and prayed, "Lord, I ask that You would stretch Mary Ann today, that You would challenge her spiritually and cause her to grow in the image of Christ."

And when he "amen"-ed his way to a close, Mary Ann looked back at him and said, "Would you mind just praying that I'd have a nice day and that the kids would behave?"

Even though I can certainly sympathize with Mary Ann, I also recognize how important it is to pray for my wife to grow spiritually—even if it requires asking for a little "stretching" to occur. The key is to *know* her and to be tuned in to her truest, deepest needs.

There are clearly times when you should pray that your wife has a good day filled with all the things that give her joy—or for your husband to be blessed with success and a sense of God's favor on his work. But there are also times when it's appropriate to pray that the Lord will deepen your wife's faith or expand her view of God. There are times to pray that the only way your husband will taste the thrill of victory is when he allows Jesus Christ to work in and through him to conquer a particular challenge in his life.

Prayer is so much more than a wish list at a candy store. Communicating and relating to God on behalf of each other means understanding that what your husband or wife wants may be the last thing he or she needs. Be willing to pray bold, farsighted prayers. And be willing to have them prayed over you.

The secret of spiritual fitness is often found in the stretching.

DISCUSS

Share with one another a couple of things that you could use prayer for—challenges you are facing.

PRAY

Ask God to continue to grow your spouse's faith and dependence upon Him.

DISCIPLING AT A DISTANCE

*The LORD longs to be gracious to you, and therefore
He waits on high to have compassion on you.*
ISAIAH 30:18

You should always consider your children your primary "disciples"—the main ones you're responsible in leading to faith in Christ and keeping infused with biblical truth and spiritual guidance. But this can become a very difficult task, especially through the teenage years, when simply keeping up a conversation can present a challenge. Many teenagers—boys especially—just don't seem to want to talk.

Don't give up. Continue to pursue them. Be prepared for that moment when the mood shifts and the words finally come out of their mouths, when the opportunity to make a connection opens up right in front of you.

We'll never forget the struggle we had when one of our teenage sons didn't want to talk to us. It was a constant challenge to initiate a relationship with him. He felt he could do just fine without us. Over and over again, Barbara and I reminded ourselves that we were the adults and he was the child, that what he needed from us was mature, adult love—not immature rejection.

It's easy in such situations to feel hurt and to withdraw, to quit caring what God wants them to learn. But that's the exact opposite of what your teen needs. When we continued to pursue a relationship with our son, time revealed the benefit he received from having two parents who never stopped loving and believing in him. Believing in your child is one of your child's greatest needs.

Our model in pursuing our children is Jesus Himself: "Behold, I stand at the door and knock; if anyone hears My voice and opens the door, I will come in to him and will dine with him, and he with Me" (Revelation 3:20). He knows better than anyone the kind of work and patience it takes to make disciples.

DISCUSS
What are the main causes of distance and separation between you and your children? Which are normal and need to be overlooked, and which ones are trouble spots that you need to pay attention to?

PRAY
Pray for persistent, active patience in developing a relationship with your kids.

Get Connected for More Information
http://www.familylife.com/moments/involvement

STILL STANDING

He who tends the fig tree will eat its fruit,
and he who cares for his master will be honored.
PROVERBS 27:18

We see a lot of advertising slogans today. Companies are always looking for newer, snazzier ways to position their products and services. But one positive feature that can never be dreamed up in a brainstorming session is a statement such as "Serving You for More than 50 Years" or "Celebrating 75 Years of Excellence."

Statements like these can't be bought from an ad agency. They can only be earned over time.

The same thing holds true in your life as a Christian. Even though all of God's promises were yours from the beginning of your walk with Christ, the awesome experience of bearing fruit over a lifetime can only be seen through the lens of many years. And when those years have been fully invested in the Lord rather than routinely squandered on foolish alternatives, the return is sure to be bountiful beyond measure.

Today's verse from Proverbs is a good reminder of this truth. Solomon was saying that our years of faithfulness will be rewarded. An orchard that is faithfully tended for many years will enjoy a much more productive yield than a new one. The more it matures, the more fruitful it becomes.

If you're still fairly young, I hope you realize that your choices now *do* matter. If you're not quite so young anymore, don't rest on the past. Keep growing a life whose fruit bears the seeds of eternity and reflects the greatness of the Gardener. Every year in His orchard is another opportunity to be used by Him in achieving His purposes in this generation.

Perhaps the "slogan" you can hope to hear on that day when you stand accountable to Him in eternity is "Well done, good and faithful servant. Enter into the joy of your Master" (see Matthew 25:21).

DISCUSS

What evidences of Christ's character in your life today were simply not true of you 5 or 10 years ago?

PRAY

Ask that you will run the race that He has set before you and that you will run well, side by side, all the way to the finish line. Pray that you will finish strong!

Get Connected for More Information
http://www.familylife.com/moments/spiritualgrowth

WHEN LOVE SAYS NO

BY BARBARA RAINEY

I do not write these things to shame you,
but to admonish you as my beloved children.
1 CORINTHIANS 4:14

One story that stands out among those contributed to my book *A Mother's Legacy* is Vonette Bright's account of the "kissing club" that she and some other teenage girls tried to start, in hopes of getting kissed by some of the boys in school. But whether through small-town "telegraph" or just a mother's intuition, Vonette's mother arrived home before the kissing had reached more than two or three pairings. Not surprisingly, she broke up the club's first (and only) meeting and incited a new regimen of mother-daughter teaching on the proper dynamics of opposite-sex relationships.

"There are only so many ways to show physical love," Vonette remembers her mother saying, "and we need to be very careful to whom we display affection." Rather than leaving her daughter to the confusing pull of peer pressure, this loving mom gave her daughter rules and reasons for making wise choices with her heart and body.

"How grateful I am that Mother loved me enough to say no many times," Vonette writes. "She took the time to develop a relationship with me where I learned I could trust her judgment and confide in her freely. It paid off. There are no skeletons in my closet, which contributed greatly to my happy and lasting relationship in marriage."

Parents must love their children enough to say no when it's necessary. Parenting is not a political campaign or a popularity contest. "No" is a very powerful and important word, if you want to shepherd your children safely through the growing-up years.

DISCUSS

Reflect back on a time when your mom said no to you and you are glad she did. In dealing with your children, where have you been letting things go when you should be saying no?

PRAY

Ask the Lord to keep you discerning and perceptive, able to see clearly what your children need. Pray, too, for courage to give them what they need, not what they want.

Get Connected for More Information
http://www.familylife.com/moments/purity

A DEBT OF LOVE

*You shall rise up before the grayheaded and honor the aged,
and you shall revere your God.*
LEVITICUS 19:32

As a teenager, I recall my dad pushing back from the dinner table and walking a few blocks to visit his mother. Sometimes I would go with him, though the visits were pretty boring. There was little more than the ticking and occasional chirping of the cuckoo clock and the creaking of Grandma Rainey's rocking chair. Not exactly high-tech entertainment for an adolescent.

But my dad's commitment to maintain a relationship with his mom made an impression on me. I've never forgotten it.

Looking back now over the 26 years my own mom lived alone after my dad's death, I wish I had done a better job of keeping up communication with her. Sure, we lived 4 hours away, and yes, we had 6 children in 10 years. Barbara had health issues. We were incredibly stretched and busy.

Even my attempts at calling Mom once a week didn't always happen. And though we went to see her several times a year, I'm convinced I didn't think often enough about the loneliness she was experiencing with her increasing age.

As I went through her bedroom after her death, I discovered a dresser drawer full of notes I had written her over the years. I believe she kept every one. It made me wonder how many times each of them had been read and re-read.

It made me wish there had been more. It made we wish I'd been as attentive to her all along as I became in the last two years of her life after she got sick—holding her hands, kissing her on the cheek, turning off the television when I visited so that we could talk without distraction.

If it's still possible, I urge you to make the sacrifices to keep your relationship intact with your parents—encouraging them, appreciating them, making sure they know how much they mean to you.

DISCUSS

If your parents are living, what could you do to keep in touch with them more often?

PRAY

While asking the Lord to keep and protect your parents, offer yourself as part of His answer.

Get Connected for More Information
http://www.familylife.com/moments/honoringparents

A DEBT OF GRATITUDE

Owe nothing to anyone except to love one another.
ROMANS 13:8

It's been both fun and extremely touching in writing these devotions to go back through the mailbag and re-read some of the letters I've received over the years. I love hearing from those who have been inspired through our ministry to invest in their families.

Here's an excerpt from one of my favorites:

> After listening to your broadcast, I was motivated and excited to write a tribute to my parents. We were planning a big eightieth birthday celebration for my dad in June, and I thought this would be the perfect gift for him.
>
> When the big day came, I had the tribute ready. I wanted to read it aloud, but there were a lot of friends and relatives there, and I knew I would get very emotional. I was about to chicken out, but my daughter said, "Mom, you can't just give it to him. You have to read it to him. It'll mean so much more." So through laughter and tears and with great emotion I made it through.
>
> When I finished, my dad said, "That is the best gift anyone has ever given me." Little did I know, however, that I would never see him again this side of heaven. He died of an aneurysm the very next day.
>
> Writing that tribute has helped me deal with my dad's death. When a loved one dies, we often have regrets of what we didn't say or do. Guilt can seep in and overwhelm us. But it has brought me great comfort knowing that I was able to express my love and gratitude to him in a way I'll never forget. I cannot thank you enough for what you've done in making my last moments with my dad a real treasure.

Her letter reminds us that we should speak our words of love and gratitude to family members when they are alive. No regrets.

DISCUSS
What is something you've always regretted not doing or not saying to honor someone? How could you go about rectifying it?

PRAY
Ask God for the gift of gratitude . . . and for clear opportunities to express it to others.

Get Connected for More Information
http://www.familylife.com/moments/honoringparents

HONORING NOT JUST ANY FATHER

Bless those who persecute you; bless and do not curse.
ROMANS 12:14

Several years ago, I began a mentoring relationship with Bryan Carter, an African-American pastor in the Dallas area. One of the first things I challenged him to do was to write a tribute to his father to thank him for the things he had done right.

This was a challenging assignment, because Bryan and his father had developed a very strained relationship as adults. That's why I challenged him with the assignment—because I knew he needed to cross this bridge of understanding and forgiveness, even toward a father who had really hurt him.

It took him nearly two years, but Bryan stepped up as a man and honored his father with a written tribute. Not only did Bryan read it eye to eye to his father, but he also took this same challenge back to his congregation. And they didn't like it either.

For four weeks he preached it. For four weeks he worked them through what the Bible says about understanding, forgiveness, returning blessing for cursing, and responding with honor. Many of those who sat within range of his pulpit came from homes where their parents were far from affirming, if they were even present at all. The prospect of finding something good to recognize in their moms and dads required sorting through mountains of debris and disappointment. It was much easier to find blame than to give thanks.

But they did it. Some reported that they called their parents on the way home from church and witnessed forgiveness flow right over the phone. Some reconnected in letters, reestablishing ties that had been long severed. Some even saw one or both parents receive Christ as their Savior.

These are the miracles God routinely orchestrates when we honor our parents—even if they've been less than honorable.

DISCUSS

Regardless of your experience growing up, I'd like to challenge you to write a tribute and read it to your parents, too. Talk together about how you feel about this assignment and about your parents.

PRAY

Ask God to give you the courage and obedience to do what you need to do.

Get Connected for More Information
http://www.familylife.com/moments/honoringparents

SEEING PARENTS AS PEOPLE

Understanding is a fountain of life to one who has it.
PROVERBS 16:22

Not everyone has fond memories of their relationship with their parents. Perhaps even now, the relationship you share with your parents is strained and distant. You may even find yourself avoiding them, weary of being hurt by the things they say or do . . . or don't do.

But one of the great opportunities of being an adult is to step back and look at your parents in a fresh way—as real people, with needs and challenges. By looking at your parents more objectively—by seeing them through the eyes of Christ—you may be able to understand them and your relationship with them. And you may also experience what happens when His grace transforms the hard edges of a strained relationship into something that bears His redemptive fingerprints.

Consider taking a fresh, careful look at your parents today. What do you see? Do you see people who experience worry, insecurity, fear, disappointment and anger—just like you? People who've made wrong and unwise choices in life—just like you? People who struggle—just like you?

I remember how, when my parents were alive, I had to grow out of my childish self-centeredness and my desire for them to meet my needs. As I began to understand what *their* needs were, I was prompted to move toward them and want to help meet those needs.

Most adult children do not know their parents as well as they think they do. By seeking to understand them, you also honor them in obedience to God's clear command (see Exodus 20:12).

You can tell when it's happening, too, because even though their behavior toward *you* may not change, you find that you don't react to them like before. You find it easier to extend grace and patience. You don't always agree with them, but at least you understand them.

DISCUSS
What are the things your parents are dealing with at this stage in their lives? How could you help meet their needs?

PRAY
Pray that God will give you true insight into your parents and help you better understand them and give them grace and honor.

WHEN REALITY EDITS THE ILLUSION

BY BARBARA RAINEY

Be devoted to one another in brotherly love ...
rejoicing in hope, persevering in tribulation.
ROMANS 12:10-12

Many of us marry with the illusion that the excitement and magic of new love will never fade away. Then, at some point in the first couple years of marriage, we wake up and realize that reality is a bit different. That's when we enter the season of *disappointed love*.

I think the secret to dealing with the inevitable disappointments we face in marriage is found in one simple word: *commitment*.

Commitment is choosing to take your husband's hand and walk through the reality God has allowed in your life, believing that on the other side you will find a deeper love and a healthier relationship than you had before.

Sometimes moving past disappointed love will mean restating your wedding vows, as one couple did at a marriage conference. Facing a time of extreme trial, they said:

> After going through a painful separation and getting back together, renewing our wedding vows had a profound effect. We both were crying so much that we barely got through it. We had not been wearing our rings for about a year and thought there was no hope. Restating our vows helped to put us on the right track. Funny how our vows meant so much more to us now than they did 19 years ago.

At other times, commitment is an inner resolve to conform to what you know to be true in spite of your feelings. Your covenant of commitment to God and each other is the heart of what remains once reality has edited the illusion of what you *thought* marriage would be.

At your wedding, you stood before God and promised to never forsake each other, "for better or for worse." Now, staring "worse" in the face, you have a choice. Will you honor that commitment?

DISCUSS

In what ways has your relationship been different from what you expected? Find your wedding vows and re-state them to one another by candlelight after the kids are in bed.

PRAY

Ask God for the absolute determination to stay together no matter what struggles you face in marriage.

Get Connected for More Information

http://www.familylife.com/moments/commitment

PRAYER WALL

But we prayed to our God, and because of them we set up a
guard against them day and night.
NEHEMIAH 4:9

After one of our many radio broadcasts in which I talked about the vital importance of praying together as a couple (I hope you're hearing that strongly in this
book, because it is so essential to the success of your marriage), a gentleman
wrote me with a new way of looking at this. I thought this was quite profound
and encouraging:

> When I was growing up, we lived in a small three-bedroom bungalow, so it
> was impossible not to hear my parents audibly praying each night before
> they went to sleep. I grew accustomed to hearing their nightly words of
> petition and gratitude for each one of us as they knelt down together
> beside their bed.
>
> Several years ago, as I was sorting through some of my own parenting
> strategies and comparing them to my parents, I received this mental pic-
> ture: I see parenting as a wall that we construct by choosing various stones.
> Some are the same ones our parents used, while others are decidedly differ-
> ent. But regardless, there will always be gaps between these irregularly
> shaped stones. None of our walls are perfectly constructed.
>
> That is where prayer comes in. Those prayers—like the ones my parents
> faithfully sent heavenward over the years—are the mortar supplier. As we
> pray, God fills in the gaps and makes the wall strong.

He's right. There are no perfect parents. There are no foolproof strategies
that work without incident every single time. But there is prayer. And there is
God. And there is a power unleashed as we humble ourselves before Him that
does more than any how-to parenting procedure on the planet.

As you build your wall, caulk it with prayer. And watch God hold back your
enemies.

DISCUSS
Talk about the noticeable changes God has brought about in your life as
you've committed to praying together.

PRAY
Pray that in the years remaining, you will be able to count on one hand the
nights you failed to pray with each other.

Get Connected for More Information
http://www.familylife.com/moments/prayer

PARENTING ON PURPOSE

That you and your son and your grandson might fear the LORD your God.
DEUTERONOMY 6:2

Many of us adopt the world's view in how we raise our children: We believe that responsible parenting means making sure they go to the best schools, wear the best clothes and participate in numerous outside activities so that they'll grow into successful adults with well-paying jobs. Sure, we want to build our children's character, but we don't know exactly how to do it. In short, we lack a true, biblical vision for parenting.

In Deuteronomy 6, God reveals why He commands parents to be fruitful—to have godly children who will pass on a godly legacy by connecting one generation to the next. This is why our best hope for renewal in a culture of weakening character and ethics is the restoration of godly homes. *The home is the best place for a child to learn about God.*

I admit it is sobering to bring children into a decadent society like ours. But in God's timing, your children will become His agents in advancing His agenda on Earth. As parents, you need to recapture the biblical imperative that parenting is a sacred calling and that children are worth the effort! God has selected parents for a work the angels must envy—the stewardship of a child's soul.

Centuries ago Otto Brunfel wrote, "If one wants to reform the world and make it Christian, one must begin with children." Now is the time to rise above the chaos and regain a vision for parenting—*biblical* parenting. From God's point of view, raising children is a high and holy calling. They are the living legacy you will send to the future.

DISCUSS

See if you can name two or three biblical goals you want to see achieved in your children. Then match them up with at least one action point you can take to begin seeing your desired results.

PRAY

Ask God to give you wisdom in being purposeful as the parent of your children. Commit to beginning each morning with your parenting goals and priorities in mind. If your children are grown, pray for them as adults and for their children daily.

Get Connected for More Information
http://www.familylife.com/moments/biblicalparenting

THE PERFECT PLACE

For God has reserved a priceless inheritance for his children.
It is kept in heaven for you, pure and undefiled.
1 PETER 1:4, NLT

We all long for the *perfect*. The perfect home, perfect spouse, perfect body, perfect job, perfect church.

In 1976, our family moved from Dallas to Little Rock and bought a little yellow three-bedroom frame house with a porch and white shutters. It was far from perfect—more like filthy, musty and dusty. But after a good six months of remodeling, that house ended up being just fine for our little family of four. I remember my dad coming to visit us there on Ashley's second birthday to help me put up some molding in her bedroom. We laughed about going to the hardware store to look for "quarter-inch putty" in hopes of filling the gap we'd left between the molding trim and the ceiling!

But after seven years and three more children, our cute little three-bedroom house was approaching the population density of Hong Kong. So in search of perfection, we moved west to the woods—just next to the edge of the earth, it seemed. It was good timing, too, because our youngest child, Laura, was already en route before we packed up the boxes.

It took us two and a half Ryder truckloads to make that move—everything from swing sets to wagons, stuffed animals and dolls, Barbara's watercolors and my fishing and hunting gear. And even though it proved to be a great move for our family, this house hasn't been perfect either, nor have the children, the neighbors, Barbara or me.

In fact, we've quit looking for perfect—either in houses or in each other. Instead, we're learning by God's grace to realize that He alone is perfect. And that the only perfect place we'll ever live will be our last move, when we go to live with Him forever in heaven.

DISCUSS

Talk about how you envision heaven.

PRAY

Until you get to heaven, pray that you two can be satisfied with what God gives you, and never more in love with anything than you are with Him.

Get Connected for More Information
http://www.familylife.com/moments/spiritualgrowth

ROAD WARRIORS

Beloved, if God so loved us, we also ought to love one another.
1 JOHN 4:11

Barbara and I know a little about building into our marriage when we are separated by travel. In fact, some of our most miserable disagreements have occurred around traveling. We've come to greatly admire those married couples who serve in the military and are separated for long periods of time because of deployments.

Travel can take a toll on a marriage. In the process of making hundreds of adjustments, we've learned a few lessons:

1. *As much as possible, don't leave packing and preparation until the last few hours at home.* If you're rushed and feeling stressed, the chances of a major misunderstanding and of provoking a conflict rise steeply.
2. *When a conflict or an argument occurs, do your best to resolve tensions before you leave.* I have to admit that I've made a few calls from the airport back to Barbara to apologize and ask for forgiveness. Do not let the sun go down on your anger.
3. *When you say goodbye, always kiss, hug and say tender words from your heart.* Leave a memory that speaks loudly of your love and commitment. Occasionally place a passionate kiss, a "smacker," on him or her—one that says, "I'll be here when you get back."
4. *Use the phone to check in.* At least once a day. If I'm in my hotel room, I turn the TV off when I call home—no ESPN on mute! She *knows* when I do that!
5. *Use email to send "I'm thinking of you" and "I love you" notes.*
6. *Pray for one another and with one another.* It's an excellent way to end a call. As much as prayer binds you together when you are at home, it's needed more when you are separated.

Consider what adjustments you two need to make to protect and build your relationship, even when traveling.

DISCUSS
What expectations do you have of one another when you travel? What can you do to improve your communication?

PRAY
Ask God to give you a supernatural ability to keep your love fresh during times of separation.

QUIET TIMELESS

BY BARBARA RAINEY

May the God of peace . . . equip you with everything good for doing his will.
HEBREWS 13:20-21, *NIV*

As our children were born and my responsibilities as a mom increased, my spiritual disciplines and devotional life became a phenomenal source of failure for me.

As a single and then as a young married woman, I had been so faithful in experiencing daily, set-aside time with God. I relished long seasons of prayer and Bible study, worshiping and basking in His presence. But children brought so many new and unpredictable interruptions into my life, and my pattern for meeting with God became impossible to plan for. I would get into a routine only to have it fall apart within a few weeks. I struggled with this issue for years.

Finally I decided to quit trying!

Understand that this was not a decision to quit *growing* but simply to stop expecting myself to fit the mental picture I had of what a spiritual Christian was supposed to look like. I still prayed every day—but not in the same way for a certain amount of time. I still worshiped and feasted on the Word—but not on a set routine schedule.

It wasn't long before my sense of oppression simply fell away. I learned that being busy as a mother didn't have to rob me of being intimate with God. It just required me to look at things in a new way, allowing my time with Him to wrap around the life He had sovereignly designed for me.

Everyone goes through seasons of added responsibility. Some are harder and longer than others, but each of them comes with new opportunities for growing in grace and drawing closer to the Lord . . . as long as our so-called "right way to do things" is replaced by a relationship with God that's less rigid and unrealistic.

DISCUSS

Talk about how you could help one another in making God be a bigger part of your busy day.

PRAY

Ask for a heart that never stops wanting to know and love God, even when there seems to be no time for either.

Get Connected for More Information
http://www.familylife.com/moments/relationshipwithgod

SOMEDAY

A time to plant and a time to uproot what is planted.
ECCLESIASTES 3:2

A number of years ago, while our house was still bursting with teenagers, I mused on what life would be like when they were gone. Here is part of what I wrote:

> Someday when the teens are gone, our car insurance payments will once again be smaller than our house payments. There won't be any more white-knuckled rides, arguing about how fast is too fast or how close is too close.
>
> Certain sounds won't echo in our home—sounds of hair spray, squeals of delight over a new boyfriend, the sound of doors being slammed in a fit of anger or our teen boys wrestling upstairs. Windows won't reverberate and bulge with bass notes coming from CD songs that no one understands the words to.
>
> Gone will be the dishes in the sink, the help for Saturday chores, discussions about whether a movie is acceptable or not, Bible studies on the book of Proverbs before school, late night knocks on our bedroom door letting us know that someone is home from a ball game. The telephone will occasionally ring for us for a change.
>
> But there will be memories . . . memories of fireside chats, grilled burgers, Dad's French toast, Mom's eggs on toast, fishing and hunting trips, vacations, cats, dates with Mom, dates with Dad, more cats, breakfast in bed on birthdays, and prayers—yes, prayers by the thousands that have been offered up on their behalf.
>
> So in the end, our home won't be empty. Instead, in the words of Bob Benson, "Every room, every corner of the house, every nick in the coffee table will be crowded with memories." And Barbara and I will "sit quietly by the fire and listen to the laughter in the walls."

DISCUSS
If this subject is present tense for you, talk about some of your favorite memories. If future tense, talk about the kinds of memories you wish to create.

PRAY
Thank God for the gift of marriage, family . . . and memory.

Get Connected for More Information
http://www.familylife.com/moments/makingmemories

EYE TROUBLE

I have made a covenant with my eyes; how then could I gaze at a virgin?
JOB 31:1

Men, this may not be an easy thing to admit with your wife sitting right next to you. But let's be honest—you'll likely relate to the story I'm about to tell.

I was seated in a car with another Christian leader—a good friend of mine. We were both away from home, without our wives, waiting for a colleague who had just gone inside a store. And as we sat there, a woman walked by who was, well, drop-dead gorgeous. I caught sight of her as she entered the store, and then turned back to our conversation.

When she walked by again, by God's grace (or the fear of my own reputation being spoiled), I summoned up enough self-control to look away. But I did notice my friend's eyes lingering as she walked on to her car. Knowing we were both fighting the same battle, I casually said, "Hey, you can look at her once, you can look at her twice, but if you look at her that long . . ."

We laughed. We knew.

Guys, there's nothing wrong with appreciating a woman's beauty. But we all know in an instant when we've reached that point where we're no longer simply noticing her but have begun enjoying her and letting our minds become a playground of lustful thoughts. That's when Fred Stoeker, coauthor of *Every Man's Battle*, says we must heed the covenant of Job 31:1. With the same impulsive quickness that makes us pull our hands back from a hot stove, we must discipline ourselves to "bounce" our eyes away from her.

Yes, it's every man's battle, all right. But it's a battle we can win.

DISCUSS
Husbands, help your wives understand that this admission of struggle is not caused by being unsatisfied with her. It's a struggle with temptation, lust, sin—a struggle with yourself.

PRAY
Wives, pray for your husbands in this area. Each of you should ask God for help with any deep areas of sin and temptation, especially those that can come between the two of you. Trust Him for the strength to be obedient.

MIDDLE OF THE ROAD

How long will you hesitate between two opinions?
1 KINGS 18:21

Barbara was driving into town from home one day when, topping a hill, she spotted a two-year-old boy standing there in his diaper—smack dab on the yellow line in the middle of the road. Without enough time to brake, she swerved wildly onto the shoulder, coming to a screeching stop a good distance past the child.

Flinging open her car door, she ran back up the street to retrieve the toddler from danger, when the mother—having heard the squealing tires and commotion—raced out into the road herself. She scooped up her crying child into her arms, trembling with shock and fright at what might have been if Barbara hadn't been driving so carefully.

Truly, the middle of the road is no place for anyone to be.

But sadly in our culture today, far too many Christian families are parked in the middle. Not sure what they believe. Not sure what they expect of their children. Not willing to take a stand on certain issues that are clearly biblical. Basing their lives on "near beliefs."

I believe that God is calling families like yours today to be counter-cultural—not in a weird, obnoxious way, but establishing a lifestyle that communicates at a glance, "This family is different. They're distinctive in their beliefs and practices. They represent Jesus Christ."

There is no reason why so many Christian marriages should end in divorce. There is no reason why people who call themselves evangelicals should account for one in every six abortions performed in America. There is no reason why more than half of our Christian teens are engaging in some form of sexual involvement to the detriment of their own hearts and futures.

We've spent enough time in the middle of the road. It's time to get in gear in the right direction and head for home.

DISCUSS

How would an outsider tell the difference between your family and one who didn't claim to be Christian?

PRAY

Pray for the courage to determine and live by your convictions—biblical convictions—no matter the cost.

Get Connected for More Information
http://www.familylife.com/moments/convictions

X-ING THE XBOX

No one can serve two masters; for either he will hate the one and love the other,
or he will be devoted to one and despise the other.
MATTHEW 6:24

In their book *Playstation Nation*, Kurt and Olivia Bruner tell the story of a mom who finally had enough.

Enough video gaming.

She had already earned high marks for unpopularity by limiting her boys' game time to one hour a day. But when she came in one night before bed to tell them, "Time's up," they wanted to "finish a level" of their game before saving their progress. So they made a fatal choice: Instead of shutting the game off, they paused it instead . . . and returned to it in the middle of the night.

When Mom woke up at 2 A.M. and noticed the light emanating from downstairs, she went ballistic at first. Then she disappeared into her bedroom and paced the floor in prayer, asking God for wisdom about how and when to strike. Finally resolved, she went in each room and began pulling plugs and boxing up every piece of game system she could find. Then—with her boys watching in horror—she opened an upstairs window in their three-story house and dropped the whole thing to the ground. Ah, the beautiful sound of smashing electronics!

Drastic? Yes. But one of those boys left soon after for college with seven of his buddies. Before the first semester was completed, four of the seven dropped out and returned home to take part-time jobs so that they could have more time for video gaming. For one young man, however, the addiction was gone, thanks to a parent who cared more about her children's character than their point totals or her popularity.

If video games have taken control of your house, maybe it's time for you, too, to bring your kids back to reality.

DISCUSS
Discuss video games and their impact on your family. What are some reasonable limits to place on your children?

PRAY
Pray that God will give you wisdom to know how to address the "addictions" that tempt and can enslave individuals, destroy marriages and devastate families.

 Get Connected for More Information
http://www.familylife.com/moments/mediachoices

TEMPERATURE CONTROL

The fruit of righteousness will be peace; the effect of righteousness
will be quietness and confidence forever.
ISAIAH 32:17, *NIV*

When you enter a room—whether it's a Sunday School class, a company meeting or maybe a lunch event—it's usually not very hard to gauge the mood of the place. It's warm, it's cold, it's engaging, it's distant, it's comfortable, it's stuffy.

Anybody can be a thermometer.

But as Donna Otto, founder of Homemakers by Choice, shared with us one day on our radio broadcast, we are not called to be thermometers in our homes but thermostats.

That's because thermostats don't just read the temperature. They guide it. They determine how warm or cool the home environment will be.

In the same way, parents determine whether a home environment will be fun, peaceful, authentic, full of grace. Will it be a quiet sanctuary from the hard press of life? Will it be a place of joy and celebration and fellowship?

Many parents today feel helpless in adjusting the climate of their home. They feel as if they can't control the predominant tempo and rhythm of the day. They've grown weary of fighting the TV-watching, video game-playing, tuned-out isolation of individual family members. In the process, far too many homes have lost a sense of purpose and direction. They've become little more than random activity centers, with no grown-ups willing to set the tone.

I encourage you to counter the frantic, frenetic pace of modern life by creating an environment that limits the endless noise of bustle and commotion. Train your children to be still and read a book, to interact, to ponder and to create.

Don't be a thermometer. Set the temperature.

DISCUSS

Take a look at the thermometer—what is the climate in your home? Now name some of the things you love best about the way your home operates. Talk about how you two can reset the temperature of your home.

PRAY

Ask the Lord to unite your family around similar convictions. And where you meet pockets of resistance, pray for the determination to keep pushing for your principles.

Get Connected for More Information
http://www.familylife.com/moments/stress

SAY YOU'RE SORRY

Godly sorrow brings repentance that leads to salvation and leaves no regret.
2 CORINTHIANS 7:10, *NIV*

A friend wrote to tell me of an incident in his home, a scene uncomfortably familiar to many of us. He and his wife had experienced some conflict—nothing major, just enough to leave the air a bit tense as the breakfast rush ended and the kids disappeared for school.

My friend, Keith, admitted that he had "developed the fine art of winning arguments at any cost, especially when I am in the wrong!" So when his wife began to come down pretty hard on him for what he had done, he was half listening and half preparing his case for a suitable response.

"As I caught my breath," he wrote, "readying my tongue for the task, something happened. Just at that moment, God did one of those surprising things it seems He loves to do. No words came. I watched my wife fall silent in turn, as she waited, girding herself for my self-defense. But in place of my impeccable logic, five simple words came out of my mouth: 'I'm sorry. I was wrong.'"

Repentance is never easy. We know. It's even bitter at times. But the fruit is sweet: Husbands and wives forgive each other and discover fresh joy, hope and oneness in their relationship. Children regain loving, attentive parents and are raised to fear God and keep His commandments. The estranged are reconciled. The haughty are humbled. The guilty find relief and rebellion. A family reformation begins.

Keith concluded, "Husband, don't argue with your wife from a position of authority or gifting or power or capacity. Don't win just because you can. Simply apologize." And ask for forgiveness.

Don't you love the way that sounds?

DISCUSS

How often do you repent to your spouse? In what situations do you argue rather than repent when your spouse points out a problem?

PRAY

Ask God for a heart that doesn't argue when caught—that your first thought would not be of self-defense but a desire to see how your actions (or inactions) are affecting your spouse. Pray that you will be quick to admit fault and ask for forgiveness.

FIGHTING WORDS

As for me and my house, we will serve the LORD.
JOSHUA 24:15

During the critical Civil War battle at Gettysburg, a key engagement occurred near the crest of a hill called Little Round Top. A Union regiment under the command of Colonel Joshua Lawrence Chamberlain was charged with defending this strategic position. If the Rebels flanked his unit, the rear of the Union army would be exposed and the battle would probably be lost.

"You are to hold your ground at all costs," Chamberlain was commanded.

Again and again, Rebel soldiers stormed the regiment's location. Again and again, Chamberlain and his men repelled the assault. They answered fire with fire and held the high ground with a tenacious stand of bravery.

Today, our nation has a Little Round Top of our own—the family. And like Colonel Chamberlain's heroic defense in 1863, our modern battle demands unwavering courage from everyone involved. The courage of husbands and wives who will turn from the seductive voices of the culture and make their marriages work. The courage of moms and dads who will reject the poisons of materialism, choosing instead to use biblical principles to shape the conscience and character of the next generation.

We are living in a culture where parents spend fewer than 15 minutes *a week* in serious discussion with their children. Where about half of marriages eventually end in divorce. Where decades of moral relativism have left many of us pessimistic about whether we can even enjoy family success under our own roof, let alone win the cultural battle at large.

Now is the time to fight for your family. And in the words of Colonel Chamberlain's superiors, I call you to "hold your ground at all costs." Stand firm!

DISCUSS
What are the leading causes of fatigue in the battle for your family? What is one critical step that you need to take to protect those you love the most?

PRAY
Pray for diligence, pray for reinforcements, and most of all, pray for each other and every member of your family that you will stand strong in the battle. Pray that none of your children will ever experience divorce.

Get Connected for More Information
http://www.familylife.com/moments/battleforfamily

A MOTHER'S INTUITION

BY BARBARA RAINEY

So that you may prove what the will of God is, that which is good and acceptable and perfect.

ROMANS 12:2

One of the most difficult days I can remember was when I drove to meet my college-age daughter with the expressed purpose of encouraging her to break off a serious dating relationship.

I assure you, my decision was not impulsive but a result of prayer. By most accounts, the young man seemed to be everything we wanted for her in a husband. But when I went walking in the mornings, thinking and praying about this whole situation, my intuition just told me it wasn't right. Dennis had questions of his own, and this confirmed my uneasiness.

It's very important that we allow our adult children to brave the hard knocks of life and establish their independence. But I also believe that when it comes to matters of romance and to life-changing decisions about marriage, there are times (not many) when we still need to make our voice heard.

Things didn't go too well that day. She appreciated my concern, she said, but she was convinced I was wrong. As we drove away and our paths diverged once again, tears began welling in my eyes. I had to pull off the road, weeping, fearing I'd lost her forever.

But the story didn't end there. Over the next few months, God brought about a change in her heart, without further comment from me. Not only Dennis and I but also some of our other children—and even a good friend who eventually became her husband—were part of God's instruments in helping her determine His will.

I learned that my mother's intuition can be very valuable and on target when I'm seeking to walk closely with Christ and please Him. I also learned that my adult daughter needed her parents' guidance and approval in this life-altering decision of choosing a mate.

DISCUSS

In what areas do your children need your guidance right now? If your children are single adults, ask them how you can encourage them.

PRAY

Ask the Lord for wisdom in dealing with your children, at every stage of life.

Get Connected for More Information

http://www.familylife.com/moments/mothers

SPIRITUAL QUESTION MARKS

*Always be prepared to give an answer to everyone who asks you
to give the reason for the hope that you have.*
1 PETER 3:15, *NIV*

I am so grateful I had a mom and dad who received Christ as their Savior and were assured of being welcomed into heaven when they died. But I know it's not that way for everyone.

Perhaps you are not sure if your parents have a real faith in Jesus. If so, I encourage you to consider three things. (And if not, I hope you'll store these suggestions away to share with people who do face this issue.)

1. *Pray.* Ask God to use you or someone else to communicate His love to them. And if words seem awkward or stiff when bringing up spiritual things, then talk less and pray more. Too often in our zeal for our parent's salvation, we can become preachy. It may be more important that you pray for them and that you show your parents honor and love and other tangible proof of the difference Christ makes in your life. Pray that they will see Him in your countenance, your attentiveness to their needs and your sacrifices on their behalf.
2. *Share a tribute.* I've heard from many people who have written tributes to parents who are not followers of Christ. And by going home and reading these expressions of love face to face, heart to heart, they've seen God thaw their parent's hearts, making it possible to share the gospel with them. I wonder how many parents are waiting on their children's honor before they receive their children's Savior.
3. *Be ready to tell them about Jesus.* Whether through your own testimony, a book you might give them or some other avenue, watch for windows of opportunity to explain your faith with them.

There's hope. Recently I had lunch with a man who was exuberant because he had just led his 71-year-old father to Christ. May God answer your prayers in the same way.

DISCUSS

What's one way you could be more Christlike when relating to your parents?

PRAY

If one or both of your parent's aren't followers of Christ, ask God to break through to them.

Get Connected for More Information
http://www.familylife.com/moments/helpingothers

STARTING FROM HOME

*Now, our God, what shall we say after this? For we have
forsaken Your commandments.*
EZRA 9:10

One spring day years ago, I stood before a small group of men at our FamilyLife office in Little Rock. I had invited them to discuss with me the concept of Family Reformation in America, something we desperately needed and felt called to initiate on a major scale.

I wrote those two words—"Family Reformation"—on the whiteboard. We talked at length about what those words meant and what they would require of us as champions for the home and family. Heaven knows that our nation and world are rife with failure in this area. Many, many sins and agendas are at war against the family.

But about an hour into our discussion, the tone of the meeting changed dramatically. Staring at those words again, each of us—one by one—fell silent. Instead of envisioning all the things that needed to occur "out there" in the culture for Family Reformation to occur, a much more daunting task began gripping our hearts: *Lord, what needs to change in* my life *for a Family Reformation to occur . . . in* my *home?*

Our meeting adjourned early that day, not because we'd come to any grand conclusions, but simply because we realized that anything of spiritual significance must always begin in one place—in personal, individual repentance. We determined that re-forming a family spiritually is a work that God must do in each of our hearts and homes.

I still believe we need a Family Reformation. I've seen it happen in place after place, marriage after marriage, home after home. I've seen God resurrect dead marriages, restoring "the hearts of the fathers to their children and the hearts of the children to their fathers" (Malachi 4:6).

The cost? Repenting of our own sins and selfishness. Before God restores, before He rebuilds and renews, He calls us to repent.

DISCUSS
Be bold enough to start now. What do you need to repent of this very moment?

PRAY
Second Corinthians 7:10 tells us, "Sorrow that is according to the will of God produces a repentance without regret." Pray it just like that.

Get Connected for More Information
http://www.familylife.com/moments/repentance

PILOT LIGHT

The unfolding of Your words gives light; it gives understanding to the simple.
PSALM 119:130

On a rainy December day in December 1925, U.S. Army pilot Carl Crane was flying a congressman's son back to Washington, DC, when he became disoriented in a thick expanse of clouds. He was 8,000 feet over Detroit. With no gyroscope on his instrument panel to tell him his rate of turn, he didn't know if he was flying level with the earth or was banking into a free fall. Soon, he had swooped into a spiral dive and had lost complete control of the aircraft.

But attempting any rescue move was a gamble. If he tried to level the wings, he was just as likely to roll upside down as right side up. If he tried to raise the nose, he might simply drive the plane more sharply into the ground. Finally, with his altitude shrinking to under 1,000 feet, he caught sight of the sign for the Statler Hotel. He had just missed clipping the top of it.

He now had only seconds to pull up. But with the lights of the buildings giving him guidance and perspective, he righted his plane and found his way to the Detroit River, which he followed back home, "shaking all the way."

For us, the words of the Scriptures are like the lights of Detroit were to Crane on that misty night. They are divine points of perspective that give us our true bearings in every situation. They explain why we behave the way we do—and which way to turn when we've lost our way. If we will follow the Scriptures like the pilot followed the river, we will be led to a safe landing. The trip may be bumpy. There may be some jostling during the flight. But the way will be made plain.

God's Word will guide us home.

DISCUSS
Think of a time when God's Word gave you clear direction. What are the Scriptures telling you about a situation you're in right now?

PRAY
Pray that you will get your *true* perspective and heading from the Bible and guide your family in doing the same thing.

WATER, WATER EVERYWHERE

This He did once for all when He offered up Himself.
HEBREWS 7:27

Every 12 years in the northern India town of Allahabad, the Hindu faithful participate in what claims to be the largest religious gathering in the world. Nearly 70 million pilgrims converge on the spot where the Ganges, Yamuna and Sarasvati Rivers come together. It's timed to coincide with the alignment of Jupiter and the sun in the astrological houses of Aquarius and Aries.

The two-month event draws Hindus and tourists from all over the world. The vast grounds are transformed into a tent city, with thousands of police on hand to maintain public safety and order.

The origins of this pilgrimage—known as the *Kumbha Mela* ("Grand Pitcher Festival")—come from a bit of Hindu mythology. According to myth, gods and demons fought a celestial war over the nectar of immortality, spilling some of it at this sacred site. But the festival's purpose is much more distinct, if no less mystical: plunging into the chilly winter waters of the revered Ganges to be purified from sin and escape the relentless cycle of reincarnation.

I try to imagine feeling the need to journey hundreds or thousands of miles in search of a peace and forgiveness that never seem complete. I try to imagine what it's like to hope that a dip in some murky waters will result in eternal life.

If we're ever tempted to take Christ's once-for-all sacrifice for granted, may we picture ourselves in the frantic throng at the Ganges, wondering if this water is really enough.

I am grateful for Jesus' claim, promise and authoritative words in John 14:6: "I am the way, and the truth, and the life; no one comes to the Father but through Me."

There is nothing murky about those words. Crystal clear. And if you believe, crystal clean!

DISCUSS

What are some of the forgotten benefits of God's remarkable, faith-based, grace-giving salvation? Stop and celebrate a few.

PRAY

Thank God for His indescribable gift of forgiveness through His Son, who knew no sin, to be sin on our behalf so that in Him we might have the righteousness of God (see 2 Corinthians 5:21).

Get Connected for More Information
http://www.familylife.com/moments/spiritualgrowth

BEWARE OF BLESSINGS?

BY BARBARA RAINEY

Then your heart will become proud and you will forget the LORD your God.
DEUTERONOMY 8:14

I remember driving home alone in my car years ago and contemplating this question: *How did I get to this place where I (and everyone else I know) feel out of breath from the daily race?*

I found myself imagining how much simpler life must have been in *Little House on the Prairie* days. If I were living on a farm in the 1800s, I wouldn't worry about having my hair cut and frosted (which is where I'd been for the past two hours). We'd be living miles from our nearest neighbors, so I wouldn't have a whole town full of people to compare my house with. Running errands would be a simple event with only one store in town that would have everything we needed.

But is living in the twenty-first century the only reason why our lives are so cluttered with lessons, parties, activities, trips, classes, events and meetings? No. We live this way because we can—and because we choose to. Because we're prosperous enough to do so. That's the only explanation for why we work countless hours earning money to spend on countless things we don't really need.

Prosperity is a blessing from God; His Word makes that clear. But He also makes it clear that prosperity can kill us, because abundance brings with it the very real danger that we will forget God, the true source of it all. Thomas Carlyle said, "For every one hundred people who can handle adversity, I can only show you one who can handle prosperity." Adversity reduces our choices and many times crystallizes our priorities. Prosperity, however, increases our options and activity. Stress soon follows!

Always be wary of prosperity and what it's capable of doing in you.

DISCUSS

What is more important to you than success? And how much of your average week is spent on those priorities?

PRAY

Commit to the daily exercise of remembering who you belong to and why you have anything.

Get Connected for More Information
http://www.familylife.com/moments/stress

TWENTY MINUTES A DAY

I thank my God in all my remembrance of you.
PHILIPPIANS 1:3

Bill Eyster, a key member of our executive team at FamilyLife, told me recently about a friend of his who had received a new guitar as a gift. It was something this man had always wanted—he had hoped he could learn to play the guitar at some point in his life. So with the encouragement of his wife and children, he started spending about 20 minutes each evening learning chords and picking out notes.

Funny what 20 minutes a night can do. Before long, he had worked up to playing a few simple songs. His family was getting a big kick out of it, singing along as he began playing things they could actually recognize. How fun! A new, learned skill was bringing music (and sometimes laughter) into his home—and the joy of accomplishment into his heart.

This resulted in Bill wondering: Everybody has at least a little free time, sprinkled here and there through the day or in the evening. Some spend it on the Internet. Some spend it watching TV or movies. Some spend it shopping or reading or scrapbooking. But what if we invested just a few of those moments—20 minutes, say—spending concentrated time and effort on our most important earthly relationship, our marriage?

What if, instead of using our free time to get better at golf or photography or Cajun cooking, we used it to become a godly wife or husband? What if we used that same amount of time to take a walk together? What if we used it just to deliberately think about how to invest in our spouse—to brainstorm our next gift idea, to plan a romantic evening, to choose a certain chore we could take off our spouse's hands?

It takes focus for a marriage relationship to grow. And focus takes time.

DISCUSS
Talk about where you could get 15 to 20 minutes together several times a week. What are the time wasters you could eliminate to get some time back for one another?

PRAY
Ask God to help you see your marriage as a daily adventure.

Get Connected for More Information
http://www.familylife.com/moments/commitment

HOME OF THE BRAVE

We were exhorting and encouraging and imploring each one of you
as a father would his own children.
1 THESSALONIANS 2:11

Maurice "Mo" Cheeks has enjoyed a long and successful career as a player and coach in the National Basketball Association. But in my opinion, his greatest moment in basketball had nothing to do with the action on the court. On this day in 2003, 13-year-old Natalie Gilbert began singing the national anthem in front of the Portland Trail Blazers' home crowd—as well as a national TV audience.

Shortly into the song, she jumbled some words, and then she froze. Panicking, she held the microphone to her forehead, as if searching her brain for the right words. But just as she was about to give up (and look for the proverbial hole to crawl in), "Mo" Cheeks stepped to her side and began singing the song with her, helping her hold the microphone in place.

Urging the crowd to join in, he stayed with her the whole way, his off-key voice shadowing hers in sweet duet. It sounded awful, but it was beautiful. And you could see (and hear) Natalie's confidence grow stronger with every line.

"He totally saved me," Natalie told an interviewer. "I was walking off afterward, and he said, 'Don't worry, kid—everyone has a bad game once in a while.'"

As our kids would say, "Cool."

The episode reminded me of the power we have as parents to come alongside and encourage our children. They need to dream big and shoot high, to put themselves out there into the battle where they run the risk of failure. And when they stumble—as they sometimes will—they need us to be there. Be all there, occasionally with the right words to see them through. They should never have to fall on their face too far from where our arms are.

DISCUSS

Regardless of your children's ages, in what areas do they need your active encouragement right now?

PRAY

Pray that your words of affirmation, belief and support will be encouraging and uplifting.

Get Connected for More Information
http://www.familylife.com/moments/involvement

THE STRONG MAN

Greater love has no one than this, that one lay down his life for his friends.
JOHN 15:13

Dick has run several dozen marathons with his son, Rick, in addition to numerous triathlons. Mind you, this was not side-by-side but with Dick *pushing his son in a wheelchair, towing him in a dinghy or propping him on the handlebars.*

How in the world? More important, why?

During his birth, Rick was strangled by the umbilical cord, leaving him severely brain damaged. Eventually, however—through modern science and his parents' love—he was fitted as a young teenager with a device that allowed him to communicate by controlling a computer cursor with the side of his head. One of the first things he typed was a request to do a five-mile charity run with his dad.

At the time, Dick had never run more than a mile at any one time. He was in his 30s and way out of shape. But he did it anyway, pushing Rick's buggy in front of him as he ran the race. When they got home that night, Rick typed on his computer, "Dad, when we were running, it felt like I wasn't disabled anymore."

That did it for Dick. He started training for marathons—with a passion. Many have asked Dick why he doesn't try doing one of these on his own, see what he could do. "No way," he says. "I do it simply for the look on Rick's face."

Recently, Dick suffered a mild heart attack during a race. The doctor said, "If you hadn't been in such great shape, you probably would have died fifteen years ago."

Being a real dad is redemptive. It has a way of saving two lives at the same time.

DISCUSS
Name and celebrate some of the things you and your children have done with each other. Is there some type of heroic achievement you could accomplish together?

PRAY
Give thanks to God for the gift of your children, and ask Him for the continued desire to make them recipients of the full investment of your love and parental vision.

Get Connected for More Information
http://www.familylife.com/moments/fathers

THE HEAT IN THE KITCHEN

Do not be eager in your heart to be angry, for anger resides in the bosom of fools.
ECCLESIASTES 7:9

We had asked two of our teenagers to clean the kitchen together. The first time I inspected their work, I found them arguing about who had done the most. I asked them kindly to keep working.

When I returned, they were bickering about who should sweep the floor. I intervened, got them quieted down and encouraged them to finish the job.

Finally—the third time—after I'd inspected their halfhearted, mediocre work, they gave me the lame excuse that they didn't really know what a clean kitchen should look like! My teenagers had been overtaken by some alien from another planet who had never seen a kitchen, let alone a clean one!

That did it. This normally unflappable dad flipped.

I went on a tirade about how disrespectful and disobedient they were. I flung a handy box of tissues at their feet in a burst of unsanctified rage. Then I stormed out the front door, slamming it shut behind me.

Standing there on the front porch, two profound thoughts came to me. The first: *It's really cold out here. Why are they in there warm? I own this house—they don't!* But the second thought pierced me in places deeper than the cold could reach: *My anger has gotten the best of me, and I'm acting like a foolish child.*

I don't recall the exact words of the apology I gave to my children. But I do recall coming to an important realization: *If I'm going to help these kids grow up emotionally and know how to appropriately express their anger, then I need to grow up myself.*

God never said we shouldn't get angry. But He did warn us not to let anger turn into sin. Or as Proverbs 14:29 cautions, "He who is slow to anger has great understanding, but he who is quickly-tempered exalts folly" (see also James 1:19).

DISCUSS
What specific situations have set you off lately? See if you can isolate the main culprits and flashpoints. What is it that makes you lose it?

PRAY
Pray that your heart will not be eager to be angry, that being "slow to anger" will be more your speed.

HANDS DOWN

Put on a heart of compassion, kindness, humility, gentleness and patience.
COLOSSIANS 3:12

In a classic Sunday comic strip from Charles Schulz, creator of *Peanuts*, Linus is eating a sandwich and Lucy is nearby as he begins to ponder. "Hands are fascinating things," he says. "I like my hands. I think I have nice hands. My hands seem to have a lot of character. These are hands which may someday accomplish great things. These are hands which may someday do marvelous works. They may build mighty bridges, or heal the sick, or hit home runs, or write soul-stirring novels. These are hands which may someday change the course of destiny!"

A moment of silence. Then Lucy's one-line reply: "They've got jelly on them."

Even as we laugh, we know that Lucy's comment is typical of the way she treats other people. And, unfortunately, it is also a picture of how you can treat your spouse. Rather than encouraging your spouse and building him or her up, you choose instead of be the voice of criticism and harsh reality.

Dr. John Gottman, a leading expert in sociological research, conducted a 10-year study to determine the types of communication—both verbal and nonverbal—that make it *least likely* for a marriage to survive and go the distance. The four critical elements he determined as being the most detrimental?

• *Criticism*—nagging, deflating, picking at each other
• *Contempt*—rolling your eyes, discounting the other's value
• *Defensiveness*—refusing to hear the truth or to deal with self
• *Stonewalling*—retreating, withdrawing, not saying anything

Do any of these behaviors characterize the way you treat your spouse? In order to minimize conflict in your home, you need to be supportive of each other by what you say and how you say it.

DISCUSS

Take a look at how you are relating with one another and see how you can use attitudes and words to strengthen and encourage one another. Would you say you are generally encouraging or critical to your spouse? How would your spouse answer that question?

PRAY

Invite the Lord to intervene in your conscience every time you feel like taking your spouse apart.

Get Connected for More Information

ALONE AND ABANDONED

I delivered the poor who cried for help, and the orphan who had no helper.
JOB 29:12

One of the things we tend to forget, overlook or just simply ignore when thinking about adoption is how desperately needy some children are. This came to mind again when hearing the story of a local couple who felt the need to share their family of six with a child from Guatemala.

All that's known about young Heidy Paola is that she was found in a cardboard box by the side of the road. She was less than a year old, abandoned to die until a policeman walked over to dispose of what he thought was an empty carton. Inside he found a sunburned, dehydrated infant, still breathing . . . somehow.

His decision to take her to a nearby orphanage probably wasn't automatic. Many children are left unwanted in underprivileged countries, where poverty and need outrank parental concern in case after case. One more wasn't a surprise. But because of God's working through one man's rescue efforts, a little baby left to die ultimately became a little girl growing up in an orphanage.

When her adoptive parents first entered the dormitory where Heidy had lived since arriving at the orphanage, she rushed from her caretaker's side and lunged into her new mommy's arms. The bond was powerful and immediate. Nothing could be closer to God's heart than this.

I firmly believe that adoption is one of the central efforts in our day that can define the Church's compassion for the world. With no one to protect them, children are in such distress. Their need is so great. May God raise up families who will reach out and give the helpless a home—a mommy and daddy who *will* protect them.

DISCUSS
One child, hurting and in need. With no hope. No one. What can you do to help a child like this experience God's love?

PRAY
Pray that your family will represent God's heart of compassion to the fatherless.

SPORTS NUTS

Jesus kept increasing in wisdom and stature, and in favor with God and men.
LUKE 2:52

I'm not saying for one minute that everything about life ought to go back to the way it was in the Eisenhower administration. But I certainly remember that in my childhood, the basketball, baseball and football seasons barely overlapped. If you have children in sports today, however, you know that just one sport can become a year-round proposition. The competition has become so fierce, and the quest for winning so passionate, there's no end to the amount of extra time your child can spend in training and competition. It's easy for parents to get sucked into this vortex.

If you're starting to feel the squeeze in your family, perhaps it's time to discuss what sports is supposed to be all about in the lives of your children:

1. *Character.* Sports can be a life laboratory for learning about finishing strong, pushing beyond fatigue and becoming better than you thought you could be. A losing team can teach valuable lessons. Did I tell you I coached Little League two years in a row? Our record was 2-15. Both years. Talk about building character!
2. *Relationships.* For the rest of their lives, your children will be on teams of some kind—at work, at church, even as a family. Giving up your own agenda for the well-being of the team is a skill that gets better with practice, and sports is a great place to refine it.
3. *Fun.* It's easy for some coaches and parents to forget this, but most kids participate in sports to have fun. When their athletic days are over, they ought to have fond memories—the type of memories I have when I look through the scrapbook my dad presented me to commemorate all those years of games and road trips. I wouldn't give anything for my memories of playing baseball and basketball.

Yeah, when it comes to sports, I guess I still like Ike.

DISCUSS
Has sports gotten out of hand in your family? What would it take to rein it back in?

PRAY
Pray that God's true priorities would be reflected in the way you parent and train your children.

Get Connected for More Information
http://www.familylife.com/moments/charactertraining

ALL I REALLY NEED

And those who know Your name will put their trust in You,
for You, O LORD, have not forsaken those who seek You.
PSALM 9:10

At the very moment Darnly Motter was giving birth to her third child in the delivery room, her husband, Larry, was one floor below having a blood clot removed from his brain.

These are the kind of paradoxes that entered the Motters' world the day their car crashed on a lonely stretch of South Dakota highway, leaving Larry in a coma with severe brain damage. When he returned to consciousness, he was partially paralyzed and his short-term memory was gone. For all intents and purposes, he was another baby in the Motter household.

There were people who advised Darnly to find Larry a comfortable place to live—to set him up in a nursing home—so that she could get on with life. But Darnly knew she couldn't do that. Making a home with Larry—even the new Larry he had become—was part of keeping her wedding vows, she believed.

Over the years, she has often cried herself to sleep at night, and she has occasionally succumbed to the heavy undertow of depression. Her lonely walk as the only "adult" in her marriage has left her feeling maddeningly desperate. But when times get the murkiest, she remembers, "I don't need answers; I just need God."

That, my friend, is a faith statement—something that people who walk by feelings can't say, because it demands that they know and trust God enough to be able to handle the challenges He often allows into life. Faith like this brings freedom and peace, even in the midst of the storms of life, known only by those who choose to set their dial and choose to live by the trusted timeless truths of Scriptures.

When life isn't fair, God is still there—to make sure you have everything you need to hang in there yourself.

DISCUSS
What do stories like these make you want to say to each other, to promise each other?

PRAY
When life is hard, ask Him to help you remember that life is short but that life with Him goes on forever.

WELL-DRIVEN NAILS (PART ONE)

The words of wise men are like goads, and masters of these collections are like well-driven nails.

ECCLESIASTES 12:11

Wisdom, which I define as skill in everyday living, is one of the greatest needs of every generation. And the writer of Ecclesiastes 12 shares about the words of a wise man being like "well-driven nails"—words that bring perspective, security and life. Over the next three days I'd like to describe three well-driven nails.

Nail Number One: Remember God

Aleksandr Solzhenitsyn, the Nobel Prize-winning author and Russian dissident during the Soviet era, said, "I have spent fifty years working on the history of the Russian Revolution. In the process, I have collected hundreds of personal testimonies, read hundreds of books and contributed eight volumes of my own. But if I were asked today to formulate as concisely as possible the main cause of the ruinous revolution that swallowed up some 60 million of our people, I could not put it more accurately than to repeat: Men have forgotten God."

These powerful words confirm that when people fail to remember God and do not recognize His presence and authority in their lives, anything goes. They develop spiritual amnesia and are unable to remember what God has done to show Himself faithful and true, not only in their own lives, but also throughout human history. When we forget God, we forget to trust Him.

If you want to drive this nail home, I would encourage you to consider three things: First, learn how to truly worship God. Second, get to know Him by spending time reading the Bible. And third, create a list together of spiritual milestones—divine acts that exemplify something significant He has done in your life or family. When we rehearse what God has done, we not only remember Him, but we also are more likely to trust Him for what we are facing today.

Remember your Creator.

DISCUSS

Recall some of your spiritual milestones together. Write them down where you can return to them again and again, adding more along the way.

PRAY

Take turns giving thanks to God for who He is and what He has done in your lives and family.

Get Connected for More Information

WELL-DRIVEN NAILS (PART TWO)

It is good that you grasp one thing and also not let go of the other;
for the one who fears God comes forth with both of them.
ECCLESIASTES 7:18

When I was a young lad growing up in southwest Missouri, it seemed as though the preacher in our little church would tilt that pulpit of his, and hellfire and brimstone would come smoking out into the pews. He preached about the almighty God who was just and righteous in His judgments. Not all of what the preacher said was healthy, but as a boy I learned to have a reverential awe of the One who held my destiny in the palm of His hand.

We rarely hear sermons today about the fear of God. Reverential awe has been largely replaced with much softer, sweeter emotions. We've traded the *fear* of God for the *love* of God, not realizing we need both of them to keep us balanced and secure.

Nail Number Two: Fear God

Believers in past centuries talked about living "in the presence" of God or living "before the eyes" of God. Keeping their view of Him high and majestic drove them to change their world, because they knew that the Lord God almighty was watching. And they never forgot it.

Living for God is not about kicking back and seeking ease. It is serious business. Rather than seeing the promises of God as ways to increase our checking-account balances and meet our own needs, the Bible calls us to "cleanse ourselves from all defilement of flesh and spirit, perfecting holiness in the fear of God" (2 Corinthians 7:1). It's not about entertainment and feeling good. It's about seeing Him for who He is and seeing ourselves accountable to Him on a moment-by-moment basis. And real life is being accountable to others who share our pursuit of reverent, holy living.

DISCUSS

What is your perception of who God is? As you look back on the past few days, what would you have done differently if you knew God was there, watching?

PRAY

Pray that God will teach you a healthy reverential fear of Him and that you will practice His presence in your life in your choices, speech and relationships.

Get Connected for More Information
http://www.familylife.com/moments/relationshipwithgod

WELL-DRIVEN NAILS (PART THREE)

*The conclusion, when all has been heard, is: fear God and
keep His commandments, because this applies to every person.*
ECCLESIASTES 12:13

A. W. Tozer said, "The word of God was not given to us to make us intelligent sinners, but obedient and authentic saints." As important as it is to *remember God*—to recall who God is and what He has done for us—and to *fear God* by practicing a reverential awe of Him and His presence in our lives, it is equally important to hammer home the final nail.

Nail Number Three: Obey God

Our lives are made up of choices—difficult forks in the road where we must decide to choose God's way or to pursue our own. And as Moses said to the children of Israel, the choice is really not between right and wrong but between life and death (see Deuteronomy 30:15-16). The prophet Amos said it very succinctly: "Seek the LORD that you may live" (Amos 5:6). Truly, the only sure path to life is found in obedience to God and His Word.

So when you don't feel like loving your spouse, obey God.
When you're tempted to steal or to compromise your integrity, obey God.
When your boss asks you to do something you shouldn't, obey God.
When your lusts and passions are telling you to give in, obey God.
When you're suffering and feel like quitting, obey God.
When the easiest thing to do is nothing, obey God.
When you feel like being lazy, obey God.
Whatever choice you may be facing, obey God . . . and live!

Thomas Carlisle wrote, "Conviction, be it ever so excellent, is worthless until it converts itself into conduct." It is not enough just to know what's right. Well-driven nails only become that way when we have the courage to sink them deep by obeying God.

DISCUSS

You need to be honest today about where you're not obeying. Come clean. Make the change. Drive the nail.

PRAY

Ask God to give you the strength and conviction to be not just His children but also His *obedient* children.

Get Connected for More Information
http://www.familylife.com/moments/relationshipwithgod

RISING TO PRAY

Where two or three have gathered together in My name, I am there in their midst.
MATTHEW 18:20

We believe—and have learned from long experience—that the true secret to spiritual intimacy in marriage is *praying together*. Yet surveys from FamilyLife's Weekend to Remember conferences indicate that less than 8 percent of couples actually do this regularly.

This really troubles me. It means that 9 out of 10 Christian couples today are resisting the number one thing that could draw them closer together spiritually.

I often receive encouraging emails from couples who understand the power of this daily spiritual discipline. One gentleman said he purchased a picture frame and places it on his pillow the moment he rolls out of bed in the morning. Inside the frame is a special reminder of something very important to do before he goes to sleep each night: "Have you prayed with Janet today? It's not too late."

Another guy wrote to tell me he had tried praying with his wife at night before bed, "but I would always find an excuse not to. One day God really convicted me that I needed to step up as a husband and commit to pray with my wife nightly. I came home that day and told her of my conviction."

In tears the wife said, "I've been praying about this for months, but I didn't want to tell you and pressure you into it. I wanted God to do the work in you."

I want to challenge you to begin praying together daily. I can promise you, on the authority of the Scripture, that if you pray together daily for two years, you will not be the same couple that you are today (see Matthew 18:19). Inviting the God of the universe into your marriage on a daily basis will change things!

DISCUSS

Settle this in your heart right now: Are the two of you going to pray together every day, no matter what comes between you or threatens to seem more important?

PRAY

Expecting immediate opposition from the enemy, ask God for the courage to be obedient in prayer. And thank Him in advance for what He's about to do in your life together.

Get Connected for More Information
http://www.familylife.com/moments/prayer

PRAYER STARTERS

Be of sound judgment and sober spirit for the purpose of prayer.
1 PETER 4:7

If you're trying to pray together regularly as a couple, here's a very workable outline and some suggestions that you can follow. Perhaps you've heard of the ACTS method, using the four letters in that word to frame your prayers for each day:

A is for *Adoration*. Worship and adore God for His love, grace and forgiveness. Praise Him for His work in your marriage and family.

C is for *Confession*. Agree with God about any sin that needs to be confessed before you make requests for His help, clearing your heart to be pure minded in your petitions.

T is for *Thanksgiving*. Thank God for your spouse, your children, your job, your home—anything He brings to mind.

S is for *Supplication*. Ask Him for those things that are heavy on your heart—a child struggling at school, physical and spiritual needs in your family, financial trouble, etc. Don't worry about impressing Him with religious language. Remember that praying is both reverential and relational.

You might also want to *take turns* praying—one of you tonight, the other tomorrow—as you each grow more comfortable doing this together. And so that you don't feel like you're always covering the same ground every time, consider having a different focus for each day's prayer. On Sunday, pray for the coming week's activities. Monday, pray for your marriage and children. Tuesday, pray for your extended family. Wednesday, pray for coworkers and other work-related issues. Thursday, pray for church leaders and needs. Friday, pray for national and international events. Saturday, devote to praise.

Finally, hold hands or hold one another when you pray. Praying together is intimate conversation together with Almighty God.

Creating expectations like these can help make your prayer together more meaningful, less routine and more natural over time. It can help you cross those hurdles that threaten to kick you back into prayerlessness.

DISCUSS

Talk about your prayer time together. What would work best for you? How can you begin to pray together every day?

PRAY

Thank God for always being there, always hearing your prayers and always wanting the best for you.

Get Connected for More Information
http://www.familylife.com/moments/prayer

WATERLOGGED?

Do not let any iniquity have dominion over me.
PSALM 119:133

The Dutch boast that God made the world, but the Dutch made Holland. That's because nearly half of Holland's land area was reclaimed from the sea and other natural waterways.

We witnessed this feat firsthand several years ago when we visited Amsterdam. We toured the famous network of dikes and levees that keep the land separated from the ocean. We also learned that, even with the most well-constructed protection, water inevitably seeps back through the dikes, requiring the use of pumps and canals to divert it back out. If the encroaching water were ever allowed to stay—even at this slow, nearly unnoticed pace—Holland would eventually sink and be submerged.

This is much more than a lesson in geography or engineering. We, too, are constantly bombarded by troubles and temptations, many of which find ways of seeping into our lives: Little sins we fail to consider as dangerous . . . waves of doubt that make us question God's goodness . . . undercurrents of discontentment that echo in our minds and whisper in our ears.

That's why we need barriers in place to protect us from inundation by the relentless tide of unbelief and moral compromise. Things like daily Bible reading, ongoing prayer, regular points of accountability, and written-out goals and value statements.

And we need built-in systems that pump out murky water that seeps in despite our best efforts at resistance. We need hearts that are quick both to repent and to forgive, marriages where communication is open and honest, and weekly worship where we are cleansed by the purity of God's presence.

Everyone takes on water from time to time. Be sure to keep it bailed out, or you'll soon find yourself sinking and submerged.

DISCUSS

Isolate some of the little things that have sneaked through your spiritual guard lately. Expose them. Confess them to God and claim the promise of God's cleansing found in 1 John 1:9. Then remove them.

PRAY

Ask the Lord for daily awareness of those sneaky sins that have wormed into your behaviors and attitudes. Pray that you will be the man or woman God created you to be: wholly obedient.

Get Connected for More Information
http://www.familylife.com/moments/spiritualgrowth

A BUG'S LIFE

We are not able to go up against the people, for they are too strong for us.
NUMBERS 13:31

I remember the first time I walked into the office of Bill Bright, founder of Campus Crusade for Christ. I was spending a college summer break working with Campus Crusade for $50 a month. When I had the opportunity to meet with Bill, I noticed that on his desk was a plaque engraved with these words: "I'm no grasshopper."

When I asked what the phrase meant, he said it referred to the spies who were sent to scope out the land of Canaan in the Old Testament book of Numbers. God said He was giving the land to the Israelites, but 10 of 12 spies reported that it was impossible for the Israelites to conquer the land: "We seemed like grasshoppers in our own eyes, and we looked the same to them" (Numbers 13:33, *NIV*).

Only two spies said they should trust in God. Unfortunately, the nation of Israel refused to believe the minority report and consequently ended up wandering aimlessly in the wilderness for 40 years, never entering their promised reward.

"When I arrive in heaven," Bill said, "I don't want my life here on Earth to have been characterized by viewing myself as a grasshopper. My God is so big, I want to expect and believe Him for great things."

Are you living in the camp of unbelief, overwhelmed by the struggles you are facing in your life, marriage, family or work? Are you paralyzed in unbelief or anger toward God for your circumstances? Do you feel like a "grasshopper"? Or are you turning in belief to the God who promises to work through you to accomplish the impossible?

No matter how foolish you've been, no matter how many times you've failed before, Jesus stands ready to work through you if you're ready to be a man or woman of faith.

DISCUSS

What issue seems so big to you right now, you don't see any way it can turn out well?

PRAY

Confess to God that you lack the power to deal with the problems you face today. Ask Him for trust in *His* power to make the changes He desires.

FAR-REACHING IMPLICATIONS

This service is not only fully supplying the needs of the saints, but is also overflowing through many thanksgivings to God.

2 CORINTHIANS 9:12

The following letter is my number one favorite. I think you'll see why.

Dear Sirs, I don't know what you did with my real mom and dad, but I love the ones you've sent me. My parents were among the hundreds of couples at your marriage conference this past weekend, and boy—are they different!

1. Every day since they got back, they've been talking over what they learned and comparing notes from their workbooks over dinner.
2. Notice I said they've been talking instead of arguing.
3. My dad now calls my mom "my wife" instead of "your mother."
4. They talk about legacies, communication, and understanding each other.
5. My mom actually asks my dad to do things instead of expecting him to offer—and he says yes!
6. They're even holding hands—creepy!

What did you do to them?

The letter goes on and on, talking about what a miracle this is. But perhaps even more encouraging is the way this woman internalized what she was seeing. God was changing her whole perspective on what to expect in her own future.

I sent to you a man and woman who had been married for 27 years and who had given up all hope of happiness. You returned me two people committed to the goal of having a fulfilling and godly relationship with one another, living out the rest of their days in love and hope. Looking at them now has made me rethink my own dreaded fears concerning marriage.

Your marriage is not just about you. It's about being a powerful example of hope to a world desensitized by divorce and disappointment. When God works in your own relationship, He uses it to make waves among your children and in the lives of people who know you best.

DISCUSS
Talk about the evidence of hope you see in the marriages of those you know best.

PRAY
When you're tempted to act selfishly, ask God to help you see that your actions affect others. Pray that your marriage will give your children hope.

Get Connected for More Information
http://www.familylife.com/moments/marriagerelationship

MAN, OH MAN

*The man said, "This is now bone of my bones and flesh of my flesh;
she shall be called 'woman,' for she was taken out of man."*
GENESIS 2:23, NIV

I'm telling you—men just have it easier. Here are some examples someone sent me. *When you're a man* . . .

- Your last name stays put.
- The garage is all yours.
- Wedding plans take care of themselves.
- You can never be pregnant.
- Wrinkles add character.
- The occasional well-rendered belch is practically expected.
- You've got one mood all the time. Usually.
- Phone conversations are over in thirty seconds flat.
- A five-day vacation requires only one suitcase.
- You can open all your own jars.
- You get extra credit for the slightest act of thoughtfulness. Usually.
- If someone forgets to invite you somewhere, he can still be your friend.
- Your underwear is $8.95—for a three-pack!
- The same hairstyle lasts for years, maybe decades.
- You only have to shave your face and neck.
- You can play with toys all your life.
- One wallet and one pair of shoes—one color for all seasons.
- You can wear shorts no matter how your legs look.
- You can "do" your nails with a pocket knife.

See what I mean?

So the next time your wife seems too complicated for you, be patient with her. You didn't marry a man. You married her because she is different.

Realize that her life comes with a lot of stuff you don't have to put up with. Take the time to genuinely listen and understand because God created her as a gift for you.

DISCUSS

If your wife is not hitting you in the arm too hard right now, take a few minutes to talk about your differences. Promise you'll try to do a better job of understanding and appreciating those differences.

PRAY

Take your wife by the hand and give God thanks for providing her with all her uniqueness.

Get Connected for More Information
http://www.familylife.com/moments/commitment

ROOM WITH A VIEW

I was asleep but my heart was awake. A voice! My beloved was knocking.
SONG OF SOLOMON 5:2

Taking time to put our physical love for each other in its proper perspective can mean excitement, delight and an opportunity to just have fun. But when the celebration becomes really adventuresome, it pays to keep one foot in reality. Just ask "Embarrassed in Arizona," who wrote me this letter after one of our Weekend to Remember marriage conferences:

Dear Dennis, when you suggested last night for us to be more creative in our romance, you never gave us warning that it could be so dangerous. Rule #1: Always be prepared—at least with a spare key!

After dinner and the sunset, my husband and I decided to take your advice and add a little romance to our evening, even to be a little daring. Staying here at the hotel, we crept out onto our fourth floor balcony where we had an incredibly romantic view, not to mention privacy. But unbeknownst to us, while we were "communicating" on the secluded balcony, the maid was turning down our bed and leaving us those ever-scrumptious mints on our pillows.

She didn't know we were on the balcony. And we didn't know she was in the room. Maybe you can guess the rest—she locked our sliding glass door! Two lovers, one romantic sky . . . and a lot more privacy than we bargained for.

I chuckled when I read her letter, wondering how they ever got back in their room! I also couldn't help but think that marriage has a way of robbing our relationship of adventure and romance. We become way too predictable. When's the last time you took a weekend away for just the two of you to have some romantic fun? Why not get out a calendar and find a time to begin your own adventure? Then write me if something unexpected happens!

DISCUSS
The next time you have time—even if you need to *make* time—what could you do to turn your romance into something a little more fun and daring?

PRAY
Ask God to bless your desires for romance with His favor and abundance.

Get Connected for More Information
http://www.familylife.com/moments/romance

NOT WITHOUT A FIGHT

It will also come to pass that before they call, I will answer;
and while they are still speaking, I will hear.
ISAIAH 65:24

Barbara and I pray together every night, and there have been times when our prayers before bedtime have been little more than two or three sentences: "Thank You, Lord, for getting us through this day. We're tired. Good night. Amen." And there have been other times when our hearts have been fraught with distress. Since we started this journey together in 1972, we've asked God for just about everything—big deals, little deals and every deal in between.

For instance, when our boys were 14 and 12, they began to maul each other like professional wrestlers. I'm not talking about fun-loving horseplay. Something about the proximity of their ages as they entered adolescence set them at odds with each other, and their fighting started getting out of hand. One night they even ripped a door off its hinges!

We disciplined them fairly severely for this, as you might imagine. We made them pay for the damage. But we knew that this wasn't enough to repair whatever had come between them. I still remember the night we offered up the prayer of desperate parents: "Lord, we feel like we're losing this battle with our boys. Will You find some way to knit their hearts together?"

Several days later our older son, Benjamin, asked to talk with us. The previous night he had dreamed that his brother, Samuel, was killed in a car accident. Benjamin woke up crying because he missed him. He felt convicted that he wasn't really appreciating Samuel like he should. He wanted to become a better older brother.

This experience did not totally end their sibling warfare. But it was exciting for Barbara and me to see God answering our prayer by divinely orchestrating this circumstance. We were reminded again that prayers aren't just spoken into thin air. Prayers are heard. And prayers are answered.

DISCUSS

As you look at your circumstances, what do you two need to ask God about? What need do you have that only God can fulfill?

PRAY

You fill in the blank: "Lord, we ask you today _____."

COMPARISON SHOPPING

BY BARBARA RAINEY

Do not judge according to appearance, but judge with righteous judgment.
JOHN 7:24

It's so easy for a woman to look at her husband and say:

"He's sure not very _____."

"He doesn't _____ or _____ or _____."

"I wish I was married to someone more like _____."

But every time you say or even think something along these lines—every time you focus on those inevitable aspects about him that are disappointing or negative—you catch him in a comparison trap. You forget that God has a plan for your man that is different from the one He has for somebody else's husband. You ignore the fact that your job is to respect him, to be used by God to help reveal that plan in his life, whatever it may be.

When I married Dennis, I had no idea we would end up doing the kinds of things God has led us to do. It hasn't always been easy to have Dennis Rainey for a husband. It would have been so easy at times to settle back and say, "I wish he was more like so-and-so," rather than being content with the one God had given me and helping him develop into the man God wanted him to be.

There are so many things that Dennis does well. There are a lot of things he doesn't. But when I'm lasering in on those things he doesn't do quite so well, I'm expecting him to be someone he's not. No, he's not perfect. Neither am I. Nobody is.

But I believe that God can change your heart as He does mine when I slip into seeing only the imperfections. The key is recognizing what you are looking at in his life and being willing to let God adjust your focus from the negative to the positive.

DISCUSS

Spend some time encouraging each other right now. I'm sure both of you could use some building up.

PRAY

Ask God to adjust your view of each other toward something more grateful and positive.

Get Connected for More Information

http://www.familylife.com/moments/wives

SUMMER'S ON ITS WAY

BY BARBARA RAINEY

One hand full of rest is better than two fists full of labor and striving after wind.
ECCLESIASTES 4:6

Before summer started, Dennis used to say to me, "Sweetheart, what do you want us to accomplish by the time we finish August and move into the school year?" He knew I was the one who had my finger closest to the pulse of our family's needs and schedules and would probably have the biggest hand in implementing the answer to his question.

Truly, the pressure to create the right kind of summertime environment in your home falls largely on Mom. Summer should be a time of rest, but it's also up to us to keep things moving in a way that integrates rest with a measure of purpose.

For me, it meant letting our kids have lots of time to play—building forts in the yard (or in the living room if it was raining), going on hikes, going swimming—anything that didn't involve wasting a perfectly good day in front of the television. It also meant having some enforced quiet time, when I would read to them or send them to their rooms to spend time alone. I wanted to discipline their hearts to enjoy solitude and to help truly recharge after the fast pace of the school year.

If you're a mom who puts a lot of emphasis on structure, I'd encourage you to tone your plans back about 50 percent as summer approaches. Take the time to let some air blow into your schedule, and resist the urge to be constantly checking your list for accomplishment.

If you're more of a free spirit who basically lets both hands off the reins, try to put a little thought into summer on the front end. Set a few goals for the type of activities you'd like to pursue, the relationships you'd like to deepen, the trips you'd like to take.

Make this a summer you'll never forget.

DISCUSS

Talk about and decide what you want to accomplish by the end of August.

PRAY

Ask the Lord to establish your plans and help you see them through . . . with lots of fun to spare.

KILLING ME SOFTLY

I have become mute, I do not open my mouth.
PSALM 39:9

A man and his wife were having some problems at home and were giving each other the silent treatment. The husband realized he needed to be awakened early one morning to catch a business flight, but he didn't want to be the first to break the silence. So he left a note on his wife's side of the bed that read, "Please wake me at 5 A.M."

By the time bright sunshine roused him the next morning, it was 9 A.M. Furious, he threw back the covers and shouted to his wife (who was nowhere to be found), "Why didn't you wake me up like I asked you to?" That's when he saw, stuck to the lamp on his bedside table, a note in her handwriting that read, "It is 5 A.M. Time to wake up."

It doesn't take much to make us angry and create emotional distance from each other. But it does take great, courageous effort to fight through the silence to a place of forgiveness and oneness. Isolation seems to offer us protection, a certain kind of self-preservation. There is a type of peace found in avoidance that appears much more appealing than the pain of dealing with reality.

Silence feels like a security blanket. But in fact, it is one of Satan's most deadly disguises. The silent treatment is perilously deceptive and ultimately destructive.

When you find yourself tempted to square off against each other, retreating to your corners and refusing to give in, remember that Jesus could have given us the cold shoulder. He could have taken one look at our many, many sins and shortcomings and never sought to draw us out. May His reaching, redemptive love be our model and motivator.

We serve a God who both seeks and speaks. Be sure you're a spouse who does the same.

DISCUSS

What, if anything, drives you into silence? Discuss what your spouse should do when you are silent.

PRAY

Pray that God will show you both what you should do if one or both of you becomes silent.

TEMPORARY DIFFICULTIES

BY BARBARA RAINEY

Have I not wept for the one whose life is hard? Was not my soul grieved for the needy?
JOB 30:25

You've been through the same type of difficulties your children are facing now, whether as preschoolers, school-age kids or teenagers. But have you forgotten what it was really like to be their age? When they suffer setbacks, are you there to give them the emotional support they need—from someone who's been there?

Our oldest daughter, Ashley, tried out for the cheerleading squad three times in a row but failed to be chosen on each occasion. Still, she decided to give it one final effort during her junior year, and this time we went all out.

I arranged for her to take lessons. I videotaped her practicing. Together we critiqued her moves. We prayed and prayed about it, feeling surer each time that God wanted her to make the team this year. It would give her a strong platform for influencing her public school for Christ.

But when the tryouts came around, she didn't make it. This time, I was as heartbroken as she was. It seemed so unfair. We cried for hours, so upset that she had to endure this loss a fourth time in a row.

I could have said to her, "Ashley, cheerleading really isn't all that important. You're making too much of a fuss over this." But this was the most important thing in her life at the time, and she needed me to let her know it was okay for her to cry, to feel sad . . . even to wonder why God had said no again.

Through an amazing set of circumstances, Ashley ended up being selected for the squad a week later. But as I look back on that experience now, I realize that the biggest thing God accomplished in our lives at that time was to knit our souls together, mother and daughter, in sorrow.

DISCUSS
Name the biggest challenges facing your children right now. How can you walk with them in the valleys yet still help them trust a sovereign and loving God?

PRAY
Pray for the words to speak . . . and the words not to speak.

Get Connected for More Information
http://www.familylife.com/moments/suffering

THE LOSS OF LEGACY

For He established a testimony in Jacob and appointed a law in Israel,
which He commanded our fathers that they should teach them to their children.
PSALM 78:5

I cringe at findings like the following from the 2000 census, as reported by the Department of Health and Human Services. These are family statistics comparing white children and African-American children:

- Living in families with a father and mother—75.2 percent of white children and 33.3 percent of African-American children
- Living in single-parent families—17.7 percent of white children and 46.2 percent of African-American children
- Living with no parent at all—3.7 percent of white children and 12 percent of African-American children

As I read these, I think of my friend Crawford Loritts sharing a tribute to his dad on our radio broadcast one day, thanking him for his faithfulness as a father:

Thank you for choosing not to get paid triple time on Christmases and other days when we needed the money living in that small Newark apartment, because you wanted to spend time with your kids. Thank you for not buying new cars until after we were grown because you wanted to have money for vacations. . . . Thank you for teaching me and telling me that I'm a man and for standing with me during hard times. Everything I am today is because of you, Dad. You never made a big splash and you never blew your own trumpet, but you quietly did the deed.

It's sobering to consider how quickly a legacy can be lost when a father is not there for his children. It's heartbreaking to think of the kids who are growing up disconnected from families and a generational heritage of faith—both in African-American homes and many others across the racial spectrum.

Oh, how today's children of all races desperately need the hearts of their fathers to return to their calling!

DISCUSS
What are you doing to secure a spiritual legacy in your family?

PRAY
Pray for the healing of all the families of our nation and world—and for children who need to know both father and Father.

Get Connected for More Information
http://www.familylife.com/moments/fathers

FROM INDULGENT TO "OUTDULGENT"

Do not merely look out for your own personal interests,
but also for the interests of others.
PHILIPPIANS 2:4

Graham Kerr became a household name when his cooking show, *The Galloping Gourmet*, emerged as an international success in the 1960s and 1970s. With achievement and acclaim came money, of course, and Graham and his wife, Treena, were indulgent in purchasing the types of goods and gadgets wealth can buy.

But at some point along the way, Graham and his wife realized that God had placed them here for much greater purposes. They knew they needed to live more simply. As if their own convictions about this weren't enough, Treena began experiencing a series of major health episodes, including a heart attack, a stroke, the onset of diabetes, and raging hypertension. God was calling them to change, not just their material footprint, but their physical lifestyle as well.

One of the stark realities of these health conditions, naturally, was the need to make changes in their eating habits. They would be consuming much less now and spending much less on their grocery bill. Then the thought struck them, *What if we could take our savings from not eating these things that once harmed us and turn that money into provision for someone else?*

So over the course of the last 20 years, the Kerrs have been calculating the money they've saved by foregoing unhealthy choices in their food budget and have redirected that money into needy areas and causes. They have been the first beneficiaries of their fit lifestyle, but those who have been helped through their generous, ongoing gifts have made it a double blessing.

Instead of living indulgent lifestyles, Graham and Treena have become, to borrow their own term, "outdulgent."

DISCUSS

Is there an area of your life that has become obviously indulgent? Are you starting to recognize the bloating effect of focusing on self and consuming just because you can? In what ways could you see yourself becoming "outdulgent" with the resources God has provided you with?

PRAY

If appropriate, confess any greed or love of possessions. Ask God to help you see the needs of others and to create a lifestyle that is generous.

Get Connected for More Information
http://www.familylife.com/moments/giving

GOOD FOR THE WHOLE FAMILY

BY BARBARA RAINEY

Determine this—not to put an obstacle or a stumbling block in a brother's way.
ROMANS 14:13

An often overlooked aspect of media use in the home is that some things that might be appropriate for an older child are not acceptable for a younger one. If you have an older sibling in your family, consider challenging him or her to be a good example. We've seen that an older teen who is making the right kinds of choices can help you establish the right standards for your younger children.

I remember once talking with our older kids about some of the music they enjoyed. I said, "I don't want you boys to listen to that stuff, because you have little sisters who don't need to hear it."

"But, Mom . . ."

"I'm sorry, but what you're doing affects everyone else in the family, not just you." They grumbled about it, but I think they realized there was good reason for being a model to their little sisters.

So although everyone has personal tastes in media—TV, movies, music—parents need to take responsibility for setting and maintaining boundaries that work for the entire family. Make this clear: As long as your child resides under your roof, you have the right to screen—and to bar—all media consumed by everyone in the household.

As your children get older and leave home, however, they will begin making more and more of their own choices. Brace yourself. Some of those decisions will not be ones that represent your values and convictions. At some point as they move into adulthood, you will need to give them the freedom to make their own mistakes. Just like you and I did.

However, while they are at home, as parents you have the responsibility to establish the boundaries and standards for your family. At times, it's going to feel like you are swimming against a mighty strong cultural current. Stand firm.

DISCUSS

What are your convictions, standards and boundaries about music, movies, the Internet and TV for your family?

PRAY

Pray that you will both stand firm in protecting your family against the various forms of evil being pushed upon our families today.

Get Connected for More Information
http://www.familylife.com/moments/mediachoices

OUTER WEAR OR INNER SPIRIT?

Your adornment must not be merely external . . .
but let it be the hidden person of the heart.
1 PETER 3:3-4

I'll never forget that spring Sunday when our church was honoring our graduating high-school seniors during the service. A couple of the students had been asked to speak to the congregation. The first was a young man, sharply dressed, who made an articulate statement about his faith and confidence in Christ. He was followed by a young lady who presented an equally strong message—but her dress was so skintight and seductive that I imagine it was hard for any of the male gender to pay attention.

I want to be quick to say that we men are fully responsible for where we allow our gaze and our thoughts to go. One hundred percent responsible. But I must ask today's Christian woman and teenage girl, what thought process goes into your clothing choices?

And dads, if your daughter dresses immodestly for church (or school, for that matter), are you willing to ask her to please go put on something more appropriate?

It's important to help our daughters understand how God hardwired a man. Barbara and I have four daughters, so you can be sure we had many conversations around this subject as they grew up. We know what it means to raise young women in a culture that's increasingly promoting immodest dress. We know what it's like to wander the stores, losing hope of ever finding anything suitable to wear.

We need to help our daughters (and sons) be more concerned with cultivating their inner spirit rather/more than their outer wear. Their appearance says a lot about who they really are. And it says a lot about the kind of man they are trying to attract. Do they really want their neckline or hemline to be what lures a guy?

DISCUSS

What are the dress codes in your family? What have you determined about how to address and enforce these?

PRAY

Pray that you will have the courage to confront difficult issues like this. And pray that you will model what you preach to your children.

KEEP GOING STRONG

These all with one mind were continually devoting themselves to prayer.
ACTS 1:14

I know how hard it can be to stay consistent with your devotions. I'm sure that in the course of reading this book together, life has served up numerous excuses not to take this so seriously. But I hope the following testimony will be as encouraging to you as it is to us—a reminder of how important your time together in prayer and God's Word really is:

Last year was kind of rough on our marriage. We've been trying to have children, but to no avail, and as a result of that frustration and a combination of being apathetic about our marriage, we both began to wonder if it was even right for us to be together. (This became quite evident at the end of a seven-day cruise we took.)

On our way home from the cruise, I found a couple's devotional book in an airport shop and showed it to my wife. She just rolled her eyes, like I was trying to make a smart remark. But when we got back home, I bought *Moments Together for Couples* and put it under the Christmas tree, labeled "To Us." My wife opened it on Christmas morning, and we made a pact that we would read it this year.

It has done wonders for us! We have communicated more in the last seven weeks than we have in our entire marriage. We have learned things about each other that we had never known. We both want our marriage to work, and now it shows. Nowadays, I can't wait to get home from work and see my wife. It reminds me of when we first started dating. I love her more each day.

For a couple that was putting the "pathetic" in apathetic, this book has helped us get out of that awful rut.

DISCUSS
Talk about some of the best benefits of being in God's presence together—things you never want to live without again.

PRAY
Pray for a steadily growing desire to be with God and each other.

NEIGHBORHOOD WATCH

He who turns a sinner from the error of his way will save his soul
from death and will cover a multitude of sins.

JAMES 5:20

When I was growing up in the small town of Ozark, Missouri, in the 1960s, I knew that if I was driving and I peeled out from a stop sign at 8 P.M. on any night of the week, I could expect my parents to know about it by 8:30. I also remember the only fight I was ever in, at the local Dairy Queen. Fifteen minutes later when I walked through the door, Mom and Dad already knew about it.

This type of parent-to-parent "instant messaging" is rare today. In our age of "non-judgmental tolerance," we reason that we don't have any right to tell another parent about a concern we have with his or her child. And children suffer for our failure to help each other.

I've called parents about behavior we observed in one of their children, and I've been told (by the parent), "I don't want to hear it." But we've also had friends—true friends—who cared enough to courageously step up and express a concern about something one of *our* kids was doing.

I think the dangers of the day demand that we drop our defensiveness and fear, and encourage others to offer observations to us about how our children are doing. Take the initiative by telling the parents of your children's friends, "If you see my son or daughter doing anything questionable, you have the freedom to tell me. I want to know." You might even want to call a meeting of the parents in your church—those with children between, say, fifth and twelfth grade—and challenge them to work together to look after one another's kids.

We're all in this thing together. This is the kind of accountability and community that followers of Christ can employ.

DISCUSS

Would you ever talk to another parent about your concern over his or her child? How would you respond if you got that call yourself?

PRAY

Pray that your love and concern will always lead to godly, redemptive actions.

LEARNING WHAT LOVE IS

BY BARBARA RAINEY

In this is love, not that we loved God, but that He loved us.
1 JOHN 4:10

I have learned more about God's love through our adopted daughter, Deborah, than from any other person on the planet. Although our five biological children certainly tested and tried us, Deborah tested our love more than all five of the others combined. Dennis and I faced countless opportunities just to walk away and say, "Look, this is too hard. We're not going to do this anymore." But we chose—over and over again—to love her, because we knew we did. And we knew God wanted us to.

I wrote in my journal:

> If Deborah were not mine, if she were not my child, would I love her? If I just passed her on the street, like I do countless other people each day, what would draw me to her? What would make me love her out of all the other people I see? She could be just another human being in my path, but she's not. God has made her ours somehow. And I have discovered a kind of love for Deborah that is unlike my love for any of our other five children. I have discovered a taste of God's unfathomable, undeserved, unexplainable, extravagant love—a supernatural love defined by His grace.

Because of Deborah, I know God in a way I could never have known Him otherwise. He has called me to lengths and depths of love I didn't know I was capable of but which I learned He can supply, because *He* is love. I don't love Deborah more than our other five children, but I do love her in a different way, and I know more love for my other kids than I would have ever known without her.

Anyone can love a child who is theirs by birth. But to love one who is adopted—this is to know the love of God.

DISCUSS

Is there someone in your life who sometimes requires great effort to love?

PRAY

Tell God, "Thank You for being love, for giving us the capacity to love and for teaching us how to love."

Get Connected for More Information
http://www.familylife.com/moments/adoption

SPLITTING HEADACHE

"For I hate divorce," says the LORD, the God of Israel.
MALACHI 2:16

This poem was written by Jen Abbas, then an 18-year-old child of divorce. I've arranged it a little differently on this page than it appears in her book, *Generation EX,* to make it fit. Its message is too important to allow form to quiet its voice. Listen to "The Eruption."

Divorce is like a trembling earthquake,
The world shakes, rumbling with rage,
And all the anger, guilt, and frustrations
That have been festering for so long below the surface
Suddenly spew upward in an inferno of hate or apathy.
At times the earth calms and you think the turmoil is over,
Settled, stable, but then the cycle begins again,
Repeating, repeating, repeating.
You are weary, you want to rest,
And that is when you realize the shaking has stopped,
But there is an eerie feeling lurking in the air.
You are hesitant to believe anything anymore,
You are so tired after struggling for so long,
And so you rest on the one solid patch of land,
Only to watch it split in two,
Two separate, distinct parts that will never come together again.
Each new patch supports part of you,
And as you watch, they pull away.

This is the type of poem that breaks my heart because it represents so many children who are torn apart by divorce. No matter what you are experiencing in your marriage, and no matter how tough it is, just remember the impact that *staying together* will have on your children.

DISCUSS
Promise each other that this will never be the heart's cry of your children. Talk about who you should consider sending this poem to right now.

PRAY
Pray for the children of divorce today, who are struggling to be loved and to belong. Pray for a friend who is moving toward a split.

Get Connected for More Information
http://www.familylife.com/moments/divorce

ROCK SOLID

He set my feet upon a rock making my footsteps firm.
PSALM 40:2

Yesterday I shared a poem that I use often when I'm speaking or talking with someone about divorce, especially about how it leaves children feeling "split in two," as Jen Abbas put it.

Actually, Jen experienced this twice—once at the age of 6 and again at the age of 18, when her mom and stepfather divorced. The second one caught her as she was leaving home for college, a time in life when she expected her family to be there for her, both to launch her and to provide that "solid patch of land" we all need when we feel unsupported or insecure.

But I want you to see again—and be blown away by—the power of the gospel as it descends upon a person who is lost and alone.

When the land cracked under Jen's feet as a college freshman, she jumped—just hoping to land somewhere. She was wide open to any belief system that would win her hand. Islam. Judaism. Taoism. Buddhism. Questioning everything, she went in search of something—anything—that wouldn't prove fickle and fleeting, the way her parents' love had.

But in her quest for spiritual security, she found every path closed and incomplete. There was only one path that stood out—the one with the element of grace embedded in it, the one that wasn't about what she did but about what she could be *given*.

Divorce had taught this young woman that if you're not always alert, constantly scanning the horizon for warning signs, love could leave. But in the person of Jesus Christ, she discovered that she was loved regardless of her performance. He changed her life.

There's hope for children of divorce—who make up 40 percent of adults today. Hope in Jesus Christ. Hope in His grace to forgive and in His power to help you forgive as well.

DISCUSS
Share with one another how the love of Jesus Christ has helped you forgive another person.

PRAY
Thank Him for His great salvation—He is the only rock any of us truly have to stand on.

GENETIC COMPLAINERS?

BY BARBARA RAINEY

Do all things without grumbling or disputing.
PHILIPPIANS 2:14

One thing we disciplined our children for was complaining. I'm not saying we did it perfectly. It seems there's a genetic disposition in our family to gripe and display an ungrateful attitude over just about anything. It is our job as parents to make sure these discontented tyrants, who masquerade as our children, aren't allowed to demand that things always go their way.

Even at the dinner table.

I can remember when our kids would whine about what had been set before them. Dennis and I would say, "I know you don't like it, but I expect you to eat one bite. After that, you don't have to eat any more, but you can't go scavenging in the kitchen for something else." (I assure you, it won't hurt an average child to skip a meal and be a little hungry the next morning.)

Sometimes, we'd save the untouched plate in the fridge and serve it again later. They weren't allowed to eat anything else until they'd disposed of what they'd earlier refused. And we wouldn't let them have dessert unless they'd finished their dinner serving.

We had a large family, and Dennis used to say to them, "Your mom is not a short-order cook for six demanding customers." Part of teaching our six kids respect and gratitude was giving them the opportunity to eat what I had worked hard to prepare.

After all, children are growing up in a world that comes with limitations. They won't always be able to "have it their way." As parents, we do them no favors by letting them be the center of their universe when God has tasked us with the responsibility of training them to become His servants.

A missed meal might just teach them to appreciate what is set before them. But developing a spirit of complaining will cost them dearly their whole lives.

DISCUSS

How much complaining do you do? Your children? Discuss how you will address this issue the next time it rears its ugly head.

PRAY

Ask the Lord to help you and your children model true gratefulness and contentment.

Get Connected for More Information
http://www.familylife.com/moments/charactertraining

FASTING

Is this not the fast which I choose, to loosen the bonds of wickedness,
to undo the bands of the yoke?
ISAIAH 58:6

Quite a few years ago, I was grappling with the state of the family in America and what God was calling me to do about it. I sensed Him leading me to embark on an extended fast. So after checking with my doctor to be sure I was physically able to consume nothing but fruit and vegetable juices for 40 days, I set out on faith to meet God in this stripped-down, bare-bones way. I cannot adequately describe what my experience with Him during that time was like.

It can be uncomfortable to talk about fasting. Some say that we shouldn't talk about fasting because it can mean we are spiritually proud. Because we seldom talk about it, fasting is the most misunderstood of all the spiritual disciplines.

Fasting is spiritually healthy because it forces us to stop feeding our unending fleshly appetites. I would say that one of my most important lessons from my time of fasting was that I got a real look at how truly selfish I am and how much of my life revolved around my appetites. I realized how much I need God.

Our culture feeds our materialistic self-absorption, which rebels and resists anything resembling sacrifice. We often live to satisfy our appetites, and we surround ourselves with luxuries and creature comforts. We deny ourselves very few things. It was good for me to throttle my flesh for an extended period of time. Part of my reason for doing it, quite honestly, was to invite God to work in my heart and subdue the stubborn tyrants of pride and self-sufficiency. I was unprepared for the "heart" surgery He performed.

Okay, here's the challenge: Start with a sunup to sundown fast to seek God in a new way and to pray. Share with one another what you learn about God and yourself.

DISCUSS

What kind of fast could you institute in your own life? What do you need to bring under the Lord's subjection?

PRAY

Pray that God will lead you to bold new ways of seeking His face.

LISTENING IN

Today if you hear His voice, do not harden your hearts.
HEBREWS 3:7-8

It's usually appropriate for our children to ask why we've come to a certain parenting decision. But sometimes, they must simply be satisfied with the answer: "I'm not sure. I just know that this is what we've decided."

Pastor, author and longtime friend Tom Elliff remembers one snowy Friday night when his daughter was returning from a school event by bus. She called home from the school building to say that she was going out with her boyfriend to get something to eat and would be home soon afterward. "I'm sorry, Beth, you can't tonight."

"Why?"

"I don't know, but I'm coming to get you."

The mood was naturally a little icy when he arrived to retrieve his daughter from school. She just couldn't understand it. Had she done something wrong? "No, I just had a reservation about it tonight. I needed you to come on home."

When they walked into the house, the phone was ringing. His daughter answered and immediately turned white as a sheet. After listening for less than a minute, she awkwardly returned the phone to its cradle and stared dumbfounded in her dad's direction.

"I will never question your authority in my life again," she said. As her boyfriend was pulling out of the school parking lot, someone shot a bullet through the passenger-side window. "He was okay at the hospital," she said, "but if I had been riding with him, I would have been dead."

Inner reservations. Checks in your spirit. They're often God's signals that something isn't right. Learn how to listen to them, and don't be afraid to follow up on what He seems to be alerting you to.

Your courageous decision to go against your teen's opinion and possible resistance could save a life.

DISCUSS
Talk about what you do when your children push back. How can you better back one another up in these situations?

PRAY
Ask God to give you a heart that is spiritually receptive to His guidance and warnings.

RAZOR'S EDGE

Flee from the midst of Babylon, and each of you save his life!
JEREMIAH 51:6

Centuries ago, a popular queen was interviewing applicants to serve on a six-man team responsible for carrying her on a portable throne on long journeys. As she interviewed each man, the queen asked, "If you were bearing me along a mountain path, how close would you go to the edge of a cliff?"

Some men would answer, "Your Royal Highness, I am so strong, I could go within a foot of the edge of a cliff." Others would boast, "Not only do I have superior strength, but I have almost perfect balance. I could go within six inches of the edge."

But a few declared, "Your Highness, I would go nowhere near the edge of a cliff. Why would I want to imperil your valuable life by leading you so close to danger?"

Guess who earned the job?

We live in a cultural landscape where it seems there are more cliffs than clearings. We spend large parts of our day within easy walking distance of all kinds of sharp drops and perilous dangers. Sexual temptation. Financial greed. Immoral entertainment. Emotional affairs. Addictions galore. Ethical compromise.

Rather than stay as far as possible from these obvious threats to our families, we often allow the enemy of our souls to lure us closer for a better look. We sample just a bit too much of what the world has to offer.

My friend Josh McDowell says, "I would rather build a rail at the top of the mountain than have an ambulance service at the bottom of the valley." I agree. But I'd suggest we take it a step further. I would prefer not putting myself in position to find out whether or not that guardrail would hold me! Safety rails aren't meant for pushing on but for steering away from.

DISCUSS

Looking back over your life, what "cliffs" draw your curiosity? Which avoidable ones do you have the hardest time keeping your distance from now?

PRAY

Ask the Lord to help you not only *spot* spiritual danger, but also to have sense enough to run from it.

Get Connected for More Information
http://www.familylife.com/moments/temptation

COVENANT-KEEPING LOVE

Therefore be imitators of God, as beloved children; and walk in love.
EPHESIANS 5:1-2

Like many couples, Barbara and I began our marriage with a commitment to love one another. But we didn't really understand what real love was all about. Now, after more than three decades together, we know that our love is much more than a feeling—it's a lifelong commitment.

I shudder when I think of the shallow love that we had for each other when we first married. I'm glad we didn't give up on our relationship when we didn't always feel "in love" as we had before, because we would never have experienced the benefits that were just around the corner. We would have missed the fruit that comes through years of building memories—raising children, working through problems and trials, enjoying romantic getaways, working together to implement a shared vision for families.

I'm reminded of a great story of covenant-keeping love. An elderly man faithfully visited his wife every day at a nursing home. She had Alzheimer's disease and would be very ugly to him some days. Yet every day he told her, "I love you."

One day the head nurse called him into her office. "Every nurse here is impressed with you," she said. "We want our husbands to be more like you. But your wife doesn't know who you are, and she doesn't know whether you come or not. You could be doing other things and leave us to take care of your wife. Don't feel like you need to come every day."

Tears began to flow down the old man's cheeks. He looked at the nurse and said, "I understand what you're saying to me, and I know that my wife doesn't know who I am. But I know who she is. She is my wife, and almost 50 years ago I made a covenant with her that in sickness and in health, I would be there for her, and I will be."

Now that's real family life and real love!

DISCUSS

In what ways is your love more mature now than it was when you first married?

PRAY

Pray that God will continue to grow your understanding and application of real love.

Get Connected for More Information
http://www.familylife.com/moments/commitment

ALL IS WELL

You who have shown me many troubles and distresses will revive me again.
PSALM 71:20

I'm sure you get the same kind of phone calls and emails that we do—reports about friends and family members facing difficulty. Perhaps it's an upcoming surgery or the loss of a job. On occasion it may involve something much more severe—a relative has been diagnosed with cancer or a friend's child has unexpectedly taken his life.

Frequently when these messages show up on our message machine or in our in-box—those times when you really don't know what to say or how to pray—I think of a moment Barbara and I shared in the county of Cornwall on the southwest coast of England. We had come across a little church on a windswept hillside, where a section of the front lawn was set apart for a cemetery filled with old, uneven tombstones, many dating back several centuries.

One tombstone bore the names of an entire family. Judging from the dates, it seemed the mother had died three weeks after giving birth. The child's name, John, also appeared, having died before he turned one. Lastly came the father's name, indicating he had lived not much more than a year after his son's death.

Etched beneath their names—in letters we could barely make out—was this simple perspective: *"We cannot, Lord, Thy purpose see, but all is well that's done by Thee."*

Here was a little family that didn't last long but had apparently responded to some tough circumstances with a resilient faith in God. They trusted that God knew what He was doing. And whenever my friends and family face problems today, I often tell them about that little Cornish hillside, where God reminded me that because He is good, "all is well."

DISCUSS
What specific circumstances in your life are desperately in need of this "all is well" reminder?

PRAY
Pray for the grace to walk through trials with a faith strong enough to still be speaking long after the situation has come and gone. Can you pray, "We cannot, Lord, Thy purpose see, but all is well that's done by Thee"?

SCRIPTURES ON STANDBY

But his delight is in the law of the LORD. . . .
He will be like a tree firmly planted by streams of water.
PSALM 1:2-3

As our children grew up, Barbara and I decided that we would "embed" Scriptures in our children's lives. We did this so that they would know how to make right choices in tempting circumstances. God's Word has a way of bearing fruit at just the right time, proving that it is living and active.

For example, as we read the Scriptures when our children were preteens, we started rehearsing different situations they would likely face later: What should a girl say to a boy who wants to park with her late at night? What should a boy do if a girl becomes sexually aggressive and starts making moves on *him*? We worked on making topics like these part of our regular conversation as we read the Bible and discussed how it intersected with real life and real decisions.

This came together one day for our daughter Ashley when she was 13 and found herself in a situation with a boy she liked as a friend. He told her he wanted to kiss her. "Well, I'm not going to let you," she replied. Undeterred, he shot back, "Well, I'm going to do it anyway."

"No, you're not."

"Yes, I am."

Finally, Ashley looked at him sternly and said, "You are *not* going to kiss me, because you are like a reed blowing in the wind, and I am a steel pole set in concrete." Not an exact quotation of Psalm 1, but close enough to let this guy know that her God had weighed in on this situation.

Do you want your children prepared to be able to withstand temptations? Embed the truth of God's Word in their hearts.

DISCUSS
Talk about how you can do a better job of relating Scriptures to the issues your children are facing today. What are the best times of the day or week to embed the Scriptures in the lives of your children?

PRAY
Ask God to burden you with training your kids in His Word and to give you wisdom to know how to do it.

Get Connected for More Information

PURITY ON THE LINE

Where there is no vision, the people are unrestrained,
but happy is he who keeps the law.
PROVERBS 29:18

A dear friend, Pat Orton, who once worked closely with me at FamilyLife, wrote me a letter several years ago to tell me about a line her parents had drawn in the sand for her as a teenager.

The waistline.

Pat's mom and dad told her that whenever she was out with a young man, the only place he was allowed to touch her was on her back, from her shoulder to her waist. Anywhere else on her body was totally off-limits. And never—never *ever*—was he to put his hand on her knee. It was a way for her to know—immediately—that if a boy's hands ever strayed out of bounds, watch out! This was leading to trouble!

Funny what boundaries can do once they are clearly established. Crossing them is still quite possible, of course, but not without knowing you're breaking trust. And for Pat and her boyfriend-turned-fiancé, this simple, clearly defined expectation remained in force throughout their four-year courtship.

Back only. Shoulder to waistline. Nothing further . . . until their wedding day. As they pulled away from the church on their way to their honeymoon, he tenderly reached over and placed his hand on her knee. "I've been waiting four years to do that!" he said with a grin so big it made her smile, too.

Isn't that just delightful? What purity! What innocence! What a testimony to the joy we help our children preserve for themselves when we draw the right boundaries, enforce the right restrictions and keep an eye out for their obedience.

That's how to start a marriage. And Mom and Dad, that's what you're here to help happen.

DISCUSS

What kind of boundaries are you challenging your children to keep with the opposite sex?

PRAY

Pray that God will keep you cautious, even when the last thing in the world you want to do is lay down the law.

Get Connected for More Information
http://www.familylife.com/moments/purity

OPEN AND SHUT

If she is a wall, we will build on her a battlement of silver;
but if she is a door, we will barricade her with planks of cedar.
SONG OF SOLOMON 8:9

As parents, one of our responsibilities is to protect the sexual purity of our children. This verse from Song of Solomon provides an interesting insight when it equates sisters with "walls" or "doors."

Those who are "walls" remain pure—they are not open to peer pressure. Their sense of sexual morality is held firmly in place. But those who are "doors" are flirtatious, prone to get emotionally involved too quickly. They're easily manipulated by someone of the opposite sex.

If you have a daughter who's a wall, honor her purity. Give her the "silver" of your praise, as the verse above says. Don't overlook her or take her integrity for granted. Instead, celebrate her steadfast morals. Cheer her on.

But if she's a door—one who seems more susceptible to being opened by the advances of young men—the Lord tells us to build a cedar barricade—hard, strong and durable—around her. Not a barricade of rules (although you'll need some of those, too) but a barricade of love, of relationship. The kind that says, "I care about you and what you're going to experience as a young lady someday in your marriage bed, so let's chat about this regularly as you become a woman."

Spend lots of time with her. Stay involved in her life. Get to know her friends. Ask questions about what's going on. Ask God for wisdom in building the "barricade . . . with planks of cedar."

Your goal is to one day present your daughters to their husbands as young women unstained, untouched by evil. In giving them a healthy view of their own sexuality, you're preparing them for the day when God says it's time to awaken those desires.

DISCUSS
Think about each of your children. Do they tend to be walls or doors? Begin to discuss practical ways you can help them be walls.

PRAY
Pray daily for the sexual purity of all your children—for the pleasures of virtue they are saving for their marriage.

Get Connected for More Information
http://www.familylife.com/moments/purity

BOYS AMONG MEN

Brothers, I urge you to bear with my word of exhortation.
HEBREWS 13:22, *NIV*

God gave us daughters who need to be protected. God made fathers to protect their daughters. And one of the ways we can do this is by getting to know the young men who ask them out.

As of today, I've conducted a sit-down interview with my daughters' dates somewhere between 30 and 40 times. A few of them have been what you might expect: boys nearly fainting in our living room. (These talks have a way of revealing the fact that even wimps can have good taste. Some boys who couldn't last one round in a character contest at least have the good sense to know a great girl when they see one.)

For the most part, however, these encounters have allowed me to get to know several young men who would make their parents proud. And I've come away from every one of these interview experiences feeling like a real man.

Even more important, these interviews have helped spare my daughters from the predatory passions of even well-meaning boys, while also protecting them from their own human natures. As a result, Barbara and I have watched our daughters enter into marriage with their virtue, not just technically intact, but also reserved—heart, soul and body—for the man God had given them to marry.

It is one of the most important investments dads can make in our girls' lives—challenging their boyfriends to be men, making sure they're clear on the high value God has placed both on them and our daughters.

These young men who like what they see in our daughters need us to look them in the eyes, man to man, and hold them accountable. When you call them to high standards of personal morality, you not only protect your daughter. You help boys become men.

DISCUSS
Talk about the requirements you're going to establish (or need to establish now) for your children and their dates.

PRAY
Pray that the Lord will protect our daughters—and our sons—from mistakes that could cost them for the rest of their lives.

THE INTERVIEW

Brace yourself like a man; I will question you, and you shall answer me.
JOB 38:3, *NIV*

I wrote yesterday about an interview I've conducted numerous times with young men who have wanted to date our daughters. Lots of parents have asked me to share some of the things I cover when I meet with these young men. Here's a "high fly by" list:

1. *A woman is God's creation, a beautiful creation, a fine creation.* You've certainly noticed that my daughter is pretty, is attractive and has a cute figure, haven't you?
2. *The attraction of a young man to a young lady is both normal and good.* I'm glad you like her and want to be with her.
3. *I understand and remember what the sex drive of a young man is like.* Believe me, I've been there, I know what you're dealing with.
4. *I'm going to hold you accountable for your relationship with my daughter.* Expect me to be asking to see if you're dealing uprightly with her.
5. *I'm challenging you to purity.* I want you to guard her innocence, not just her virginity.
6. *I want you to respect and uphold the dignity of my daughter by keeping your hands off of her.* Keeping this one precaution in mind will help keep you from getting into further trouble.
7. *Do you understand all of what I've just said to you?* Are we clear on what I'm expecting and what you can expect from me?
8. *When you're a dad someday, I hope you will challenge your own children to abide by these standards and will interview your daughter's dates.* My prayer is that you will never forget this conversation.

One of the greatest privileges God has given me is to stand alongside our four daughters and honorably and gently attempt to protect their innocence. Meeting with these young men has been one of the highlights of being a dad.

DISCUSS
Dads, discuss with your wife why this can be a little awkward to do. Moms, share with your husband how it makes you feel when you see him protecting your daughter.

PRAY
Pray for courage to follow through with what you know to be right.

Get Connected for More Information
http://www.familylife.com/moments/dating

DAD RULES

Hear, O sons, the instruction of a father, and give attention
that you may gain understanding.
PROVERBS 4:1

I came across a tongue-in-cheek list of "Dad Rules" recently on the Internet—little warnings you might want to keep in mind as boys start wanting to date your daughter (or daughters):

> If you pull into my driveway and honk your horn, you'd better be delivering a package, because you're sure not picking anything up.

> It is usually understood that to get to know each other, we should talk about sports, politics and other issues of the day. Please do not do this. The only information I require from you is an indication of when you expect to have my daughter safely back at my house. And the only word I need from you on the subject is: "Early."

> As you stand in my front hallway, waiting for my daughter to appear, and more than an hour goes by, do not sigh and fidget. If you want to be on time for a movie, you should not be dating. Instead of just standing there, why don't you do something useful, like changing the oil in my car?

> The following places are not appropriate for a date with my daughter: Places where there are beds, sofas or anything softer than a wooden stool. Places where there is darkness. Places where there is dancing, holding hands or happiness. Places where the ambient temperature is warm enough to induce my daughter to wear shorts, tank tops, midriff T-shirts or anything other than overalls, a sweater and a goose-down parka zipped up to her throat. Hockey games are okay. Old folks homes are better.

Okay, I'm not really suggesting that you use these rules (I don't think). This is just a fun way of reminding you that protecting your daughter's moral purity is a responsibility you need to take on with purpose, intent and diligence. Seriously.

DISCUSS

I didn't have room to list all the "Dad Rules." Maybe you'd like to come up with a few more of your own.

PRAY

Pray for a heart that's not too busy, preoccupied or overly trusting when it comes to defending your daughter.

Get Connected for More Information
http://www.familylife.com/moments/dating

Fourth Quarter

See to it that no one comes short of the grace of God.
HEBREWS 12:15

Pat Summerall is a man living in the fourth quarter of life. His first quarter was spent in the home of his grandmother—he was born into a broken home and his parents abandoned him at an early age. His second quarter was filled with athletic success, first as a college football standout at the University of Arkansas ("Go Hogs!") and then as an NFL great with the New York Giants.

The third quarter, though, was a volatile mix of success and failure. Professionally, he became one of the premier broadcast voices on sports television—for many years he was famous as the partner of John Madden as they covered NFL football. But severe alcoholism was eroding his family life, destroying his marriage and threatening his friendships.

So Pat's third quarter came to a close with a surprise meeting attended by 14 friends, including some of the most prominent people in professional sports. Each had a letter to read and an appeal to make: "Will you go for help?"

Anger hardened him at first against the things he was hearing, but the surprising confrontation was too much to withstand. He checked in to a recovery clinic . . . and met Jesus in the process. At 66 years of age, he was baptized in a Texas church and has been living for Christ ever since.

So now Pat Summerall is in the fourth quarter of life—coming from behind, restoring his family relationships and proclaiming a vital message: "It's never too late."

No matter what you've done, no matter how far you've slipped away, there is always hope. There is always possibility. There is always more to be gained in Christ than you've lost along the way.

DISCUSS
How do you handle success? Failure? Has there ever been a moment in your life when you wondered if it was too late?

PRAY
As you come to a deeper awareness of sin, pray for not only a deeper repentance but also a deeper view of what God can do.

EXUBERANTLY HAPPY

You have turned for me my mourning into dancing;
you have loosed my sackcloth and girded me with gladness.
PSALM 30:11

Bob Russell, longtime pastor of Southeast Christian Church in Louisville, Kentucky, shared this in a sermon one evening:

What if I asked you tonight, on a scale of 1 to 10, how happy you are right now? If you answered with anything other than a 9 or a 10, you'd probably go on to qualify your answer by saying, "Well, there are some circumstances in my life today that are less than ideal."

I'll bet, though, that I could make you exuberantly happy within twenty-four hours without changing even one of the circumstances you're living in right now.

But it would be a brutal twenty-four hours.

I'd have your lawyer call to tell you that you were being sued, that it looked like you were going to lose every dime you had. Then I'd have your doctor call to tell you that he's looked at your latest tests and thinks you have a terminal disease—you've got just six months to live. Then I'd have a trusted friend call to tell you that the three people who are closest to you in life had just been killed in a traffic accident. Then I'd have a theologian that you trust submit an article saying that the Bible is not true—that he no longer believes in Christ.

Then, after twenty-four hours, I'd say to you, "None of this is true. You still have your nest egg, you still have your loved ones, you still have your health, and you still have your church and your hope in Christ."

You'd probably want to punch me out, but you'd be exuberantly happy, even with the same circumstances you started with.

Happiness is largely a matter of perspective, isn't it? No matter what your circumstances, God can make you "exuberantly happy" . . . as long as you are keeping your eyes on Him.

DISCUSS

What circumstances are causing you to feel anxiety rather than "exuberant happiness"?

PRAY

Pray for a deeper dependence on God, a greater contentment with His good gifts and a deeper compassion for others' suffering.

Get Connected for More Information
http://www.familylife.com/moments/spiritualgrowth

TOTALLY EXPOSED

BY BARBARA RAINEY

With all humility and gentleness, with patience, showing tolerance
for one another in love.
EPHESIANS 4:2

One weekend our two family photographers—daughter-in-law Stephanie and oldest daughter, Ashley—were together taking photos of Ashley's little boys. My favorite is one of little James, who was about 18 months old at the time, in his birthday suit. The dark backdrop in the photo highlighted the purity of his new little body with its clear, soft skin. The pose they captured showed James innocently and playfully on his hands and knees, looking to the side with a precious grin on his face. It will be a treasured photo for years to come.

As photographers, Stephanie and Ashley had a choice. They could have placed little James in the backyard mud and then irritated him to make him mad so that they could capture his little sin nature on film forever (which would have been much easier to do)! Instead they chose to focus on his best qualities. And because he was naked, they carefully chose an angle that hid his male parts from view, knowing it would be distracting in the final photo and that James would likely be embarrassed by it someday.

Like little James, we are naked and exposed before each other in marriage. No one knows your wife's or husband's sin, shame and failures the way you do. But marriage was designed by God to be a place of comfort and safety, not condemnation and critique.

Each of us brings our own set of flaws with us when we marry, and unfortunately, we add new ones to them as time goes along. But marriage should be the best place for two imperfect people to find acceptance and ongoing forgiveness . . . as well as the courage to change and grow.

DISCUSS

Share some of your favorite things about your mate—and in so doing, repent of your critical focus.

PRAY

Pray that forgiveness will flow freely in your marriage, creating an environment and inducement for godly change.

Get Connected for More Information
http://www.familylife.com/moments/marriagerelationship

FINDERS KEEPERS

What therefore God has joined together, let no man separate.
MARK 10:9

Research has shown that about two-thirds of all divorces today are occurring in low-conflict marriages. That is, they're ending without a death blow like infidelity or physical abuse. Instead, a couple simply accumulates enough disagreement and disharmony that they begin believing that the best option for doing away with the headaches is just to do away with the marriage.

If you know people in that situation, urge them to fight for their marriage. Tell them not to quit without taking another lap around the track—without stopping to realize that the best marriage to be in is the one they already have.

I received an email not long ago from a radio listener who was convicted by an interview he had heard on one of our broadcasts. He and his wife were divorced, and he was close to marrying another woman. He wasn't sure what he should do.

I couldn't get away from his message. I read it and reread it. Finally, I just sat down to call him, and asked, "Is there any possibility of reconciling with your wife before you move on to remarriage? Look, you're still going to be married to an imperfect person, even if you swap one spouse for another. Only now you're going to be bringing all that divorce baggage into your new relationship."

One researcher told me that if a couple can find as little as 20 percent of their marriage that they would call satisfactory, they have a better than 90 percent chance of making their marriage better in two years—*if* they stick with it, *if* they keep fighting, *if* they don't give up and throw in the towel too soon.

DISCUSS
Do you know a couple who appears to be close to giving up? Talk about what you can do to help.

PRAY
Pray hard for the struggling marriages you know.

A MATTER OF CONSCIENCE

It is better, if God should will it so, that you suffer for doing what is right rather than for doing what is wrong.
1 PETER 3:17

Barbara was working on her needlepoint, and I was reading the newspaper. It was any weeknight in America—just the way Norman Rockwell pictured it.

At least it was until our eighth grader, Benjamin, popped his head up from behind his school-assigned book and said, "Dad, I don't think I should be reading this."

"What do you mean, buddy?" I asked.

"This story—it's got some pretty graphic details about a man and a woman in it. You know, sex!" He blushed a bit and shot a nervous glance at his mom, who nearly jabbed her finger with that sewing needle.

"Let me see that book," I said. Quickly flipping through a few pages, I could see right away why he was concerned. He was dead on. This book was explicit and graphic as it spun a romantic tale.

As it turned out, we were able to help him get an alternate assignment. After his teacher originally threatened him with a zero for not reading this particular book, we came to a meeting of the minds and were happy with the result. But nothing made us happier than seeing our son's conscience in action, knowing that at 14 he already had an acute sense of right and wrong—and the courage to choose what he knew was best.

I can promise you that living-room stories like these don't happen without lots of work on the part of parents. Lots of Scripture. Lots of prayer together. Lots of offhand conversations, teachable moments and direct disciplinary actions.

If you're doing it right, parenthood often means being a pain to your children, interfering with what they want. But those early years of character development are so important. That's when you play the role of your children's consciences—calling them, training them, prodding them on to a higher good, helping them learn the value of refusing evil.

DISCUSS
How have you seen your children's consciences fire into action?

PRAY
Pray that the Lord will always keep your kids' consciences tender to His touch.

Get Connected for More Information
http://www.familylife.com/moments/charactertraining

LACKING NOTHING

*He did not leave Himself without witness, in that He did good
and gave you rains from heaven and fruitful seasons.*
ACTS 14:17

Dollar dilemmas. If you're like most couples, you've already had some high-thermostat conversations about money. In many marriages, one spouse grips a dollar bill so tight that Washington has tears on his cheeks, while the other has greasy fingers.

Barbara shared recently that when we started our marriage, she felt as if she had to ask before spending virtually any money. I recall that as a new husband, I had no idea of how she felt about what I thought of as *our* money. We were not on the same page in how we looked at our finances.

We realized that if we hoped to reconcile our differences or our account balances, then we needed to develop a mutual understanding about our finances that was the same as God's.

Over time, we learned that the foundation of our attitudes about money should be our understanding of Him as Provider. When Jesus' disciples returned from a trip, He asked them if they had lacked anything along the way (see Luke 22:35). Their answer? "No, nothing." They trusted Christ and their needs were met.

This spiritual principle is true today. During our entire marriage, Barbara and I have relied on His provision through His people. Simply put, we receive a set salary if (and only if) our supporters give enough to cover that amount every month. Every month is like Christmas, seeing how God has provided. (In fact, we also do not take royalty payments for our books or receive honorariums when we speak at FamilyLife events or conferences.)

Over the years, we've experienced God's provision in hundreds of ways. Every paycheck is hand to mouth . . . His hand to our mouths! Even now, He melts our hearts as we find Him knowing our situation, understanding where we are and moving with faith-building power to supply our genuine needs.

DISCUSS
What are some ways God has provided for your needs together as a couple?

PRAY
Thank God for His provision. Ask Him to help you recognize Him as Provider during times of abundance or times of need.

Get Connected for More Information

BOUNCING BALL

*I considered all my activities which my hands had done and
the labor which I had exerted, and behold all was vanity.*
ECCLESIASTES 2:11

There are seasons in life when our work requires more of us than it does at other times. Tax season for the accountant. Christmas season for the retailer. Whatever your line of work, it likely has a natural rhythm that spikes at certain times.

But increasingly in our success-driven culture, busy seasons have run together into *all* seasons. We have allowed the pace to perpetuate itself, driving us at full throttle month after month, year after year. Things begin to come totally unraveled at home, in our marriage, in our relationship with our children. It can happen, seemingly, in a blink.

This reminds me of a commencement address attributed to Brian Dyson, who held several senior management positions with Coca-Cola during his long career. He told a class of Georgia Tech graduates, "Imagine life as a game in which you are juggling five balls in the air: work, family, health, friends and spirit. You're keeping all of these in the air.

"You soon understand that work is a rubber ball. If you drop it, it will bounce back. But the other four balls are made of glass. If you drop one of these, it will be irrevocably scuffed, marked, nicked, damaged, or even shattered. It will never be the same."

You may not get as many pats on the back for being at home to dry the dishes or settle a disagreement or help a child study for a test. You may not receive the same sense of affirmation you feel from accomplishing a work goal or achieving recognition among your peers. But you will be living proof that winning at home *first* is the key to winning anything of value.

Marriages and families don't bounce. They shatter. For generations.

DISCUSS

What is your "busy season"? What are the first signs that work is getting out of balance? How can you help each other handle those seasons that demand more of you than usual?

PRAY

Pray for the ability to juggle well . . . and to know which balls can drop without causing major damage.

Get Connected for More Information
http://www.familylife.com/moments/stress

NEVER TOO LATE

*He will restore the hearts of the fathers to their children and
the hearts of the children to their fathers.*
MALACHI 4:6

I'm always grieved when I hear about dads who are too busy or self-absorbed to invest themselves in their children. This neglect often produces a wound in a child that rarely heals right. But when it does heal, you can be sure God has done it.

A radio listener wrote me not long ago with a story like this, and it touched my heart. He told of the first full day he ever remembered spending with his father. It didn't happen until the boy was 21 years old and was legally allowed to visit the bar where his dad spent so much of his time.

But this encounter became a start. And even though his father apologized for "not being there," the young man never heard the words every child aches to hear: "I love you" and "I'm proud of you."

The father died when his son was 25, and the loss sent him into his own bout with alcoholism. That led to many years of struggle and eventual recovery—including a life-changing encounter with Jesus Christ.

Then one day he was listening to our broadcast on *FamilyLife Today* about the pain of past hurts and the healing power of forgiveness. "For the first time ever," he wrote, "I felt my dad's hurt, and my heart was moved with compassion." He began to talk to his father, just as though they were in the same room together. And with each sentence, the tears flowed. Relief came. All the pent-up anger and anguish melted.

He was whole. He was free.

Healing like this can take many long years, as it did for this man. But never stop believing that God can mend your heart, no matter how deep the hurt or how afraid you are to risk opening the wound again.

DISCUSS

What still stands between you and the forgiveness of a parent (or someone else) who has hurt you deeply? Will you forgive him or her?

PRAY

Ask the Lord to enable and empower you to "keep short accounts."

TAKING SIDES

He Himself is our peace, who made both groups into one and broke down the barrier of the dividing wall.

EPHESIANS 2:14

Simon and Chana Taub of Brooklyn broke up housekeeping after 20 years of marriage—divorcing and going their separate ways. Sort of.

He went to the living room on the first floor, and she took the bedroom level on the third floor. And just to be sure they didn't bump into each other on the *second* floor—to which they both had partial access—a judge ordered that a partition be erected at the staircase, blocking them from accidentally crossing paths.

Now, I've seen the pictures of it myself on the Internet. An actual slab of white drywall, cut to fit a doorway opening in their richly ornate home. It's a stark representation of the stubborn walls of isolation that are nailed up in far too many homes across our land. Walls of silence. Walls of distance. Walls of unresolved issues. Walls built to the thickest dimensions with the materials of misunderstanding, impatience, annoyance and ridicule.

But just as Jesus came to destroy the dividing line between Jew and Gentile, He also comes into our homes and marriages today, offering us all the tools required to dismantle the walls that so easily and quickly grow up between us. He offers the tools of forgiveness. The tools of honor and grace and repentance.

It may take a whole lot of hammering and demolition *and selflessness* to get these walls down, but keep going through your house until you've found them all . . . and have torn them to the ground.

Let's hope Simon and Chana get theirs down, too, and find some way to meet in the middle. A marriage with walls is not what God intended.

DISCUSS

What walls have you allowed to stay standing in your home? Where have you built those walls? In the kitchen? Living room? Bedroom? What will be your first steps to remove them?

PRAY

Pray that God will help you spot any walls going up between you before they get filled in with resentment and bitterness. Ask God to help you grow in oneness.

Get Connected for More Information
http://www.familylife.com/moments/conflict

OUT IN THE OPEN

The man and his wife were both naked and were not ashamed.
GENESIS 2:25

Being "naked" but "not ashamed."

This is why we get married—not just to have sex, but also to become emotionally intimate with another person. We want someone we can be openly transparent with, someone who accepts us, even when we're being our real selves.

Yet although this is what our souls long for, many couples—especially young couples—hide this need behind the mere act of sexual togetherness. They find having sex easier than opening up to each other *spiritually*, where the potential for hypocrisy and awkwardness always exists. Sex can be easier than opening up *emotionally*, letting someone else in on their fears and worries and dreams and deepest feelings.

That's why, even when the level of sexual intimacy is high in a marriage, the level of real transparency can still be surprisingly low . . . and subtly debilitating.

I recall a young single man stopping by Barbara's and my table at Wendy's one evening. He had heard us speak at a recent singles event at church and wanted to thank us for helping him see again why keeping the sexual element out of a budding romance gives a young man and woman the chance to really develop their relationship. It helps them do the authentic work of getting to know each other, not just settling for what comes naturally and without thinking.

But you know what? The same thing can happen inside marriage. We can let sex become a substitute for real relationship—even as husband and wife! We can be *together* but not be transparent.

Certainly, transparency isn't something we achieve overnight. It's a process—a lifelong process of growing increasingly comfortable being honest with each other without fear of rejection. But it's what makes marriage a continually richer blessing.

To be in love is good. To be in love and perfectly transparent is as good as it gets.

DISCUSS

What have been your greatest obstacles to true transparency? Talk about one of the following: your greatest fear, your most courageous act or your biggest doubt.

PRAY

Pray for your love to grow into one that more readily reveals and never rejects.

Get Connected for More Information
http://www.familylife.com/moments/communication

It Only Takes a Spark . . .

I can do all things through Him who strengthens me.
PHILIPPIANS 4:13

For a firefighter, one of the most terrible phrases in the English language is "blow-up." In a firefighter's world, blowing up occurs when a manageable forest fire suddenly explodes into an inferno that rages through the grass and trees at a deadly speed.

To me, "blow-up" is an appropriate description of what's happened during the last decade at the heart of American society. A searing fireball of destruction has engulfed a priceless part of our culture—the family.

I remember speaking to 700 college students at a Campus Crusade for Christ conference in Dallas. When I asked those who had been affected by divorce (through their immediate or extended family) to stand, *80 percent* of the audience responded.

Afterward, a young man came forward to talk to me about his parents' divorce. His father had been a leading evangelical pastor. "My dad was my hero," he said. "He taught me everything I know. And now he's gone. I'm the only one left in my family that is still walking with God."

Far too many Christians today feel this same type of impotence. They are filled with fear—and burned by the heat of our cultural blow-up.

If you are tempted to lose hope and courage, take heart: You can make a difference! As today's verse tells us, God can give you the strength and power to withstand the heat.

In fact, when a firefighter cannot outrun a blow-up, one common tactic is to ignite a fire of his own to burn the area around him before the fireball reaches him. If you feel threatened by the fires of today's culture, *it's time to start a fire of your own.* You can do that by returning to God's Word and walking daily in obedience to Jesus Christ.

DISCUSS
What issues in our cultural blow-up cause you to lose courage and hope? Choose one way you can start a fire of your own that protects your family.

PRAY
Ask God for the courage to make a difference in your home and in your culture in the coming week.

COURAGEOUS PARENTING (PART ONE)

Wait for the LORD; be strong and let your heart take courage.
PSALM 27:14

One of my favorite conversation starters when I'm eating with other men or with a group of couples is "What is the single most courageous thing that you have ever done in your lifetime?"

When most people think of courage, they think of heroic deeds—like those done on battlefields distant in time and geography. But I think we need massive doses of courage if we are going to raise families according to the Scriptures.

Courage is demanded of parents who desire to do the following:

- Establish godly standards and boundaries for how their sons and daughters are to relate to the opposite sex
- Impart God's perspective of sexual identity for men and women in contrast to a culture that is promoting perverted distortions of what God created
- "Intrude" into the lives of their children when they sense something isn't right
- Avoid conforming to the values of other Christian parents in terms of curfews, acceptable dress, movies, language, Internet use, etc.

Parental courage is needed if we want to raise a generation of young people who know how to withstand sexual temptation. It takes a battlefield mentality if we are going to give our children the kinds of standards they need to maintain sexual purity.

It takes courage to look your sons in the eye when they're 13, 18 or 24 and ask them if they've been looking at pornography on the Internet. But your sons need you to ask them. And, Dad, *you* need to be able to ask them with your own conscience clean.

It takes courage to talk to your sons straight about keeping their hands off the girls. And it takes courage to meet with a young man who wants to take one of your daughters out for the evening—asking him to keep his hands and lips off *your* daughter!

The easiest thing to do is nothing. But that's how battles are lost.

DISCUSS
What is the most courageous thing you've ever done?

PRAY
Ask God for the courage you need to stand strong in the battle for the souls of your children.

Get Connected for More Information
http://www.familylife.com/moments/biblicalparenting

COURAGEOUS PARENTING (PART TWO)

Be strong and courageous, do not be afraid or tremble at them, for the LORD your God is the one who goes with you. He will not fail you or forsake you.
DEUTERONOMY 31:6

It takes courage to raise children today according to biblical standards, especially when the culture doesn't exactly support us in our striving to courageously protect our sons and daughters.

So what's a parent to do?

First, *resolve that you will* not *be a parent who does the easiest thing: nothing.* Loving children today will mean that you will make some mistakes. Perhaps you will go too far in setting some standards; but if your child has a secure, loving relationship with you, then I would rather you challenge your children to a high standard rather than one that is too low.

Second, *pray.* Someone has said, "Courage is fear that has said its prayers." Parents need to pray that they will be courageous. Barbara and I did—continually. We needed God's wisdom and strength.

Third, *meet as a couple and establish courageous boundaries for your family.* Set some clear rules about the following:

- Movies
- Use of the Internet and the phone
- Dating (i.e., if so, when, how and whom to date?)
- Relating to the opposite sex (i.e., how far do you want your child to go with the opposite sex prior to marriage?)
- Curfews
- Dress

Remember the question I mentioned yesterday? Whatever courageous acts you have accomplished in your lifetime, it could be that the *most* courageous is determining that you will remain involved in the lives of your children. Being a parent calls for repeated, heroic action. Doing your duty.

In the struggle against evil, our generation needs men and women who can stare at critical choices and not blink. It's this private brand of courage that should set a Christian family apart—the fortitude that turns a mom and dad into spiritual warriors on behalf of their family.

DISCUSS

What biblical standards would require the most courage to uphold in your family right now?

PRAY

Ask God for the courage to take specific steps to uphold these standards.

Get Connected for More Information

http://www.familylife.com/moments/biblicalparenting

WITHOUT A FRIEND

Better is a neighbor who is near than a brother far away.
PROVERBS 27:10

We've never had so many options for connecting with people—mail, email, phone, text-messaging, even Internet video. Yet recent findings reported in the *American Sociological Review* show that the number of people who claim to have *no one* to confide in on important matters is up from 10 percent to 25 percent since 1985.

True friendship—what's happened to it?

Some people, of course, claim to have a multitude of friends. One college student said, "You go on some people's online profiles, and they say they have a thousand friends. Truth is, they probably don't even *know* half of them."

So these days, in this high-tech, low-touch culture, is genuine friendship even necessary? More specifically, once you're married and settled as a couple, is there still a great need for you to maintain friendships?

Hopefully, your best friend is the person you're sharing this devotional moment with. That's the way it's supposed to be. But husbands and wives both need at least one close Christian friend of the same sex. It's also important for you to have at least one other couple you can share with—mutual friends you can turn to for fellowship and accountability.

Barbara and I have a handful of true friends upon whom we frequently lean for counsel, advice and balance. We've discussed everything from discipling our children to finances, areas of struggle, managing pressure, and the seasons of life.

As you look at today's culture of high-tech communication, one of the greatest needs you have is to be connected to some true friends—kindred spirits, followers of Jesus Christ who will tell you what you need to hear—friends who won't hesitate to weep with you or bring comfort or encouragement (or even correction) in a time of need.

DISCUSS

Who are your closest friends? What do you need to do to keep those friendships healthy and vibrant?

PRAY

If the two of you need some friends to come alongside you, ask God to direct you and another couple together. Be patient, and expect Him to provide.

Get Connected for More Information
http://www.familylife.com/moments/friendship

BOLD RESISTANCE

Have salt in yourselves, and be at peace with one another.
MARK 9:50

I still remember hearing about the 1995 murder of three children in their Little Rock home. Riley Noel and three accomplices wheeled into the driveway of Mary Hussian's house that night, high on drugs. They were certain that either Mary or one of her kids had been involved in a recent drive-by shooting that had taken the life of Noel's brother.

Riley Noel ordered the three children in the home—ages 10, 12 and 17—to lie down on the living-room floor, where he shot them execution style. Their mother escaped after a struggle. But she spoke these chilling words at a news conference soon after the tragic event: "I stand here with the blood of my children still under my fingernails. My kids were all I had. I plead with the youth today—don't send another woman to bed crying the way I'm going to cry tonight!"

Unfortunately, Barbara and I can't write this book fast enough to keep up with the latest news story out of another major city, or even a secluded farmland, about a young person who has gunned down even more of our nation's children. But no matter what the papers are reporting as you're reading this today, I urge you to put an end to your fear and apathy.

I urge you to pray, as 600 or so of us did in a city-wide prayer service soon after the Hussian children's deaths, confessing our sins and committing to action.

I urge you to confront immorality when you witness it within your home or in public settings.

I urge you not to be ashamed to call others to godly accountability, from governmental leaders to pastors to the people you work and associate with.

And I urge you to demand righteousness of yourself, because societal change always begins with one person, one home, one man or woman, one boy or girl, willing to make a difference.

DISCUSS

Be specific: What could you, your church or your neighborhood do to reclaim this nation for righteousness?

PRAY

Pray for the safety of our children, the courage of our people and the mercy of our God.

DREAMING DREAMS

So then, while we have opportunity, let us do good to all people.
GALATIANS 6:10

I think one of the greatest needs in the Christian community is for individual laymen and laywomen to dream some dreams about how they can use their talents to impact people's lives for Christ.

Let me tell you about a family that is making a difference. A small family ministry called Standing with Hope provides prosthetic limbs for below-the-knee amputees, not only in the United States, but also in Ghana, Africa.

The process of adding "skin" covering to make a prosthetic look real can cost thousands of dollars—far too costly for an outreach whose goal is to help as many people as possible be able to walk again. That's where the family's 15-year-old son, Grayson Rosenberger, comes in. While noodling over an entry idea for a nationwide science contest, Grayson came across one of his mom's old, discarded prosthetic legs. He found that by wrapping it in a very common household item, he could give the mechanical limb a realistic shape.

His inexpensive solution? Bubble wrap.

Total cost for application? About one dollar.

No, it doesn't look like skin. But with the right hose or stockings, the prosthetic leg can be made to look real. And for poverty-stricken adults and children in Africa who are often ostracized and teased for the primitive, bare-bones appearance of a fake leg, this is a confidence-creating alternative.

Bubble wrap. Who'd have thought?

Could it be that there's a right-under-your-nose opportunity to make a difference in people's lives—right where you are? Could it be that, if you slowed down and set your mind on seeking God for a way you could really serve Him, He might lay out an idea that's so simple, you'll be shocked you didn't think of it earlier?

Just think. Bubble wrap.

DISCUSS

Every person and every couple has an assignment from God—a ministry. What's yours? If you can't articulate your ministry, plan a time when you can begin to pray and think together.

PRAY

Express your availability to God, and ask Him to show you the best way to serve.

BIG BROTHERS AND SISTERS

Am I my brother's keeper?
GENESIS 4:9

We were having dinner recently with four couples. As the evening progressed, one of them shared her struggle with a sister, who at the age of 45 is chronically ill and likely a hypochondriac. This prompted another friend to share how his brother was in an unhealthy, codependent relationship with his 90-year-old mother. Around the table it went—each of them with their own story to tell about strain with an adult sibling.

As Barbara and I drove home, the thought struck me: *The problem with families is that all of us come from one!* They can indeed be stormy at times, defying predictability, routinely disruptive—a lot like Cain and Abel in Genesis 4.

Perhaps one of you is estranged from a brother or sister. Perhaps many months or even years have gone by since you've talked with or seen each other. Perhaps you have a sibling who still doesn't have his or her life together and continues taking advantage of your parents. Perhaps no matter what you or anyone else does to help, he or she cannot walk a straight line, keep a job or stay out of trouble.

I believe wisdom offers us three principles in trying to deal with this:

1. *Realize you're not alone.* Sibling difficulty was an issue in the very first family—something between Cain and Abel, as I recall—and it continues to stain most families today as they age and expand. What you're dealing with is unfortunately more normal than abnormal.
2. *Stop trying to change them.* If you have a tendency to be the 9-1-1 rescue responder, resign from that role. Put your trust in a big God, and turn the job over to Him. He's good at it.
3. *Forgive them.* Resist resentment. Stop punishing them. Give them the grace and mercy you have received from the Lord, and choose to love them, even if it must be from a safe distance.

DISCUSS
Rather than recounting the troubles between you and your adult siblings (or your parents), take this time to discuss how you could apply these three principles to your situation.

PRAY
Pray for them. Never stop praying for them. *Really* praying.

Get Connected for More Information
http://www.familylife.com/moments/siblings

PASS IT DOWN

I will instruct you and teach you in the way which you should go.
PSALM 32:8

How can you tell if the spiritual-sounding words coming out of your children's mouths are evidence of a true faith?

The fact is, you may not really know until they're somewhat older, because most children are clever enough to say what they know Mom and Dad want to hear. It often takes some severe testing to determine the veracity of your children's faith, and that doesn't usually happen until they're well along in their teen years, perhaps even college-age or older.

Our children began to have their faith tested in middle school. They started coming home with questions like, "What does the Bible say about evolution?" or "What does God think about being gay?" We had many lively discussions at the dinner table as I played devil's advocate to help them think through their beliefs. That's when they began to discover truth on their own from Scripture.

I don't know how to emphasize enough the importance of this kind of training. Depending upon whose research numbers you believe, the rate of young adults who abandon the faith of their parents is somewhere in the 50- to 80-percent range. We're talking about a major problem.

If we are to avoid the fate of many other nations where Christianity has dwindled into irrelevance, it must begin in homes like yours. Your children can only hitchhike on your faith for so long. You must constantly be looking ahead to the day when you release them to take their own journey of Christian belief.

May we raise children to invade and infiltrate the twenty-first century, not with faith standards blindly adopted from their parents, but with biblical beliefs honed into convictions.

DISCUSS

What are the key messages and convictions from the Bible that you want to pass on to your children? Discuss how you can both do a better job of diligently teaching and training your children.

PRAY

Ask God for the passion to make biblical training a top priority in your home, as well as the peace not to worry about being a super-theologian—just to share what you're experiencing and learning about God.

DOLLARS FROM HEAVEN

*Give, and it will be given to you. They will pour into your lap a good measure—
pressed down, shaken together, and running over.*
LUKE 6:38

Our children are better students of us than we are of them. They know—*really
know*—more of what's going on in your marriage than you think they do.

This was certainly the case for a couple who were invited by the wife's
brother and sister-in-law to attend one of our Weekend to Remember marriage conferences. Times had been hard for this couple, from the typical
stress of raising four teenage daughters to the strain of having one daughter
preparing to graduate and another preparing to marry to the added pressure
of temporarily providing a home for a friend and *her* two children. Truly, this
was a couple in need of some refreshment.

But even with their relatives' offer to pay for the airfare, they still didn't feel
as if they could handle the cost of the hotel, meals and conference fee.
Disappointed, they said, "As much as we'd love to go, we just can't afford it."

But when they returned home that same night, they were met by an incredible sight in their bedroom: 400 one-dollar bills—on the bed, on the floor, even
taped to the walls—as well as a card that read: "We love you, Mom and Dad.
Have a great time!" Their youngest daughters (ages 10 and 13), knowing what
was going on, had scraped together every cent they had saved to give their parents a gift and the trip of a lifetime.

Don't ever forget that your children are like little radar units, locked on to the
two most important people in their lives. They *know* how you are doing. That's
why it's so important to invest regularly in your marriage by getting away.

DISCUSS

When was the last time you took time away to work on your marriage? Pull
out a schedule and talk about finding two weekends in the coming year to
invest in your marriage.

PRAY

Ask the Lord to help you be sensitive to how your children gain strength and
stability from your relationship with one another.

ROCKY ROAD

By Barbara Rainey

We know that God causes all things to work together for good to those who love God, to those who are called according to His purpose.
ROMANS 8:28

Many couples experience a season of disappointed love in their marriage relationship. For our son Samuel and his wife, Stephanie, that season began the day after the wedding.

Watching these two get married was one of the greatest delights of my life. Their wedding day rivaled any fairy tale with their long-anticipated first kiss at the altar, the *Star Wars* theme recessional music, and a horse-drawn white-carriage ride around historic Franklin, Tennessee, in absolutely perfect weather.

And then began what they call the "honeymoon from hell"—missing their plane flight, a lost driver's license, no heat in their romantic hideaway, and more. Over the next few months, they clashed over their expectations about married life, their assumptions about their roles, and many other issues. Although most of these flash points were mistakes and misunderstandings, they still led to some raw feelings of grief and hurt. It was a long way from the horse-drawn carriage ride on their wedding day!

I share this to remind you that disappointed love can occur at any point in your marriage, even after times of peak romance and unusual oneness. This season calls for a level of hard work that you never expected your marriage to actually require. This is when you discover that the love you're looking for can't be self-produced; it requires an understanding and compassion that can come from God alone and a courageous commitment from each spouse.

When love disappoints, as it does for all of us, don't give up. God allows these times to bring us face to face with what we really value and to see that we can only love well when we are depending on Him. Disappointed love can be transformed by God into a deeper love that I call *cherishing, committed love.* And that kind of love is far better than fairy-tale love.

DISCUSS
Are you able to talk openly about your seasons of marital disappointment? Talk together about how you can share the burden of your disappointments.

PRAY
Pray for a courageous commitment to weather the inevitable hard times of disappointed love.

I'M THERE

I have no one else of kindred spirit who will genuinely be concerned for your welfare.
PHILIPPIANS 2:20

Gary Thomas, author of such inspiring books as *Sacred Marriage* and *Authentic Faith: The Power of a Fire-Tested Life*, tells the story of two American soldiers who became fast friends during their preparations for combat in World War I. Though they had known each other only a short time, the camaraderie of battle and their shared dreams of postwar life quickly cemented their relationship.

One day, these two buddies crawled from their foxhole with the rest of their unit in an attack on the German forces. After a valiant fight, the order was given to retreat. But only one of the two friends returned to the trench. The other had been hit by German gunfire and was lying about 50 yards out of reach.

Against his commanding officer's orders, the other soldier crawled out of the ditch to go find his fallen comrade. Hugging the ground and dodging enemy bullets, he worked his way across the bloody, corpse-littered ground until he finally located the friend he sought. Finding him semi-conscious, they were left with only a few seconds together before he died.

When the man returned to the trench with the body of his soldier friend, the ranking officer flew into a rage for this flaunting of his order. "Was it worth it for you to risk your life?"

"Absolutely, sir. Because when I turned him over, he looked up at me and said, 'I knew you'd come.'"

That's the kind of loyalty we are called to in all our relationships—especially in our homes and families. Your spouse needs to know without a doubt that when you are needed, you will be there. Your children need to know they can count on you, not just in a pinch, but also in their most routine of expectations. When they need you, can they be sure you'll come?

DISCUSS
How can your marriage and family practically demonstrate this kind of love for one another?

PRAY
Pray that the Lord will keep you sensitive to each other, anticipating when you're needed most.

Get Connected for More Information
http://www.familylife.com/moments/parentinginvolvement

CALL TO ARMS

*Valiant men, men who bore shield and sword and
shot with bow and were skillful in battle.*
1 CHRONICLES 5:18

It's hard starting out in marriage. Money is usually tight. You're getting used
to new responsibilities. Even though your love is young and energetic, you
find yourself dealing with disagreements and expectations you didn't really
see coming.

As Barbara and I watched our children marry, we wondered what we should
do to help. At the same time, we didn't want to meddle.

As an older man, I wanted to encourage my sons and sons-in-law as they
began to shoulder a husband's responsibility. I decided to bless them and give
them a man-to-man charge.

Before their weddings, I've given my sons and sons-in-law a copy of a poem
that I titled "Be the Man." I personalized each one, framed it and then read it
to him as a verbal challenge and charge for him to step up to his responsibilities. I want each young man to know I believe in him and am standing alongside him as he sacrificially leads his family.

But there's something else I've chosen to give these young men: *a sword.*
Not a toy sword or cheap imitation. These swords are sharp as razors, craft-
ed of finely honed steel. Their weight and presence convey not just the grav-
ity of the gift, but the significance I place on their calling to protect their
wives and family.

Each of these men now have a sword hanging in his home as a statement of
passage, a clear declaration that each has been charged with duty, service and
purpose—to "Be the Man." My prayer for each is that each time he looks at it,
he remembers not only that he's locked in battle, charged with the commission of protecting his wife and family, but also that he's equipped with everything required to carry out his orders.

And that we believe in him.

DISCUSS
Think of something significant you could do to bless and encourage your
children as they move through key passages in life.

PRAY
Ask God for wisdom to raise young men who will "Be the Man."

WHEN PRAYER LISTENS

Give ear, O LORD, to my prayer; and give heed to the voice of my supplications!
PSALM 86:6

I heard a wife talking about how prayer had enhanced her relationship with her husband. "When we pray together," she said, "we are communicating with God, but we are also communicating with each other and sharing our common love for our Savior."

I hope this doesn't sound either irreverent or intrusive to you. I hope it doesn't make you feel threatened or bashful to know that part of what is happening when you're praying together is this: Your spouse is listening to you and gaining a deeper understanding for what's going on in your heart.

The truth is, when you actively listen to each other in prayer, you are able to empathize at the deepest, most honest level. You are putting yourself in your spouse's shoes. Prayer becomes a much more significant experience when you are listening carefully to the burdens your spouse is repeatedly bringing to the Lord so that you can join him or her in praying for those same things, as well.

This can only happen, of course, when each of you is willing to honestly verbalize what's on your heart, when prayer is not a routine exercise devoid of real-life substance and content, when prayer becomes your heart's genuine cry before the Father. Only then can you go to the Lord God almighty together—with both humility and confidence—asking the Lord to encourage your wife when she feels like a failure as a mom or asking God to grant your husband increased wisdom when he struggles to be the leader of your family.

From our own experience, Barbara and I can assure you that your times of prayer together will be greatly enriched and more productive if you communicate openly and listen attentively.

DISCUSS
Talk about how praying together enriches your relationship. Share what you are facing today that could use your spouse's prayers.

PRAY
Turn your prayer today to the needs of your spouse, interceding for him or her with the understanding gained from knowing each other so well.

Get Connected for More Information
http://www.familylife.com/moments/prayer

KIDS AND MUSIC

BY BARBARA RAINEY

Whatever is pure, whatever is lovely, . . . dwell on these things.
PHILIPPIANS 4:8

One of the thorniest issues to tackle when raising children is music. Many children become devoted to music while in grade school, and its influence upon their lives can be huge.

What types of music will you allow your children to listen to? The apostle Paul provides a great media filter in Philippians 4:8: "Whatever is true, whatever is honorable, whatever is right, whatever is pure, whatever is lovely, . . . if there is any excellence and if anything worthy of praise, dwell on these things."

Parents should approach this issue shrewdly and wisely. As your children grow older, your ability to understand their taste in music—and how music affects their emotions—is critical.

It's important to engage them in ongoing discussions. When one of our daughters was about 16, she began listening to a radio station that played Top 40 pop songs from the 1980s and the 1990s. As I paused to listen at different times, I was surprised by the suggestive lyrics in some of the songs. I would ask her, "Do you know what that is saying?"

"I turn it off when the bad stuff comes on," she'd answer.

"So you've listened to it long enough to know the song well enough to know the bad parts so that you can turn it off? By then it is already in your head."

We talked this through a number of times over a period of several months. Slowly she quit listening to that music. I never told her she couldn't listen to it, but I did challenge her convictions with timely questions that made her think about what she was hearing and how it was affecting her decisions.

Never forget: You are the parent by divine decree. Use your appointment strategically.

DISCUSS

Take an inventory of your children's music. What do you think of the music your children listen to? What's your game plan to address this issue?

PRAY

Ask God to give you wisdom about how to establish boundaries and challenge your children to develop convictions regarding the media they watch and listen to.

Get Connected for More Information
http://www.familylife.com/moments/mediachoices

MENTAL IMPRINTS

These days were to be remembered and celebrated throughout every generation.
ESTHER 9:28

Memories are what make each family unique. They give your marriage and family a mental imprint of shared laughter and reflections. As someone has said, "God gave us memories so that we could enjoy roses in January."

But there is an art to memory-making. Here are a few perspectives Barbara and I have gleaned over the years:

Memories are best made with loved ones. Sure, memories can be made with coworkers and church friends, but don't let others get all your best times. Your marriage and family is a ready-made unit for the rich production and harvest of memories. Plant your fields wide and deep with them.

Memories take time. Our best memories have usually been born out of extended time together. Don't expect them to be created in three-minute sound bites.

Memories are made of varied adventures. Be creative. Do something different. If you can, travel together—especially on short-term mission trips.

Memories are both planned and unplanned. Memories are made through family traditions, such as summer vacations or an annual family Christmas tree cutting. But watch for the serendipitous memory. One special memory for us is the midwinter night when the power went off and we cooked supper in the fireplace. Don't lose your ability to be spontaneous and impulsive.

Memories should be celebrated. A memory isn't a memory if you don't revisit it and talk about it, look at pictures of it, laugh or cry about it. "Do you remember the time . . ." can be a joyful introduction to a family conversation. One of our favorite questions to revisit as a couple or as a family is, "If you could keep only one memory of all our years together, what would it be?"

So go ahead: Get out there and leave the unique imprint of memories in your family's life.

DISCUSS

What's your favorite ongoing family tradition? If you could keep only one memory of all your years together, what would it be?

PRAY

Ask the Lord God, the Creator of the heavens, to help you create and celebrate the unique mental imprints of memories for your family.

MAKING THE GETAWAY

*[Jesus] said to them, "Come away by yourselves
to a secluded place and rest a while."*
MARK 6:31

Every family needs the anticipation, experiences and memories of a well-planned vacation. But in today's "time is money" way of thinking, the family vacation is fast becoming a thing of the past.

When asked recently by Gallup pollsters whether or not they had any summer vacation plans, 43 percent of adult respondents said no. And for many of those who do get away, their vacations are hardly conducive to getting relaxed and unplugged. Since 1995, the number of vacationers who bring their work along—by way of cell phones and laptop computers—has nearly doubled. All in all, about half of us do.

As couples and families, you need to buck this trend. Just as the romance of a marriage relationship is enhanced by cozy getaways, the romance of a relationship with your children is built on the memories you create together.

And one of the best places to do this is on vacation. *Real* vacation. One thing my parents did right was to instill in me a lot of memories: making ice cream at Grandma's house, fishing trips, relatives, parties. We didn't go all over the United States on fancy trips, but they did leave me with an enormous reservoir of memories that I still draw on today as a husband and father. We certainly did the same thing with our children as well.

Consider this goal for your family in the coming year: *Our family will be found guilty of having too much fun rather than too little.* But to get there, you'll need to carve some time out of your schedule—*on purpose!* Memories are not built by default. Memories are made by couples and parents who are intentional about being together.

DISCUSS

Reflect on your memories from childhood. What made the great trips truly great? Think about what you'd like to do on your next getaway as a couple or as a family.

PRAY

Ask the Lord to give you wisdom and to help you resist the constant, relentless tug of work so that you can truly pull away with your family.

Get Connected for More Information
http://www.familylife.com/moments/familyfun

MEMORY CATCHING

BY BARBARA RAINEY

*A book of remembrance was written before Him for those
who fear the LORD and who esteem His name.*
MALACHI 3:16

When I was home-schooling our children during their early grades, I had them keep a daily journal as a way of teaching them writing skills. We found that this idea extended naturally into our vacations. I would bring my camera along and take pictures throughout the trips we took, and the children later glued the photos into their "vacation books."

Many times the children didn't want to journal, but I made them do it anyway. With the younger ones, I acted as scribe. I would say, "Tell me what you did today," and then I'd write what they told me as fast as I could. They would scribble pictures in the margins and at the bottom of the pages.

These vacation books are humorous, but they record serious memories, too. One of the entries from Benjamin's journal, written on a trip to Colorado in 1984, has a drawing of what must be an oil pump. Next to it, in his own handwriting, are the words "We saw 200 oil pumps." And then, just as matter-of-factly, "Samuel invited Jesus into his heart, age 6." What a great way to have this moment captured in time, in context and in writing.

I'm not so sure our kids appreciated the discipline of journaling when they were young, but I know they appreciate having their books now. I've seen them pull the journals off the shelf many times and enjoy looking at their drawings and pictures. Many details about these events would have been lost and forgotten if not kept and treasured along the way.

I encourage one of you to take on the role of family historian and curator. It can take some extra effort and planning ahead, but I promise you it'll be worth it. Your family will be glad they had a memory catcher in their midst.

DISCUSS
Which one of you will promise to take the lead in memory-catching? How will you collect the memories?

PRAY
Take a few moments to recall what God has done in your marriage and family and give thanks.

Get Connected for More Information
http://www.familylife.com/moments/makingmemories

TABLE TALK

She rises also while it is still night and gives food to her household.
PROVERBS 31:15

R. V. Brown was the sixteenth of 17 children. As he and his siblings arrived at the dinner table, he never understood why his mother stood in the corner with a bowed head. When he was older, he learned that she was praying that the butter beans and cornbread would make it to one end of the table and back without running out!

Of all the rich memories forged in his childhood home, this was the best: dinnertime. Everybody gathered around. Talking, listening and enjoying the laughter and noise of family togetherness.

He can still hear the older kids talking about the work they'd been doing that day. Or about what had happened at school. Another might tell a story he remembered from his stint in the army. And before they finished, R.V.'s daddy, who couldn't read or write, would lean back in his chair and begin sharing from his heart in that soft, arresting voice of his. Little bits of wisdom. Nuggets about how to treat people. Pearls about how to always give your best, settling little problems by using some patience and understanding and not hurting anybody.

I hate to think what the pace of life in today's families has done to memories like these. How many kids, when they grow up and look back on their childhood, will reflect on how much it meant for them to wolf down a fast-food hamburger in the car between ball practice and youth group? I think that what we stand to lose by consistently eating on the run may be a generation that has learned to value activity over relationship . . . and continues to feed self when they could be feasting together.

Give your children something they'll always remember: Give them dinnertime.

DISCUSS
Be honest about your dinnertime habits. Are they what they should be? What's one thing you want to do differently about your dinnertime?

PRAY
Ask God to help you place more value on being together than on doing it all.

Get Connected for More Information
http://www.familylife.com/moments/makingmemories

BLOW US AWAY

Since the creation of the world His invisible attributes,
His eternal power and divine nature, have been clearly seen.
ROMANS 1:20

My son Benjamin and I played a round of golf recently at a beautiful course in Beaver Creek, Colorado. He even bagged a hole in one.

As we stood there in that tee box—after we'd sufficiently celebrated his remarkable feat—I couldn't help but admire the beauty of this location.

Just that one hole, the tenth, is absolutely stunning in its layout and contour. It's truly a magnificent piece of golf architecture. But as my eyes lifted a bit, scanning the foothills that surrounded the property, the golf course suddenly appeared a little smaller and less spectacular.

From there, I looked farther to the visible range of mountains that runs all the way to Vail. Snow-capped splendor, majesty and rugged beauty—as far as the eye can see. And if I could have flown in an airplane and climbed high above the clouds, I could have seen the western United States—the Tetons, the Sierra Nevadas, the West Coast. Beyond that, the windswept Pacific Ocean—vast and mysterious—covered by a canopy of blue by day and a sparkling array of stars by night.

If I could have gone beyond planet Earth, even it would be dwarfed by the expanse of our solar system—one of innumerable others that comprise the Milky Way galaxy—which itself is one of a billion other galaxies in God's unfathomable universe of wonders.

From that vantage point, the tenth hole at Beaver Creek loses a good bit of its luster. Because truly, we serve a God whose ingenuity has no peer, whose power and might and knowledge of us overwhelms with its sheer magnitude.

Almighty God, who slung a billion galaxies into space, cares about you. He knows everything about you, yet He loves you. And He wants you to trust Him with your problems and worship Him with your heart.

DISCUSS

See if your current worries shrink in size a little when you compare them to Almighty God.

PRAY

Don't ask for anything more today than the chance to worship, honor and give thanks to God for being who He is.

Get Connected for More Information

http://www.familylife.com/moments/relationshipwithgod

GRACEFUL LANDINGS

The grace of the Lord Jesus be with you.
1 CORINTHIANS 16:23

Far too frequently, we hear about the indiscretion of a public figure or religious leader being exposed in some kind of tabloid-style news flash. For a few days, the person's name and all the titillating details are near the top of every news broadcast.

How should Christian parents handle these kinds of reports?

I ask this question because I fear that the way we discuss these things around the dinner table can have longer-lasting implications for our kids than we realize. When we rant about what these individuals have done, judging them with little grace or calling them names and considering them despicable, what does that say to our teenage sons and daughters about what they can expect if they ever need to come to us and confess some secret sin?

Whether we like to think it or not, our children all struggle with sinful desires. They are growing up in a world riddled with promiscuity, drugs, alcohol, pornography, gluttony and dozens of other addictions and seductions. Even if they never act on all these temptations, their human desires cause them the same difficulties from day to day as ours do.

But if they know that your response to human guilt is abrupt and merciless, what will they likely say to themselves if they mess up badly in the future? "I could never come clean with Mom and Dad. I could never be real with them about what I'm struggling with."

Your children should know that if they ever fail morally, you will not intervene to spare them from the consequences. But they should also know that no matter how hard they fall, there is always grace in your household. They are always safe in your embrace. They can never slip so far away that your love won't still be there to reach out to them and welcome them home.

DISCUSS

Use an example from the recent news to start a healthy discussion of man's failures and God's healing grace. Talk with your children about truth, consequences and God's forgiveness.

PRAY

Pray that you and your family will be a safe harbor of forgiveness, grace and hope for those who fail.

Get Connected for More Information

http://www.familylife.com/moments/charactertraining

WRITTEN IN INK

I said, "I will never break My covenant with you."
JUDGES 2:1

In the summer of 1997, I was sitting at my computer writing an article, praying and asking myself, *How can we rebuild the family in America?* I wasn't just pondering this because it was my job to do so or because I had spent my entire adult life focused on this calling and endeavor. More importantly and specifically, I was thinking about my oldest daughter's wedding, which at the time was just a few days away. *Was there something I could say or do that would help Ashley and Michael begin a marriage that would go the distance?*

That's when God brought to mind the concept of *covenant*, which means literally "to cut." Many scholars believe that in Old Testament days, a covenant between two people was often made by splitting an animal in half, laying the two sides apart from each other on the ground, walking between these bloody pieces and pledging, "May God do the same thing to me if I break my covenant with you" (see Genesis 15). Well, I thought that would make a real mess on the church carpet, but I still wanted to incorporate "covenant" into their wedding ceremony in some visible way.

So I took their wedding vows to a calligrapher, who inscribed them on a sheet of pure cotton paper. And immediately after Ashley and Michael exchanged their vows verbally during the ceremony, they signed this marriage covenant. The pastor then asked if anyone in the audience wanted to come forward and sign it as well, as witnesses to the covenant this couple had entered into. A line formed quickly of friends and family members, promising to help hold them accountable to their wedding vows.

Today, their marriage covenant hangs above the fireplace in their home as a constant reminder of the pledge they once made at a wedding altar, just as you once did. May you always be true to your covenant.

DISCUSS
Think of something special you could do—even now—to remind yourselves of the seriousness of your marriage covenant.

PRAY
Come before God today and rekindle your wedding promises.

Get Connected for More Information
http://www.familylife.com/moments/commitment

I GIVE UP!

Search me, O God, and know my heart; try me and know my anxious thoughts.
PSALM 139:23

In July 1995, we were in Fort Collins, Colorado, for the U.S. Staff Conference of Campus Crusade for Christ. More than 3,000 staff members and volunteers had made similar treks to be there, expecting to enjoy a rousing time of worship, rejuvenation and fellowship.

We got a lot more than that.

On the fourth day of the conference, Nancy Leigh DeMoss (now an author and radio host but at the time simply a writer and speaker for Life Action Ministries) gave a message that ignited a fire. She spoke of our desperate need to turn from pride to humility in true spiritual brokenness. Following Nancy's address, God orchestrated what became three days of holy introspection, confession and cleansing.

Scheduled meetings were cancelled. Speakers who had traveled from across the country never presented their talks. Instead, men and women streamed to the platform and poured their hearts out in confession, repentance and reconciliation.

Staff members made phone calls seeking forgiveness for years of bitterness harbored against a father, mother, sibling or friend. Brokenhearted parents sought prayer for wayward sons and daughters. I remember sobbing in anguish beside a friend who confessed to deceit and adultery. More than 100 people surrounded this man to pray for healing in his marriage and family.

None of us felt any inclination to judge. All of us knew we were sinners. And the ripple effects of that one event continue to be felt in our family relationships.

Now let me ask you a very personal question: Is there anything in your life, your marriage or your family that needs to be confessed to God and perhaps to one another? This could be one of the most important questions you answer in this entire book.

REFLECT AND PRAY

Take some time as individuals to prayerfully ask God if there's anything you need to confess to Him and possibly to your spouse. If necessary, make a list and confess that list to God. Tell Him that whatever He needs to say, you're willing to listen—whatever He asks, you're willing to do.

If appropriate, discuss your lists as a couple.

Get Connected for More Information
http://www.familylife.com/moments/repentance

KEEPING IT QUIET

BY BARBARA RAINEY

LORD, you have assigned me my portion and my cup.
PSALM 16:5, *NIV*

Barely a year after my mother and father married, her parents decided to divorce. My mother traveled to Chicago and spent an entire week pleading with her parents to restore their relationship. Unsuccessful, she returned emotionally exhausted, needing more than ever a warm, accepting relationship with her mother-in-law, who lived nearby. But for reasons still unknown to us, she was never embraced by my father's mother.

You'd think, then, that my childhood would be one of growing up with a mother embittered by her loss of parental affection and support. You'd think my relationship with my grandparents would be distant and suspicious. Yet quite the opposite was true. That's because my childhood was protected by a mother who quietly accepted the circumstances God had ordered for her life and refused to pass along her pain to the next generation.

My mother could have poisoned my brothers and me against both sets of grandparents, spewing angry tirades about the hurt and rejection their failures had caused her. She could have criticized my father, making him the scapegoat for his mother's attitude toward her.

But she didn't. She never once said any negative words about these important people in our lives. As a result, we grew up confident of our parents' love for us, secure in their commitment to each other and free to enjoy our extended family relationships.

Each of us enters marriage with our own share of pain and baggage. But you don't have to pass it on and load down your children with it. You can stop the cycle in your generation by refusing to become embittered and by speaking well of your family.

DISCUSS

If you've been guilty of this kind of complaining about family, now is the time to admit it and ask for forgiveness. Commit to handling your pain God's way. Discuss how you can help one another process pain.

PRAY

Ask the Lord for the grace and maturity to protect your children from living with pain they didn't cause. Consider giving thanks to God for the imperfect circumstances that created your pain in the first place.

Get Connected for More Information
http://www.familylife.com/moments/marriagerelationship

THE MAN NEXT DOOR

I have been crucified with Christ; and it is no longer I who live, but Christ lives in me.
GALATIANS 2:20

Mike Wallace of *60 Minutes* once interviewed Yehiel Dinur, a Holocaust survivor and witness at the Nuremberg trials. During the show, Wallace played a 1961 clip of Dinur walking into the Israeli courtroom where Adolf Eichmann was on trial. A principal architect of the Holocaust, Eichmann had evaded capture for years but had finally been found and brought to justice.

As Dinur spied Eichmann for the first time in 18 years—he had last seen the German mastermind at Auschwitz, the notorious death camp—he stopped still in his tracks. He began to sob uncontrollably. He fainted and collapsed to the floor.

Was he overcome by hatred? Fear? Horrid memories? Actually, as he said later, it was none of these. What overwhelmed Dinur was this: Suddenly he realized Eichmann was not the godlike army officer who had sent so many to their cruel deaths.

Adolf Eichmann was just an ordinary man.

Wallace captured it best when he asked, "How is it possible for a man to act as Eichmann did? Was he a monster? A madman? Or was he perhaps something even more terrifying—was he normal?"

"Eichmann," Dinur said, "is in all of us."

This hard truth about ourselves is difficult to swallow. If not for fear of consequences or a liking for our own reputation or the healing flow of God's grace, we are capable of anything.

May the Lord keep us from ever believing that our goodness is something we've worked up from within. May we realize again that whatever goodness lives in us is the goodness of God shining through . . . the One who gave His Son to give us life. And to save us from ourselves.

DISCUSS
What evidence exists in you that we are all born sinful and self-centered and are in desperate need of Christ?

PRAY
Ask God to reveal again the full extent of His salvation. Thank God for His redemption, not only from hell, but also from being enslaved to self.

HOME WRECKER

*We demolish arguments and every pretension that sets itself up
against the knowledge of God.*
2 CORINTHIANS 10:5, *NIV*

I am always encouraged when I hear people say, "You're helping us raise our family through your ministry." But not long ago, I had one of those experiences that . . . well . . . I'd never heard anybody say it just this way before.

A few years ago, while visiting our daughter Rebecca while she was living in Atlanta, she took us to meet some faithful listeners to our radio broadcast. When we drove up, we caught the mother outside doing yard work. Then her teenage son came around the corner of the house. He looked like he was ready to go to one of the service academies. A sharp young man.

"So you're Dennis Rainey," he said.

"Yes, I am."

"Well, I have you to blame for wrecking my teenage years," he said, extending his hand. A sly grin crept across his face as he added, "If I hear your name another time in this house, I think I might throw up!"

After talking with him for a few minutes, it became clear his comment was a compliment. His parents had anchored him in Christ and as a result had "wrecked" some of his plans as a teenager.

As I drove away from that home, I had a smile of my own. I love to hear of parents who have an infectious love for Jesus Christ and the Scriptures and are passing it on to their children. One of the most important purposes of a Christian family is to equip the next generation with an accurate knowledge of God, with godly skill in everyday living and with the mandate of reaching their generation with the gospel of Jesus Christ. That's what these parents had done. And I guess if I helped them "wreck" a young man's teenage years in doing that, then I'll gladly accept part of the blame!

DISCUSS
Talk about the fundamentals of the Christian faith and how you are passing these on to your children—or, if you don't have children, to others.

PRAY
Ask God for wisdom to know how to complete your mission as parents or as a couple.

Get Connected for More Information
http://www.familylife.com/moments/biblicalparenting

THE LEAKY BALLOON

But I want you to be wise in what is good and innocent in what is evil.
ROMANS 16:19

Early one evening, I drove Rebecca—then 14—to meet some girlfriends for a bunking party. But her friends were running late, and as we sat there waiting in a parking lot, God orchestrated a great teaching moment.

We were talking about how she was going to relate to the opposite sex as she got older—about how far she would go sexually with a young man. A water balloon was lying in the console between us; it was stashed ammo from a balloon fight at our home a few days before. Picking it up, I got an idea.

"Let's say this water balloon is filled with your sexual purity and innocence. This is all you have. How much of it would you want to give away before you're married?"

"None of it," she answered. "I want to give it all to my husband!"

Then I put it in teenage terms. "Let's say a young man comes to you and just wants a little kiss—your first kiss—just a little bit of your innocence." I held up the balloon and pretended to pierce it with an imaginary needle. Then another boy comes along, and *he* just wants a little more. Then later on, you fall in love and decide it's okay to give away even more."

I paused and looked deeply into her wide eyes. "How much innocence and purity will you have left to give the man you marry?"

"It would be all gone," she said, "little by little."

Now I have a question for parents: As you look at how this culture is seducing our teenagers, how do you need to teach and instruct your teens? If you don't hold the standard high for your children, then who will?

DISCUSS

As parents, what is your game plan to help your children "be wise in what is good and innocent in what is evil"? Talk about one or two convictions that you want to pass on to your children.

PRAY

Pray for wisdom to know when God is designing teaching opportunities.

Get Connected for More Information
http://www.familylife.com/moments/purity

PEER PRESSURE GROWS UP

The fear of man brings a snare, but he who trusts in the LORD will be exalted.
PROVERBS 29:25

I used to think peer pressure only showed up in parenting books and situations facing teenagers. I thought it was something you outgrew. But I remember sitting in a business meeting with a roomful of Christian leaders and being asked to vote on a particular issue. The man seated next to me—a very good friend of mine—held a strong opinion that was different from mine. And during the debate that ensued, I chose to keep silent about my convictions.

Finally, we were asked to stand up to indicate a yes vote on the measure. My friend stood quickly to his feet. He wasn't the only one. Many others were rising in support.

I can still feel the rumblings that clashed inside me. *Even though I'm against this,* I thought, *how can I stay seated when one of my best friends is standing—when this whole place appears to be standing?*

So I did what every preadolescent and teenager is tempted to do: I caved in, and I stood up. And from that vantage point, I could clearly see two who remained seated, opposing the motion. Just two. I still remember them because of their courage and convictions.

Peer pressure. It happens, not just in school locker rooms and hallways, but around the lunch table with work associates, in the homes of people who are more affluent, during adult conversations when you don't want to admit who you really are or what you truly believe. The fear of being different or disagreeable doesn't leave you when you reach adulthood. It changes clothes but keeps the same skeleton.

What I needed that day was integrity. I needed the character to vote for what I knew was right.

DISCUSS
Be honest: Where are you still susceptible to peer pressure? Do you need to go against the herd today on some issues that you're facing?

PRAY
Pray the same prayer you may have prayed as a teenager—that God will give you convictions so that you can stand firm.

Get Connected for More Information
http://www.familylife.com/moments/peerpressure

SAFELY THROUGH

The LORD is my rock and my fortress and my deliverer.
PSALM 18:2

God has given Barbara and me a real heart for the military wife. Her courage and tenacity at keeping the home fires burning while her soldier is in training or on duty or perhaps gone for many months overseas makes her an unsung hero. Military wives are every bit as much a part of our nation's defense as their husbands who wear the uniform.

But the weight of such responsibility can sometimes become more than one woman can bear. That's what happened to Patty, a mother of five at Fort Leonard Wood in the Missouri Ozarks. Trying hard to keep their family's finances from falling apart, she took on two jobs and ran up huge credit-card bills just to keep basic necessities on the table.

But the pressure mounted beyond her ability to cope. One night while driving home from work, nearing a steep drop in the road, Patty decided to drive off the side and find at its gravelly bottom escape from her stress.

While these dark thoughts swirled in her mind, the sounds of the car radio cut into her conscious mind. It was a *FamilyLife Today* broadcast, targeted specifically at the needs and concerns of military wives. Patty felt like she was hearing her life described on the air—her same thoughts, same challenges, same struggles, yet wrapped in the big arms of God and in His boundless ability to supply. It was all she needed to get through the night. God had sent her His hope, just when she needed it most.

If you're a military family, I pray you'll never doubt God's power to help you through the many hardships you face. And if you're not a military family, ask Him to lead your family to one that is—especially to a wife who's doing her best to go it alone. She could really benefit from your voice of comfort and companionship.

DISCUSS
What could you do to offer friendship and support to a military family? Discuss what your church could do.

PRAY
Pray for those in harm's way—and for the wives and children who keep going while they're gone.

GOOD FRIENDS

A friend loves at all times, and a brother is born for adversity.
PROVERBS 17:17

H. Clark Bentall once headed the Bentall Corporation, a construction company headquartered in Vancouver, British Columbia. Five downtown office towers in that city bear his family's name. He was a major player in the commercial construction and real estate business.

But late in life, after a 50-year career with the company, he found himself in a disagreement with his brothers, who leveraged Clark out of the day-to-day operations and eventually out of the business altogether. Shortly thereafter, his wife of 57 years lost her battle with cancer, and Clark himself was soon stricken with Alzheimer's disease.

There he was—in his early 80s, alone with no work and no wife—and with his ability to grasp what was going on around him beginning to slowly evaporate. A man who once had everything now had nothing.

But in the years before the fog of Alzheimer's engulfed him, Clark Bentall had invested thoroughly and genuinely in his friendships. And now, in his time of need, every Tuesday and Thursday morning some of his best friends would come over for breakfast, just to talk and say thanks . . . for everything. As the weeks and months went by, Clark had less and less to contribute to the stimulating conversation and shared memories. But still they came, for over four years.

That could be you one day. Alone. Dependent on the obligations of family members and the goodwill of neighbors and friends. Will you have invested enough in people's lives to make them want to come see you, even when you're not as much fun as you used to be?

Now is the time to pour your heart into others—not just to look ahead to the future, but also to make a difference in their lives today.

DISCUSS
Talk about your friendships. List your best ones. Talk about how you could help one another do a better job of building friendships.

PRAY
Give thanks to God for "kindred spirit" friends. And if you don't have many, ask Him to bless your life with a few more.

PURE INTIMACY

BY BARBARA RAINEY

If two of you agree on earth about anything that they may ask,
it shall be done for them by My Father who is in heaven.
MATTHEW 18:19

Romance is certainly not the foundation of marriage, but it sure makes the relationship warm and secure. At times it's the best way to say, "I really love you." In order for romance to flow most freely, however, a husband and wife must be committed to putting God first. And that includes praying together as a couple.

Our wedding day on September 2, 1972, was filled with the usual—family, friends, celebration, vows and (yes) romance. After enjoying the reception and saying our good-byes to everyone, we were off to our wedding night at the historic Warwick Hotel in Houston.

Dennis had planned every detail. After checking in, he encouraged me to take a nap while he went out and bought some flowers. Fine dining, dancing and an elegant, silent elevator ride overlooking the city skyline made the romantic evening truly magical. But back in our room, before we enjoyed becoming one, we knelt beside our bed and prayed, committing this part of our married life to the Lord and asking Him to bless us.

Since then, we have done much to enhance the romance in our marriage: going on Sunday night dates, taking drives together, having private dinners in our bedroom after the kids had gone to bed, splurging on short getaways and other surprise trips.

But whether we've been in a tent in the Rockies or at a fine New York City hotel, through prayer we have invited God to join our relationship, including the romantic aspect of it. There's nothing quite like holding one another tightly as we pray together. In fact, there may not be a more secure feeling in all the world.

DISCUSS

Decide together to do something romantic this week. And make sure to invite God to be a part of every aspect of it.

PRAY

Thank the Lord for not keeping romance off in its own little world, disconnected from your relationship with Him. Thank Him for giving full life to His children.

Get Connected for More Information
http://www.familylife.com/moments/romance

THE MEDIA MONSTER (PART ONE)

Above all else, guard your heart, for it is the wellspring of life.
PROVERBS 4:23

What if I told that every day a legion of competitors was lining up to enter your home, your workplace, your car and even your phone to seduce you and your spouse?

They are. Each day assorted voices and images lure your spouse and you away from each other: television, cable, Internet, email, blogs, chat rooms, radio, magazines, newspapers, music, movies, books and video games. Media is competing with you for your spouse's attention and affection!

Media takes time away from your relationship with your spouse. Keep track sometime of how many hours you spend each week just watching television. Then think of what you could have done together during that same time.

Media twists your sense of reality, creating unreasonable expectations for your spouse. The media usually present a distorted picture of relationships. For example, how often in a movie or on a television program do you see a man and woman fall in love, get married and remain committed for a lifetime? More often, the norm is two people falling in love and into the sack without much thought about moral issues. If you constantly feed these images into your head, doesn't your spouse stand to lose in the long run? Competing with fantasy is difficult.

Media facilitates emotional adultery through pornography and Internet liaisons. Although the benefits of using the Internet are obvious, its costs and risks are not always so plain. Pornography is a click away on computers and now phones. It can be as damaging to the mental and emotional health of a marriage as a physically realized affair. And just as bad, people use Internet chat rooms to meet strangers and engage in intimate, sexually oriented conversations.

With all these temptations lining up outside our lives, isn't it time you took an inventory of your media consumption?

DISCUSS
What type of media is the biggest threat to your marriage? To your family?

PRAY
Pray for unity as a couple to know how to keep these competitors out of your marriage.

Get Connected for More Information
http://www.familylife.com/moments/mediachoices

THE MEDIA MONSTER (PART TWO)

Whatever is true, . . . whatever is pure, whatever is lovely, . . . dwell on these things.
PHILIPPIANS 4:8

Yesterday I talked about the way the media monster can damage your marriage. Here are some thoughts about how to master the media instead of being manipulated by the messages:

Know what you believe. How will you be able to distinguish the truth from lies in media if you don't know the truth of the Scriptures on a variety of issues? Knowing what the Scriptures teach about guarding my heart has empowered me many times to turn off a television show or TV movie.

Be aggressive—not passive—about the media. A media monster will seep into our eyes, ears, minds, hearts and families if you allow it. Set some standards!

Guard your mind and heart. If you allow yourself to create fantasy lovers through media sources, you stand in the courtyard of the house of adultery. This includes advertising as much as programming.

Don't depend on the movie rating system and on movie reviews. Find out about movies from friends who share your values. Consult reviewers with a similar Christian worldview.

Control Internet access. Subscribe to a provider that screens out offensive material. Place computers in very public places in your home, such as the kitchen or family room. Speak to your kids about Internet challenges and help them monitor both the type of usage and the amount of time they're online. If necessary, consider using software designed for parents that helps you monitor your children's traffic and use.

Consider cutting back on or even fasting from media use. Have you ever tried going a whole day or week without watching television? What might happen in your marriage if you did? You miss out on many enjoyable activities when you are lazy about unhooking your media umbilical cord.

Why not consider joining us for our "Turn Off the TV Fast" in the month of August? I promise that you'll benefit from this 31-day fast from television.

DISCUSS
Talk about the changes you need to make personally or as a family in media use. Consider pulling your children into this one, listing ideas. Pick one.

PRAY
Ask God to begin making you more sensitive as a couple to how media impacts your marriage and family. Pray for courage to do what you need to do.

Get Connected for More Information
http://www.familylife.com/moments/mediachoices

THE MISSING INGREDIENT

Husbands ought also to love their own wives as their own bodies.
He who loves his own wife loves himself.
EPHESIANS 5:28

See if you can spot the problem in this couple's relationship:

The first few years of our marriage were good, but the sweet talk and little whispers in the ear diminished, and we became just another married couple. My husband, however, still wanted all the perks that go with marriage. I began to resent his touch because I didn't feel like he really loved me, just my body. I remember after making love with him on occasion, I would cry because I felt cheap and used. He, of course, was angry because he knew this wasn't the way a marriage was supposed to be.

Stalemate. Sexual impasse. But is it just a matter of misunderstanding and unmet expectations? Insensitivity and selfishness?
Keep reading.

I'm finding my physical desire for sexual intimacy dwindling. But I would still love to be romantically head-over-heels in love with my husband like I once was. I would love to have him touch my heart. The sad thing is, we just don't really have a spiritual link between us.

Ah, there it is. Underneath all the surface issues, beneath all the uncomfortable moments and silent frustrations, lies the deep spiritual need that resides in every one of us. Far too many husbands fail to recognize that *what your wife wants and needs most from you is your concern for her soul*—your daily desire to take her needs before the Father and unite with her in shared dependence on Him.

When you step up and take your place as the spiritual leader in your family, you create an environment where bitterness can't easily survive but where relationship and romance can grow.

DISCUSS
Talk about how you can truly lead your wife spiritually. Ask what it looks like to her. Then take her hand and pray for one or two of her needs.

PRAY
Husbands, pray for the courage to keep leading spiritually, even though you won't do it perfectly. Wives, pray that your husband will be encouraged as he leads you and your family spiritually.

Get Connected for More Information
http://www.familylife.com/moments/husbands

MINISTERING PURITY

BY BARBARA RAINEY

Drink water from your own cistern and fresh water from your own well.
PROVERBS 5:15

Do you find it interesting that the warnings about sexual temptation in Proverbs are directed at men? Proverbs 7, for example, describes the wily harlot seducing the foolish young man who wanders too close to her door.

While women are certainly not immune from being tempted in this area, I find it remarkable that the Scriptures are almost exclusive in giving examples of men falling into this sin:

- Judah sleeping with his daughter-in-law, thinking she was a prostitute (see Genesis 38)
- David and Bathsheba (see 2 Samuel 11)
- Samson and Delilah (see Judges 16)

A wife must understand that men are prime targets for sexual temptation. And one of the easiest ways for this sin to get a foothold in a man's life is for his sexual needs to remain unmet at home. In a man's world, there are many voices tempting him to fulfill his needs through illicit and perverted recreational outlets. Counterfeit pleasures beckon from every street corner, every magazine rack and every modem.

Because God's perspective on sex in marriage is so misunderstood by most of us, the potential for men and women to miss each other is enormous. A wife can easily misinterpret her husband's sexual need and interest as a weakness or, at worst, a selfish demand. And sometimes his timing may not be ideal.

But we as women have a unique and powerful opportunity in marriage—not just to affirm our husbands in an area central to his manhood, but also to be used of God to help him remain pure. A wife who understands this power she has with her husband is a woman who is pleasing to God.

Remembering the big picture of God's purposes and His good intentions helps keep the momentary challenges of marriage in correct perspective.

DISCUSS

It's not unspiritual to talk about your sexual needs. Make time soon to open up with each other, being honest to share . . . and eager to respond and meet one another's needs.

PRAY

Thank God for the way He created each of you—as perfect matches for one another.

Get Connected for More Information

http://www.familylife.com/moments/wives

GENEROUSLY SPEAKING

For they all out of their surplus put into the offering;
but she out of her poverty put in all that she had.
LUKE 21:4

Let me tell you the true story of a really generous giver.

Christian financial expert Ron Blue and his oldest son ate breakfast together on a regular basis at a local fast-food restaurant. The same place, every week. And each time they went, the same Hispanic woman would wait on them at the counter, always greeting them with a warm smile and a radiant spirit.

The weeks turned into years until one day, spurred by a passing thought of pure generosity, Ron decided to do something unusual in the fast-food world. He decided to give her a tip. Twenty dollars seemed amply big-hearted, but when he reached into his billfold, he sensed the Holy Spirit instructing him to do more. So he put together five twenties, folded them over, and asked the waitress if she would be willing to accept it. She did.

But that's not the big story I'm talking about.

This woman was a single mom with five kids. She had immigrated to America to provide new opportunities for her family and was working a fast-food counter to keep basic necessities on the table. When Ron gave her the money, she knew immediately what to do with it. Her car needed a new set of tires, and she figured a hundred dollars would probably cover it.

But when she arrived home that night, one of her high-school children told her about a fire at an apartment building nearby, where several of their friends had suffered substantial losses. As the woman told Ron several weeks later, "I knew there was a better use for that hundred dollars. We gave it to a family that had lost everything."

What we all shouldn't give for generosity like that.

DISCUSS

What are your goals for giving?

PRAY

Ask God to give you opportunities to be used as a generous giver toward others. Pray it like you mean it. And give like it doesn't really belong to you in the first place. It doesn't.

A USE FOR OUR REFUSE

But if we are afflicted, it is for your comfort and salvation.
2 CORINTHIANS 1:6

What do you have that could be of benefit to others?

That's the question you may ask yourself every time you go exploring through your attic or garage. You realize how much you tend to keep and accumulate, even when your need for these items has long subsided. Often the stuff you find crammed deep into your closets isn't even worthy of charitable donation. It's just junk, better thrown out with the garbage.

But when it comes to the junk in your own personal life—the mistakes you've made, the poor judgment you've exercised, the hurt you've caused each other—God may have a purpose for it even still. Over the years, I've challenged many couples to step forward as mentors. But they have their own reservations and excuses. Many feel they just aren't qualified. They say they have nothing to share with younger adults. They don't think they know the Bible well enough.

Many of them are simply haunted by their own mistakes—their own junk. They don't realize that those mistakes may be among the most valuable tools they possess in teaching a younger couple about how to grow a marriage and family God's way.

Everyone struggles with marriage and family issues. Everyone. That's why the core curriculum for learning how to minister to other couples includes the textbook of true-life experience. Weakness and disappointment provide some of our best resources for sharing life messages with others. They provide both content and context to our instruction.

You see, it's not junk if somebody else can use it. The only way it becomes a waste is if we're afraid to admit we've still got it, if we're unwilling to let God use our garbage for His glory.

DISCUSS

Talk honestly about some of the mistakes you've made. Have you seen any good come from them?

PRAY

Pray that God would open your heart of compassion so wide for another couple that you wouldn't let anything hinder you from helping them.

KINDER AND GENTLER

What do you desire? Shall I come to you with a rod,
or with love and a spirit of gentleness?
1 CORINTHIANS 4:21

Ellie Kay, the wife of an Air Force pilot and the author of *Heroes at Home: Help and Hope for America's Military Families*, reveals what can sometimes happen when her husband, Bob, returns from a turn of military duty. After months of flying and fighting and barking commands, he is often still in a giving-orders mood when he re-enters civilian life. That's when Ellie uses a little code phrase to bring him back to her world: "K and G."

Kinder and gentler.

It's a signal to her husband, who likely doesn't even realize how harsh his words may sound, to throttle back. To tone it down. Save it for his subordinates.

We all know you don't have to be a soldier in uniform to bring home a military manner at the end of the day. You can be in a business suit, casual pants or coveralls and still treat your wife as though she's just another item on your checklist, just one more employee needing a grade on her efficiency. It can work the same for women who work outside the home.

Like Bob, we often aren't aware that we're doing this. We're still in our office or job mode without realizing we've left it on. If our wives confronted this attitude, would we listen? Would we respond?

My suggestion is to find a spot along your usual way home—some recognizable milestone or visual marker—to remind you that it's time to shed the necktie and get ready to meet your wife. Leave the workday behind someplace where you can pick it up again tomorrow. And go home ready to love and listen, not to push and prod.

Be K and G.

DISCUSS

How often do you bring the pressures and attitudes of work home with you? How do they manifest themselves at home? Talk about how you can remind one another to be K and G.

PRAY

Instead of bucking your mate for confronting a bad attitude in you, thank the Lord for putting someone in your life to help you be more like Christ.

Get Connected for More Information

ISLANDS OF CLARITY

*I would have despaired unless I had believed that I would
see the goodness of the LORD in the land of the living.*
PSALM 27:13

Barbara and I have long enjoyed the benefits of carving out time together as a couple. It was something we committed to early in our marriage. Even with six kids and all the natural activity that ensued, we pretty much stuck to our guns, and everybody reaped the benefits.

For us, these became islands of clarity—stolen moments when we chose to set aside the rush, distractions and noise of life long enough to reflect and hear from God. Here are three tips for finding uninterrupted time to help you regain perspective in the midst of the family circus:

Do it daily. The mere fact that you're reading this book tells me you understand your need for at least a few minutes each day to square up and seek the Lord together.

Do it weekly. I've been telling people for years about Barbara's and my selecting Sunday night as our sacred time to grab a booth at our favorite cozy little restaurant, The Purple Cow, and sync up our schedules. We have seen God supply answers as we talked about the children's school needs, various discipline issues, major purchases and other elements of our marriage relationship.

Do it twice a year. It doesn't have to be anything fancy, but we found that squirreling ourselves away without the kids helped us clear our heads and renew our sense of partnership and purpose. Many couples use the Weekend to Remember as an annual getaway to refresh and refuel their relationship.

Marriage often resembles a shootout between Siamese twins—two people joined together at the hip but fighting to control the direction they go. Islands of clarity are good places for the two of you, not just to sign peace treaties, but also to chart a course for the future and build romantic fires as well.

DISCUSS

What has been your favorite getaway as a couple? What made it so memorable? Schedule your next one.

PRAY

Pray that God will help you never to lose the ability to set aside some time away together as a couple to seek Him and one another.

ARE YOU REALLY BIBLE BASED?

I am the true vine, and My Father is the vinedresser.
JOHN 15:1

This may seem like a shocking thing to say, but I firmly believe that most Christian marriages are actually patterned after the world, with a few threads of Christianity woven in. Couples know certain Bible verses, but few really practice the Word of God and use it as the defining standard for their lives.

Here is a litmus test: Could you lead a group of couples through a Bible study for several hours on what the Scriptures have to say about marriage and family issues—everything from raising children to God's blueprints and purposes for marriage? Most churchgoers couldn't last more than a few minutes.

But the very fact that you're reading this book today at all is a testimony to your desire to know more of God's Word and apply it to your lives. If you want your marriage to become all that God intended, then I hope this inspires you to keep digging deeply to His truth and let it become the "source" of your lives together.

Jesus painted the picture when He declared Himself the vine, with us as the branches. He said, "Abide in Me, and I in you. As the branch cannot bear fruit of itself unless it abides in the vine, so neither can you unless you abide in Me" (John 15:4). The word "abide" here is used to describe drawing the source of life from Jesus, like a branch draws its life from the vine. It means to make Jesus Christ and His Word the source of your convictions, decisions and mission in life. Just as branches draw their nutrients from the vine, so too we are only able to grow spiritually when we're firmly attached to Christ, drawing our life from the source of all truth.

DISCUSS
Talk honestly about your values, convictions and mission. How much are these shaped by abiding in Christ and His Word? Talk about how you can help one another do a better job of abiding in the Word.

PRAY
Pray for one another that you will grow spiritually together as a couple by abiding in Christ.

THE HOLY SPIRIT

Do not get drunk on wine, which leads to debauchery.
Instead, be filled with the Spirit.
EPHESIANS 5:18, *NIV*

When I was a little boy growing up, I remember people in our church referring to the Holy Spirit as the "Holy Ghost." For a long time I had this image in my mind of the Holy Ghost being something like Casper the Friendly Ghost, floating through walls like a puff of smoke.

I was also wrong about something else: I used to refer to the Holy Ghost as an "it"—as if He were some kind of impersonal machine or space alien. But the Holy Ghost that Jesus talked about is a living, active, personal being, sent to glorify Christ as well as to be our Counselor, Advisor, Advocate, Defender, Director, Encourager and Guide.

If you are interested in living life the way Jesus promised—and if you want a marriage where the two of you are growing spiritually—then a good understanding of the Holy Spirit is vital. Being "filled with the Spirit" is not just a suggestion but a clear command of Scripture. What Paul wrote to the Ephesians in the above verse means being controlled by Him in much the same way that alcohol controls a person's mind and actions.

When we're angry with each other about something, for instance, being filled with the Spirit enables us to control our tempers and impatience. He keeps us from saying things we'll later regret. He battles the selfishness within us, bringing our hearts under His authority and bending our wills to God's.

We don't always let Him win, of course. We still fail Him far too often. But every time we submit ourselves to His control, He grows in us the character traits that please Him and bless our spouses. "For the mind set on the flesh is death, but the mind set on the Spirit is life and peace" (Romans 8:6).

DISCUSS
What have you learned about the Holy Spirit? How much of your understanding of Him has been inaccurate over the years?

PRAY
Pray for hearts that are constantly cleaned and confessed, leaving ample room for the Spirit to dwell in.

DON'T HURT ME

One who is married is concerned about . . . how she may please her husband.
1 CORINTHIANS 7:34

What usually happens when you and your spouse get into a disagreement? If you're like most couples—according to the research of Dr. John Gottman, professor emeritus at the University of Washington—the wife does six times the amount of fussing and scolding, and the husband is 85 percent more likely to be the one who goes into stone-wall mode.

But as Emerson Eggerich told our radio audience recently, it's not merely the amount of the wife's talking that pushes her husband into silence and rejection. It's the *way* she talks.

To every wife reading this, I know that this just seems to confirm that every man is overly sensitive and not willing to deal with the truth. But Emerson, who has over two decades of experience helping couples, asks you to take this challenge: "After you've had a fight with your husband, go into the bathroom, shut the door and reenact your responses as best as you can in front of the mirror. Look at yourself and how you're coming across. Is there any man in your husband's world who talks to him that way? Is there *anybody* in his world who talks to him that way?"

Usually, all you have to do to avoid his stonewalling is to soften the tone, brighten the facial expression and control the pointing finger. You can pretty much talk to him all day long—even with deep, impassioned emotion—if you avoid berating, dismissing and emasculating him.

Men are typically able to handle negative content. We do it all day long. We just can't easily handle it when it comes across with the volume turned up on contempt. The disrespect drowns out the message from being heard.

If the goal is communication, the gateway to his heart is through respect, even when you don't think he deserves it.

DISCUSS
Is this pattern true of your marriage? What makes you want to attack verbally? What makes you want to clam up?

PRAY
Pray that you will better understand how to communicate with one another with mutual respect.

Get Connected for More Information
http://www.familylife.com/moments/conflict

I WAS JUST THINKING

I have seen You in the sanctuary, to see Your power and Your glory.
PSALM 63:2

Where is your place to ponder?

Maybe it's a certain chair in a quiet corner of your home. Maybe it's the back deck at sunrise or under the porch light after dark, with only the rhythmic hum of the crickets to disrupt your quiet. Maybe it's a nearby creek or a nice place to walk or jog. Maybe it's a garage workshop or a cozy cafe.

Or maybe it's nowhere. Maybe you and a "place to ponder" aren't seen together in the same spot very often.

Over the years when I come home from work or when Barbara comes home from her many errands, we take one another by the hand after dinner and sneak out for a walk. (With six kids you have to be a sneak sometimes. We did this so many times, they knew where to find us!)

We'll stroll through our garden beds, looking at what's blooming at certain seasons of the year. The garden is hardly professional—it's in constant need of repair and weeding. In fact, one of the problems with our place to ponder is that we often find ourselves pondering the work that needs doing out there.

But most important, it's simply our time away from the needs of other people. You know, the phone and email and all the other interruptions. We may share something we've been thinking about. We may dial up a sweet memory. We may stop and pray, or we may just walk along glad to be at home together.

If there's one reason why marriages wither under the pressures and demands of daily life, it may be the lack of having regular times and places where we deliberately go to pray, share and regain perspective. It may be because we're always puttering and planning and doing and moving from one place to the next but never stopping . . . and listening . . . and recharging . . . and pondering. Together.

DISCUSS

If you don't have a "place to ponder," where could it be? How could you make a habit of going there?

PRAY

Ask God to help you see the value of getting quiet before Him.

Get Connected for More Information

http://www.familylife.com/moments/stress

I'LL PROTECT YOU

Have I not commanded you? Be strong and courageous! Do not tremble or be dismayed, for the LORD your God is with you wherever you go.
JOSHUA 1:9

One day during Rebecca's first year of junior high, she came home from school with an unusually unhappy look on her face. Some boy had been making ugly remarks about her figure (or more precisely, her lack of one).

"What's this guy's name?" I inquired. She told me what it was. "What's his phone number?" I asked. "Sounds like we need to have a little man-to-man chat."

When the boy's father answered the phone, I told him I needed to talk to his son. I said I wasn't going to be mean, but he had been making derogatory comments about my daughter and I wanted to tell him that such comments are inappropriate.

"Okay, here he is." (I could just imagine the look on this young man's face as the phone receiver came his direction.) "Hullo?" he said in that teenage monotone.

"Hello, I'm Mr. Rainey. Rebecca's dad. From school. She came home today telling me about some things you said about her body, and I just wanted you to know I don't appreciate it. This is not the way to treat a young lady, and I'd like you to respect her dignity enough to stop teasing her about the way she looks. You understand?"

That was it. Didn't take long. I remember it took some courage to make the call, but I just remember Rebecca standing there beaming. And though I'd like to think it made a statement to the young man on the other end of the line, I know for a fact it made a statement to my daughter.

She saw the way a man is supposed to protect a woman, the way a dad is supposed to protect his little girl.

How will they know if they don't see us doing it?

DISCUSS
Do you think I did the right thing? Name some issues where, as parents, you need to step in, protect and be strong for your children.

PRAY
Ask God to keep you alert and wise to what's happening in your children's lives and hearts.

ROOTLESS RELIGION

These things you have done and I kept silence; you thought that I was just like you.
PSALM 50:21

A Christian leader told me about boarding a small commuter plane for a short flight out of Nashville. Moments after he settled in, a flight attendant's voice came on the loudspeaker and said, "When the pilot steps onto the plane, I want you to clap for him. He just found out his fiancée is expecting twins." When the captain appeared, the passengers erupted into a raucous ovation. My friend sat there thinking, *I can't believe it. We're applauding immorality.*

This is in a country where reliable research tells us that nearly 85 percent profess to have some kind of religious convictions, and 90 percent believe there is a God. But it's also a country where a solid majority personalize religion with little regard for the need to submit themselves to any kind of accountability or authority. In essence, everyone does what is right in their eyes (see Judges 17:6).

We've become a nation made up of very small humans playing God.

As a result, many people treat religion more like a hobby. It's a free-flowing, do-as-you-please, spiritual smorgasbord where they pick and choose what they want, when they want it. A little dab of truth here, a little dab there. But never too much truth. As someone has said, "God created man in His own image; then man returned the favor."

It is time for us as Christians to clean up our own house, to let the Bible's truth become not just our standard for belief but also our standard of *behavior*, both personally and in our families. Then we must take it a step further, calling those around us to the good news of Jesus Christ and exhorting those who know Him to internalize, apply and proclaim His life-giving message.

The future of your family and our nation depends on it.

DISCUSS
Try to define a practical step you could take to influence your sphere for Christ. What is one need you could embrace as your spiritual calling?

PRAY
Humble yourselves before the face of God, and ask Him for the spiritual reformation of your family and our country.

Get Connected for More Information
http://www.familylife.com/moments/convictions

PRAYER AROUND THE WORLD

*I urge that entreaties and prayers, petitions and thanksgivings,
be made on behalf of all men.*
1 TIMOTHY 2:1

In November 1970, at the height of tensions in Vietnam, a pair of college students launched a campaign to bring awareness to the plight of American POWs and MIAs. Their plan was to create inexpensive metal bracelets, each bearing a soldier's name and the date of his capture, and distribute them across the country as reminders for the average citizen.

Sharon Denney, now a 40-something college admissions counselor, remembers sending off her $2.50 for one of those bracelets in the early '70s. Hers was etched with the name of First Lieutenant Ralph Galati, whose Air Force jet had been shot down in North Vietnam. Galati suffered through a year-long ordeal of torture and deprivation, including more than two months of solitary confinement.

But back in her hometown of Morrow, Georgia, young Sharon Denney was praying for Galati—for his safety and for his release or rescue.

Many years passed before Sharon came across her POW bracelet again while going through some things in her parents' home. A few Internet searches and phone calls later, she had not only learned of Galati's release in March 1973 but had also found his home phone number. And when she was finally able to make contact with him, the former POW told her that she was one of more than a hundred he had heard from over the years—men and women, boys and girls, who had worn his bracelet, had remembered his suffering and had prayed, prayed, prayed for their prisoner soldier.

Prayer knows no boundaries of time or space, no limits of age or distance. Prayer is simply our link to the heart of God and to people's lives all over the world. Never underestimate what prayer can do in the short run or the long haul. Don't give up. Keep praying.

DISCUSS

Why don't we pray more as individuals and as a couple? Who have you been forgetting to pray for?

PRAY

Take turns bringing some requests before God today for people who seem to be facing impossible situations.

Get Connected for More Information
http://www.familylife.com/moments/prayer

GROWING GARDENS AND GROWING CHILDREN

BY BARBARA RAINEY

Let us not lose heart in doing good, for in due time we will reap if we do not grow weary.
GALATIANS 6:9

I love the way a garden looks when it's clean and neat, when all the soil is evened out and the weeds are pulled up. But I know too well that the hard work of a Saturday morning will be repeated again and again, all season long. It never takes more than a week or two of neglect before weeds are sprouting all over the place.

Parenting is a lot like that. Just when you think you've finally mastered one area, you wake up the next day and a whole new issue is facing you. It's so easy to forget that parenting is a process. A long, long process.

You go to bed at night sometimes relishing those little victories, thinking all is secure and right with the world. But it's not very long before something else crops up. Infant issues morph into young-toddler issues. Toddler issues become school-age issues—the unmade bed, the homework, not coming to the table when we call. Then it's on to adolescent issues—the emotional turbulence, the anger, the words they hear and pick up at school (and at church!).

Remember that *building character is the most important goal in parenting.* Imprinting a child's heart with the image of God takes time and repeated effort, often reworking the same ground repeatedly to keep bad behaviors from becoming habits.

So I encourage you today not to give up. Don't lose heart. The Bible promises great reward to those who faithfully persevere through the long days, the long battles that often don't even stop for bedtime. I assure you, all that weeding will pay off.

DISCUSS

Name the biggest issues you're dealing with in the lives of your children. Or name one issue that is just around the corner.

PRAY

Thank Him for the wisdom, energy and ability He provides to get through each day, knowing that His supply is sufficient and His promises are sure. Pray for one another in this long process of child rearing.

INSIDE BASEBALL

Behold, You desire truth in the innermost being.
PSALM 51:6

Sometimes in the midst of correcting your kids, you can easily lose sight of the main reason you discipline them in the first place. It's not just to get their clothes picked up or to eat the meal you've prepared or to stop hitting a sibling. The reason for discipline is to develop *inner* character, the kind that knows and is learning how to respond to life's challenges.

The core of a baseball is made of hard rubber. But imagine if the core were marshmallow. What would happen as the string wrapped around it or when a bat smacked it hard several times? It would smush into a mess.

It's the inside that counts—the character you're growing in your children. As life begins to happen, as circumstances and decisions begin to wrap around them, it's their character that will hold them together.

Barbara and I define character as "response-ability"—the ability to make the right choices in response to authority and to life's circumstances. From the time your children leave the cradle, your work as a parent is to turn life situations into teaching situations, growing their "response-ability" one day at a time, teaching them how to respond to you, to others, to life and to God.

In the next few days, you'll have plenty of opportunities either to overreact to your children's behavior or to address the roots of their development—to deal with externals or to train their hearts. Remember, you're growing character here. It's only the ones who grow strong at the center—especially as character is strengthened by commitment to God's Word—who are able to hold up to the challenges they will face in life.

DISCUSS

One of the biggest challenges to a parent is building character on the fly—in the midst of a busy schedule and a family with a multitude of different needs. Talk about how you can take advantage of natural teaching opportunities to train your children in how they should respond.

PRAY

Pray for God to give you the discernment to know what issues need to be addressed and what issues you need to let go.

Get Connected for More Information
http://www.familylife.com/moments/charactertraining

PARCHEESI CHEATER

There is one who speaks rashly like the thrusts of a sword,
but the tongue of the wise brings healing.
PROVERBS 12:18

Stu Weber, who pastors a church in Portland, Oregon, and is the author of such best-selling books as *Tender Warrior: God's Intention for a Man*, remembers an evening he spent many years ago as a seven-year-old boy playing Parcheesi with his grandparents. (Now *there's* a game you don't hear much about anymore.)

Well, the last thing Stu wanted to do that night was lose to his grandma. So, sensing the tide swinging in her direction, he scanned the board, looking for options, and found only one that offered him much hope of winning.

Cheating.

Not everyone, however, has the poker face to pull this off. Stu didn't. And not everyone has parents or grandparents who are courageous enough to take character seriously—enough to hand it down at every opportunity. Stu did.

Stu still remembers his grandfather—seeing what was going on—peering over his glasses at his grandson and saying, "You're a Weber, boy; and Weber boys don't lie, cheat or steal." This grandfather was a wise man; not only was he calling his grandson to obey the Scriptures, but he also wanted Stu to realize he was part of a family of character.

There would be times later in life—as a Green Beret in the military, as a father, as a pastor—when Stu would be faced again with the chance to cheat his way out of a bad situation. But he would always hear these words in the back of his head: "You're a Weber, boy; and Weber boys don't lie, cheat or steal."

A family legacy is powerful. Your children (or grandchildren) need to hear those kinds of memorable words from you.

DISCUSS

Think of an opportunity you've had recently to communicate character to your kids. How'd you do?

PRAY

Pray that your words of challenge and affirmation will stick in your kids' minds a long time.

LYING IN WAIT

Who may walk on Your holy hill? He who walks with integrity . . .
and speaks truth in his heart.
PSALM 15:1-2

When dealing with our young children, we sometimes forget what we're up against: the deceit that is a natural part of a child's heart.

It's intriguing that when God identifies seven things He really hates (see Proverbs 6:16-19), two of the seven concern deceit: "a lying tongue" (verse 17) and "a false witness who utters lies" (verse 19). Deceit seems to fall into two major types:

1. *Lying.* Every one of our children lied to us. Multiple times. Some of them lied about lying! When children are tempted to misrepresent the truth and are caught, they must be disciplined. Whatever amount of protesting and defending they choose to make, they must ultimately admit wrong and receive the penalty for their deceit. It was an automatic spanking for our children under the age of eight or nine. The older children were grounded.
2. *Habitual craftiness.* This murky, constant shading of the truth can create exhaustion and a sense of hopelessness in a parent. You may look into the sweet eyes of your little one and see the makings of a crafty riverboat gambler. One way to get through to this child is to share situations from your life where you stepped into a deceitful snare. Talk about the consequences that resulted. Help your child see that everyone is capable of this sin—even you—but no one escapes the damage it causes. You will need to help this child experience the full pain of his or her lies. Do not shield your child from the consequences.

Deceit is a natural reaction that starts early in life. Be ready for it in your children. Train them with ample doses of God's Word and remind them who they are ultimately dealing with.

DISCUSS
How have you been burned by your own deceit? If you're detecting a deceitful streak in your children, what is your game plan to address it?

PRAY
Pray that in leading your children toward honesty and truth-telling, you will be modeling and internalizing it yourself.

Get Connected for More Information
http://www.familylife.com/moments/charactertraining

GAME OVER

All things become visible when they are exposed by the light.
EPHESIANS 5:13

Our son Samuel was a top-rated tennis player at age 14, before he was diagnosed with a rare neurological disease. But he struggled at times with getting angry at himself. I warned him often about dealing with this. And although he tested our limits periodically, he always seemed to get himself under control before we felt the need to take drastic action.

Except at one particular tournament. Samuel was well ahead of his opponent but still missed shots he thought he should have made. Soon, he began beating the air with his racquet.

I looked sternly in his direction, making eye contact.

Not long after, he slammed a ball into the chain-link fence.

I stood up.

Finally, he angrily whacked the fence with his racquet.

That did it. I walked out onto the court and declared, "This match is over. My son forfeits for poor sportsmanship."

It was a difficult moment. You could have heard a pin drop. The look of shock on Samuel's face was one I'll never forget. But it didn't matter. It was character-training time. And however hot the attention felt on my back from both the spectators and from Samuel, I was determined to make my point. And believe me—I did!

There will be times—if you haven't experienced them already—when your children will need to be stunned by what their misbehavior can cost them. They need to know that the game they are playing is not the ultimate objective. It is an opportunity to grow their character. To win the game and lose at life is not the goal.

DISCUSS
What is important: the game or life? What misbehavior in your children could force you to conduct some out-in-the-open correction?

PRAY
Pray that God will give you the courage to do what is needed to shape the character of your children.

Get Connected for More Information
http://www.familylife.com/moments/charactertraining

MOUTH GUARDS

The mouth of the righteous is a fountain of life.
PROVERBS 10:11

It didn't happen often. I only remember hearing it on a couple of occasions. But I guarantee you that in those rare moments when my father let loose with a foul word, it made a deep impression on me. It shocked and surprised me.

He was a man of few words. And even fewer foul words or disrespectful words. I doubt that I heard him use 10 curse words my entire life. And over the 46 years of his marriage, I never recall hearing him speak harshly to my mother even once.

I guarantee you, your children are watching. And listening.

If you hope to control the wild tongues in your family, you must first clean up the words that flow from your own. The way you speak to each other, and to your children, must set the course. If you speak respectfully to one another, you can reasonably expect your children to do the same.

What kind of boundaries have you chosen to set on your speech? Cursing is clearly wrong, of course, but what about slang words that are right on the edge of foul language? What about other toxins of the tongue, like gossiping and criticizing people behind their backs?

Do your children hear you using unwholesome speech to describe your neighbors or coworkers? What comments do they hear you making about your boss, your pastor or your political leaders? What do you say when somebody cuts you off in traffic or dumps trash in your yard? Do you obey God's commandment to honor your parents, or do you grumble about the burden they've become?

Never forget that mutual respect is the foundation of all healthy relationships. The way we relate to each other as a couple is the best model for helping children learn the pleasing use of the tongue.

DISCUSS
How would your children describe the model you are setting in your home of your vocabulary and how you speak to one another?

PRAY
Pray that the meditation of your heart and the words of your mouth will be acceptable in the sight of God.

HEAVEN IN HIS EYES

Blessed are the pure in heart, for they shall see God.
MATTHEW 5:8

When I was a boy, the thought of going to heaven sounded boring. As a young lad, I thought that there is so much more here that I wanted to experience. Places to go. Thrills to embrace. The thought of sitting around for all eternity strumming a harp didn't appeal to me.

I had a very immature perspective of heaven back then. But in the last few years I've closed some of my letters and emails in a unique way:

God is good.
Life is a challenge.
Heaven looks better and better all of the time.
—Dennis

As I've read the Scriptures, I've realized that heaven looks much better than anything the world offers. I think life is one long process of God weaning us from this world and its pleasures and showing us that what we yearn for isn't here.

Do you long for heaven? On those days when you desire heaven the most, is it because you're exhausted, so you long for heaven's rest? Is it because you're drained by the burden of carrying life's troubles and you long to be free? Is it because you've lost your sense of happiness and you long for a place of lasting peace and joy?

I don't think it's wrong to ache for a place of real sanctuary, a home in heaven where every tear will be wiped away, where "there will no longer be any mourning, or crying, or pain" (Revelation 21:4). But the true joy of heaven is not just pain relief. The true joy will be found in seeing our living Lord and Master, Jesus Christ, face to face. As Martyn Lloyd-Jones asked, "To stand in the very presence of God, to gaze and gaze on Thee . . . Is that heaven to us? Is that the thing we want above everything else?"

When you long for heaven, long for Him.

DISCUSS
How deeply do you yearn for heaven? If not, what do you long for? What keeps it from being what you desire?

PRAY
Pray that you will better see who Jesus is today and, in turn, set your affections "on things above," not the world.

Get Connected for More Information
http://www.familylife.com/moments/spiritualgrowth

HOUSE RULES

If a house is divided against itself, that house will not be able to stand.
MARK 3:25

Mia had been married for 20 years and was the mother of 4 teenagers at the time she wrote us:

"My husband and I bought a house I totally hate—a 30-year-old log home that's falling apart. We've been in it for three years now, and I hate it more every day. My husband has worked on it day and night all these years, but this is just adding more stress to our marriage."

Their family life, too, was beginning to suffer: "Our kids have felt abandoned by their dad, who doesn't spend any time with them because he's always working on the house." It was also eating into their pocketbook: "We had the money to buy the house," she said, "but not to fix it up."

She closed her note this way: "I have fully admitted to my husband that I have bitterness in my heart toward him because of what the house has robbed us of. I'd like to sell it, but my husband would rather see me walk out the door than to sell this house."

What's the real problem here? There are several, but the main one is that this husband and wife don't share the same values. They haven't discussed the desires and priorities in their lives. What matters to one is not important to the other. Chances are, they never sat down along the way to define their core convictions on money, family, faith and other priorities.

Before this happens to you, or even if you find yourself experiencing this level of contention already, look each other in the eye. Make a promise. You're going to decide what should really matter—to both of you—together. And you're going to move into the future based on your shared values, honoring one another's preferences in the process.

DISCUSS
List the top 10 things that are most important to you. Then compare lists. When you're done, hammer out the top 5 core values of your family.

PRAY
Pray for oneness in your marriage and a heart that knows how to sacrifice for one another to maintain that oneness.

FIFTY YEARS FAITHFUL

For love is as strong as death.
SONG OF SOLOMON 8:6

Only 10 months into their marriage, during an otherwise calm Sunday drive to church one July morning, a young Navy couple's car was broadsided by a streaking ambulance racing through an intersection. The driver of the car, R. L. Alford, sustained some minor injuries. But his wife, Hilda, was thrown from the vehicle, suffering a massive head injury that left her not only a quadriplegic, but also legally blind and unable to speak.

That was 50 years ago—50 years of communicating with his wife through little more than the nods of her head. Fifty years of pushing her wheelchair or (his preferred way) carrying her in his arms. Fifty years of emptying her urine pan and cleaning up her bowel movements. And in the last few years, even feeding her through a tracheal tube and learning how to insert her catheters.

Along the way, R. L.'s brand of marital loyalty has drawn some unexpected notice. ("Undeserved," to hear him say it.) When a longtime family friend spearheaded a drive in the mid-'80s to raise funds to build the Alfords a new home, help came from such high-ranking places as Florida governor Bob Martinez, who not only gave them a brand-new refrigerator but also spent a day working at the construction site. President Ronald Reagan sent a check for $500, followed by another for $1,000.

"When R. L. was asked to repeat the vow 'for better or worse,'" a neighbor said, "he heard it real loud. Medically, it's a miracle Hilda is still alive. But she's not alive because of all those doctors. She's alive because R. L. gave his life to her."

In September 2006, the Alfords celebrated their golden anniversary. Looking back, R. L. humbly remarked, "Sure, it's been rough in some ways. But it's been rewarding."

Fifty years of being there. May all our promises to each other be that long lasting.

DISCUSS
Talk about what you would do for one another if the unthinkable happened. Promise you'll be there, regardless.

PRAY
While asking God for many more years together, pray it with a promise that you'll remain faithful no matter what those years entail.

GET 'EM WHILE THEY'RE YOUNG

How can a young man keep his way pure? By keeping it according to Your word.
PSALM 119:9

For many years George Barna has been a leading researcher on Church and cultural trends in America. When he appeared on our radio broadcast, I posed a question I'd always wanted to ask him: "What was the most stunning set of data you ever received?"

This is a man who isn't stunned by much. Even though he's become well known for exposing very troubling patterns in our society, his findings rarely surprise him.

This one did. He took a national sample of 13-year-olds and compared them with a sampling of adults comprising every age segment. On 12 core spiritual perspectives, *he discovered no difference between any of the groups.* In other words, the things a person believes by age 13 are pretty much what he or she will die believing.

This tells me something: We don't need to wait until our children are teenagers before we expect them to be able to understand major biblical truths. Things like being saved by grace through faith, not by good deeds. Things like how our hearts are naturally inclined to sin and that as a result, they need forgiveness. As Charles Spurgeon said, "A child who knowingly sins can savingly believe."

Dwight Moody was speaking to a group of children in Scotland when he rhetorically asked them, "What is sin?" One of the children replied, "Sin is transgression of the law of God"—straight out of the catechism. Amazed, Moody responded, "Children, you must thank God that you have grown up in Scotland"—where they were systematically taught the Bible from an early age.

I pray that our children will thank God they have grown up in *our* homes, where they are learning the Scriptures and learning how to live.

DISCUSS

See if you can list 8 to 10 vital Christian truths or concepts that you need to begin to teach (or continue teaching) to your kids.

PRAY

Pray that God would cement your own beliefs and convictions more clearly in your mind and show you how to communicate them in real-life ways to your family and others.

Get Connected for More Information
http://www.familylife.com/moments/spiritualtraining

TROUBLE BREWING

*By faith Noah, being warned by God about things not yet seen,
in reverence prepared an ark for the salvation of his household.*
HEBREWS 11:7

His name was Harry Truman.

No, not "The buck stops here" Harry Truman. Not the "Dewey Defeats Truman" Harry Truman.

No, this Harry Truman lived in a rustic log cabin near pristine Spirit Lake in the crisp, cool timberland of Washington. But at some point in the early part of 1980, geologists and government officials came to his home and said he needed to leave his homestead. Pressure was brewing in a nearby volcano, and Harry's life was in danger.

I recall watching him one night on television as he told the news media how all the learned authorities didn't know what they were talking about. Even more vividly, I recall a helicopter ride I took one afternoon a year later over the gray-streaked remains of Mount St. Helens. Somewhere down below, under hundreds of feet of molten ash, lay the bones of one Harry Truman—and the dusty, empty hole that used to be Spirit Lake.

I often think of Harry when I see marriages and families teetering on the brink of destruction, while the husband or wife—or both—are ignoring all the warning signs. Meanwhile, the pressure keeps mounting. The alarmed spouse is trying to get the other's attention. People who care about them are doing everything they can to advise and intervene. The volcano is set to blow, yet they foolishly want to wait it out, doing nothing.

If that's where you find yourself right now, I urge you to realize that looming destruction can't be avoided by wishing it away. It requires prayer, counsel, adjustments and repentance.

Remember Harry Truman and don't just sit there. Get some help.

DISCUSS

Identify any pressure points you're seeing in your home today. Address the most critical pressure by establishing a plan of action.

PRAY

Pray to God, "Father, make us aware of reality, and give us courage to address those pressures that would destroy our marriage, family and legacy."

Get Connected for More Information

http://www.familylife.com/moments/conflict

TWO BY TWO

The things which you have heard from me, . . .
entrust these to faithful men who will be able to teach others also.
2 TIMOTHY 2:2

Christianity has become too much of a spectator sport. Like football, it's 22 players on the field desperately in need of rest, being watched by thousands who are in need of exercise.

Over the past 10 years, Barbara and I have enjoyed the *spiritual exercise* of mentoring a small number of younger individuals and couples. We've enjoyed coaching and passing on to the next generation lessons we've learned.

If you're a seasoned, experienced couple that is relatively happy—not perfect, not infallible, but *relatively* happy and satisfied with your relationship—you have all the qualifications you need to become a marriage mentor. You don't have to be certified or board trained. You just need to have lived. Experienced a few failures. Learned a few lessons.

It's as simple as praying and asking God to lead you to a particular couple who are starting their journey together. Invite them over for dinner and say you'd like to get to know them. Then let God take it from there. Get together once a month for a couple of hours and tell them about the most important spiritual lessons you've learned.

There is a generation of young couples who are hungry for this kind of mentoring. We live in a high-tech, low-touch society that doesn't know how to do relationships very well. What better place for this to happen than in a very informal, very supportive, very personal, couple-to-couple relationship where people are intentionally building into each other's lives?

I believe this is one of the greatest opportunities before us today—to reach down to a younger generation and give them the coaching they need to step up.

DISCUSS

Think of one thing you've learned along the way in areas like communication, conflict resolution, money management and sexuality. Do you feel you're at the point where you could mentor a younger couple? Make a short list of younger couples and pray about which one you should invite over.

PRAY

Ask God for the courage and the ability to build your lives into one or two other couples.

Get Connected for More Information

http://www.familylife.com/moments/mentoring

TV TYRANNY

All things are lawful for me, . . . but I will not be mastered by anything.
1 CORINTHIANS 6:12

To me, one of the saddest scenes in marriage is when a husband and wife retire after dinner to either end of the house—she to watch *her* television shows, he to watch his. But perhaps it's only slightly worse than sitting together in the same room, night after night, with the television talking over anything else that might be of interest in sharing with one another.

Truly, the TV has the power to take over a relationship.

This reminds me of a joke I heard about a woman who had brought her purchases to the check-out line in a department store. When the cashier asked if she'd be paying with cash, check or credit card, the woman began fumbling in her purse for her wallet, agitatedly placing various *non*-wallet items on the counter while she looked for it. Unable to keep from noticing that one of the things she'd pulled from her purse was a TV remote control, the cashier humorously asked if she always carried one of these with her.

"No," the woman replied, "but my husband refused to come shopping with me today, and I figured this was the worst thing I could do to him legally."

It's easy to let your lives becomes dominated by television. It can even take over the evening meal; you might even find yourself hooked on a steady diet of take-out food and microwavable dinners—things you can eat while watching the evening news and digesting a nightly dose of TV sitcoms and crime-solving dramas. Little by little, without even realizing it, you begin the process of shutting each other out of your lives, while giving hour upon hour to the make-believe world of television.

DISCUSS

Talk about your television habits. Is turning it on just a natural reflex now? Does it have too much of you?

PRAY

Pray that nothing—not even acceptable things—will come between you and your spouse's affections and attention.

Get Connected for More Information
http://www.familylife.com/moments/mediachoices

COLD TURKEY TELEVISION

I will walk within my house in the integrity of my heart.
I will set no worthless thing before my eyes.
PSALM 101:2–3

We Americans recently passed one of those cultural milestones we've been slouching toward for years: We now have more television sets in our homes than people.

Nielsen Media Research found that about half of us now have three or more TVs, with a sizable number boasting as many as seven or eight. And, believe it or not, 25 percent of two-year-olds have a TV in their room.

A few years ago, after reading Bob DeMoss's book *TV: The Great Escape,* a wild thought occurred to me: *What if we encouraged families to take a whole month off from television every year? What if we declared a TV fast for the month of August?* We have now done it for five years. We call it, "Turn Off the TV Fast."

So, here we are nearing the end of summer. We're all kind of tired of the break by now. Vacation has probably come and gone. In some states, school is set to start in a few days.

What do you say? Are you and your family game for a TV fast? This means you can't even watch nature shows or war documentaries.

Imagine the calories you could burn or the neighbors you could meet by taking walks together in the evening. Imagine the conversations you could have in the quietness of your own home. Imagine the yard work and other household jobs you could accomplish—the ones you keep complaining about not having time to do. I'm giving that time back to you right now, every evening, for 31 days straight!

Hey, it's just a suggestion. But a lot of people who felt the color rush from their faces at the first mention of a TV fast have written to say what a gift it's been to their families.

Try it. You might like it.

DISCUSS
Name some things you and your family could do with the TV off for a month.

PRAY
If this has struck you as something you should do, ask God for the courage and self-control to see it through.

WHITE-GLOVE TEST

You are already clean because of the word which I have spoken to you.
JOHN 15:3

Whenever our Weekend to Remember speaker team gets together—as we're passing each other in the hallway or stepping onto the elevator—we often ask each other one probing question: "Are you clean?" We're calling each other to personal holiness—we don't want anyone who represents our Lord and our ministry to stand before others with an unexamined heart.

"Are you clean?" It's a good question to ask, don't you think? Few of us like being presented with something that pries this hard—something so personal, something we might not be able to answer yes to.

I remember when I came across a friend—a fairly well-known Christian leader—at a convention. I shook his hand, looked him in the eye and surprised him by asking, "Are you clean?" He answered back, "Well, yeah, I'm clean." But he wasn't clean. I could tell.

A couple of days later, this same man tapped me on the shoulder and said, "Dennis, I need to talk to you privately about something." We eased off to a corner of the room, where he said, "I lied to you. I'm not clean. I've got a problem with pornography. It's causing me to fail as a husband and a father. I'm not the man other people think I am."

I was so proud of him for responding to the Holy Spirit with that kind of honesty and remorse. We talked for quite a while, prayed together and laid out some accountability steps we both knew would help.

A few years later, I crossed paths with him again. But this time I didn't even need to ask him the question. His whole countenance and posture answered it for me. He was clean. And confident. He'd been sprung from that whole demoralizing trap of phony sexual fulfillment.

How about you? Are you clean?

DISCUSS
Who could use someone like you to ask this kind of question of them?

PRAY
Pray for a life that is so clean and pure, you'll want to share the blessings of obedience with others.

IF YOU PLEASE

Each of us is to please his neighbor for his good, to his edification.
ROMANS 15:2

I'll never forget one particularly hectic period in our family's life when my schedule had gotten so busy that I didn't feel like I had time to even change a light bulb. The stress of keeping it all going was occupying just about every waking moment of the week, and our house was really beginning to suffer for it.

Specifically, our garage.

I don't how many times I'd go in there, wishing for just one good Saturday with half my brain cells functioning to do nothing but straighten up and thin down. The entire family used it like a toxic dumping ground. The kids had been hauling stuff in there left and right—even trash that the neighbors were throwing away! (Don't get me started. You don't want to know.)

But one day during this stretch of time, I came home late in the afternoon and as I pulled up to the garage, the door was standing wide open, *and everything inside was clean and organized!*

I did a quick double-check on the house number to be sure I hadn't turned up the wrong driveway by mistake. But sure enough: It was our house and our stuff. Barbara had known how heavily this undone task had been weighing on my shoulders, and she had marshaled the troops to get out there and "Do the deed for Dad."

Wow, it felt good. But not just to have a garage I could squeeze the car into again. Not just because I finally knew where some of my long-lost tools were. It felt good because I had a wife who knew what was bothering me and took it upon herself to take that load off my mind.

Marriage is about having someone to please and having someone to please you. It's knowing that when you've had a bad day, someone's there who really cares.

Does your mate have a "garage" that needs your help?

DISCUSS
What's a particular weight or concern that your spouse is carrying around that you could relieve?

PRAY
Ask God to make you sensitive to your mate's needs and to show you opportunities to fulfill them.

PASSIVE FATHERS, ANGRY CHILDREN

Fathers, do not provoke your children to anger,
but bring them up in the discipline and instruction of the Lord.
EPHESIANS 6:4

Look at the verse above again—it contains one negative command and two positive ones. From our experience, the three commands work together; if you obey the negative command, you are able to fulfill the others as well.

We have established a list of common things a dad does to provoke anger in his children. Many more could be listed, but here are our top five:

- Shows a dictatorial style of relating to his children, over-emphasizing authority without an underlying relationship of love, affection and fun times together
- Exhibits a critical spirit, consistently tearing down his children with the tone of his voice and the words of his mouth
- Is passive and neglects his children outright
- Fails to provide clear expectations about boundaries, limits and rules
- Fails to develop a relationship with each of his children, either rejecting or withdrawing from the relationship

Fathers need to realize that they can provoke their children to anger or guide them to greatness. It's interesting that the same Scripture gives fathers two practical ways of developing children into the men and women God designed them to be: discipline and instruction.

When a father cares enough about his children to enter their world and develop a relationship with them and, when needed, discipline them, he expresses love to his children. When we had four teenagers at one time, Barbara leaned on me a lot when it came to discipline. And I want to tell you, it's during these exhausting moments at the end of the day that the easiest thing to do is nothing.

The same is true for instruction. Dads, you need to turn off the television or the computer and crawl out of your easy chair to formally engage your children's moral and spiritual education.

Step on up and be the man!

DISCUSS
On a 1- to 10-point scale (1 being poor and 10 being outstanding), discuss how you are doing with your children in each of the three commands of Ephesians 6:4.

PRAY
Pray that God will grant you favor as you seek to be God's man in raising your children.

Get Connected for More Information
http://www.familylife.com/moments/fathers

PEACE TALKS

*Be kind to one another, tender-hearted, forgiving each other,
just as God in Christ also has forgiven you.*
EPHESIANS 4:32

There was only one problem when Tara Barthel and Judy Dabler set out to write their book *Peacemaking Women:* No sooner had they started than they weren't speaking to each other.

Judy had been Tara's first choice as co-author for a book about resolving conflicts. Everything from her conciliation expertise to her Christian experience made her the ideal partner.

Tara was pregnant with her first child when the writing process began, and in her task-oriented mind, it was imperative that the manuscript be completed before the baby came. Judy, however, was blindsided by a series of major setbacks, including personal health issues, her husband's hospitalization after a lawn-mowing accident, her mother's hip replacement, her father-in-law's bout with lung cancer, the loss of two employees in her counseling ministry and an unusually taxing caseload.

But Judy isn't one to make excuses. And though Tara would have probably understood why Judy's work wasn't coming in on time if she had known what her friend was up against, all she could see was a colleague who wasn't making good on a promise.

Everything at this point became email driven—the kind of communication that strips itself of personality and voice inflection, leaving the real meanings obscured by cold keyboard strokes. And every time the other's name would appear in the in-box, stomachs would churn.

This wasn't going well. Not at all. Two peacemaking professionals in a standoff. In need of peace.

You'll be glad to know that both of them finally applied the truth of their book. The hurt came out, understanding occurred, and forgiveness was expressed and granted. And their book had an extra chapter about very up-close-and-personal conflict.

Their story teaches a lesson. When people disappoint you, be patient. There may be more going on underneath the surface than you realize.

DISCUSS

Talk about a relationship you avoid because you haven't met the person's expectations. Keeping in mind Paul's challenge in Ephesians 4:32, read Romans 12:18 and discuss what, if anything, is left for you to do.

PRAY

Pray for honesty, understanding, forgiveness and peace in your most challenging relationships.

Get Connected for More Information
http://www.familylife.com/moments/conflict

HOME FIRES

We will not conceal them from their children,
but tell to the generation to come the praises of the LORD.
PSALM 78:4

Five grown siblings came together at the event of their parents' fiftieth wedding anniversary. When the time came to express their thanks to each parent for the one thing that stood out above all in their memories, each of them—without consulting the others—thanked their father for his leadership in family worship.

One of the brothers said, "The oldest memory I have, Dad, is of tears streaming down your face as you taught us from *Pilgrim's Progress* on Sunday evenings. No matter how far I went astray in later years, I could never seriously question the reality of Christianity. I had seen it in you."

Whenever the subject of family worship comes up, you may feel guilt at your failure in this area. I understand that. Few things seem harder to pull off or easier to be put off. But when you consider the impact this one commitment could make on your own children for a lifetime, what could be more important?

It doesn't have to be tightly preplanned. Take five or ten minutes before school to read a devotional with your children. Schedule one night a week when you'll all be home to read a story and Scripture, sing (or make a joyful noise) and have some outrageous fun. Watch for those opportunities to practice "sandbox theology," turning your children's everyday events into spiritual training moments.

Don't miss this: Dad and Mom, your ultimate assignment as parents is to introduce your children to God; His Son, Jesus Christ; and His Word. It may be hard to start and a challenge to continue, but it will make a huge difference in how they finish.

DISCUSS

Talk about what each of you can do to be helpful and encouraging to each other in getting family worship started or in keeping it going.

PRAY

Pray for priorities to firm up in your life, for incidentals to be seen for the waste of time they are and for God's Word to recapture each of your hearts.

Get Connected for More Information
http://www.familylife.com/moments/familyworship

MARCHING ORDERS

*For our struggle is not against flesh and blood, but against the rulers . . .
the powers . . . the world forces of this darkness.*
EPHESIANS 6:12

Whether you realize it or not, you are engaged in a spiritual battle every day. You live in a culture that is increasingly hostile to your faith. The devil and those who promote his self-indulgent agenda are relentless in their assault on your mind and affections. You can't afford to drop your guard for a minute.

Here are some suggestions for surviving—and thriving—in the battle:

1. *Don't engage the enemy alone.* Ephesians 6:10 says, "Be strong in the Lord and in the strength of His might." Whatever temptations you're facing right now, it is His strength alone—not yours—that can see you through. Keep on surrendering daily to the Master.
2. *Employ every piece of your spiritual armor.* As Ephesians 6:13 says, to resist the schemes of the devil, you must "take up the full armor of God." Not just the belt of truth, but also the shoes of His gospel, the breastplate of His righteousness, the shield of faith, the helmet of His salvation and the sword of His Spirit—the Word of God (see verses 14-17). Don't head off into battle without them.
3. *Go on the offensive.* It's not enough just to play defense. Though people without Christ may seem fulfilled and self-satisfied, the truth is that they need to know God's forgiveness.
4. *Quit wasting time.* You and I are fighting for the soul of future generations. So turn off the television. Put down the sports page. Unplug from the Internet. The consequences of your life are too eternal to waste on forgettable moments.

Never forget that your marriage is taking place on a spiritual battlefield, not on a romantic balcony. Help one another maintain your "war footing." If you do, you won't be a casualty.

DISCUSS
Identify two or three areas where the constant pull of the world has been wearing down your spiritual sharpness lately. Talk about what you need to do.

PRAY
Pray for strength when you're weak, attentiveness when you're tired and new discoveries of what it means to put your trust in God.

Get Connected for More Information
http://www.familylife.com/moments/battleforfamily

ARE YOU MY MOTHER?

Though my father and mother forsake me, the LORD will receive me.
PSALM 27:10, *NIV*

Many of us have read the old P. D. Eastman book *Are You My Mother?* to our children. But not many of us have had to grow up asking that question over and over again, to one person after another, growing increasingly convinced that no one was . . . or at least no one wanted to be.

Yet that was life for Mattie. Born to a substance-abusing, unmarried teenager, she fell out of the nest at an early age after police stopped her mom's car and found drugs inside. Both Mattie and her sister were placed into state custody and deposited in foster care. When the last family decided they didn't want Mattie and her sister anymore, she finally decided—somewhere between eight and nine years old—that the mother she longed for was nowhere to be found.

That was before Jenifer came into her life. With a family already bustling with two sons and a daughter, it would have been easy to ignore the nudge she and her husband were feeling from the Lord to adopt. Life was complicated enough without adding a new dynamic and personality type to the fold, with all the potential baggage the child would likely be bringing with her.

But somewhere a little girl was toughening her heart against a question she had grown tired of asking—"Are you my mother?"—only to be told no every time.

Mattie's life is now filled with safety and stability and camping in the summer, with an extended family gathered around to give love and support to a young girl and her sister who once had neither. "I thank God every day that I was adopted," she says, "because now I know who my mother is."

DISCUSS
What could you and your church do to help orphans?

PRAY
Pray for orphans in need . . . and for godly men and women who need to come to their aid.

EMPTY NESTING

BY BARBARA RAINEY

Do not cast me off in the time of old age; do not forsake me when my strength fails.
PSALM 71:9

It was not easy for me when our youngest child, Laura, left our home for college. There's a sense of importance that comes from your children being dependent on you. It becomes your identity. Motherhood defines who you are. And when that is taken away as children leave your home, a life-sized portion of your sense of importance, self-esteem and purpose goes with it.

When she left, I felt as if I had been fired from my job. Downsized and shown the door! Who was I now? What was my purpose?

Even though we had talked a great deal about this transition in advance, I discovered I needed my husband to help me evaluate this new season of life. Even though the change was also drastic for him, for me it was much more.

I had seen some women fly into anything just to stay busy. But when you ask your husband to listen and guide and process this new chapter together, it gives you the opportunity as a couple to face your future *on purpose.* Walking this strange, unfamiliar road together can bring a new level of unity to the marriage.

When I was going through this process, I needed a lot of talk time with Dennis. One day I'd wake up feeling excited about my new freedom; then I'd find myself sad all over again at the loss. It was unpredictable. Few of our discussions ended with clear direction.

But there's no other way that God's purposes for you and God's purposes for your spouse can become God's purposes for *us* unless you're walking through this together. God has more planned for your lives beyond the years of raising children. And that can be exciting!

DISCUSS

What do each of you see your life looking like once the children are grown and gone? How can you practically prepare for that?

PRAY

Pray for the grace and patience to care for each other well in all the seasons of marriage.

Get Connected for More Information
http://www.familylife.com/moments/emptynest

READY FOR PRIME TIME?

Even when I am old and gray, O God, do not forsake me,
until I declare Your strength to this generation.
PSALM 71:18

All parents eventually face the empty-nest years. And many do not look forward to them. But I want to challenge you to think of the empty nest as a brief parenthesis—a chance to catch your breath, a time to seriously evaluate what the next fruit-producing years of your life will look like.

I like to call the next phase "prime time"—the season on the other side of the empty nest when you transition from childrearing to new goals that are equally as noble. It's a process of listening to God and to each other, trying to determine a sense of direction and affirming the priorities that will define the rest of your lives.

Ideally these priorities should hinge around two commands in Scripture:

1. *The Great Commandment.* Perhaps you've heard this phrase from the Westminster Catechism: "Man's chief end is to glorify God and to enjoy Him forever." You do this by being obedient to Christ's Great Commandment: Love the Lord with all your heart, and love your neighbor as yourself (see Matthew 22:36-39).
2. *The Great Commission.* This is the greatest job assignment ever given to man: "Go and make disciples of all nations" (Matthew 28:19, *NIV*). Jesus was saying that your life is about proclaiming and teaching the gospel of redemption and reconciliation to those who are lost, while also influencing and commissioning a new generation of believers to do the same (see also verse 20).

If your "prime-time mission" doesn't include these priorities, you will miss much of life as you move into your later years. Regardless of your season, now is the time for you two to enlist in the Great Commission army and engage in the greatest commandment ever given to man.

DISCUSS
Whether you're nearing the empty nest or not, name one or two planned activities you could begin doing together to mirror these two biblical objectives.

PRAY
Ask the Lord for courage to face periods of transition with hope and purpose. Ask for guidance and trust Him to reveal His will in His way, in His time.

Get Connected for More Information
http://www.familylife.com/moments/emptynest

JOIN THE CLUB

BY BARBARA RAINEY

Encourage one another and build up one another, just as you also are doing.
1 THESSALONIANS 5:11

Soon after our youngest child left for college, I was invited to a baby shower for a young woman expecting her first baby. I anticipated this one to be just like the dozens of other showers I've attended over the years. Or so I thought.

As I sat there listening to a roomful of conversations about babysitters and laundry and little ones getting sick in the night, I was suddenly struck with the realization—for the first time in my life—that I wasn't part of this club anymore.

It was a very strange feeling, one that for some reason caught me totally off guard. I sat there thinking, *I want out of here.* Only one other woman at the party was in my season of life. Unfortunately, she pretty much just whizzed in, dropped off her gift and departed.

That's when I remembered something I was told once by a woman about 10 years ahead of me in this empty-nest transition. She remarked how important it is for us to talk with one another, to get together often to share our common experiences, to remind ourselves that we're not alone in feeling like we do. In my baby-shower moment, I discovered she was right.

Maybe for you right now, your struggle is not about adjusting to life without children. Maybe you're up to your ears in them! (I know how that feels.) But no matter where you are in the journey, don't hold your feelings in. Find a veteran mother who can share what you're dealing with. Together, you can cheer one another on.

DISCUSS

What's some of the best advice or counsel you've heard about handling your current season of life? Identify a couple of women or couples that you could get together with for support now and in the season you'll soon face.

PRAY

Husbands, pray for your wife. Wives, ask God for the discernment to know when you need help, when you need a listening ear. Each of you should pray for the humility required to be real, to admit loss, to share each other's pain.

INTENSIVE PRAYER UNIT

Let them pray for him continually; let them bless him all day long.
PSALM 72:15

If there's one thing Barbara and I have learned during our many years of raising children, it's that prayer is indispensable. Irreplaceable. Life giving. That's why we went before God often with our children's personal matters in mind. And we urge you to do the same, being careful to do the following:

Pray offensively. Pray for your children's peer groups—that they will each have at least one strong Christian friend they can count on through the years. Ask God to protect your children daily from those who would be an evil influence. Also consider asking God to help you catch your children *doing things right* so that you can encourage them in making good choices.

Pray defensively. From time to time we felt that a child might be deceiving us, but we could never be absolutely certain. In those situations, we asked God to help us catch the child if he or she was doing something wrong. God seems to honor parents who pray this prayer!

Pray intensely. One of the most misunderstood spiritual disciplines of the Christian life is prayer accompanied by fasting (the giving up of food or something that you love for a prescribed period of time). According to the Scriptures, God assumes that we will fast and pray (see Matthew 6:16-18), and He promises to reward us if we do it with a pure heart and motive. We know one couple that set aside each Monday to fast, from sunrise to sundown, praying for their struggling teenager.

Any time God brings your children to mind is the perfect moment to bring their names and needs back before Him. As James 5:16 tells us, "The effective prayer of a righteous man can accomplish much."

God delights in hearing the prayers of the "helpless parent."

DISCUSS
What are the top needs of each of your children?

PRAY
Make your prayer time today focused on each of your children. If you don't have children, consider praying for a niece or nephew.

Get Connected for More Information
http://www.familylife.com/moments/prayer

THE PERFECT SETTING (PART ONE)

BY BARBARA RAINEY

You husbands in the same way, live with your wives in an understanding way.
1 PETER 3:7

Our sixth year of marriage was a season of suffering. It included financial problems, the death of Dennis's father and a serious health scare of my own, followed by an unplanned pregnancy.

That summer, our friends Dr. Jim and Ann Arkins, seeing our struggles and exhaustion, invited us to join them for a four-day getaway to Mazatlan, Mexico. It seemed to be just what the doctor ordered.

After a wonderful dinner with our friends on that first full day, we returned to our room. A gentle breeze was blowing, and the moon was peeking around a thunderstorm on the horizon. As we lingered on the tiny balcony watching the last fading colors of the distant sunset, we were serenaded by the music from a nearby cabana.

While the setting was close to perfect, the two people were not. And we were about to find out how different our needs were.

Dennis began lighting some candles. He was making assumptions that seemed logical to him. There were no children to interrupt us . . . the room was warm and quiet . . . it was the perfect time for love.

I also had some assumptions. Even though we'd had a relaxing day, we hadn't had much time alone for the two of us to just talk. Since my health scare and pregnancy, I had become fearful, timid, confused and introspective. I hardly knew what I was feeling or how to express it.

So on this perfect night in this perfect location, what I needed was not what my husband needed. I wasn't opposed to making love eventually, but first I needed him to help me sort through what I was feeling and reassure me that everything would be okay in my life.

How did we resolve our differing needs?

I'll finish my story tomorrow!

DISCUSS
Can you relate to the story I've just told? What do you do when one of you is "in the mood" and the other is not?

PRAY
Ask God to give each of you a discerning spirit so that you can know how to meet each other's needs regarding sex and intimacy.

Get Connected for More Information
http://www.familylife.com/moments/suffering

THE PERFECT SETTING (PART TWO)

BY BARBARA RAINEY

My beloved is mine, and I am his.
SONG OF SOLOMON 2:16

So how did we resolve our differing needs on that perfect night for love in Mazatlan?

We had a fight!

Not right away, of course. Dennis tried to talk to me. He tried to love me. I wanted to talk, but I didn't know what to say. I knew he wanted to make love and he needed me, but I just couldn't respond in that moment.

I felt guilty—I hated myself for being so complicated. Dennis was frustrated over his inability to love me enough to make me forget my fears.

Finally the tension became too much, and Dennis grabbed a bottle of hand lotion on the side of the bed and threw it across the room. Instead of hitting the wall, the bottle broke a small pane of glass in the window!

The room became very still. I began to cry. I loved my husband and didn't want to hurt him.

Then Dennis said something that I never expected to hear. Something that became a milestone in our marriage. He tenderly cupped my face in his hands and said from his heart, "Barbara, I want you to know that I love you, and I am committed to you. I will love you for the rest of your life, even if we never, ever make love again."

Then he kissed me on the forehead and gathered me into a warm embrace with no strings attached, and we eventually fell asleep in each other's arms. No gift of any price could have meant more.

That evening in Mazatlan was a make-it-or-break-it moment in our marriage. We learned that *sacrifice is the language of romance,* and selfishness is the language of isolation and rejection. Commitment inspires one to sacrifice, and sacrifice makes commitment a rare jewel to be cherished.

PS. My husband's sincere proclamation of love made me want to be with him physically more than ever the next day!

DISCUSS
Turn to each other right now and make your own statement of forever love.

PRAY
Ask God to help you put to death the demands of self and to help you find ways to serve one another.

Get Connected for More Information
http://www.familylife.com/moments/romance

WHAT IN THE WORLD?

My soul is greatly dismayed; but You, O LORD—how long?
PSALM 6:3

Barbara shared yesterday about some events that occurred during one of the most challenging seasons of our marriage. On top of the crises she mentioned, our one-year-old son, Benjamin, had to be rushed into emergency surgery; we were cheated out of a substantial amount of money on a home we had just bought; and after returning to southwest Missouri to temporarily run my deceased father's propane business, I had a medical episode of my own.

I remember lying down on the very bed my dad had died in only months before, feeling my heart beginning to race at a frightening level. It turned out to be a panic attack. Dangerous only to my ego.

Two nights later I found myself on top of a tank car at 2 A.M., pumping propane and battling subzero temperatures. I had never been more confused in my whole life.

It was pitch black except for the twinkling stars on that brutally cold night. There I was, totally confused about what was going on in my life. Exhausted from the strain. I remember raising my fist and face heavenward against that winter sky and crying out loud to God, "What in the world are You doing?"

That's a fair question sometimes, isn't it? Have you ever been confused and cried out to God in a similar way? Are you in a situation right now where the only thing you know to say or think is, "What in the world are You doing, God?"

These are never times for pat answers or spiritual clichés. But every now and then, it is good to be in a situation where you are forced to throw your full weight of dependence back onto the only shoulders strong enough to carry you. In crying out to God, you find out in time how good, how redemptive He really is.

He is there. And He cares.

DISCUSS
If not you, think of someone you know who's enduring a season like this. Determine how you can be an encouragement to him or her.

PRAY
Thank God for being there, for hearing our desperate cries, for always caring about us.

LOVE AT SUBLEVEL

Love one another, even as I have loved you.
JOHN 13:34

Danny Akin, a seminary president with the bold audacity to write a book on sexual intimacy, shares this true, touching story:

> A woman had been diagnosed with breast cancer so severe that the doctors had no choice but to do a radical mastectomy. And like most any woman who awakes from this unsettling surgery, the blow to her self-esteem was deep and profound. Not only was she dealing with the loss of her breast, but she could see in the mirror how her hair was matted and her face swollen from reaction to the antibiotics. One day during her hospital stay, when her husband entered the room, she burst into tears. "Look at what I look like!" she moaned through her sobs.
>
> Immediately, he left the room and returned soon thereafter with a cart of shampoo, creams, and lotions. He picked her up in his arms, carried her to the sink, and set her down on his lap. Then leaning her head back over the basin, he washed her hair. He combed it out. He blew it dry. Then with unsteady hand, he applied her makeup the best he could—blush, lipstick, mascara.
>
> She looked at herself in the same mirror that had earlier sent her into convulsions of vanity, and saw someone she recognized: herself. She was back again. All because her man had loved her well through those crucial moments when her world had been crumbling around her.

Today, even though this woman's experience with breast cancer qualifies as perhaps the lowest point in her life, one of her favorite moments from all of her marriage has become those few precious moments in her hospital room—when her husband loved her in a way any woman would have understood.

"Husbands . . . , live with your wives in an understanding way" (1 Peter 3:7).

DISCUSS
Tell each other about a time when your spouse's love spoke volumes to you.

PRAY
Pray that God will always keep you sensitive to the exact expressions of love your mate needs from you—at any individual moment.

MISSING SOMETHING?

But we also exult in our tribulations.
ROMANS 5:3

Gary Smalley told me one day about being in a Kansas City church where he'd been leading a weekend conference. When the final session was over and he went to retrieve his bag to leave, it was gone.

You know how it feels when something like this happens? After the mad scramble to search and check and double-check to see if you might have laid it down somewhere, you feel that sharp, gnawing regret and anger. "Why didn't I–? What was I thinking? Who wouldn't have known to–?"

On-site surveillance cameras recorded video of a tall kid in a striped shirt walking out the door with Gary's bag, but nobody knew who he was. There was no chance of finding it.

Gone were Gary's laptop with all his lecture notes, as well as hard copies he had printed out to read on the plane to Chicago for his next seminar. Add to that the loss of a ruby ring and necklace he had bought for his wife to celebrate their fortieth wedding anniversary.

Gary was nauseated. But then, the Holy Spirit convicted him. And Gary started thinking, *Wait a minute, the Scriptures are clear: We're supposed to rejoice in our tribulations, "knowing that tribulation brings about perseverance" (Romans 5:3). The Lord tells me to "boast about my weaknesses"—even the weakness of being a little absent-minded—"so that the power of Christ may dwell in me" (2 Corinthians 12:9).*

Not immediately, but before the day was out, Gary had found his peace again . . . in the replenishing power of God's truth.

Truly, the Scriptures have the power to realign our thinking with the heart of God, showing us how to act, respond and live—even in the pressure-packed, disappointing moments of life.

DISCUSS
Which Scripture verses above seem to speak the clearest in regard to one of your present circumstances?

PRAY
Ask the Spirit to continually bring His Word to mind, just when you need it most.

DOUSING AN OLD FLAME

There is no fear in love; but perfect love casts out fear.
1 JOHN 4:18

Before you were married, was there someone else?

If so, you need to realize it's not abnormal for your spouse to feel insecure about an old flame. Even one that went out years ago.

Barbara and I were cleaning up around the house not long ago, and we came across a box of pictures we hadn't opened since early in our marriage. It was just a bunch of loose photographs, mostly from our college years. A good many of the pictures were of me and other girls I'd dated. (I had 16 blind dates in one month!)

I told Barbara, "Let's pitch it." I didn't really want these snapshots handed down for our children to sort through.

There was nothing inappropriate in the pictures; I just wanted Barbara and my children to know that I am a one-woman man. She is all that matters to me. And I don't want any temptation around that could entice me to look back and linger and wonder.

Have you seen or heard from an old flame recently? Been tempted to search the Internet for an old flicker? Do you still have a box of letters or memorabilia from relationships of long ago? There's only enough room in marriage for two.

The best thing to do with an old flame that suddenly reappears is to put it out. And if your spouse struggles with jealousy, the best way to cast out fear in the spirit of the biblical command at the top of this page is to cut off every ounce of oxygen from your mate's insecurities, until he or she feels totally safe in your love. Leave nothing behind to feed the fears or fan the flames of an extramarital affair.

DISCUSS

Do you still wonder about any feelings your spouse may have for an old flame? Have you dealt with yours, as well? Be honest with one another.

PRAY

The God who loves us jealously knows how to help us forsake all others. Ask Him to help both of you guard your relationship from old or new flickers and flames.

Get Connected for More Information
http://www.familylife.com/moments/commitment

YOU'RE MAKING THIS WORSE

He who separates himself seeks his own desire, he quarrels against all sound wisdom.
PROVERBS 18:1

I had spent a busy day wrapping up last-minute details, preparing to leave for a conference the next morning. I came home that evening, however, to a wife who had experienced a hard day herself—a *very* hard day with the kids. She needed to talk. But I was still busy.

I remember picking up the phone to make one last important call, when Barbara said, "Please don't get on the phone right now. If you do, I'm going upstairs."

I couldn't help it. I really needed to make that call. So I did. And that was the first of my mistakes. The moment I hung up, my mom called. We chatted for about 20 minutes. Then, feeling a little guilty, I began cleaning the kitchen, snapping on the television to keep me company. But by the time I finished, I was halfway interested in a show.

When Barbara finally came down to demand I make some time for her, there I was—sitting in front of the TV.

Busted.

I'm sure it would come as no surprise to tell you that the temperature dropped to about 40 below zero in our home that night. Barbara got so mad that when our disagreement headed to the bedroom, she whacked me hard on the head with a pillow. I remember turning my face to the wall as I tried to go to sleep, consumed with anger and how to get even. (Don't tell me you've never done that.) It was bad.

I think I'll leave it there for today and finish the story tomorrow. But till then, I want you to see how one mistake in judgment led to another. Every attempt to avoid confrontation did nothing but make the final confrontation worse. When you realize you're acting up, *now* is the time to stop it and make things right. Do *not* keep adding fuel to the fire.

DISCUSS
In what ways do you get yourself into trouble with your spouse?

PRAY
Desire self-control. It's a fruit of the Spirit. Ask God how to make it grow in you.

Get Connected for More Information

YOU CAN DO BETTER

Do not let the sun go down on your anger.
EPHESIANS 4:26

Every so often—through an aspect of His grace that feels much more like a punch in the stomach—God will crash His way into a pity party and spoil all the fun we get from sulking. That's exactly what happened on the night I was telling you about yesterday.

As I lay in bed feeling sorry for myself and angry at Barbara, God began the process of convicting me of my selfishness. He reminded me that the very next day, I would be speaking to a large conference crowd, telling them what they should do in situations just like this one.

Oh, yeah . . . I forgot.

And with that little revelation of reality and honesty, all the air went out of my argument. I didn't turn over to face Barbara right away, but I did promise myself I was going to be the first to set things straight in the morning. I was going to apologize. She was right. It was my fault. All my fault.

Things were still a little tense when we sat down together at breakfast the next morning, but I looked Barbara in the eye and admitted how selfish and preoccupied I had been, how I should have responded to her first distress signal. "It was very insensitive of me. I blew it. I'm sorry."

"Well," she said, "I'm sorry, too. It was pretty childish of me to hit you with that pillow. But finding you sitting there watching TV when I needed you, it just . . . that was the last straw."

We talked a while longer. Then I headed out to catch my plane. But by the time I left, we were both feeling a lot better. Even though we didn't feel like it, we forgave each other anyway—by an act of the will.

Reconciliation. It's better than American Express. Don't leave home without it.

DISCUSS

Is there any unresolved anger standing between you right now? Wouldn't right now be a good time to reconcile those issues?

PRAY

Ask God to use the sun as a daily reminder to resolve your issues. Never let it win the race to reconciliation.

Get Connected for More Information
http://www.familylife.com/moments/conflict

UNDERGROUND WARFARE

Not returning evil for evil or insult for insult, but giving a blessing instead;
for you were called for the very purpose that you might inherit a blessing.
1 PETER 3:9

Some couples just don't seem to know any other way to relate to one another than with digs, comebacks and put-downs. But sometimes, that same bitterness of spirit can show itself in less vocal ways, when one or the other spouse stews underneath and passively retaliates. There's more than one way to get back at your spouse.

This reminds me of the old story—supposedly true—about some soldiers who were living off base during the Korean War. They hired a local houseboy to do cooking and cleaning and other odd jobs for them, but they also took delight in playing tricks on him—just for meanness.

One morning when the boy got up and put on his slippers, he awkwardly fell forward to the ground—his shoes had been nailed to the floor. One night when he crawled into bed, he found shaving cream under his pillow. But no matter what pranks the soldiers pulled—whether short-sheeting his bed or setting buckets of water over his door—he always appeared to respond without much visible anger. "That's okay," he would say.

Finally, the young men realized they'd been inhumane in their treatment of the boy. They went to him and apologized. "We're sorry for what we've been doing to you. It won't happen again."

"You no more nail shoes to the floor?" No.

"You no more short-sheet bed? No more shave cream under pillow?" That's right.

A little smile crept across the boy's lips. Then he said, "Okay. Then me no more spit in soup."

There are many, many ways to spit in each other's soup in marriage. I am amazed at how quickly my mind can creatively come up with ways to retaliate. The Scriptures tell us that it isn't wrong to be tempted. But it *is* wrong to "spit in your spouse's soup!" In the spirit of 1 Peter 3:9, find a way to give a blessing instead of an insult.

DISCUSS

Be honest: When and how have you undercut each other like this? What are your little tricks for getting even? How can you begin to practice "giving a blessing instead"?

PRAY

Ask the Holy Spirit to help you turn away from hurting your spouse and to help you give your spouse a blessing in the heat of the moment.

Get Connected for More Information
http://www.familylife.com/moments/conflict

FORK IN THE ROAD

Before destruction the heart of man is haughty, but humility goes before honor.
PROVERBS 18:12

Years ago, I conducted a public interview with Bill and Vonette Bright, who founded Campus Crusade for Christ. I asked them, "Was there ever a time in your marriage where you were at a real crisis? A true fork in the road that could have ended in disaster?"

Bill's eyes filled with tears, his head dropped a bit, and he began to nod. There was shame and sorrow in his voice as he began to tell about a disagreement that had momentarily threatened their marriage.

It began when Bill had begun to make some key ministry decisions without consulting Vonette, even though the choices he was making directly affected her. One day as they argued about one of these issues, Bill declared, "The decision has been made, and it's too late to change our plans now."

Suddenly, all the resentment building inside Vonette erupted. "Okay, Bill Bright! I'll just leave! I'm not going to live where I have nothing to say about what goes on." She whisked the children into the car, got in the driver's seat, and then slumped. Where would she go?

At this point, their young son Zac made a statement that cut to the core: "Mom, this shows me the kind of person you really are." As her son's words stung her, Bill burst through the front door and deliberately got in front of her car. He pleaded, "Don't go, Vonette."

He went on to apologize, and she did too. Then Bill backed up his words of apology by changing the decision they had argued about. Later, Vonette wrote, "I stayed because he took the first step toward reconciliation and working out our problems. It took a real man of God to admit he was wrong, and this gave me the courage to confess my poor attitude."

The Brights' marriage flourished for more than 50 years until Bill's death in 2003. They never quit. Neither should you.

DISCUSS

Have you faced any forks in the road? What key decisions have strengthened your marriage?

PRAY

Pray for a heart of humility so that you will always take the first step toward reconciliation.

GO GET HER

You, therefore, who teach another, do you not teach yourself?
ROMANS 2:21

I'll never forget the email I received from a husband who described in point-by-point detail what he hoped to get from one of our marriage conferences he and his wife were scheduled to attend. I can't squeeze all of them onto this page, but you'll get the idea.

I need you to talk to my wife about:

1. Getting her to stop watching bad TV shows
2. Getting her to read the Bible
3. Getting her to listen to Christian music
4. Getting her to support the charity work I do
5. Getting her to realize that she's a sinner
6. Getting her to stop drinking beer
7. Getting her to stop wasting our family's money
8. Getting her to stop worrying about fixing up our home
9. Getting her to realize she's setting a bad example

After reading this email, I wanted to say to him, "Well, sir, I've got a better idea. What if instead of making this long list of things you'd like to see changed about your wife, you made a list of what *you* needed to change? What if you made a list of what you most appreciate about her? What if you made a list of her top-three needs from you, along with a deadline for you meet them?"

I know this is an extreme example. It's easy to pick on someone like this. But ask yourself, *Am I too quick to think that fixing my mate is the solution to our marriage problems?*

DISCUSS
Promise each other you're going to make at least one of the three lists I mentioned. Plan a time when you can share them.

PRAY
Pray that God will stop the temptation to accuse and point fingers, using whatever red flags and warnings get your attention the best.

CLOTHED IN RIGHTEOUSNESS

Everyone who has this hope fixed on Him purifies himself, just as He is pure.
1 JOHN 3:3

Barbara and I were eating in a fast-food restaurant when we noticed a couple of college kids wearing T-shirts with gross, sexual vulgarities on them.

Maybe it was because we were out of town—or maybe it was because I was eating a cheeseburger when I should have been having a green salad! But something made me want to appeal to these two young men, man to man. So Barbara and I talked it over, and I said to her, "Go unlock the car and have the motor running, just in case I need to make a quick getaway."

I walked over and smiled as I introduced myself. "Young men," I said, "I don't know how you'd feel if your mom walked in right now, but I want you to know that my wife was sitting over there and saw what was written on your T-shirts, and she found it deeply offensive."

As they began to back away from their burgers, I continued to smile but said firmly, "One day when you're a dad like me, and your boys want to wear shirts like these, I hope you'll teach them what it means to be a man and to have respect for the opposite sex."

Now, I'm not suggesting that this approach is always a good idea. But be sure to tell your children, "Never forget that the way you dress is a reflection of who you are. You are a member of this family, and you are a child of God."

It has been said that all that is necessary for evil to triumph is for good men to do nothing. I don't take on every issue, but I am determined to take on those that God clearly sets before me. What about you?

DISCUSS
Are you content with the way your children are dressing? Identify any areas that need to be addressed. Make plans to talk to your children about them.

PRAY
Thank Him for giving you the privilege of shaping your children's conscience. Thank Him for the responsibility you and your children have to honor God with your lives.

Get Connected for More Information
http://www.familylife.com/moments/helpingothers

WHY SETTLE FOR LESS?

Whatever you do in word or deed, do all in the name of the Lord Jesus.
COLOSSIANS 3:17

John Flanagan, Jr., was flying a routine Air Force mission during the Vietnam War, seeking to confirm a radio report of 300 enemy Vietcong troops spotted in a nearby area. Flying low above the coordinates of the site zone, he could see nothing that aroused his suspicions or indicated the presence of enemy forces.

But just before he pulled up and headed back for base, the memory of his high-school English teacher flashed through his mind. Father John Mulroy was one of those instructors who never allowed halfhearted work to be passed off as acceptable. His students—like John Flanagan—either gave it their very best or got the consequences for just getting by.

So with a new resolve to swing around and look more closely this time, he spotted a gathering of Vietcong. Not only that, he noticed a squad of American gunships zooming into position to blow them away.

But something didn't look right. Sinking lower, skimming just above the treetops, Flanagan buzzed his plane right into harm's way and recognized that the troops on the ground were not Vietcong but South Vietnamese forces—friendlies! By blocking the ensuing battle at the risk of his own life, he stopped a dose of bad reconnaissance from leading to regrettable bloodshed.

The disaster John Flanagan courageously helped avoid by going the extra mile that day earned him a Distinguished Flying Cross and the admiration of his fellow airmen. But many of the accolades could have legitimately gone to a tough-minded teacher who wouldn't let his students settle for second best.

Are you challenging one another and your children to be the very best you can be?

DISCUSS
Share about a person in your past who really challenged you to do your very best and to never quit before the job was done. Discuss what kind of challenge you want to give your children.

PRAY
Ask God for the perseverance to model excellence and a job well done, realizing that it is ultimately Him that you are seeking to please.

Get Connected for More Information
http://www.familylife.com/moments/biblicalparenting

FAITH TESTED

To the one we are the smell of death; to the other, the fragrance of life.
And who is equal to such a task?
2 CORINTHIANS 2:16, *NIV*

Within all of us, I believe, is a lingering self-doubt. We may look like we've got life totally wired, but *we* know we don't. So it hurts when our own insecurities are thrown back in our face—especially when they involve our desire to follow Christ wholly and fully.

That's exactly what happened to a friend who sensed God's calling on his life to enter Christian ministry as a vocation. When he informed his mom of his decision, she said, "There was a time when I was extremely proud of you. It's a shame that you're throwing six years of education and two degrees down the drain."

His aunt was no kinder in her assessment. She wrote him to say, "You may think you're about to do a noble thing. However, my dear nephew, that is not the case at all. What you're about to become is another blood-sucking leech on the neck of society, draining the hard-earned resources of the people of this land. If you were my son, I would have you see a psychiatrist, for only a sick person would be sold a bill of goods as you have been."

How does a person respond to words like these? Even devoted followers of Christ know how hard it can be to discern the inaudible voice of an invisible God. So when others belittle a choice you've made because of your relationship with Him, whom do you believe?

It's natural to feel unsure sometimes about the specifics of His will. And you do need people in your life who will provide balance and hold you accountable. Ultimately, you must develop a confidence in God that sustains you when others doubt you. Let His pleasure with you be your source of confidence.

DISCUSS
Has there been a time when others questioned a decision you made out of obedience to Christ? Is God leading you in a direction today that you need to obey?

PRAY
Pray that you will have the faith, courage and perseverance to obey God . . . regardless.

NEAR BELIEFS

Continue in the things you have learned and become convinced of,
knowing from whom you have learned them.
2 TIMOTHY 3:14

I'm afraid too many of us Christians don't know what we really believe. Like a cork in the ocean, driven and tossed by the waves, we bounce from opinion to opinion, influenced more by the last book we read than by a lifetime of biblical study. We've become activity junkies, seldom stopping long enough to decide what really matters to us, too busy to determine what's really worth living for, let alone worth dying for.

As a result we live our lives based upon "near beliefs." Near beliefs have just enough truth in them to sound strangely familiar to convictions, yet they're too weak to inspire us or our actions. Too anemic to influence us to make a decision that demands a sacrifice.

Near beliefs wimp out when a teenager is pushing you out of his or her life. Near beliefs won't keep a marriage together when romance fades. Near beliefs almost always fall silent on such issues as same-sex marriages and homosexuals adopting children. Near beliefs don't inspire the courage to change a behavior or to press on against disapproval or opposition from "the herd."

Near beliefs are to blame for a new brand of Christianity that is epidemic in our homes and churches—a faith that has little flavor, little light and little influence. When near beliefs are our only source of motivation, tough stands are never taken, feathers are never ruffled, and absolutes are held very loosely. Without core convictions to help us navigate, we stand uneasily on shifting sand, and we lack the solid footing with which to stage a life of principle and character.

Today is a call to biblical conviction. A call to spending time studying the Word. A clarion call to challenge you to determine: *What do I believe?*

What is needed today is a battalion of believers who follow Christ and stand for Him and His truth.

DISCUSS
If you were on trial for being a Christian, would there be enough evidence to convict you?

PRAY
Ask God for the courage to stand for that which you know to be true.

Get Connected for More Information

DON'T PUSH IT

Love is patient.
1 CORINTHIANS 13:4

I'll be the first to admit it: When I go places, I like to be on time. Punctuality is a big deal to me. I am usually not obsessive about it, but I think it says something about your character and about the value you place on the event you're attending or the person you're scheduled to meet. That's just me.

But it's not Barbara. And on a few occasions in our many years of marriage, whatever character I thought I was displaying through being on time was more than cancelled out by the character I revealed through my impatience and angry words directed toward Barbara and the kids when they ran a little behind my schedule.

Cookie (that's my pet name for Barbara) is an artist at heart. God has wonderfully wired her with imagination and originality. But numbers just don't add up in her abstract mind. As a result, being punctual is a challenge for her. Fifteen minutes either side is considered an on-time arrival. Close enough. It simply doesn't faze her.

I chuckle when I recall one of the greatest moments in my relationship with my father-in-law, Bob, who was an engineer. He said to me, "Dennis, all these years, you've arrived late to every one of our family gatherings. I always thought it was you. But as I sit back and think about it, I realize I was wrong. It's not you. It's my own child." I smiled! There is justice!

But you know what's *not* right? I have occasionally let punctuality become more important than people. I've lost sight of the fact that human relationships are more valuable than any human expectations of structure. And even though being on time may be important to me, it's not more important than my wife and kids.

It is better to be a little late and still be in love.

DISCUSS
Do the two of you feel differently about the importance of punctuality? How has this been a factor in your marriage? How can you help one another be on time?

PRAY
Ask God for patience.

Get Connected for More Information
http://www.familylife.com/moments/marriagerelationship

Blessed is the man who trusts in the LORD.
JEREMIAH 17:7

For some reason I stayed home from work on September 11, 2001. I had just finished a three-mile run when Barbara met me on the highway near our home with a concerned look on her face. She blurted out the words, "We've been attacked!"

After watching television and learning more about the terrorist attacks, I showered and rushed to the office, where I met with leaders of our ministry. We prayed and discussed how we would encourage followers of Christ to respond to days that were filled with fear and uncertainty.

Many of the reflections that I captured in the days following 9/11 are just as appropriate in these days of insecurity:

1. *Trust in God, not men* (see Jeremiah 17:5-8). God and His plans are not upset by the actions of men. He is the anchor in a storm.
2. *Live for eternity and God's kingdom* (see Matthew 25:14-30). The things of the world seem trivial in a time of crisis. Determine God's purpose for you. How does He want to use you to reach, influence and serve others in the cause of Christ?
3. *Share the gospel boldly* (see 2 Corinthians 5:20-21). People could be one breath from meeting God face to face.
4. *Embrace biblical family values now, not just when there's a crisis* (see 2 Peter 3:10-13).
5. *Give others courage to live for Christ today and not wait for tomorrow* (see Hebrews 3:13).

One of my favorite hymns in the days after 9/11 was Martin Luther's "A Mighty Fortress Is Our God." Perhaps you sang it in your church:

A mighty fortress is our God, a bulwark never failing;
Our helper He, amid the flood of mortal ills prevailing:
For still our ancient foe doth seek to work us woe;
His craft and power are great, and, armed with cruel hate,
On earth is not his equal.

Those are words to remember whenever we need courage to live in these troubled times.

DISCUSS
What do you remember from 9/11? How was your faith affected?

PRAY
Pray that you and your family would make God your "mighty fortress" in the days to come.

Get Connected for More Information
http://www.familylife.com/moments/relationshipwithgod

READY, WILLING AND ABLE

The horse is prepared for the day of battle, but victory belongs to the LORD.
PROVERBS 21:31

On the morning of September 11, 2001, former Staff Sgt. David Karnes was watching the horrific events unfold on television at his office in Connecticut. But this ex-Marine, now an accountant, felt more than pain and sympathy. He felt a call to action.

Leaving his office, he proceeded to the barbershop for a "high and tight" haircut. Then he picked up his starched camouflage fatigues at home. Grabbing some basic rappelling gear, he jumped back into his car, swung by his church for prayer with his pastor and then headed for lower Manhattan.

Despite numerous roadblocks, his military demeanor provided him clear passage right into the heart of Ground Zero. And from there, along with another volunteer, he helped pull the final two survivors from the smoldering wreckage of the World Trade Center.

We can learn a lot from David Karnes about how to deal with the crises that we all face at times in life. *First, he was ready.* When the time came to respond, he knew where his stuff was. He wasn't caught careless and unprepared.

Second, he was humble. Despite his warrior mentality, his first response was to pray and to seek God's direction and strength.

Third, he acted. He threw his courage and convictions into the fight at the risk of his life.

Are you spiritually prepared for what may come ahead? Are you ready to act when the time comes? I believe the great need today is for men and women who are willing to engage real-life issues, instead of doing nothing.

DISCUSS
While you're reflecting on 9/11 today, discuss opportunities that may exist around you that may need your help. Talk about your willingness and readiness to step into the life of another.

PRAY
Pray that the Lord will protect our nation and world in the future from such pointless evils as happened on 9/11. Also pray that He will use you as a couple to touch the lives of others.

Get Connected for More Information

WRONG OR RIGHT

He has made everything beautiful in its time.
ECCLESIASTES 3:11, *NIV*

When you made a covenant to your spouse, it wasn't just a promise to stay married. It wasn't a pass/fail exam. It was a sacred pledge to care for and nourish each other—to meet the other's needs and receive the other—to accept and embrace each other as God's personal provision for your needs.

But obviously, your wedding vows are made long before you *really* know the person you are marrying—before years of sharing the same house, the same bathroom, the same dishwasher, the same everything. By then you are aware of the maddening little things that just get under your skin.

It's at points like these when some husbands and wives conclude, "I think I married the wrong person." That thought is not abnormal, but it is dangerous.

If that thought has ever crossed your mind, I ask you to think carefully about this timeless advice from author and motivational speaker Zig Ziglar: "I have no way of knowing whether or not you married the wrong person. But I do know that if you treat the wrong person like the right person, you could well end up having married the right person after all. It is far more important to *be* the right kind of person than it is to *marry* the right person."

All of us inevitably come to places in marriage where our objectives and attitudes clash with each other, sometimes pretty strongly. We don't make it all the way through without encountering stretches of road that are filled with potholes, bridges out and some steep grades. But what would happen if we chose to accept rather than reject, to be thankful rather than spiteful, to give encouragement rather than disapproval?

I guarantee you, Mr. and Mrs. Right are the people in your wedding pictures, even if it hasn't been looking like it recently.

DISCUSS
In what ways has your perspective changed toward your spouse since you were married? Reaffirm your commitment to one another in a short letter to one another.

PRAY
Ask the Lord to keep your heart contented, committed to a lifetime of not just living but loving one another well.

Get Connected for More Information

STANDING-DOWN SIBLINGS

I tell you this so that no one may deceive you by fine-sounding arguments.
COLOSSIANS 2:4, *NIV*

Every family with more than one child at home faces sibling rivalry. Even when it's not showing itself in fights and raised voices and loud cries of "Mom!" you can be sure it's going on! They're jockeying for position. They're watching to see who's getting more and who's getting away with less.

I remember coming home frequently to a spat or dispute between sons and daughters. Somebody had taken something without asking . . . somebody had left something out with the cap off and ruined it . . . somebody had been goofing off when they were supposed to be helping out. Sibling rivalry was the never-ending story.

There were times when Barbara and I wondered if these kids of ours would ever be able to get along. Would they grow up to hate each other the way they so often seemed to at home?

But I want to encourage you today: Even when you're bone tired and worn down and feel particularly ill-equipped to handle these relational "muggers," jump in the middle and work to get these warring factions back together.

I'm convinced that one of the reasons sibling rivalry exists is to give you the opportunity to prepare and train your children for lifelong relationships in their marriage and families. When your children learn to settle their differences with each other, admit their own faults and ask for forgiveness, they are learning methods of conflict management that will serve them throughout their lives.

One of our most endearing joys today is to watch our grown children—the same kids who got under each other's skin so often when they lived under our roof—rally around a brother or sister in moments of crisis or need. I assure you, the time you spend training them is well worth the effort, even when you're not sure it's getting results. Trust me: They are getting it—even if they are acting like they aren't!

DISCUSS
How are you currently using sibling rivalry to train your children in conflict resolution? What could you do differently?

PRAY
Pray for perseverance. You'll need it.

Get Connected for More Information
http://www.familylife.com/moments/siblings

THE PLOTLINE OF LIFE

Trust in the LORD with all your heart and do not lean on your own understanding. In all your ways acknowledge Him, and He will make your paths straight.
PROVERBS 3:5-6

A few days after 9/11, one of my daughters and I met with a businessman and his daughter for an early-morning Bible study. It was always easier to get our kids into the Scriptures with the promise of a fresh doughnut or a breakfast with Dad.

We had been reading through the book of Proverbs, and on this particular day we looked at the passage that appears at the top of this page. As you can imagine, those words had a little extra octane as we repeated them so soon after the terrorist attacks. We began talking about what it means to trust in God with "all" our heart, to acknowledge Him in "all" our ways. During our discussion, my friend read aloud this interesting question from his Bible commentary: "Is Jesus Christ the One who gets the credits in the movie of your life, or is He the plot?"

Times of tragedy and loss have a way of answering this question for us. If you have been basically doing things on your own while occasionally expressing a semi-sense of dependence on Him for your life and work and family, then you may not be prepared for suffering. But if you build a habit of daily acknowledging Him as your source and sustainer, you will feel welcome rushing to His side in an emergency.

"Seek first His kingdom and His righteousness," Jesus told His followers, "and all these things will be added to you" (Matthew 6:33)—peace in the midst of anxious moments, courage in the midst of fear, and contentment and joy in the midst of lack. These are the sweet rewards for those who have made Jesus Christ the plotline of their lives.

DISCUSS
How would you describe the plotline of your life? What is standing in the way of making Jesus Christ the plotline of your life?

PRAY
Thank God that He pursues you and responds with love, grace and forgiveness to your multiple failures.

GOD'S BUILDING PROGRAM

*Therefore everyone who hears these words of Mine and acts on them,
may be compared to a wise man who built his house on a rock.*
MATTHEW 7:24

This is a true story.

In the 1870s, when the citizens of Swan Quarter, North Carolina, began looking for a piece of property for a new Methodist church building, their sights fell on a nice piece of elevated land where the structure would be reasonably protected from coastal flooding. But the landowner had more lucrative plans for the property and declined their offer.

So the church was built on another site and dedicated on September 16, 1876. Within a matter of days, however, a monster hurricane reached landfall at this precise location. One casualty of the storm was the brand-new Swan Quarter United Methodist Church, which was lifted up off its pilings by the surging tide of storm water and was carried north—floating, intact—and then inexplicably east, eventually coming to rest *on the very tract of land its leaders had originally requested.* As legend tells it, the property owner came with trembling hand to sign over the title deed to the church.

Yes, God is in control. Since 1968, as I have attempted to walk with God, on more than one occasion I have had to admit that I don't have the foggiest idea about what He is up to. He is God and I am not. I don't understand: infertility or the loss of a child, a chronic or terminal illness, the death of a young mom or dad, and a thousand other things that make zero sense, humanly.

What I do know from the Scriptures is that God has a unique purpose for every person and for every thing that happens to us. I have come to the conclusion that either He is the sovereign God, totally in control, or He is not in control at all (which I do not believe at all).

He made us to trust Him, regardless of the circumstances. And that is reflected in the new name of that Methodist church in North Carolina that God moved to solid ground:

Providence United Methodist Church.

DISCUSS

What are you or a family member facing right now that is testing your trust in God? What are your alternatives?

PRAY

Confess any lack of belief in God that He is in control, and express your faith that you want to trust Him because He does know what He is doing, even if you don't.

ONE HOME AT A TIME

A smoldering wick He will not put out, until He leads justice to victory.
MATTHEW 12:20

Major General Robert Dees (U.S. Army, Retired) was one of a rugged group of alumni from the 101st Airborne Division—the "Screaming Eagles"—who commemorated the fiftieth anniversary of World War II's Operation Market Garden by parachuting into the same drop zone in Eindhoven, Holland, as their heroic predecessors.

By almost any historian's accounts, the aerial assault initiated on this date in 1944 was a tactical failure. Yet it was part of an overall march to victory . . . and for some, the gift of life. Though on one hand it miscalculated the offensive's ability to secure "a bridge too far" (as portrayed in the well-known book and movie of that title), for some it became a bridge to hope and a future.

That's what General Dees discovered this September day in 1994.

After his parachute landed, he was greeted by an elderly Dutch woman who fell to her knees and grasped him around the legs. Through her tears, through the words of an interpreter, she told this gripping story: In September 1944, the Germans were executing five fathers a day in Eindhoven—to keep the population in submission and deter the brave Dutch underground. On the day this woman's father was to be shot, the American troopers fell from the sky, saving his life. She had not yet been born, she said, so she was alive because of Operation Market Garden.

General Dees's story reminded me that each home is important in the battle for the family. Your small courageous choices—to stand for truth, to remain committed to one another and to raise a family that honors Jesus Christ—will yield a victory of some kind. Don't give up. Just like that little Dutch girl and her dad, the next generation is at stake.

DISCUSS
Even if your efforts to strengthen your marriage and family haven't visibly made a difference lately, what little victories is God enabling you to win?

PRAY
Pray for the perspective to see bright spots in the midst of battle and for the courage to liberate your family and others from the cultural battle for the family.

Get Connected for More Information
http://www.familylife.com/moments/battleforfamily

LITTLE INTERRUPTIONS

BY BARBARA RAINEY

Make my joy complete by being of the same mind, maintaining the same love, united in spirit, intent on one purpose.
PHILIPPIANS 2:2

As moms, we get to deal with such exciting things as spit up, poopy pull-ups, and frogs and lizards escaping in the house. So how do you balance all of that with the desire to be an attractive, romantic, interesting wife?

One key is to remember that *your children are third on your list of priorities.* They cannot be more important to you than their father and certainly not more important than your heavenly Father.

A wise woman said to me years ago, "Honey, one child will take all your time, two children will take all your time and so will three. It doesn't matter how many children you have; they will take all your time." And she's right . . . if you let them. It's up to you whether or not you save at least some of your energy, time and attention for your husband.

When you pay attention to your husband, children begin to see that their needs and desires don't have to be met immediately. They learn patience when they have to wait for you to finish your tasks, your conversation . . . or your kiss! A healthy marriage creates security in their hearts and minds. Plus they can learn responsibility and greater independence when you and your husband leave them (well supervised, of course) to go on a date or a weekend away. They need an occasional break from you, just like you do from them!

Yes, children are often little interruptions, but keeping your husband a higher priority is the first step in balancing the roles of wife and mother.

DISCUSS

Perhaps this sounds very freeing for you. Or perhaps it sounds selfish and unkind. Talk about how you feel about putting limits on the time you spend with your children so that you can spend time with each other. Discuss a regular time each week when you can have a date night together.

PRAY

Ask God for the wisdom to set aside time for one another to invest in your marriage relationship.

INVESTING IN PEOPLE

*Admonish the unruly, encourage the fainthearted, help the weak,
be patient with everyone.*
1 THESSALONIANS 5:14

Who are the people that have meant the most to you in your life? Who has had the most influence in your life? Your parents? A coach, a teacher or a Sunday School teacher? Undoubtedly they challenged you to rise above the status quo. I remember people who cared about my character and who inspired me to a solid standard of holiness, devotion and diligence.

The bottom line? They all called me to noble, pure virtues.

Others have also stepped out of the herd and stepped up. Consider the famed scientist and inventor George Washington Carver who once wrote down what he called the "eight cardinal virtues":

1. Be clean both inside and outside.
2. Neither look up to the rich nor down on the poor.
3. Lose, if need be, without squealing.
4. Win without bragging.
5. Always be considerate of women, children and old people.
6. Be too brave to lie.
7. Be too generous to cheat.
8. Take your share of the world and let others take theirs.

Virtuous words. Yet even from a distance of nearly 100 years, they touch us at a deep level of our souls and call us higher than the selfish parts of our natures typically want to go.

I encourage you today to be careful where you look for inspiration—be sure that the people who influence you are those who can be counted on to lead you in the paths of purity and righteousness. And I encourage you to become an influencer, one who has the thick-skinned courage to step out and up and motivate others to be Christ followers. For Christ is the One who *truly* embodies noble virtue.

DISCUSS
Talk about your greatest role models and influencers. What did they do that called you to something greater?

PRAY
Pray that your head will only be turned by those who both preach and practice godliness.

OLD NEWS

BY BARBARA RAINEY

That which has been is that which will be. . . . There is nothing new under the sun.
ECCLESIASTES 1:9

We had just returned to the United States after a three-week trip to South Africa. We were glad to be back, of course, but it's always a mixed bag to return to our country. International travel has a way of clearing the fog from one's own nationalistic view of life. America is wonderful, and we are so blessed to experience its freedom and abundance, but returning home provides an opportunity to see this way of life with much more clarity.

After landing and clearing customs at JFK airport in New York, we stopped at a coffee shop in the airport terminal. Since we hadn't seen any news at all on our trip (other than front-page headlines in the South African papers), we sat where we could watch a television and find out what we'd missed.

The incessant chatter of ever-present televisions filled the air—a noise that quickly became irritating after having been away from it for a while. After watching for half an hour, we looked at each other and realized that our three weeks without access to American news information had been no great loss. Nothing very new or significant was being offered on the morning parade of programs. Most of it actually seemed quite silly, empty and valueless.

The conclusion was obvious. We Americans are not comfortable with silence and quiet. We are addicted, it seems, to celebrity twaddle and random acts of mayhem caught on cell-phone cameras. What a waste of time.

There really is nothing new under the sun. Especially on cable news channels.

DISCUSS

Evaluate the television shows you watched this past week and determine if there was anything you just *really couldn't have done without.* Then evaluate the amount of time you spend absorbing it all. Discuss any needed changes in your viewing habits.

PRAY

Ask the Lord for a discerning spirit, one that understands how valuable your time is, and for wisdom to know how to not let television rob you of your most important relationships.

Get Connected for More Information
http://www.familylife.com/moments/mediachoices

CARRYING CHARGE

Live with your wives in an understanding way, as with someone weaker,
since she is a woman.
1 PETER 3:7

Each fall, a ski resort in Maine hosts an event that is little known to the rest of the nation: the North American Wife Carrying Championship. To compete, husbands transport their wives through a hilly, 278-yard obstacle course that includes a 20-foot trough of water and 2 log hurdles. They can carry their wives in whatever way suits their running style—piggyback, fireman's carry or the more popular "Estonian" method, with the wife upside down across his back, legs crossed around his neck, arms held around his waist. The only enforceable rule is that she not touch the ground.

Ex-Olympians are sometimes among the contestants, while others are probably just there hoping for the first prize: the wife's weight in beer, plus five times her weight in cash and a thousand-dollar voucher toward a trip to the World Wife-Carrying Championship in Finland. (I'm serious.)

Admittedly, this event sounds a bit crude and primitive. But there is nothing archaic about a wife needing her husband to carry her sometimes—to be her strength during a tough stretch of circumstances, to stand with her in prayer, to be the broad shoulders she leans on when life gets heavy.

Yes, I've "dropped" Barbara a few times over the years. But I've had the privilege of shouldering her load in life-and-death health issues, a teenager's rebellion and dozens of those pesky parenting issues that can wear a mom down. We have our own race to run and it's an honor to carry her.

Husbands, be there for your wife. Listen. Care. And if need be, carry her.

And, wives, don't try to do it all by yourself. Lean on your husband. Let him help you. God will give him the strength. We need to be there for each other.

DISCUSS

Husbands, do you "carry" your wife well? What is one area of life right now where you need to be doing a better job of bearing her load?

PRAY

Pray that you will learn appropriate dependence on each other.

Get Connected for More Information
http://www.familylife.com/moments/husbands

LOVING YOUR MAN

BY BARBARA RAINEY

The wise woman builds her house, but the foolish tears it down with her own hands.
PROVERBS 14:1

I often give three pieces of advice to young women before their wedding day. But because these remain just as important as we go through marriage and because they are fashioned by the Scriptures and proven by experience, I share them with you today—at whatever stage you find yourself in marriage:

1. *Believe in your husband.* This is the most valuable gift Dennis says I've given him. You know your husband better than anyone. To see his faults and weaknesses and yet to believe in your husband's God-given potential as a man and his leadership of your home does more than you can imagine for his spiritual growth.
2. *Be willing to confront your husband in love.* Too many wives mistakenly believe they are following the biblical pattern of submission by ignoring or denying deficits in their husband's life. But being submissive does not mean being silent. It simply means being wise and loving in how you approach him, treating him with kindness and respect. Say to your husband, "Could I talk to you about something?" Asking permission to broach a difficult subject may make it easier to get your message across. He is far less threatened and insecure this way.
3. *Pursue intimacy with him on every level.* Most men consider physical intimacy the most important part of marriage. I've come to learn that it is central to my husband's manhood. It's the way God made him, and it is good. So rather than resenting it, learn to appreciate this aspect of your marriage as God's design. And be willing to learn and grow, becoming God's woman for your man. It's not always easy, but with God, nothing is impossible.

DISCUSS
Both of you should answer this one: Which one of these principles is most in need of your attention right now? Wives, what can you do to begin practicing love for your husbands in this area?

PRAY
Wives, thank the Lord for your man. And husbands, thank the Lord for your woman. Hold each other's hand and specifically thank God for things about one another.

A FEW GOOD MEN

There is a friend who sticks closer than a brother.
PROVERBS 18:24

Tim Kimmel, who along with his wife, Darcy, is a frequent speaker at our Weekend to Remember marriage conferences, remembers the two of them going out to eat sometime around his fortieth birthday. As they were waiting for their meal to arrive, he began doodling a crude picture of a casket on his paper napkin.

Turning it around to face his wife, he asked, "Darcy, how many people does it take to carry one of these things?"

"I don't know," she answered. "Six. Or eight."

"Okay, if I were to die tonight," he asked, "who would you call to be my pallbearers?" She began giving him a name or two, followed by the names of his brothers.

"No, not by brothers. They don't count. They'd be required to be there anyway. I want you to think of people who wouldn't feel like they *had* to come but who would drop whatever they were doing if you called them." Unfortunately, those names didn't fire so quickly to mind. And that's when Tim realized that he couldn't be sure he had enough real friends to answer his roll call for casket carriers.

That bothered him. He realized that, like so many other men, he had not really worked on building friendships. And *that* bothered him.

Since that night, Tim has been spending time with men, pouring his life into them. He is choosing to invest himself in people rather than fritter his time away on trivial, temporary matters.

You have a lot of choices in front of you—all kinds of ways you could spend your time and energy in the remaining years of your life. Will you use them to draw you closer to others or more deeply within yourself?

DISCUSS
Who would your six or eight pallbearers probably be?

PRAY
Ask the Lord to show you the value of other people . . . and the mirage of most everything else.

LOVE-HATE RELATIONSHIP

BY BARBARA RAINEY

You love every harmful word, O you deceitful tongue.
PSALM 52:4, *NIV*

I had been a mom for about six years when I first began to experience significant anger. And as the pressures of parenthood increased and our older children moved into adolescence, I started getting angry more severely and more often. It was inappropriate, and it was really becoming a problem.

One Thanksgiving weekend, my 13-year-old son and I got into a raging argument about . . . something. I don't even remember what. I just remember I couldn't control him, and I couldn't control *me*. For years, I had justified my anger by saying I was so tired and worn out every day. Now, for the first time, I realized it had gotten bigger than I was. I could justify my behavior no longer.

Dennis was a part of the solution. As we talked it over, we agreed that it would be healthy for me to go through a period of counseling. As I sought help, the Lord sensitized my heart one summer day to the words of Psalm 52. As I was reading the fourth verse—the one above—my eyes filled with tears.

Suddenly I knew that in all my years of struggling, the only thing I really hated about my anger was that I couldn't control it. Yet in those few moments of holy conviction, I realized I needed to hate my anger simply because it was sin. Before, I had only hated what I did with it. Now, I hated it for *what it was*.

Perhaps you're still rationalizing a certain harmful behavior of yours by claiming your right to it. Perhaps, if you dug a little deeper, you might even discover, like I did, that you enjoy the power and control it gives you.

If this is you, don't you think it's time to confess (agree with God about it) and deal with it?

DISCUSS
In what ways might you love your sins, even the ones that grieve you the most?

PRAY
Ask God to give you the courage to confront those things about yourself that need to be dealt with.

Get Connected for More Information
http://www.familylife.com/moments/anger

LISTEN UP

But everyone must be quick to hear, slow to speak and slow to anger.
JAMES 1:19

I was reading the paper one day and came across an excerpt from a book called *The Mistress' Survival Manual,* written by the founder of Mistresses Anonymous. (Now, I didn't read this book. Honest. I simply read an article that mentioned it.) One of the quotes in the excerpt spoke volumes about a great need in today's marriages. The author, who had spent her whole adult life engaged in adultery, said, "Many people think a mistress is a shapely young woman who wears flimsy negligees and lounges on satin sheets. But more likely than not, she's just an extremely good listener."

How many affairs have begun when one hurting person turned to another, sharing his or her disappointments with someone who was eager and motivated to listen to his or her problems? A woman wrote to us recently, telling how she had merely been talking with a young single man at church about a girl he was interested in dating. When the conversation turned to her marriage, she knew she shouldn't go there—she shouldn't tell him how unhappy she was. But pretty soon they were spending more time together, talking on the phone, wishing they could be together even when they weren't.

"Every time I meet someone new who takes the time to listen and spend time with me," she says, "I find myself drawn to him. Maybe I'll get out of this one friendship on time, but what about the next person who comes around? Please pray for me."

One of the greatest gifts we can give each other is the promise to be a good listener—tearing ourselves away from all our distractions and preoccupations, just to listen. To listen and understand. I can almost guarantee that your spouse needs you to be "an extremely good listener."

DISCUSS
Talk honestly about the way you listen (or don't listen) to each other. Share ways you both can encourage and sharpen your listening skills.

PRAY
Pray for your ability to listen and really hear what your spouse is saying.

Get Connected for More Information
http://www.familylife.com/moments/communication

YOU'RE STILL THE ONE

Above all, keep fervent in your love for one another,
because love covers a multitude of sins.
1 PETER 4:8

I can't attribute this story to its source, but a number of years ago I read a story about Babe Ruth. At the end of his legendary baseball career, the Babe had become obviously overweight. During one of his final contests, he bungled several fly balls in the outfield and struck out weakly with every plate appearance. Fans who had seen or heard about his once-proud exploits were now quick with catcalls, mocking this man who had hit twice as many home runs as anyone else in baseball.

But as the jeering got louder and louder, a little boy leaped over the railing and onto the playing field. With tears streaming down his face, he ran to the Babe and threw his arms around the legs of the fading athlete. Babe Ruth reached down, picked up the boy and hugged him tight. Then setting him down and patting him on the head, they walked hand in hand toward the dugout, while the jeers turned to cheers. Hardly an eye remained dry in the whole place.

The crowd had been correct in their assessment, of course. The Babe had let much of his athletic prowess go to seed. Yet a little boy had remembered him for who he was . . . and had covered over his errors with love.

This is not unlike what marriage was established to be—two people saying to each other, "I know you've failed me and disappointed me at times (as I have you), but I'm still going to put my arm around you and tell you, 'I love you.' I'm on this journey with you one way or the other."

I believe the angels burst into praise when they hear that, because this is the visitation of God's love on two imperfect people.

DISCUSS

How are you two doing right now? Are you standing by one another in the midst of life's turbulence? Perhaps you need to just look one another in the eyes and smile at one another.

PRAY

Thank God for His love that has already covered a multitude of your sins.

BAD APPLES

Do not be deceived: "Bad company corrupts good morals."
1 CORINTHIANS 15:33

One of my favorite object lessons in the sixth-grade Sunday School class I taught for many years was the "bad apples" demonstration. During a class at the beginning of the year, I brought some apples with me into the room—a beautiful, shiny red one that I called a "good apple" and a couple of others that looked nice but had at least one bruise.

"These two apples with the bruises represent a couple of buddies you really shouldn't spend time with in junior high," I would say. "They have a dark side to them—a compromised area of their lives. This good apple represents you, a nice Christian teenager but one who doesn't see any problem with bruised apples. 'These are my buddies,' the good apple says.

"So these three apples are going to hang out together for a few months. We'll check on them at the end of the year and see what happens." Then I would put the apples together in a plastic bag and place them in the closet.

Several of the students would become curious over the next few months about what had happened to our little "buddies," but I wouldn't return the bag until the last class of the year. Then I'd read the verse we're focusing on today—about bad company and its impact on good morals.

It never failed, of course. Nine months of hang time always took a toll on the good apple. The identity of all three apples had long been lost. All that was left was sort of a gross, discolored, mushy apple soup.

The buddies our children spend time with will inevitably influence them, either for good or for bad. That's why parents need to be fruit inspectors, helping their kids spot the bad apples and encouraging their kids to build friendships with the good ones.

DISCUSS

Do your children have some bad buddies? Discuss how you can take steps to wean them away from the wrong crowd and encourage them to spend time with some "good apples."

PRAY

Ask for discernment to spot problems ahead of time and for wisdom and courage to go about correcting them.

Get Connected for More Information
http://www.familylife.com/moments/peerpressure

MOM ALARM

My children, with whom I am again in labor until Christ is formed in you.
GALATIANS 4:19

Sharon's 15-year-old daughter, Kristin, went to the movies with friends, but then she sent her mom a text message saying they couldn't find anything to watch and were going over to Dory's house.

"Dory? Who's Dory?" Sharon asked.

"She's in my biology class, Mom," Kristin texted back. "It'll be great."

But something on Mom's radar told her it *wasn't* great. She suspected there were no parents at Dory's house. She knew she needed to go find Kristin—no matter what her daughter might think about it. But Kristin wasn't answering her phone, and Sharon didn't know where Dory lived. However, through a combination of caller ID and an Internet mapping site, she located directions to Dory's house.

Sharon had to ring the doorbell twice when she arrived. An older boy holding a can of beer looked out a window and yelled, "Oh no, it's somebody's mother!" She rang again. Finally, someone came to the door. "Would you please tell Kristin Hersh that her mother is here for her?"

After a minute, Kristin appeared, an ashen look on her face. Sharon feared they were in for a long ride home. But as they walked to the car, Kristin asked, "Mom, how did you know? How did you know I needed you?"

It turned out that some guys from a different school had arrived at the party, talking trash and getting aggressive. It looked like there might be a fight.

Even when your children are resisting your efforts at care and protection, they still need you more than ever. When they get stubborn, keep coming. When they become unlovable, keep loving.

Don't let them push you out. Don't cave in or capitulate to their culture. Be there for them.

DISCUSS
Did you push your parents out of your life when you were a teenager? Discuss how you will handle the lack of popularity with your teen.

PRAY
Pray for God to help you and provide a full-screen spiritual radar to discern what is happening in the lives of your children. And pray for the courage and wisdom to use your data well.

THE SECRET OF SUCCESS

What does the LORD require of you but to do justice, to love kindness, and to walk humbly with your God?
MICAH 6:8

A friend sent me an email posting from Ruth McGinnis, a Nashville recording artist and author, who had recently been diagnosed with ovarian cancer. In the midst of her ordeal, God began reframing the definition of success in her life:

> One of the most powerful insights I've had as a result of this unexpected detour in my well-planned life is truly understanding that the value of my work—the books I've written, my instrumental recordings, the speaking and performing I've done for countless years—has nothing to do with commercial success. I always thought that to be "successful," I would have to register in the marketplace with some measurable impact, like making the *New York Times* best-sellers list. As a result, even though I've enjoyed a rewarding career as a creative person, I've always felt that somehow I'd never quite arrived—that my life was incomplete.
>
> Having cancer has forever changed this. The cards, letters, gifts, phone calls, and emails I've received from people I know—and many I've never met—have revealed to me that the reach of my work and the value of my simply being here is greater than I ever could have imagined.
>
> I am convinced this is true for each one of us. That we all tend to be hard on ourselves and measure our achievements against harsh standards. We fail to appreciate our own contributions, and we forget to acknowledge the gifts, beauty and efforts of others.
>
> I will never think of success, fulfillment and contentment the way I used to. Cancer has swept the veil away from my eyes—has given me a new way of looking at life and rethinking everything. It is an unexpected gift.

Your life will be measured, not by the amount of money or power or fame you gain, but by the way you allow God to touch others through you.

DISCUSS
How would you define "success" in your life? In your family? Talk about Ruth McGinnis's perspective.

PRAY
Pray that you will be content just being who God has called you to be.

Get Connected for More Information

BEHIND CLOSED DOORS

Let her breasts satisfy you at all times; be exhilarated always with her love.
PROVERBS 5:19

One night, one of our teenagers came into our bedroom and said to us, "You know, it really bugs me that you shut the door to your room at 10:00 or 10:30 every night. I feel like you're shutting us out of your lives."

We replied that this was by design! Being alone with each other gives us a chance to talk and to know each other better. Of course, neither of us explained *how* we might be "knowing" each other on any given night, but Barbara and I understand that we need the opportunity for intimacy—not just spiritually and relationally, but also sexually.

God intended for us to become one flesh, to be drawn together toward each other. Adam and Eve didn't just shake hands when they met each other in the garden and began their lives together. They had sexual intercourse with each other, and God blessed their union. Sex is not all there is to marriage, of course, but it is a vital dimension that we shouldn't always sacrifice to the pressures of life or even the incessant demands of our children.

God is not down on sexual pleasure in marriage. The verse above is not from *Playboy* 5:19 but from *Proverbs* 5:19—right there with all the more well-known nuggets of scriptural truth about fearing God and being kind to your neighbors and not spending money you don't have. God even inspired an entire book of the Bible—Song of Solomon—that talks about little other than sexual love in marriage.

No matter how our culture twists and perverts the idea of sex, and no matter how squeezed we may feel by our children's and others' expectations, we need to keep our sexual relationship central and celebrated. That's the way God designed it.

DISCUSS
In light of the demands of children, discuss what you must both do to protect this important area of your marriage.

PRAY
Pray that God will give you wisdom to know how best to meet one another's needs in this area.

ACID RELIEF

Put on a heart of compassion, kindness, humility,
gentleness and patience; . . . forgiving each other, whoever has
a complaint against anyone; just as the Lord forgave you.
COLOSSIANS 3:12-13

A number of years ago, there was a person in my life who had hurt and wronged me, and every time his name came up, my stomach did a sort of little twist.

I thought the problem was that this person never recognized how deeply he had hurt me. He never apologized. But the real problem was that *I hadn't forgiven him.* No matter what he had or hadn't done, God's expectation was for me to forgive him regardless.

Forgiveness is not conditional. It is a command of God—"just as the Lord forgave you." This means you stop blaming. You stop pouring on guilt, and you stop referring to the offense as a trump card to win an argument.

You may not feel like forgiving. But by an act of your will, you need to operate out of a spiritual mandate: To forgive a friend—or a spouse—means giving up the right to punish that person.

For some offenses, there may always be a twinge of pain involved that never goes away. But when you say, "I can't forgive you," what you're really saying is, "I choose not to forgive you. I'm hurt so deeply, I can't move to forgiveness."

In some cases you may need to seek out a wise counselor to help you deal with your pain. But if you ever want your stomach to stop churning, you have to obey.

Marriage was designed by God to be the union of two forgivers who have been forgiven.

DISCUSS
Now would be a good time to put this principle into practice. Whatever it is, whatever it was, look your spouse in the eyes and tell him or her, "I forgive you."

PRAY
Our Lord knows this isn't easy. How well He remembers the cross. Lean on Him today, letting Him help you take this beyond words and into action. As you pray, open your hand as a symbol of releasing the punishment, and then take your spouse's hands in yours to signify your forgiveness.

UP-CLOSE FORGIVENESS

If you forgive others for their transgressions, your heavenly Father will also forgive you.
MATTHEW 6:14

I am often reminded of what C. S. Lewis said: "Everyone thinks forgiveness is a lovely idea until he has something to forgive." How true. It's not until forgiveness becomes personal and costly that it takes on its actual size and weight.

But perhaps some of what troubles us about forgiveness is that we don't understand what it is . . . and what it isn't. Forgiveness doesn't mean:

- Excusing what someone did to you
- Forgetting what happened
- Denying, or stuffing, your feelings
- Reconciling instantly every time

It *does* mean:

- Embracing the offender—Christ modeled forgiveness at its best when He forgave and welcomed back those who hurt Him the most.
- Being proactive—When Jesus said from the cross, "Father, forgive them; for they do not know what they are doing" (Luke 23:34), He was forgiving people before they even asked for it.
- Surrendering the right to get even—The essence of forgiveness, especially in marriage, is letting go of our rights to punish and see justice done. Forgiveness is evident when one spouse ceases to demand restitution for hurt feelings and wounded pride.

The other night when Barbara and I were praying together, I turned to Barbara and said, "Sweetheart, before we pray, there's something I need to ask forgiveness for." Then after some dialogue, the words "I forgive you" were spoken by Barbara. That's when you know your marriage is what it was meant to be—a relationship in which forgiveness can flow at the slightest offense. Forgiveness is one of the most important qualities you must practice if your marriage is to become great.

DISCUSS
Talk about the definition of forgiveness . . . surrendering the right to get even. Is there anything you need to ask forgiveness for?

PRAY
Pray that God will show you both how to be aggressive in pursuing forgiveness and appropriately quick in granting forgiveness.

Get Connected for More Information
http://www.familylife.com/moments/forgiveness

ONE IMPOSSIBLE POSSIBILITY

Bearing with one another, and forgiving each other, whoever has a complaint against anyone; just as the Lord forgave you, so also should you.
COLOSSIANS 3:13

Are there things that someone has done to you that you think you could never forgive?

You are not alone. Ron Luce, president of Teen Mania Ministries, shares a story that many can identify with.

Ron came to faith in Christ as a teenager after enduring an abusive home life. Not long after his conversion, God began to convict him of his need to forgive his mom for the evil things she had done and said to him as a boy. Things like hitting him in the face. Crushing a cigarette butt out on his back. Telling him when he was 13 years old, "Why don't you do me a favor and kill yourself?"

Initially, Ron reacted with typical human disbelief. How could he forgive his mom? She didn't deserve it. But in time, God broke through, and Ron decided he needed to forgive his mother.

So Ron started carrying around Scriptures on little cards—verses about forgiveness he could meditate on and memorize. He began desperately praying that God would give him the ability to give up his right to punish her. It wasn't easy, and it didn't happen overnight. But one day as a senior in high school, he remembers praying, "Lord, You need to reach my mom and touch her, because I love her."

He couldn't believe what he'd just said. "I love her?" He had never spoken those three words before in his entire life! "But I *do* love her. I *do* love my mom. And You're the One who put it there, Lord. You must have done it."

We can forgive, because He forgave us. He shows us a better way. A way of freedom from bitterness and punishment.

Christ does it through us. And He can do it through you.

DISCUSS

What impossible injustices—things you've grown weary of dealing with on your own—do you need to hand over to Christ? Make a list and ask Him to lead you to full forgiveness.

PRAY

Pray for whatever He must do in you to free you to forgive.

Get Connected for More Information
http://www.familylife.com/moments/forgiveness

FORGIVENESS FOR A PRICE

Above all, keep fervent in your love for one another,
because love covers a multitude of sins.
1 PETER 4:8

I don't know anything at all about what caused it, what led up to it or even what came of it. But I'm sure it was hard for people not to notice a full-page ad in the Jacksonville newspaper one morning that read: "Please believe the words in my letter. They are true from my heart. I can only hope you will give me the chance to prove my unending love for you. Life without you is empty and meaningless."

It was a full-page $17,000 advertisement and plea for forgiveness.

According to the ad's author, his wife of 17 years had left him two weeks earlier. She was living temporarily with her parents in a gated community, beyond the reach of her husband. Even her cell-phone number had been changed to keep him from contacting her. But relatives told him that she had indeed seen the large display ad and had left the room crying.

I pray that they were able to work things out. But—again, not knowing the circumstances—this still goes to show you that marriage, unlike any other human relationship, is the joining of two hearts into one flesh. The pain of living at a distance, even temporarily, feels like a limb being torn away. We can't think straight. We can't enjoy ourselves.

That's why your marriage must be a place where mercy and forgiveness are regularly being asked for and extended. Given, received and embraced. None of us are able to always be everything our spouse wants us to be. But only through the power of grace and forgiveness can you live through seasons of disappointment—with yourself and with one another—and come out feeling united again.

It might even save you $17,000 and even more heartache.

DISCUSS
Is there anything between you two today? Anything that you need to ask forgiveness for . . . or forgive one another for . . . right now? Just do it.

PRAY
Thank the Lord for His full forgiveness of us and for the ability to extend the same to each other.

GOOD QUESTION

Jesus asked them a question: "What do you think about the Christ?"
MATTHEW 22:42

Have you ever been moved to write a letter to someone who was making some bad decisions in life and needed a good dose of "talking to"? In a situation like this, it is difficult to avoid becoming fairly pious and preachy, even when trying to say things in a nice, persuasive, tough-love kind of way.

I know a man who felt compelled to write one of those letters not too long ago. A business acquaintance of his was getting dangerously close to walking away from his wife and family, and my friend wanted to be a voice of godly perspective in this man's life. But instead of filling his letter with direct warnings and admonishments, he simply asked his friend a series of questions. With each one, he took his friend farther out in years. He asked him things like, "What do you want your life to look like at the end?" and "How do you expect your children to eulogize you?"

Questions, not answers.

If you feel bottled up and ineffective as a Christian witness, is it possible that it is because you think you need to know everything? Is it any coincidence that the greatest Christian witness of all time—Jesus Christ Himself—so often responded to people's questions by asking them questions in return?

Who do you think Jesus Christ is?

If Christ doesn't pay the penalty for your sins, then who will?

If you were to die right now and God were to ask you what right you have to heaven and eternal life, how would you answer Him?

When you ask questions of your neighbors and others in your life, you can open true lines of dialogue. Don't feel the need to do all the talking. The doors you open by getting others to wrestle with God—and not argue with you—are usually the widest ones for people to walk through.

DISCUSS
Think of some questions you could use naturally in your interactions with others to get them thinking about their relationship with God.

PRAY
That He would give you His heart and eyesight for lost sheep.

THE GIFT OF CHILDREN

How blessed is the man whose quiver is full of them.
PSALM 127:5

For the most part, we raised all of our children the same way. Lived in the same house. Ate the same food. Passed around the same germs. But I'm convinced that if we had raised six more, they would all have been as different from each other as the first six have been.

Children are the most unique and creative of all God's gifts. And each one must be received this way—as God's unique gift to you.

Part of this gift means that you will be transformed into someone you'd never have become without them. It's a gift of spiritual growth and discovery, experienced each day as you relearn life through the eyes of your children.

For example, I would never have gone shopping for dresses with four daughters if God hadn't given them to me. I would never have attended high-school plays, science fairs or art shows or appreciated all the creativity and hard work that go into them. If not for six up-close, in-my-face reasons for stretching me beyond my normal backdrops and surroundings, I would have missed out on so much of what He wanted to show me and teach me.

Perhaps you're not seeing your children as gifts from God right now. Perhaps, if you were honest, you'd admit that some of the activities your children are involved in don't interest you much at all. You have a hard time being as supportive and enthusiastic as you know you should be.

How about making a conscious decision to receive each child as God's gift to you? Know that He is working through him or her to do some work in you as well.

DISCUSS
Is there a child who is different from you, one you have not embraced? How do your children take you out of your comfort zone? Talk about how you and your spouse need to grow.

PRAY
Pray for a heart that's always open to the unique gifts of God. Give thanks for each of your children.

SEEK GOD, NOT SIN

Seek good and not evil, that you may live.
AMOS 5:14

Over the next seven days, I want to walk you through what I call "the seven non-negotiables of life"—biblical benchmarks that are true simply because *He* is true.

We're familiar with some of the non-negotiables of our lives. For example, when we buy an automobile, we also get an owner's manual that outlines the maintenance schedule for keeping the car in good working order. If we follow the plan, we should enjoy many years of reliable use of the car. But if we maintain the car improperly, we can expect big trouble—and probably at a time when we least expect it and can least afford it.

The same is true in life. Depending on how we treat God's non-negotiables, they will either protect us or destroy us.

So . . . ready to go?

Non-negotiable Number One: Seek God, Not Sin

One of the great hymns of the Church that always strikes me with its profound truth is the song "Come, Thou Fount of Every Blessing." The lyric from this hymn that probes at the deepest level of honesty and understanding is this line: "Prone to wander—Lord, I feel it; prone to leave the God I love."

Does that resonate with you as it does with me? Even when we are genuinely denying ourselves and experiencing nearness to Christ, we still know—deep down—that this never happens without a struggle. We are "prone to wander." O Lord, how we feel it.

This is why God steps out of eternity to tell us in His Word, "Seek good and not evil, that you may live." He is the life giver. And though our feet are indeed made of clay, our souls know that life is only found in one place—in Christ, in God, through the righteousness given to us at new birth.

Seek God, not sin. And live.

DISCUSS

Share how you've "wandered" in the past. What is an example of how we are prone to seek sin rather than God?

PRAY

Pray for one another that your hearts will seek God and that when you or your children do wander, it will not be a lengthy journey.

FEAR GOD, NOT MAN

The fear of the LORD leads to life, so that one may sleep satisfied, untouched by evil.
PROVERBS 19:23

There are few things in life sweeter than lying down in bed after a long, hard day and sinking into a dreamless, uninterrupted, eight-hour sleep. No one enjoys this kind of rest on more of a regular basis than those who have learned to reverence God and practice His presence in their lives. The Bible repeatedly teaches that the fear of God turns us away from evil and from the fear of man.

Non-negotiable Number Two: Fear God, Not Man

Fearing God means we reverence Him. We set Him apart and live our lives under His watchful eyes. To be sure, He is the God of love, but He is also the Lord God Almighty, who was and is and is to come! He is a righteous Judge who should be feared. You and I are accountable to Him for the life we live and choices we make.

Do you fear men more than God? Are you preoccupied with what people think about you? Are you living your life for the grandstands of heaven or Earth? Only the fear of God is able to deliver you from the fear of man.

It was A. W. Tozer who said, "What you think about God is the most important thing you think." Knowing God—really knowing Him and who He is—calibrates all of life. He is the ultimate measurement because He is in control. When we see God as Creator, Maker, Redeemer, Judge, Consuming Fire, Sovereign King and the One who knows all things, we begin to practice His presence in our lives.

He is God. He is holy. And as fervently as He is to be loved, He should also be fiercely feared. He is worthy of it. And we are in need of fearing Him.

DISCUSS

Who do you fear more: man or God? Share with one another your understanding of who God is and how that understanding impacts your life daily.

PRAY

Ask God to teach you to fear Him.

LOVE GOD, NOT THE WORLD

If anyone loves the world, the love of the Father is not in him.
1 JOHN 2:15

I don't have to tell you how hard the world is vying for your affections. It beckons you and me with the lure of lesser loyalties. The world wants you to have a better car, a bigger house, more-fashionable clothing, a sleeker cell phone, a snazzier computer. And nearly every day in the mail, you are offered a brand-new credit card to buy it all with.

But what you may not realize is that money and possessions are not the only things the world offers to demand your affections and compromise on one of the Bible's clearest commands.

Non-negotiable Number Three: Love God, Not the World

What in the world do you love? Why not complete a year-end inventory of your heart and its affections? Just like a year-end inventory in a big warehouse, walk down the aisles of your heart and take note of what clutters the shelves. How do you use your time? What do you think about and talk about?

Perhaps you'll find some "old inventory" that should be moved out of your heart. Perhaps there are some habits you've developed over the years—and if you are honest, you really love these old habits more than you love God. Things like hobbies or television—or perhaps even addictions like food, alcohol, drugs or pornography.

Perhaps the inventory will reveal a possession that you realize owns you. It is in competition with God for your love.

Perhaps it's time to clear out some inventory and replace it with some fresh obedience to God's commands.

Wasn't it Jesus who said the greatest commandment was to "love the Lord your God with all your heart" (Matthew 22:37)?

Love God. Love His people. Love His mission and will. When you're consumed with love for Him, you won't have much room left to love the world.

DISCUSS

Discuss a year-end inventory of your hearts. What is competing for the affections of your heart today?

PRAY

Spend some time together expressing your love, praise and adoration of God. Whatever else may compete for your affections, ask Him to be your first love.

Get Connected for More Information

BELIEVE GOD, NOT THE DECEIVER

Whenever he speaks a lie, he speaks from his own nature,
for he is a liar and the father of lies.
JOHN 8:44

A Long Island businessman in the 1930s bought an expensive brass barometer to mount in his home. However, when the man pulled the instrument out of the box and started to hang it, the arrow that indicated current weather conditions was pointing hard to "Hurricane."

Angrily, he pounded his palm on the glass face of the barometer. The arrow didn't move. He shook it and then banged it on the table. The arrow still didn't move. This thing was obviously defective. So the next morning he fired off a nasty letter to the manufacturer and dropped it in a mailbox on his way to work in Manhattan.

But sure enough, a storm did roar through Long Island that day. And when he drove home in the afternoon, his house was destroyed . . . in a hurricane.

You see, there is absolute truth and there is deception.

Non-negotiable Number Four: Believe God, Not the Deceiver
All of life is a choice of who you will believe. Life is a battle between believing the truth or swallowing lies. And because the nature of our hearts—like that of the man in this story—is to doubt the truth and believe deceptions, it takes a deliberate effort to embrace God's truth as non-negotiable. If we don't keep our minds in the truth of the Scriptures on a daily basis, we become easy marks for our constant foe, the devil, who is both "an angel of light" (2 Corinthians 11:14) and "the father of lies."

So even when the Scriptures teach something you don't like, it's always the right choice to believe God anyway. It's better to know the truth that a hurricane is coming than to mistakenly think you're in the clear.

DISCUSS
What deceptions have you fallen prey to in the past? How have they burned you? What is God asking you to believe today?

PRAY
Pray for daily, deliberate, ongoing discernment.

Get Connected for More Information
http://www.familylife.com/moments/relationshipwithgod

OBEY GOD, NOT YOUR APPETITES

Everyone who competes in the games exercises self-control in all things.
1 CORINTHIANS 9:25

The choices you make today or tomorrow are not confined to today or tomorrow. A baby step of obedience may be all the ground you need to cover today in order to put yourself in position to launch a major spiritual breakthrough later on.

Non-negotiable Number Five: Obey God, Not Your Appetites

As C. S. Lewis wrote, "Good and evil both increase at compound interest. That is why the little decisions you and I make every day are of such infinite importance. The smallest good act today is the capture of a strategic point from which, a few months later, you may be able to go on to victories you never dreamed of."

What an incredible proposition!

But as with all non-negotiables, it works the other way, too. Even a trivial indulgence in lust or anger today represents the loss of territory in our hearts that the enemy can secure, giving him an inroad to launch an attack against you—an attack that otherwise would have been impossible. Each misstep offers him a stronger foothold for marshaling his counteroffensives against you, against your marriage, against your family—if not right now, then at a later time when he knows he can inflict the greatest amount of damage.

So it is absolutely crucial that you submit your passions to Jesus Christ each day, denying yourself the temporary pleasures of sin and therefore gaining ground that can only be won through consistent, ongoing, long-term obedience. It takes a great deal of courage to say no to the appetites of the flesh, especially over time.

Someone has said, "It is upon the little hinges of obedience that the door of opportunity swings." God wants to open those "doors" for us. The question is: Will we be obedient?

DISCUSS

Confess the sinful, human appetites that demand to be fed in your life. What do you need to do today that would starve them out tomorrow?

PRAY

Pray for daily victory that leads to a lifetime of spiritual progress.

Get Connected for More Information
http://www.familylife.com/moments/relationshipwithgod

SERVE GOD, NOT SELF

*I heard the voice of the Lord, saying, "Whom shall I send,
and who will go for Us?" Then I said, "Here am I. Send me!"*
ISAIAH 6:8

There can be only one Lord in this relationship, or it just doesn't work. Any other combination of play-callers in this game plan results in confusion, distraction and disobedience.

Non-negotiable Number Six: Serve God, Not Self

The Bible exhorts us to become "slaves" or "bond-servants" of Jesus Christ (see Ephesians 6:6; Acts 16:17; 2 Corinthians 4:5). We are all slaves of some master. If that master is sin, we will be enslaved to evil. If that master is self, we will be in bondage to our pride. It is Jesus Christ who gives us the power to break free from these masters and find life in Him as our true Master.

Barbara and I have written on a number of occasions about a document we created in our first year of marriage in 1972. It was our first Christmas together and we decided that before we gave anything to each other, we would give God what we called "The Title Deed to Our Lives."

Each of us sat down and wrote out a document that signed over all our rights, all our possessions and all our dreams of what we'd ever hope to have. We gave ourselves as fully and completely to God as we could at the time. We became bond-slaves of Jesus Christ. I cannot begin to tell you how liberating that decision was.

Nearly 20 years later, we opened the envelopes that contained our "Title Deeds." I laughed as I read back over all that we gave God on that day. What we gave Him on that day could hardly be considered a loss when we compared what He had given us as His bond-slaves. I cannot imagine what our lives would have looked like if we had chosen a lesser master.

Serve God, not self. When He is Lord, you have the best Master on Earth.

DISCUSS

What would it be like for you to sign a "Title Deed of Our Lives"? What would you give up? What would you gain?

PRAY

Pray that God will make you willing to be willing to be His bond-slaves.

Get Connected for More Information
http://www.familylife.com/moments/relationshipwithgod

WORSHIP GOD, NOT COMFORT

Though He slay me, I will hope in Him.
JOB 13:15

When I go to church, I love to worship God in song. I've found that closing my eyes and singing to Him without being distracted by people is a very satisfying experience. I love what happens when the Holy Spirit speaks through the Scriptures, realigns my attitude and calls my heart to worship and reflect on His goodness and mercy. I love all the things that make worship services so full—the choir, the baptisms, the Lord's Supper.

But if we really want to learn how to worship, we must do it when the microphones are turned off and the singers have gone home, when the room is quiet and our hearts aren't fueled by feelings that swell with the music. We must learn to worship in the midst of life . . . and even in the midst of suffering.

Non-negotiable Number Seven: Worship God, Not Comfort

You may be in the midst of a true season of pain. Perhaps this season has lingered and has now become two seasons. Perhaps you've looked for comfort but haven't found much. Maybe your heart aches and feels empty. Has your lack of comfort dried up your words of worship? Has the loss of ease emptied your heart of gratitude?

It may be that the most important thing you could do is also one of the most unnatural things you could ever imagine doing: Giving thanks to God, praising and worshiping Him. Regardless of your circumstances.

Worship in its truest form ascribes and acknowledges that the truth is about God. Worship reminds us of who He is and who we aren't. He alone is God. He is in control. He is the just God, the compassionate and loving God. He knows everything. He knows our condition.

God-centered worship ultimately comforts us because it reminds us of the truth about life. It brings hope.

When life seems most uncomfortable, worship God.

DISCUSS

Talk about how you best worship God. Discuss how you could encourage one another to engage in real worship each day.

PRAY

Ask God to teach you how to truly worship Him when things aren't comfortable.

Get Connected for More Information
http://www.familylife.com/moments/relationshipwithgod

LIVING BY THE LIST

*Seek first His kingdom and His righteousness,
and all these things will be added to you.*
MATTHEW 6:33

I want to spend just one more day wrapping up these seven non-negotiables of life—because when you see them together like this, it becomes much clearer what they're all about.

1. *Seek God*, not sin.
2. *Fear God*, not man.
3. *Love God*, not the world.
4. *Believe God*, not the deceiver.
5. *Obey God*, not your appetites.
6. *Serve God*, not self.
7. *Worship God*, not comfort.

We know in our heads that we should put God first and ourselves last. What we're not always sure about, though, is how to apply that theoretical truth in real life—during a routine business meeting or a normal Thursday afternoon or an encounter with a child.

That's what these seven simple action points are all about. When every intersection of life begins with an eye toward God—the way each of the statements in this list does—our lives begin to more closely resemble our professed beliefs.

I urge you to type out and print these seven non-negotiables, put them in your pocket or purse and discover how often they apply to the choices you make in the course of an average day. They'll help you not just remember your need to put God first, but also see how to do it.

DISCUSS
Choose one of these non-negotiables right now, and talk about how applying it in the circumstance you are facing would make a huge difference.

PRAY
Taking turns, pray your way through these seven. Pray for your spouse as you take your turn.

Get Connected for More Information

ALONE IN THE DARK?

How long, O LORD? Will You forget me forever?
How long will You hide Your face from me?
PSALM 13:1

Some people believe the words "Christian" and "depression" should never appear in the same sentence. They believe that a person whose Bible proclaims, "The joy of the LORD is your strength" (Nehemiah 8:10), should know better than to be unhappy.

It makes you wonder, though, if that was the case with William Cowper, author of such classic hymn lyrics as "God moves in a mysterious way, His wonders to perform" and "There is a fountain filled with blood, drawn from Emmanuel's veins." Severe depression forced him early in life to abandon his career in law. If not for the patient mentorship of John Newton (composer of "Amazing Grace"), who knows how low Cowper's depression would have taken him?

Charles Spurgeon struggled mightily with depression, particularly after a false cry of "Fire!" set off a stampede in his packed-house congregation, killing several in attendance. He often talked about hearing his "own chains clank" as he delivered his sermons, comparing his feelings to a chariot stuck in the mud.

King David, we know, cried out in melancholy many times through the psalms. Paul, who wrote, "God, who comforts the depressed, comforted us by the coming of Titus" (2 Corinthians 7:6), certainly knew seasons of darkness and despair. Biblical figures such as Moses, Job and Elijah went through overwhelming valleys of doubt and fear.

So if either of you find yourself under the heavy weight of depression today, grappling to work free but not always able to win the fight, you're not alone in your struggle. Your suffering is not unknown by God. Your dark circumstances are not beyond His power to heal, restore and redeem.

As you seek God for relief, take a measure of comfort in your good company.

DISCUSS
What purpose could possibly be served by depression? Why would some of God's greatest servants be touched with it?

PRAY
Comfort one another in praying for each other, casting one another's burdens on Him, because He cares for both of you.

MY-FAULT REMORSE

Now all these things are from God, who reconciled us to Himself through Christ and gave us the ministry of reconciliation.
2 CORINTHIANS 5:18

Ken Sande, who heads up a wonderful group called Peacemaker Ministries, told me about a woman who had just found out that her husband of 20 years had been unfaithful. She clearly had biblical grounds for divorce. And she wanted one. Badly.

But the pastor who was counseling them insisted that she take some time to consider whether exercising her right for divorce was the best step to take. For several weeks they worked together, getting nowhere. The wife—the one who appeared innocent in this situation—was still seething with anger. The husband—the obvious bad guy—was clamming up and shutting down.

Stalemate.

But as the wife was completing a homework assignment for her next session, the Holy Spirit convicted her with an overwhelming sense of remorse and responsibility. Moments into the next counseling session, her body trembling, she blurted out through sobs, "It's my fault! It's all my fault! Years ago, I began pulling away from him. I set him up for this!"

Across the room, her usually stoic husband fell into sobs himself. "No! It was *my* fault! No matter what you did, I had no excuse. You cannot blame yourself for this." And in a transcendent moment of inconsolable grief, God knitted a marriage back together—through the power of confession.

Hopefully, any conflict you may be experiencing today doesn't reach anywhere close to this depth of pain and harm. But whatever it is, let's say you are the offended party; if you put both sides on the scale, your guilt load would be legitimately less than the other's. What would change in the dynamic of this disagreement if you asked God to expose the extent of your own bad attitudes, actions and responses? What would your spouse do if you took the first step toward reconciliation?

DISCUSS

What are issues that have become off-limits to discuss in your relationship? What part of them is yours to admit and confess?

PRAY

Invite God to restore His peace in your relationship.

Get Connected for More Information
http://www.familylife.com/moments/conflict

FOUL BALL

Therefore be careful how you walk, not as unwise men but as wise.
EPHESIANS 5:15

I've often wondered why more people don't get hurt by foul balls that are hit into the stands during a baseball game. You'd think it would happen almost every time, especially those line drives that carom through an entire seating section. But even on those occasions when a stray ball does leave a lump or a bruise, you can hardly blame the batter, can you? I mean, he's not out to intentionally harm anyone. It's just what happens in the flow of the game, right?

That's probably not the way Baltimore Orioles' Jay Gibbons felt not long ago when he fouled a pitch straight back over the screen. That's because this time, his wayward swing didn't threaten a nine-year-old sitting there with his cap and glove or a hot-dog vendor walking the steps or a pair of buddies taking in a game together.

No, Jay's foul ball hit his own wife right in the ribcage.

He didn't mean to. It wasn't intentional.

This story reminded me of those sarcastic remarks we sometimes let slip.

Or those little unkind things we foul off. Or those grunts we utter when we think the magazine article we're reading is much more interesting and important than what the wife is saying.

A foul ball can hurt as much as a direct hit. A fairly insignificant slight or accusation—especially when it's allowed to fester and accumulate and build on the last one—can bruise your relationship. That's why you must guard against minor, offhand offenses. Stop occasionally and go see if your words are hurting anyone—your spouse, a child or a friend.

Careless words. A lapse in judgment. Foul balls. And foul words. But whether intended or not, they can still carom with enough speed to wound and injure the ones you love the most.

DISCUSS

How do you two usually handle the little "foul tips" that occur from time to time in your relationship?

PRAY

Ask God to make you immediately aware of any offense you commit toward your spouse.

A NEW LEGACY

This book of the law shall not depart from your mouth, but you shall meditate on it day and night, so that you may be careful to do according to all that is written in it; for then you will make your way prosperous, and then you will have success.

JOSHUA 1:8

As a people, we are healthier but not happier. We are drenched in knowledge but parched for wisdom. Materially we are wealthy, but we suffer a profound poverty of the soul. The longer I live, the more I see that our nation needs a spiritual reformation in its inner spirit.

Nowhere is this more apparent than in the state of the family. The biblical values that built our great nation—once passed on from each generation to the next as a national treasure—are being questioned and dismissed. As a result, never before have we seen such deterioration in our homes:

Never before have so many children grown up in broken homes.

Never before has the definition of marriage been altered to allow for two people of the same sex.

Never before has the marriage covenant been viewed with such contempt by a generation of young people.

Never before have parents been ridiculed for seeking to raise children with biblical values.

Never before have so many Christians laughed, shrugged their shoulders or did nothing about adultery, divorce and sin.

Never before has materialism been so flagrantly embraced over relationships.

Never before has the family been in such need of *a new legacy*.

The pivotal national issue today is not crime; neither is it welfare, health care, education, politics, the economy, the media or the environment. *The pivotal issue today is the spiritual and moral condition of individual men and women, husbands and wives, mothers and fathers, and families.*

Nations are never changed until people are changed. The true hope for genuine change in the heart lies only in the life-changing power of Jesus Christ. Through Him, lives can be rebuilt. Through Him, families can be reformed.

DISCUSS

How has the deterioration of our homes affected your family? Your extended family?

PRAY

Pray that change in our country will begin with change in your lives and home.

Get Connected for More Information

http://www.familylife.com/moments/battleforfamily

FINISHING WELL

I have fought the good fight, I have finished the course, I have kept the faith.
2 TIMOTHY 4:7

Bill Bright, founder of Campus Crusade for Christ, experienced the ultimate graduation, to heaven, on July 19, 2003. And other than my parents, no person has had a greater influence on my life. My mind fails trying to lay a yardstick beside the many, many ways he shaped and influenced me.

Shortly before his homecoming, I wrote him a personal letter—a very inadequate attempt at expressing how much he meant to me. Among other things, I thanked him for the following:

- Modeling what it looks like to be a bond slave of Christ
- Constantly reminding me that our God is not small
- Having a great sense of humor and for being real
- Never thinking about quitting—*never!*
- Allowing me the freedom to disagree
- Making tough decisions
- Telling me there is no amount of money that God won't give the man who doesn't allow it to stick to his fingers
- Allowing God to use him to build a platform that so many could follow, using it to reach nations for God's glory
- Being committed to his wife, Vonette, for more than 53 years—for running the race and finishing well

Pulmonary fibrosis kept him in constant pain during his final years. Yet amazingly, these years were some of his most productive. "It's a win-win situation for me," he said. "If I live, I go on serving Him. If I die, I'm in heaven with Him."

I am a better man for having known and worked for Bill Bright for more than 30 years. How we need more friends and mentors with that kind of faith and life!

DISCUSS
Of these nine statements of Christian character, which one or two are you most eager to exemplify?

PRAY
Pray that God would grow His nature and character in you so that the first thing people see in you is your faithfulness—and your faithful Lord.

Get Connected for More Information
http://www.familylife.com/moments/mentoring

PASTOR'S HELPER

Who is weak without my being weak? Who is led into sin without my intense concern?
2 CORINTHIANS 11:29

In a famous scene from the film *Gone with the Wind*, Scarlett O'Hara searches for a doctor to help her sister-in-law, Melanie, who is about to give birth. As she weaves through stretcher after stretcher of bleeding, dying soldiers, the camera pans back to reveal a swath of misery—a huge square teeming with desperate, injured soldiers lying in the sun.

Finally she finds her friend Dr. Mead, who is exhausted from facing an endless parade of need and hopelessness. "Are you crazy?" he tells Scarlett. "I can't leave these men for a baby. They're dying. . . . Look at them, bleeding to death in front of my eyes. No chloroform, no bandages, nothing! Nothing to even ease their pain."

That scene reminds me of the day Dr. Robert Lewis, my friend and former pastor, made the startling statement that the church staff was spending more time dealing with preventing divorce, comforting those going through a divorce and helping people recover from a divorce than with all other spiritual needs and issues combined. The consequences of this "war" were littered from one end of the church to the other—marriages shot through with deception, adultery, distrust, financial woes, and bitterness. But what could our paid ministers do among so many?

October is Pastor's Appreciation Month, and you may not be formally trained as a counselor. You may not know the textbook definition for some of the crises people are dealing with. But what could you do to step in and serve your pastors, to relieve them of some of the weight and show some of the same "intense concern" that the apostle Paul describes in 2 Corinthians 11:29?

Rather than asking our pastors to do more, we need to come alongside and get involved. And not worry about getting a little blood on our hands.

DISCUSS
Are you aware of one couple nearby who may be having some trouble? How could you help them?

PRAY
Pray for your pastor, and ask God to show you the people He's already arranged for you to minister to.

Get Connected for More Information
http://www.familylife.com/moments/helpingothers

KNOWN BY NAME

The bird also has found a house, and the swallow a nest for herself,
. . . even Your altars, O LORD of hosts.
PSALM 84:3

I heard the story recently of a couple who, by their tenth anniversary, had been unable to conceive any children. Those of you who have experienced this heart-break can readily relate to the frustration they felt, the void that remained so senselessly empty in their lives.

On days when they allowed themselves to think about it, they'd ponder what they might name a child if they were ever to have one. They had always been able to settle on a boy's name, but they both had a different favorite for a girl. The wife liked the name Autumn; the husband preferred Amanda.

But still, no child came. Boy *or* girl. So they went to Plan B and decided to adopt siblings.

You can imagine how they prayed for this opportunity to develop. They asked God to work His perfect will, to bind their hearts with just the right children from just the right situation. One day the adoption agency called with the news that two sisters—ages three and five—had been relinquished by their mother. Though she wasn't a believer herself, the woman had requested that her daughters be placed with a Christian family. That had moved this couple's name to the top of the list.

When they asked the social worker to tell them more about the girls, here's what she said: "They're both green-eyed blondes. The five-year-old is named Autumn. The three-year-old is named Amanda."

How amazing it is when God mends a broken heart and parts the curtain at times, showing us beyond the shadow of a doubt that He hears our prayers and knows our hearts. If you've been praying for a similar answer to your need, know that He never loses sight of you, that He knows where you are . . . that He knows your name.

DISCUSS
Be honest about where your faith level is right now. Are you discouraged? Fearful? Encouraged?

PRAY
Even when it seems and feels like it's getting you nowhere, keep praying. Keep praying.

Get Connected for More Information
http://www.familylife.com/moments/adoption

AVOIDING THE TRAPS

You will pull me out of the net which they have secretly laid for me,
for You are my strength.
PSALM 31:4

Try to picture this scene: With 50,000 men watching intensely, a 15-year-old young man, Trent—blindfolded and barefoot—begins stepping cautiously across an outdoor stage. Before him are a dozen steel animal traps with their jaws wide open. Each is labeled with words like "peer pressure," "drugs and alcohol," "sexual immorality," "rebellion" and "pornography"—the "traps" that can easily ensnare teenagers today.

Right beside me, on the opposite end of the platform and the traps, stands the boy's father, Tom, anticipating his son's every move. After two tentative steps, the boy's third step places him directly in the path of the biggest snare on the stage—a bear trap powerful enough to absolutely crush his leg. (It had taken three grown men just to set it.)

Before his son can raise another foot, Tom yells into the microphone, "Trent, stop! Don't take another step!" Circling the traps, he positions himself in between his son and the bear trap. After whispering some instructions, he turns his back to the boy. Trent eagerly places his hands on his father's shoulders. Then slowly, they begin navigating the trap field together.

When the two finally reached me and we took the blindfold off, father and son hugged each other. Applause at this Promise Keepers event swelled to a thunderous standing ovation across the stadium. Above the roar, I shouted through the sound system, "Men, that's what God has called us to as fathers—to be there and guide our children through the traps of adolescence!"

For Tom and Trent, the trap demonstration was a setup on a stage. But for you and your teen, the traps of adolescence are all too real and treacherous. Don't allow your children to risk the journey on their own. Grab them by the hand, watch your step, and move out together. Let God guide you through.

DISCUSS
What do you not know about the traps in your teenager's world? Make plans to find out.

PRAY
Pray for God's ongoing protection over your children and for your ongoing vigilance as their parents.

PRIVILEGED PARENTS

I have no greater joy than this, to hear of my children walking in the truth.
3 JOHN 4

I didn't quite finish telling the story of what happened at the Promise Keepers event I mentioned yesterday. After we finished the demonstration with the traps, a large stream of boys (sons of the dads in attendance) began pouring into the stadium after listening to another speaker in a separate area. Their entrance was the only sound you could hear because I had asked the men to remain quiet as their sons filed in. Then these fathers began standing, baseball caps in hand, as they watched the next generation parade by in a mass of teenage energy and potential.

Once all the boys were inside, I said to the dads, "These young men are our sons, the leaders of the families of the future. Let them hear what you think of them!" I'll never forget the deafening roar that immediately erupted. Clapping. Stomping. Yelling. The enthusiastic affection cascaded down the stadium aisles for several raucous minutes. Tears of unbridled pride and joy filled the eyes of fathers throughout the stadium.

It's too bad that rearing children can't always be as exhilarating as those moments were. On most days, parenting is rather lonely by comparison. There are few cheers, mostly challenges. It's hard work and long hours with no guarantees.

But there are plenty of rewards. Nothing can compare to the joy of seeing children grow up to walk in the truth. Nothing can match the fun of having them right here in our homes, letting us feed off their creative, spontaneous humor and their raw zest for life. And nothing is as exhilarating as watching our children bravely walk around and stay out of our culture's traps and snares, advancing the banner of Jesus Christ in their generation.

It might be a good idea to give your teen a standing ovation for a choice he or she has made recently. Cheer them on.

Trust me. They *need* your cheers!

DISCUSS
What have you been forgetting to celebrate lately about your children? Celebrate it now.

PRAY
Thank God for the joy—and the journey—of parenthood.

Get Connected for More Information

FIFTEEN WAYS TO PLEASE YOUR HUSBAND

BY BARBARA RAINEY

Each of us is to please his neighbor for his good, to his edification.
ROMANS 15:2

Who is your closest neighbor? Your husband. And how can you edify (build or improve) your husband and thereby enhance his self-worth, the way the verse above instructs? By discovering—and doing—what pleases him. Here are a few ideas:

1. Write him a letter and send it to his office, or put a love note in his lunch box or his briefcase.
2. Prepare his favorite meal.
3. Arrange an evening out for just the two of you.
4. Wear his favorite dress with your hair done the way he likes it.
5. Purchase something small and frivolous for him that he won't buy himself.
6. Give him a nicely framed picture of yourself, or of you and the children, for his office.
7. Surprise him with a trip to do something he likes.
8. Put the children to bed early and prepare a candlelight dinner.
9. Do something that especially pleased him back when you were dating.
10. Pray and read the Scriptures with him daily.
11. Take walks together.
12. Keep your junk out of the garage.
13. Greet your husband warmly after work.
14. Wear his favorite negligee, or buy a new nightgown to add sizzle to your evening attire.
15. Clean out the car for him.

Sometimes the smallest gesture can make the biggest difference. Pick out something you haven't tried before. Don't give complacency a foothold in your marriage relationship.

DISCUSS

Husbands, share something your wife has done lately that has pleased you. Why was it so encouraging?

PRAY

Wives, ask God to help you think of his needs, making you sensitive to find ways that truly encourage him and put wind beneath his wings.

Get Connected for More Information
http://www.familylife.com/moments/wives

FIFTEEN WAYS TO PLEASE YOUR WIFE

How beautiful you are, my darling, how beautiful you are!
SONG OF SOLOMON 1:15

Not to be outdone by Barbara's choice selection of husband-pleasers from yesterday's reading, here are some ideas from the man's side of the equation. See what you both think about these:

1. Hug and kiss her every morning before leaving the house.
2. Go to bed at the same time she does.
3. Brush her hair while complimenting her eyes and appearance.
4. When she's studying herself in the mirror, tell her, "You are so beautiful."
5. Evict late-night television from your bedroom.
6. During mid-afternoon, call or send her an email to ask how her day's going.
7. Try your hand at making breakfast on Saturday morning.
8. Put gas in her car, vacuum the floor mats, and clean the windows.
9. Write her a short love letter. List several ways she has blessed you this year.
10. Resurrect common courtesies: Hold the car door open. Offer her your arm.
11. Put the toilet seat down.
12. If you hear her engaged in a tough situation, compliment the way she handled it.
13. When you're together in a crowd, find a way to brag on her.
14. Help her put the kids to bed.
15. Pray with her every day. Every day!

If this sounds like a lot of work or if it's out of character for the kind of guy you are, do it anyway. You'll get better at it. And I guarantee your wife will love you for it.

DISCUSS
Wives, what is something your husband has done to please you lately? Why was it so encouraging?

PRAY
Husbands, expect God to give you creativity and sensitivity as you focus your affection and attention on your wife.

FULL STEAM AHEAD

Commit your works to the LORD and your plans will be established.
PROVERBS 16:3

When young William Borden—heir to the Borden dairy fortune—graduated from high school more than 100 years ago, his father gave him three things for his graduation gift: enough money for a trip around the world, a servant to accompany him and a brand-new Bible. So at just 16 years of age, William traveled throughout Africa, Asia and the Middle East, experiencing a mix of cultures and people.

But the combination of seeing human suffering while simultaneously acquainting himself with the Scriptures caused William's heart to be stirred with a calling from God. He committed his life to prepare for the mission field, and he wrote two words in the back of his Bible: "No reserve."

Returning home, he enrolled at Yale University, where his spiritual devotion and his ministry to the poor and destitute became well known among the students, faculty and community in New Haven. And though he was courted by both Wall Street and the family business upon graduation, he stayed firm in his desire to serve God overseas. During this time he wrote two additional words in the back of his Bible: "No retreat."

While traveling through Egypt on his way to a mission in China, William contracted a form of spinal meningitis. Within a month, he died. He was only 25. Weeks later, as his father was going through William's things, he came across the Bible he had given his son as a high-school graduation present. The list of short handwritten statements in the back now included a third: "No regrets."

No reserve. No retreat. No regrets. Those six words should challenge all of us to be radical followers of Christ. We should live purposefully in our marriages and families, investing ourselves wholeheartedly in the primary people God has given us to love and to lead. Always forward. Always faithful.

No going back.

DISCUSS
What areas of your life and marriage are crying out for these words (and actions) of resolve right now?

PRAY
Pray that you will both be radical followers of Christ, who don't hold back, don't go back and don't look back with any regrets.

DON'T WALK ON BY

All Scripture is inspired by God and profitable for teaching, for reproof,
for correction, for training in righteousness.
2 TIMOTHY 3:16

General Norman Schwarzkopf, the commander of operations for Desert Shield and Desert Storm in the early 1990s, exercised this simple premise of authority: *A leader never walks by a mistake.*

I think he's got a point, not only in how to lead a military unit, but also in how we raise our children. Barbara and I have often talked about how much easier it would be to ignore our children's shortcomings. We naturally wish to avoid the discomfort of confronting and correcting their selfish, sinful ways.

Some parents default to a soft, indulgent love, thinking their kids will grow up fine on an exclusive, pain-free diet of praise and permission. But the concept of "reproof" that Paul used in the above certainly suggests pain. "Reproof" means pointing out a wrong, bringing someone to a place where he or she can admit what he or she has done. And there's nearly always an element of pain involved in doing that.

Yet as writer James Litter has said, "One thought driven home is better than three left on base." That's really your assignment as parents: Drive home the key issues that need to be laid bare and exposed if your children are going to finish growing up. You must help them embrace these lessons while they're young so that they won't have to learn them in a much more painful way later on as adults.

Our culture today is rushed and weary. You may have so much going on that it's difficult to slow down and address a defect in your child's character. But if you've taken on the mantle of parenthood, you've also taken on the responsibility of bringing occasional pain into the life of each of your children—even as painful as it can be on you as a parent.

DISCUSS

Of course, you can't discipline for *everything*. But be honest: Are there some issues in your children's lives that you may be deliberately overlooking? Evaluate one another as parents in this area.

PRAY

Pray that God will bring conviction for any areas where you are allowing fear, laziness or indifference to determine your parenting style. Ask for strength.

Get Connected for More Information
http://www.familylife.com/moments/discipline

DOLLARS TO DOUGHNUTS

If we hope for what we do not see, with perseverance we wait eagerly for it.
ROMANS 8:25

Not long after I graduated from the University of Arkansas, a female friend came to me for counsel. She was dating a young man who happened to be my best friend. And though she wanted to marry him, he was uncertain about committing to her.

I had doubts, too, about whether they should marry. So I told her a parable I had recently heard, about a boy who'd been playing in his front yard when his uncle stopped by to visit. After talking for a bit, the man sprung a philosophical question on his five-year-old nephew: "If I gave you the choice, would you like a dime today or a dollar next week?"

The boy stood and thought. A dollar could buy him that rubber ball he'd seen at the corner store, but a "dime today" could mean a package of potato chips for his hungry late-afternoon stomach. So he took the dime, bought his snack and went home happy.

But about a week later, a buddy passed his house bouncing a new rubber ball. The boy then thought about his uncle's offer. The chips were a distant memory, along with the dime that had seemed so valuable at the moment. If only he'd been willing to wait for that rubber ball later on.

There's a lot of truth to that story, you know. Sometimes we're so glamorized by the glint and gleam of the one thing we want right *now* that we're not willing to wait and trust God for the something better He planned for us down the line.

I should know. Because just over a year later, this female friend of mine decided to marry someone else—my best friend's best friend.

Me.

And even though there's been a lot of inflation since then, Barbara says she got her dollar!

DISCUSS
Does the parable of the "dime now or a dollar later" seem relevant to any decisions you are facing right now? Decisions that you need to trust that God knows what He's doing?

PRAY
Ask for God's wisdom and discernment to help you rightly value each new opportunity.

Get Connected for More Information
http://www.familylife.com/moments/relationshipwithgod

SOCCER-MOM SYNDROME

BY BARBARA RAINEY

O LORD, You have searched me and known me. . . . [You] are intimately
acquainted with all my ways.
PSALM 139:1-3

Over the years, Dennis and I have attended hundreds of events involving our children. Baseball games. Volleyball matches. Cheerleading events. Gymnastics competitions. Evangelistic outreaches. Music recitals. Sometimes they all seemed like a blur! But there is one trap we worked hard to avoid: the Soccer-Mom Syndrome—the belief that attending your children's activities automatically means you're involved in their lives.

In reality, involvement means much more. It means crawling inside the head and heart of each of your kids. Finding out what he or she is thinking and feeling. Diving into the often turbulent waves caused by uncertain emotions.

This can be scary and uncomfortable at times. That's why so many parents run from real heart-and-soul involvement with their children and withdraw to much safer territory.

The sobering truth is that you can be in the same house or the same gym with your children but be clueless about what's really going on in their lives. Yet connecting can be something as simple as walking into each child's bedroom, sitting down and asking a few questions. It can be a quick outing for a milkshake or a hamburger. It can be stepping out on the porch together on a Sunday afternoon, just to check his or her plans for the week or ask if he or she needs to talk, to let your child know you're there to listen.

When you pursue this kind of heart-to-heart relationship with your children, you're actually following God's example. Wouldn't it be wonderful (someday) if your kids could say of you, "My parents have 'searched me and known me.' They know not just 'when I sit down and when I rise up,' but they also 'understand my thought' and are 'intimately acquainted' with who I am and what I'm like"?

That's the definition of an involved parent. Not just watching how well they turn a somersault.

DISCUSS

Ask yourselves this question: "Are we just going and doing, or are we living and listening?"

PRAY

Pray for ways not just to *get* there, but also to *be* there for your kids.

Get Connected for More Information
http://www.familylife.com/moments/involvement

SHOW UP, LORD

Ah Lord GOD! . . . Nothing is too difficult for You.
JEREMIAH 32:17

How many times have you prayed for God to "show up"—that He would reveal His purpose and power and presence in an unmistakable way?

Some people might say, "Aw, that's just the way Christians talk. No one really expects God to 'show up' or do anything." Well, it's not just talk if God can actually do it. Look at the context for today's verse:

Ah Lord GOD! Behold, You have made the heavens and the earth by Your great power and by Your outstretched arm! Nothing is too difficult for You, who shows lovingkindness to thousands, but repays the iniquity of fathers into the bosom of their children after them, O great and mighty God. The LORD of hosts is His name; great in counsel and mighty in deed, whose eyes are open to all the ways of the sons of men, giving to everyone according to his ways and according to the fruit of his deeds (Jeremiah 32:17-19).

This passage tells me that God can break through the most desperate situations in your lives and transform them into trophies of His grace. He can intervene in the lives of your friends and family members—even those who are running hard from Him right now—and turn their whole world around.

Sometimes we grow weary of praying for God to act. When an answer to prayer doesn't immediately come, we can become impatient. We're tempted to quit after a while. But never misjudge God's silence as inactivity. He is working and waiting for the right time to show up, to leave no doubt that He's the One who makes all the difference (see also Isaiah 64:4).

Persevere in prayer.

DISCUSS

In what areas do you need God to intervene in your life? Who in your family needs God to show up?

PRAY

Pray for God to show up in your life and in the lives of the people you're praying for—that He would make His presence real in your lives.

PRAYER AT ITS SIMPLEST

It is He who sits above the circle of the earth, . . .
who stretches out the heavens like a curtain.
ISAIAH 40:22

Ask almost any gathering of Christians to name one thing they wish they knew more about and prayer would be near the top of every list. I understand that. Yet perhaps in longing for those far-off secrets of spiritual success, we overlook prayer's simplicity and beauty. Perhaps in searching for answers, we forget that prayer in its simplest form is a reverent conversation with God.

One of my favorite places to go on our little piece of property in the woods is the picnic table down by our fire pit. I often find myself there, not on the bench, but sitting on the table itself—looking out at the sky, the treetops, the hills in the distance. Usually within the first minute or two of leaning back on my open palms, I find myself reflecting upon God, His greatness and the beauty of His creation. It's easy to see from my picnic table: "In the beginning God created the heavens and the earth" (Genesis 1:1). We are His. We are here only because . . . He is.

It's so simple, isn't it? The perspective from my picnic table says that it is.

Perhaps it's because all we see sometimes are sidewalks and skyscrapers. Shopping centers and new construction. Office walls and commuter traffic. In the midst of a noisy, hectic life, we don't notice the pinks and purples of a morning sunrise. Our prayer life takes the staccato form of our non-stop lifestyle, with all the depth of a coffee-break conversation.

But what if you knew that all it took to kick-start your prayer experience with God was to locate one of His billowy clouds floating effortlessly across a city skyline . . . and begin to remember who made it . . . and who made you . . . and who has the affairs of your marriage and family safely in the grasp of His loving, caring arms?

DISCUSS
Do you make prayer harder than it is? What helps remind you most often that God is there?

PRAY
Pray simply but deeply. Yes, you can do both at the same time, you know.

Get Connected for More Information

CHILDLIKE FAITH

Whoever then humbles himself as this child, he is the greatest
in the kingdom of heaven.
MATTHEW 18:4

Thomas Epting's young body began showing its first signs of leukemia when he was only two years old. By age four, there was no doubt. And after the disease had ebbed and resurfaced once again at age seven, his family understood that Thomas's childhood was not going to be normal . . . at least not in the way our world defines "normal."

They were right. But not just because of the complications and chemo treatments.

How normal is it for a young boy to never complain about shot needles and hospital stays—not even once? How normal is it to hear a child say, after being told of his need for yet another procedure, "I just want God to be glorified in this, and I don't want to embarrass Him"?

Thomas was a remarkable boy, indeed.

There was a period of years when Thomas's physical suffering was graciously relieved by the hand of God. His leukemia was gone. Undetectable. He used the time to read every book written by A. W. Tozer. He wrote profound Christian poetry. He took the SAT at 13 and outscored his parents' high-school marks.

But at 15, he received bad news. Not one but five malignant, inoperable brain tumors had been seen on an X-ray. The setback sent his mom and dad into a parent's tailspin.

But his mom, Amy, remembers a day, barely a month before his death, when she was talking with Thomas about how she should pray for him. He flashed those twinkling eyes at her and said, "Mom, you think too much! God sent His Son to die for me! If He never did anything else for me, sending Jesus is enough for me to praise Him as long as I live. Just focus on that, Mom, and quit worrying about the tumors!"

Give me Thomas Epting's brand of normal. I could use some of it today. Couldn't you?

DISCUSS
Apply Thomas's wisdom to one of your own struggles right now.

PRAY
Pray as Thomas did: "Sending Jesus to die for my sins is enough for me to praise You as long as I live."

TRASH TALKING

His song will be with me in the night, a prayer to the God of my life.
PSALM 42:8

Barbara and I diligently tried to teach our children about God and His Word. We studied the Scriptures with them. We prayed with them. We dialogued often about life issues, casting them in terms of biblical worldview and morality. And yet, some of the most encouraging moments came when we saw God Himself reaching out to them.

One story stands out. Our son Samuel went through some tough times as a teenager when he was stricken with a rare neurological disorder that slowly robbed him of his athletic abilities. Boys he once trounced on his way to becoming one of the top-ranked tennis players in the state were now beating him and laughing at his failure.

On another occasion, he was trying to add some memory to my computer and ended up erasing the hard drive and eliminating a substantial chunk of written material that I had created. He felt terrible about that. Soon after, the engine burned out on his truck . . . not just one time, but *three* times! It was one trial after another, over and over. I felt like I'd lost all ability to encourage him. My words, though true, sounded so hollow sometimes.

But one day as he was taking out the trash at home, he slung one of the cans into place at the top of the hill, and out of it—incredibly—floated a crumpled piece of paper that fell to the ground at his feet. On it were written all the words to the Twila Paris worship song "God Is in Control."

It was just what Samuel needed to hear.

When Samuel told me about this experience, it was a powerful and emotional moment for me as a parent. I knew God was reaching down and inviting Samuel to trust Him and have a relationship with Him.

God is in control, indeed.

DISCUSS
How are you teaching your children to believe the truth about Him and trust Him with their lives?

PRAY
Pray that your children will increasingly know and trust Jesus as *their* Lord, the lover of *their* souls.

TOUGH TIMES, TOGETHER

*We who are strong ought to bear the weaknesses of those
without strength and not just please ourselves.*
ROMANS 15:1

Life in a fallen world can be tough. But what makes suffering and hardship
worse is that they often turn us *against* each other rather than toward each other.
Here are a few ways to keep that from happening as you negotiate the common
speed bumps and detours of life:

Give your spouse time and freedom to process trials differently. Fight the urge to
discount each other's emotions or grow impatient with the time it's taking
your spouse to deal with something. Some of us are quick to move on. Some
process slowly and are more introspective. Give your spouse freedom to not be
like you.

*Recognize the temptation to withdraw from each other during periods of intense chal-
lenges.* As a result, you end up thinking your spouse doesn't understand you or
isn't taking the tough time seriously enough, which makes you want to pull
back even more.

Respond to trials by embracing God's perspective of suffering. Search the Scriptures for God's counsel and point of view. Verses like "In everything give
thanks" (1 Thessalonians 5:18) help to strengthen you through seasons of
suffering by reminding you that God is good and He is in control.

Remember that your mate is never your enemy. As my friend Dr. Dan Allender
says, your spouse is your "intimate ally," a fellow burden bearer for a difficult time.

If the burden or suffering persists, seek outside help. If you feel as if you're slipping
off into a deep ditch as a couple, don't wait until you have all four wheels
stuck before you seek help. Find godly counsel by calling a mature mentoring
couple, your pastor or a biblical counselor to gain some traction.

DISCUSS

Talk about the way each of you responds to periods of suffering, stress or a
major challenge—and why. What do you need the other to understand about
how you process difficulty?

PRAY

Take some time to pray for one another around an issue you are facing. Express
your trust in God to guide, strengthen and see you through . . . together.

Get Connected for More Information
http://www.familylife.com/moments/suffering

VALLEY VIEWS

*Even though I walk through the valley of the shadow of death,
I fear no evil, for You are with me.*
PSALM 23:4

I know a man whose son has battled a serious illness his entire life. His whole family has been shaped around the requirements of this boy's chronic care. Never a full night's sleep. Never a trip where he and his wife could totally unwind. Always the possibility of a bad-news phone call and another long stay in the hospital.

When I asked him what this odyssey has really been like for him and his wife, he said, "Dennis, when you face an ordeal like this as a couple, there is an intimacy with your spouse that grows incredibly sweet, incredibly deep. God has taught us some things about Himself—such profound ways of trusting Him and knowing Him and walking with Him—that I really wouldn't trade it for a life of ease."

Can you believe that? This man ought to feel cheated and angry. But he has a smile on his face because he can look back and see where God has taken him and his wife.

It's so easy for us as couples to have those dejected conversations: "Life is horrible . . . God has forgotten us . . . our Christian faith doesn't seem to work anymore." That's why Barbara and I try to frequently look back over the dozen or more serious trials we've endured in our marriage, just to get a new perspective. From that vantage point, you can see progress—the things God has done, the intimacy He's grown in you, the trust, the faith, the spiritual muscle.

Why not pull off to the side of the road sometime. Look back into the valley. See how far you've come. And be glad He's given you each other for the journey.

DISCUSS
Which difficulties have forced you to grow the most? How much stronger are you now than you were then?

PRAY
Thank God for using crises—the valleys you would never choose to enter on our own—as places to grow us, even when they feel like they're destroying us.

MAN TO MAN

I have directed you in the way of wisdom; I have led you in upright paths.
PROVERBS 4:11

When each of our sons, Benjamin and Samuel, graduated from high school, I treated them to one of the most unusual breakfasts they had ever enjoyed.

It was a simple meal held in a local hotel meeting room. Also in attendance were some men who wanted to help Barbara and me send each of these young men off to college with some godly advice. Man to man.

Each man talked about what he wished someone had shared with him before he started college. They talked frankly about the challenges and temptations our boys would face, and they exhorted them to grow spiritually, intellectually and morally.

At Samuel's breakfast, for example, Bob Lepine, my friend and co-host on *FamilyLife Today*, recalled that when he attended college, his goal was to earn a high grade-point average. But he challenged Samuel to focus on growing in character and wisdom. Bob said that after college, "people look at the mark of a man's life, what his reputation is in the community. Grade points aren't the issue. The issue is learning what God has you there to learn."

Another man in the room that day was Bill Bright, president and founder of Campus Crusade for Christ. "I would like to recommend more than anything else, Samuel, that you master this Holy Word," he said. "Every day I get on my knees to read this Word, because it was inspired by God. It is living."

Now, 10 years later, I'm encouraged to see how both of my sons took the advice of those godly men. Third John 1:4 says, "I have no greater joy than this, to hear of my children walking in the truth." From this dad's standpoint, my heart soars to see what fine men Ben and Samuel have become.

DISCUSS

Who are some friends you can use to speak truth into the lives of your children and encourage them to stand strong and follow Christ?

PRAY

Ask God for a handful of adults who will build into the lives of each of your children.

WHY NOT NOW?

Behold, now is "the acceptable time," behold, now is "the day of salvation."
2 CORINTHIANS 6:2

R. V. Brown is a giant of a man, a four-year college football letterman who received Christ while still on campus and was turned loose with a fire to introduce his Savior to the youth of America. But one night, this man with the bulging biceps and the evangelist's heart woke up in a sweat, worried sick about the condition of his dad's soul.

Willie "Fish" Brown had been a model of faithfulness and sacrifice. The son of a slave, he had shielded his family from the bitterness felt by so many of his race because of the discrimination they had endured throughout their lives. Instead—illiterate and uneducated though he was—he had imparted to his 17 children the qualities of hard work, generosity, deep love for wife and family, and kindness to fellow men.

Still, R. V. didn't know if his father was a Christian or not. So on his next visit home, he sat down with his dad—who was then over 100 years old—and asked him if he was assured of going to heaven when he died. Willie said he wasn't.

So R. V. opened the Word and showed his father what was required of a man to embrace the salvation of God. He got down on his knees with his aged father, led him to the base of the cross and opened for him the throne room of heaven.

That's not easy to do. Parents, grandparents, brothers and sisters, aunts, uncles and cousins are often the hardest ones for us to engage in spiritual conversation or ask eternal questions. But the risk of offending them is miniscule compared to the issue of their eternal destiny. Humbly engage in a conversation. God in His grace may use you to break through to even a 100-year-old heart!

DISCUSS
Do you have parents and family members who are not followers of Christ, who are unsure of where they'll spend eternity?

PRAY
Just pray for an opportunity to talk in as non-threatening a way as possible. Then expect God to open the door for that conversation. Know He'll be there to help you.

Get Connected for More Information
http://www.familylife.com/moments/helpingothers

ONE AGAINST NONE

That their hearts may be encouraged, having been knit together in love.
COLOSSIANS 2:2

One of our favorite games that our children absolutely loved playing was Reverse Hide and Seek. We'd turn out all the lights in our house. Then, instead of having one person look for everyone else, one person hid and all the others would try to find him or her. When you located the hidden person, you would quietly slip into the same space to hide with him or her. The game would keep going until only one person was left seeking all the others in a pitch black, totally silent house.

It wasn't easy being the last man standing. Swiftly, the house would become very quiet and still. All you could hear was the sound of your own panting and your appeals for everyone to show themselves. But usually, the giggles and snickers of seven people huddling in the bathtub or under a table would give away their location. When the last person finally joined the crowd, it was a huge relief—almost like a family reunion, full of laughter, hugs and silly recaps of the highlights.

What a picture of how marriage and family relationships ought to be. Rather than allowing anyone to isolate himself or herself, we should seek each other out, huddle together and reconfirm the fact that we're sharing life together. No one's going it alone. Not in this house.

So I'm appointing you today to the office of Seeker. I challenge you to commit yourself to watching for signs of isolation in each other and in your children. Sure, there are times when we all need our space—the opportunity to pray and process things. But always stay sensitive to the first feelings of distance that creep into your relationship.

Don't let it stay quiet for long. Go on the prowl. Look behind the curtains. Pursue one another and God, together.

DISCUSS
Is there any hiding going on in your home? Any isolation? Talk about how you should seek out one another.

PRAY
Pray that you will know when your spouse or a child is withdrawing into isolation and that you will know what to do.

BACK ON LINE

Therefore, confess your sins to one another, and pray for one another that you may be healed.
JAMES 5:16

Every time couples get together for one of our Weekend to Remember conferences, the Lord does something special . . . and almost always leaves us with stories like this one:

I had been leading an online extramarital affair with someone from college for almost three years. My husband had no idea. But one night I told him I didn't love him anymore and that I was finished. I was numb inside and felt very much alone. I just wanted out. We began to seek help from our church counseling ministry, and although I went, I was still living a lie.

One day my husband came home excited that he had won a registration to a Weekend to Remember conference. I didn't want to go. If I went, it meant pretending that I wanted to work on my marriage. But through the weekend, I began to feel a softening in my heart for my marriage and the husband God had gifted me with.

It wasn't until six months later that all the deception was on the table and my sin was out. I felt so released from my bondage and free to truly love my husband as God intended. So we are working through the hurt of my affair and through all the other issues that brought us to that point in our marriage. We are on the road to recovery. I believe that with the blessing of your conference last winter, my marriage took a U-turn.

I want to thank you so much for the hard work you do and for the love you have for hurting marriages. We are attending the conference again this November. And this time I am so excited!

So are we.

DISCUSS

When was the last time you got away with your spouse for a weekend? Take a look at your calendar and discuss a weekend getaway like this. It may be time for a 12,000 mile, 12-month wheel alignment.

PRAY

Bring to God any outstanding balance (unreconciled issues) in your relationship today, and let Him get to work reconciling the differences.

Get Connected for More Information
http://www.familylife.com/moments/marriagerelationship

COMEBACK OF THE YEAR

Therefore, since we have this ministry, as we received mercy, we do not lose heart.
2 CORINTHIANS 4:1

It's easy to become discouraged when we fail. It's easy to lose heart and stop trying. That's why I love stories like this one:

> For many years Bob Brenly was the starting catcher for the San Francisco Giants. But because of a last-minute lineup change on this very date in 1986, he was pressed into duty at third base. Everything was going fine . . . until the fourth inning.
>
> That's when he committed not one, not two, not three, but a record-tying *four errors* in the same inning—including two on the same play. In fact, he almost had a fifth error. "I missed a head-high line drive that tipped off the webbing of my glove and went into left field," Brenly said. "If they hadn't called that one a hit, my name would have stood alone in the record books."
>
> The home crowd booed. His coaches and teammates avoided even looking at him. But his manager left him in the game. Good thing.
>
> When Bob came up to bat the following inning, he smashed a solo home run. His next at-bat was a two-run single in the seventh to tie the game. And with his final plate appearance of the day in the ninth inning, he stroked a game-winning homer. His manager later commented, "This man deserves to be the Comeback Player of the Year for this game alone."

If you've been trying to branch out of the ordinary—at home, at work, in your walk with Jesus Christ—don't let a few setbacks get you down. Keep swinging for the fences. And if it's your spouse who's failing . . . like the manager, keep on believing in your teammate.

DISCUSS

Talk about any recent failures in your life or your spouse's life. Discuss how you can encourage each other to stay with it.

PRAY

Thank God for His Holy Spirit, who comforts us, continually invites us to greater challenges and empowers us to keep stepping out in faith. Pray for the perseverance to press on despite setbacks in life, at work and in your marriage and family.

Get Connected for More Information
http://www.familylife.com/moments/commitment

CONVERSATION STARTERS

You will do well to send them on their way in a manner worthy of God.
3 JOHN 6

Between interaction with the culture, media and their peers, this year your teenagers will be exposed to one hundred thousand messages about sex. How many of these will come from you?

That's the question Sharon Hersh posed on one of our *FamilyLife Today* broadcasts recently, and it is a good one. Sex is talked about incessantly in the predominant media channels that today's teens are wired into. It's almost impossible to avoid. It's also a frequent topic for discussion in hallways, in Internet chat rooms, in emails and on the phone. And although this generation has become more comfortable talking about this subject than any generation before them, parents still find it nearly impossible to bring up.

But we'd better—because 99 percent of what they're hearing in those one hundred thousand messages is wrong!

I assure you, most of the mistakes we made in this area were not because we were too involved. Rather, they occurred when we made some dangerous assumptions that our children's convictions and standards were more firmly in place than we thought. We also erred in thinking that peers from excellent Christian homes embraced biblical convictions as well. In the words of our teens, "NOT!"

A letter we received from a young woman, who became pregnant as a teenager, cemented this resolve in us. I hope it will in you, as well. After telling her story, she wrote, "Parents, talk to your kids. Let them get angry. I would rather my children say, 'I hate you and your rules' than say later, 'Why didn't you tell me I was headed for trouble?'"

Please don't sit back and let your children negotiate these sexual traps alone. They need you to guide them through. They need to hear the truth—from you—not just once, but repeatedly.

DISCUSS

What do you think you know about your children's sexual standards? What will you do to find out for sure?

PRAY

Pray for God's protection of your children's sexual purity and for their convictions, and ask for the courage to repeatedly break through the conversation barrier.

Get Connected for More Information
http://www.familylife.com/moments/purity

ENCOURAGING THE STRONG

*Mighty men of valor, men trained for war, who could handle shield
and spear, and whose faces were like the faces of lions.*

1 CHRONICLES 12:8

Recently I had the distinct honor and privilege of meeting with a high-ranking officer at the Pentagon in Washington. What was planned as a 15-minute appointment turned into more like 45. He told me that two of his sons were currently serving in the same unit in Iraq. A war takes on a different face when you talk to dads and moms whose sons and daughters are in harm's way every day. He said he starts his day by reviewing a list of names of the men and women who have died in battle.

We closed our time by praying for this officer and his family. As I prepared to leave—after praying with him for his work and the safety of his family—he handed me a pair of bronze medallions. On one side were these four statements that are especially meaningful to soldiers:

> Mission first.
> Never accept defeat.
> Never quit.
> Never leave a fallen comrade.

As he pressed the medallions into my palm, he left me with instructions to give each one to a soldier who I met during my travels. "Tell him not to lose heart and to be courageous."

About a month later, I had my first opportunity to accept his commission, placing one of these medallions into the hand of an officer at one of our Weekend to Remember conferences. He was preparing to return to Baghdad for the seventh time, and tears welled in my eyes as I thanked him for protecting our country, my family, my kids and my grandkids.

As you have the opportunity, I hope you'll encourage these brave men and women as well.

DISCUSS

How do the four admonishments on the medallions pertain to your own wars at home, at work and in the prevailing culture?

PRAY

Pray for our soldiers, sailors, airmen, Marines and Coast Guardsmen who are out there right now, sacrificing all to honor our nation and keep us safe.

Get Connected for More Information

http://www.familylife.com/moments/military

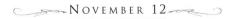
MEDIA RELATIONS

If there is any excellence and if anything worthy of praise, dwell on these things.
PHILIPPIANS 4:8

Some time ago, I was working at home during a weekday and flipped on the television to check the weather. What popped on instead was one of those midday talk shows about some sleazy topic.

It shocked me. I couldn't believe what I was seeing.

In fact, I dropped what I was doing and called the director of the local station that was airing the program. I was careful to be very kind and not beat the guy up verbally. He listened to me for a few minutes but gave me little in the way of a satisfactory answer for why he would promote such questionable content. So I followed up my telephone complaint with a letter, challenging him to do the right thing as a business leader, as a father, as a man morally responsible for what he broadcast into the community. Here's some of what he wrote back:

Many of the programs aired on television are not to the taste of my family either, and we, like you, choose not to watch them. However, one of the things I fear most of all in any form of communication is censorship, and the Nielsen ratings are a true test of what most viewers want or do not want to watch.

As weak (and utterly predictable) as his response was, I fear that too many of us are no different. We may disagree with the shows our teenagers like to watch or the music they listen to or the movies they enjoy. But we don't want to cause too much of a fuss or appear too overbearing. We're not sure it's a good way to spend our parental capital.

But the shows that reach out to our kids through the television or computer screens are shaping their minds, defining what's normal, deceiving their hearts. It's you—not Nielsen—who knows what's right.

DISCUSS
Evaluate the viewing habits of your family and children. Is there something that concerns you?

PRAY
Knowing He has placed you in this position of responsibility, ask for both the courage and tools to address the problem.

Get Connected for More Information
http://www.familylife.com/moments/mediachoices

COMFORT FOOD

I have remembered Your ordinances from of old, O Lord, and comfort myself.
PSALM 119:52

We live in a world with constant turmoil, with terrorist threats and with head-strong dictators forming a constant cloud in the back of our minds. But it won't always be like this.

A day is coming when we will be free from all fear, totally out of harm's way. That's a promise of God shouted from one of those Old Testament outposts we don't find ourselves in very often—the book of Micah, chapter 4, verses 1 to 5:

> It will come about in the last days that the mountain of the Lord will be established as the chief of the mountains. It will be raised above the hills, and the peoples will stream to it.
>
> Many nations will come and say, "Come and let us go up to the mountain of the Lord and to the house of the God of Jacob, that He may teach us about His ways and that we may walk in His paths." For from Zion will go forth the law, even the word of the Lord from Jerusalem.
>
> And He will judge between many peoples and render decisions for mighty, distant nations. Then they will hammer their swords into plowshares and their spears into pruning hooks; nation will not lift up sword against nation, and never again will they train for war.
>
> Each of them will sit under his own vine and under his fig tree, with no one to make him afraid, for the mouth of the Lord of hosts has spoken. Though all the peoples walk each in the name of his god, as for us, we will walk in the name of the Lord our God forever and ever.

Couldn't have said it better myself.
Are you ready?

DISCUSS

What are your and your family's greatest fears and anxieties? How does this passage speak to them?

PRAY

Pray for a deeper trust in God, a deeper sense of impending eternity and a deeper patience in how you live in the meantime.

Get Connected for More Information
http://www.familylife.com/moments/suffering

PARTY DOWN?

I will also put an end to the arrogance of the proud.
ISAIAH 13:11

After deciding on a ballerina theme for her daughter's sixth birthday party, a young mother drove all over town to find little dancers for the cake. She even added 50 little Beefeaters (those fancy-dressed guards) around the edges, layering them in white icing and peppermint trim.

Only one catch: The kids at the party wouldn't eat it. They wanted to play.

This comes from the "disaster story" file gathered by a parent's group in St. Paul, Minnesota, that is trying to curb the runaway epidemic of outlandish birthday parties for kids.

There are more: A one-year-old whose gift opening lasted more than two hours (she slept through most of it). Seven-year-olds picked up in stretch limos. A six-year-old who took one look at the contents of his gift bag and declared, "This is a rip-off!"

Listen, I'm all for having fun and making memories. The Raineys have always been high on celebrations and traditions. We love turning milestones into unforgettable moments. But I find myself applauding this group's ideas for ramping down the competition, stress and showmanship of children's party planning. In some areas of the country, it's way over the top!

The group suggests, for example, holding parties without gift bags for everyone who attends. (As one mom said, "Do they really need another pencil, another rubber ball, another whistle?") They also endorse inviting kids only, not their parents, and letting them just go outside and play rather than trying to orchestrate fun with wildly elaborate games and activities.

Happiness is being together as family and friends, not feeling the pressure to turn your backyard into a five-star amusement park.

Freeze Tag, anyone? Simon Says?

DISCUSS

In what other ways do you feel the pressure to compete with other families or to outdo others?

PRAY

Ask the Lord to keep you content with simple pleasures.

SHE FED HER HUSBAND DOG FOOD

To sum up, all of you be harmonious . . . kindhearted, and humble in spirit.
1 PETER 3:8

This is no joke. Real people. Real struggles. Real reality.

Brett returned home from work one night, took a bite from the meal his wife, Tina, had prepared, and declared, "This tastes like dog food!"

"Fine," Tina snapped back. "You don't have to eat it!"

The next night Brett took a couple bites from dinner and practically choked. "What on earth is this?" he said.

"Last night you said my meal tasted like dog food," Tina replied. "So tonight I decided not to waste my time making anything special for you. I just fed you dog food!"

Many would have said this was a marriage without hope. Brett and Tina were typical of many couples today—struggling through life with no game plan for how they could be successful in their marriage.

They decided to attend a Weekend to Remember conference because someone gave them a free registration. What did they have to lose?

Midway through the weekend, Brett recommitted his life to Jesus Christ. For Tina it was a different experience. She disagreed with many of the messages she heard.

On the final morning, she stormed out and demanded that they leave. Brett drove Tina home and then returned to the conference by himself.

Over the next few months, Brett began to demonstrate to Tina that he was a changed man. He applied some of the lessons he learned at the conference and gradually began to win Tina over through real love. Tina's heart softened, and eventually she invited Jesus Christ to be her Savior and the Lord of her life.

A year after they first attended the marriage conference, they came back, walking hand in hand. They still struggled, but now they possessed a relationship with the God who designed marriage in the first place.

Brett has learned to appreciate Tina. And her cooking.

DISCUSS
If God could change a marriage like this, what could He change in your marriage?

PRAY
Ask that God will give you the power to truly live in harmony with each other, in the spirit of 1 Peter 3:8-9.

Get Connected for More Information
http://www.familylife.com/moments/conflict

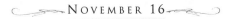
OPEN ARMS

He makes the barren woman abide in the house as a joyful mother of children.
PSALM 113:9

Recently a young man named Ryan shared with me this very personal story:

When my sister was born, there were problems during my mom's pregnancy that made her unable to have more children. So my parents decided to pray for a miracle. They got down on their knees and prayed at the side of their bed every night for an entire year, but nothing happened. One year turned into two. Two quickly turned into three. Three turned into four. Four years of praying. Four years of hurting. Still, nothing happened.

Right about that time, there was a young couple in high school. They had been dating for a while, but the girl said, "This isn't the guy I want to marry, and if I'm not going to marry him, I don't want to keep dating him." So they broke up. But a short time later, she found out she was pregnant with his baby. She didn't know what to do—didn't know if she should tell her parents, didn't want them to be upset or mad or disappointed.

Finally, she just couldn't take it anymore. She broke down one night and told them. They didn't know what to do either. They already had four kids. One more mouth wasn't going to help things. . . . They started meeting with a counselor, looking at options, shedding a lot of tears, and trying to decide what to do.

But the Lord took my parents' inability to have more kids, and He took that young couple's high-school indiscretion, and He meshed them together. On August 31, 1970, my parents, Jim and Shirley, brought me home from an adoption center.

That's how I became a Dobson.

That's the power of prayer. That's the power of adoption. And that's the power of a family.

DISCUSS
Infertility strikes so close to the heart, but talk about adoption is its redemptive response.

PRAY
Ask God to increasingly make Christian families like yours available and open—havens of hope to millions of orphans. And if you know an infertile couple, please pray for them.

Get Connected for More Information

http://www.familylife.com/moments/adoption

UNLIKELY HEROES

This matter is your responsibility, but we will be with you; be courageous and act.
EZRA 10:4

I used yesterday's reading to let Jim and Shirley Dobson's son, Ryan, tell his own adoption story. Stories like this are so rich with the loving sovereignty of God—how He takes two needy situations and unites them in one holy purpose. For His glory.

We must never forget that the choice of a young, frightened girl to stand in the face of a personal storm and believe God for something better is an act of sheer courage. Being pregnant and unmarried, though sadly not as uncommon as it used to be, still invites sideways looks and quick glances at the young girl's ring finger. To carry a child to term instead of choosing abortion, to endure the feelings of shame that rise up as a young girl begins to show, is an unavoidable embarrassment like few others.

Ryan, reflecting on the experience of his own birth mother, said, "I talk to adopted kids all the time who think somehow they've been abandoned, and I say, 'No, no, you have no idea what it means to go through a pregnancy.' I've seen my wife go through it. I've seen how tired she is. And to think that a young 17-year-old girl did that for me, not being married—and on top of it all gave me up to give me a better life, never to see the rewards of it . . ."

Yes, Ryan, it's truly amazing.

Perhaps you're watching an unmarried pregnancy up close in your neighborhood, your church, your extended family . . . maybe even in your own. I pray that you will be the one who offers encouragement, strengthening her in the heroic decision to choose life for her child.

DISCUSS

What is your typical response to seeing a young, unmarried, very pregnant girl? Talk about how the Christian community can celebrate the protection of unborn life with a young girl who's made a mistake.

PRAY

Pray for the Christian community to welcome those who've made mistakes, offer the healing balm of love and celebrate the heroism of those who choose life and not death.

Get Connected for More Information
http://www.familylife.com/moments/adoption

MASTER BUILDERS

By Barbara Rainey

The words of wise men are like goads, and masters of these collections are like well-driven nails.

ECCLESIASTES 12:11

When your marriage relationship hits a trouble spot, it may be difficult to find much to praise about each other. Yet those are the times we need praise the most. So I urge you to initiate praising your spouse. Make it a deliberate effort. Bring the power of positive words to him or her in the midst of trouble.

In the verse above, the author (who may have been Solomon) gave some very descriptive characteristics of well-spoken words. When you choose to encourage and praise your spouse, your words carry the ability to prod, or goad, him or her in the right direction. And notice the result: Those words become like "well-driven nails," the kind that secure all types of building projects.

In the hands of God, your words can be used like nails to secure your mate's self-esteem. Your wise and truthful words bring perspective to his or her life, to your relationship and to your situation as a couple. They make finding solutions to your problems a real possibility.

You may be asking, "What if all this praise goes to my spouse's head? Won't he become prideful?" There's a difference between truthful praise and flattery. Flattery gratifies a person's vanity, but praise is based on a person's character and deeds. When you truthfully praise and applaud your spouse's choices, you reinforce the value of building godly character.

Paul exhorts us, "Speak truth each one of you with his neighbor" (Ephesians 4:25). A keyword in that phrase is "truth," which is the only real standard for bringing value to another person. Truth results in assurance and security, in worth and value. It becomes the compass during the storm that confidently steers us in the right direction.

So praise your spouse in all situations, using wisdom to meet the need of the moment, speaking truthfully to help construct character. Your words of affirmation can help rebuild what life has torn apart.

DISCUSS

What's been blocking the flow of affirming words in your relationship? Share three real compliments with each other.

PRAY

Pray for a heart that longs to build up, not tear down.

Get Connected for More Information

http://www.familylife.com/moments/communication

SEXUAL STANDARDS

I want you to be wise in what is good and innocent in what is evil.
ROMANS 16:19

Have you ever had that wave of paralyzing dread—the one where you fear you'll come off looking and feeling like a hypocrite if you challenge your child to uphold standards you didn't keep too well yourself when you were younger?

For many, this feeling is especially acute when talking to children about sexual behavior. I believe this is one of the ways the enemy attempts to silence parents. But don't allow past failures to prevent you from calling your child to the standard of God's Word.

After all, every one of us has lied, haven't we? Yet we still teach our children to tell the truth. When it comes to talking frankly with your preteens and teenagers about what God expects of them sexually, you dare not let the fear of an embarrassing question force you into silence.

Most children won't ask whether or not you were a virgin prior to marriage. But even if they do—and even if you weren't—you could answer, "That's a good question, and someday when you're an adult, I want to answer you more fully. But for now, that information is off-limits." If your child isn't satisfied and persists in digging further, you may want to admit, "Yes, I made some mistakes I really regret," but not go into details.

Children need role models, especially in their parents. And it's better if they don't know certain things about you when they're too young to understand. When your child is grown, in the context of an adult relationship, you can decide how much you want to reveal. But for now, don't let vivid descriptions become stumbling blocks in their lives and in your discussions.

Keep the subject on God's standards and on His desire for their welfare and purity. They need to hear from you what God expects of them.

DISCUSS

Talk about how you can challenge your children to embrace biblical standards. Also discuss how you will discuss past mistakes with them.

PRAY

Pray for the courage to instruct with God's standards, even when it's uncomfortable and potentially embarrassing.

PRAYER COVERING

The report of your obedience has reached to all.
ROMANS 16:19

Another inspiring story that arose from the life of young Thomas Epting, the boy I told you about in the November 1 reading, began with a batch of prayer cards his family printed to hand out in the community. A total stranger offered to produce 50,000 cards at no charge, each featuring a picture of Thomas and describing what he was up against and how he was handling it with praise and perseverance.

One day near the end of Thomas's life, his mom, Amy, wondered why, with all of these prayer cards in circulation and with so many people interceding on Thomas's behalf, the Lord had not yet brought the healing they so desperately wanted. Thomas replied, "Mom, God is using those prayer cards, just not the way you want Him to."

Those words came rushing back to mind one day when Amy's telephone rang not long after Thomas had died. The woman on the other end of the line said she had been sitting in her attorney's office, where she had gone to file for divorce, and had caught sight of one of Thomas's prayer cards lying on a table in the waiting area. She couldn't believe what she was reading—a young teenage boy fighting for survival but more full of faith than most people who have their whole lives ahead of them.

This woman walked out of her lawyer's office that day, not with divorce papers, but with a new resolve to make her marriage work. God had used a sick child's faith to spread healing ointment on a sick marriage—the same God who assured us in His Word that all things are possible.

Especially when it comes to prayer.

DISCUSS

Is there someone you know who needs to hear Thomas's story? And what are your deepest, biggest personal prayer concerns today?

PRAY

Never stop praying. Only eternity will reveal all God has done with your prayers.

SEAGOING GRATITUDE

BY BARBARA RAINEY

Those who go down to the sea in ships, . . . they have seen the works of the LORD.
PSALM 107:23-24

One song that really gets me in the mood for Thanksgiving—even though it's not really a Thanksgiving song—is the official U.S. Navy hymn: "Eternal Father, Strong to Save." I didn't grow up hearing it (my father was in the Army, after all), but it has become one of those captivating songs that reminds me of God's protection in times of great stress and worry.

If you saw the film *The Perfect Storm,* you may remember hearing this song at the end of that movie. Its roots actually go back to the mid-1800s, when William Whiting wrote these words to encourage a student who was traveling by ship from Great Britain to America and was paralyzed with fear that the vessel would sink and that he would be drowned.

Eternal Father, strong to save
Whose arm hath bound the restless wave,
Who bid'st the mighty ocean deep
Its own appointed limits keep;
Oh hear us when we cry to Thee,
For those in peril on the sea!

Some years later, it seems, an American sailor heard this song while on duty in England and brought it back to the Naval Academy choir, where it's still sung today at the close of Sunday services.

I'm sure your year has had its share of "peril on the sea" in one form or another—health scares or job insecurities, money troubles or family tensions, close calls or lingering pressures. Like a stormy tempest on the ocean, some things are simply more powerful than we are. But whether sailor or not, we all need to know that nothing is more powerful than the One who measures our path and guards our way—the One who calms the seas—the One we praise in this season of Thanksgiving.

DISCUSS

What peril has God brought you out of—or is even now seeing you through?

PRAY

Thank God for His great and mighty power in the midst of our perfectly harrowing storms.

Get Connected for More Information

http://www.familylife.com/moments/holidays

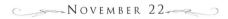
GIVING THANKS

BY BARBARA RAINEY

It is good to give thanks to the LORD and to sing praises to Your name, O Most High.
PSALM 92:1

As Psalm 92 tells us, "It is good to give thanks to the LORD . . . to declare Your lovingkindness in the morning and Your faithfulness by night." With a little effort, you can make Thanksgiving a cherished family time devoted to thanking God for what He has done in your lives.

One tradition we've kept for years is to have each family member write five things for which he or she is thankful. On our plates are five kernels of corn—a reminder of the Pilgrims' daily ration during one of their first difficult winters. Before we eat, we pass a basket around the table five times, and each person places one kernel of corn at a time into the basket and tells one thing he or she is thankful for.

Here are some of the things our children wrote one year:

- "I'm thankful for being able to have a family."
- "I'm thankful Ashley got to come home from college for Thanksgiving."
- "I'm thankful for God in my life."
- "I'm thankful for my ministry at my high school."
- "I'm thankful for my sisters and all they've taught me about relationships."
- "I'm thankful I got to shoot a deer!"
- "I'm thankful for a great brother."

Dennis and I were thrilled to hear the kids actually thank God *for each other*! After so many years of sibling rivalry, they were finally beginning to show each other the affection we hoped would continue throughout their lives.

That year we also were touched by something our son Samuel wrote: "I'm thankful for my muscular dystrophy." He had been diagnosed with the disease earlier in the year, and we had been through some wrenching months. Thanking God was a big step of faith for him. And it provided another sign that our children were learning the true spirit of Thanksgiving—a heart of gratitude that gives thanks in *all* things.

DISCUSS

How has God worked in your lives this past year?

PRAY

Spend time thanking God for His love, His provision and His work in your lives.

THANKSGIVING DAY AFTER DAY

BY BARBARA RAINEY

He who offers a sacrifice of thanksgiving honors Me.
PSALM 50:23

Has it ever seemed surprising to you that God made the Israelites wander in the wilderness for 40 years just for grumbling and complaining? My kids may have spent 30 minutes in their rooms for griping, but 40 years? That's some severe discipline!

One thing is crystal clear from this biblical account: *God is obviously not pleased with grumbling, ungrateful hearts.* And we should not tolerate grumbling either—in ourselves or in our children.

Being grateful is a choice that we readily and ritually express on Thanksgiving Day. But what do we do on other days of the year when the mood is less festive or the atmosphere is more ordinary?

I like the contented way the Pilgrims approached life. They did not allow their feelings or circumstances to determine whether or not they would exercise gratitude and thanksgiving. They believed that God was in control—"providence," they called it. Following this belief to its logical conclusion, they responded to challenges with a perspective that said, "God has allowed this for our good." They chose to believe—rightly so—that their dependence on a holy, faithful God was well placed and that even though much was against them, there was always much more for which to be grateful.

Developing a heart of gratitude is essential to growing a stronger faith. As John Piper stated in his book *A Godward Life,* "If we do not believe that we are deeply dependent on God for all we have or hope to have, the very spring of gratitude and faith runs dry."

Make the choice today to take your eyes off yourself and your circumstances, gratefully acknowledging who God is and what He is doing. Deny yourself the right to complain, embracing instead the deep-seated joy of thanksgiving . . . in all things.

A grateful heart pleases God.

DISCUSS

How would a more thankful spirit alter your approach to the situations you're facing as a family? Make a list together of some things you need to be grateful for right now.

PRAY

"Bless the LORD, O my soul, and all that is within me, bless His holy name" (Psalm 103:1).

Get Connected for More Information
http://www.familylife.com/moments/holidays

STEPPING ON TOES

His father had never crossed him at any time by asking, "Why have you done so?"
1 KINGS 1:6

Maybe he was too busy. Maybe he didn't feel like his own sinful past gave him the right to enforce morality. For whatever reason, the verse above tells us that David didn't train his son Adonijah to become a man. He didn't correct him but instead spoiled him. And it cost them both dearly.

Barbara and I learned a lot of lessons with our own six kids. These action points will serve you well along the way:

1. *Ask questions.* Ask who they've been talking to on the phone. Find out who their friends are. When they are teenagers, make them tell you where they went on their dates and who they hung out with. Don't be bashful about checking up on them.
2. *Avoid isolation.* As children grow older, they start wanting more space, which is fine within limits. But they'll push you away altogether if you let them. What they need is not distance but a relationship with wise counselors—their parents.
3. *Believe in them.* The teenage years are especially clouded with self-doubt and insecurities, and the social pecking order in junior high and high school can be brutal. Express your belief and confidence in your children as often as you can.
4. *Establish boundaries.* Determine where they can go. When they need to be home. What movies they can watch. What they can wear. God has given you the assignment of drawing lines and boxes—and to *in*spect what you *ex*pect.
5. *Confront sin.* Kids need parents who will restrain them from evil, loving them enough to watch carefully and discipline faithfully.

David lost his son because he refused to make him face the consequences of his choices. Don't let it happen in your house.

DISCUSS
In your family, which of the five action points is a strength? A weakness? Talk about how you are going to team up to do a better job as a couple.

PRAY
Ask for the courage to keep pressing in, even when your kids push back. Pray for consistency to correct and train, even when they don't appear to be listening.

Get Connected for More Information
http://www.familylife.com/moments/biblicalparenting

CRUCIBLE

Although He was a Son, He learned obedience from the things which He suffered.
HEBREWS 5:8

It's easy to focus on the struggles in our lives and not recognize what God may be doing. I've always thought this historical summary I read from Ted Engstrom, who headed Youth for Christ and World Vision in his fruitful lifetime, was encouraging:

> Cripple a man, and you have Sir Walter Scott. Lock him in a prison cell, and you have John Bunyan. Bury him in the snows of Valley Forge, and you have George Washington. Raise him in abject poverty, and you have Abraham Lincoln.
>
> Strike him down with infantile paralysis, and he becomes Franklin Delano Roosevelt. Burn him so severely in a schoolhouse fire that doctors say he'll never walk again, and you have Glenn Cunningham, who set the world record in 1934 by running a mile in four minutes and six seconds.
>
> Call him a slow learner, retarded, write him off as unable to be educated, and you have Albert Einstein. Have him or her born black in a society filled with racial discrimination, and you have Booker T. Washington, Harriet Tubman, Marian Anderson, George Washington Carver, and Martin Luther King.

We could add many others to that list. People like Corrie ten Boom, Dietrich Bonhoeffer and Aleksandr Solzhenitsyn, whose incarceration in a concentration camp or prison cell became their classroom. Or Joni Eareckson Tada, whose wheelchair has become her platform for amazing ministry. I could tell of others whose names you wouldn't know, just as you could add names from your own life. Each is proof of what Charles Spurgeon said: "The Lord gets His best soldiers out of the highlands of affliction."

Could it be that even now—on the front lines of your current ordeal—God is making you more battle-worthy than ever before?

DISCUSS

In what ways has God used trials and adversity to make you stronger, wiser and more usable? Or have you allowed hardship to merely harden you into stubbornness and bitterness?

PRAY

Ask God to use the "highlands of affliction" in your life to mold you into a good soldier. And ask Him to do the same with your children.

Get Connected for More Information
http://www.familylife.com/moments/suffering

THAT LOVIN' FEELING

May he kiss me with the kisses of his mouth! For your love is better than wine.
SONG OF SOLOMON 1:2

When Barbara and I were working on our book *Rekindling the Romance*, I went online and typed "romance" in the Google search engine. Guess how many of the top 10 sites listed were for married couples? One!

Makes you wonder if romance has become an endangered experience after marriage. Is it like the way the late comedian Minnie Pearl put it? "Gettin' married's a lot like gettin' into a tub of hot water," she said. "After you get used to it, it ain't so hot."

Believe me, it doesn't have to be that way. Sure, there are a lot of barriers to romance in your marriage—primarily the hectic pace of your lives. But you married each other to become intimate partners, not traffic controllers, and that requires time just being together.

Barbara and I certainly felt the tug in our own lives when our schedules got crowded and the kids started adding up. With six children constantly chirping with needs, we found that we had to plan regular date nights just to get away by ourselves. Frankly, if we hadn't had this touch point in our lives, our marriage could have easily dissolved into two high-performance people doing their *own* thing. Existing individually without really sharing life.

When our children were little, we would either get a babysitter or we'd plan a fun date at home after the kids had gone to bed. Sometimes we'd create our own restaurant atmosphere, complete with candlelight and a gourmet meal we'd prepared together. When we finally sat down to eat, we'd just focus on one another.

Don't let the romance slip out of your life. It isn't dependent on the newness of your marriage but only on the freshness of your heart, the tenacious desire not to let the crush of life keep you from having a crush on each other.

DISCUSS
How could a weekly date night become a reality for you and your spouse?

PRAY
Ask the Lord to help you both for the creativity and for the perseverance to keep the home fires burning.

RUT BUSTERS

Come, my beloved, let us go out into the country. . . . There I will give you my love.
SONG OF SOLOMON 7:11-12

I don't know what "routine" means to you, but this was ours when the kids were still at home:

Up before sunrise, have a few words together, maybe enjoy a little breakfast or a cup of coffee, exchange a kiss on the cheek and it's goodbye for the day.

I take kids to school and then drive on to the office, while Barbara stays home to get busy with her own work. She deals with endless issues involving the children—school, laundry, chores, errands, doctors and conflicts. Meanwhile, I juggle budgets and meetings and problem solving all day long.

Our paths cross again around 6 P.M., after both of us have emptied about 90 percent of our tanks. We take a glance at the news, eat dinner, flip through the mail, pay some bills, clean up the dishes, help with school work. Then an hour of getting the kids to bed. Barbara tries to get in some reading before sleep overtakes her.

That's the drill.

But there is no imagination in that. I'm not saying that a typical day can routinely accommodate wild swings of adventure, but I'll tell you this (if you haven't noticed already): A routine is just a few letters away from being short-ened to a rut. A rut you will never escape unless you make a deliberate effort to do so. And I guarantee that your "rut" will never be on the same page as "romance" in your marital dictionary.

When the TV show *Desperate Housewives* first began its iconic rise into our national awareness, *Newsweek* did a feature article on the phenomenon. I remem-ber one of the women who was interviewed lamenting, "Don't you remember the time when he kissed you with a kiss that launched a thousand kisses?"

Is there ever room for *that* in the middle of your routine?

DISCUSS

Ready to spice up the routine? How would you do it if you could? (You can, you know.)

PRAY

Ask the Creator for a delightful dose of His creativity to give you a break from the routine.

Get Connected for More Information
http://www.familylife.com/moments/marriagerelationship

KEEPING COVENANT

A cord of three strands is not quickly torn apart.
ECCLESIASTES 4:12

Modern society is still suffering from the sickness of the "Me Generation," which has contaminated the covenant of marriage. The selfish Me-Gen person says in effect, "When marriage serves my purpose, I'm on board. But when it ceases to make me happy, when it's too much effort, when the unexpected shows up and creates additional pressure, I'm outta here." Some leave physically; others leave emotionally and withdraw.

But those who do have forgotten three basic truths about their commitment to each other:

1. *Marriage is a covenant between three, not two.* On our wedding day, I entered into a covenant both with Barbara and with God. Our marriage is not a contract but a sacred cord of three strands that will not be easily broken.
2. *Marriage vows require us to forgive each other.* No marriage is a perpetual walk through the daisies. There will be unmet expectations, unwise decisions, troubles with schedules and finances, and other unexpected pressures that will rattle our relationship until we think it's about to fall apart. But when hurt and disappointment come, our vows demand that we forgive one another. This is not an optional accessory. It is the life and breath of our marriage.
3. *Marriage vows are enduring.* When the pressure becomes relentless and intense—when the cultural voices around us entice us to look out only for ourselves and quit—our vows shout, "DON'T!" (Or, as my kids say, "Deal with it.")

Quitting on your marriage may temporarily reduce the pressure you feel, but I promise you that a broken marriage and family will add truckloads of new pressures over a lifetime. It takes courage to do what you know is right. Remaining devoted to your spouse becomes your living testimony to the faithfulness of God and the strength of your marriage covenant.

DISCUSS
Think of the marriages you've seen fail. To what extent did selfishness play a part in the breakup of those relationships?

PRAY
Pray that you will always love as God loves, forgive as He forgives and endure as He endures.

Get Connected for More Information
http://www.familylife.com/moments/commitment

Pride, Prodigals and Holy Scars

For we all stumble in many ways.
James 3:2

When two parents set out to raise their children, it's easy to begin with the thought, *We can do a better job at this than everybody else.* Despite our inexperience, we believe that by mixing in ample amounts of prayer, Scripture memory, family devotions, worldview teaching and church attendance, we can almost guarantee our children will turn out the way we want them to. Put the right stuff in, we'll get the right stuff out.

There's a term for this kind of attitude, however: "spiritual pride." I know, because Barbara and I felt the same way when we started out on our parenting journey.

But we learned one thing really quickly about children: If you want a guarantee, buy a new set of tires or a car battery . . . because children don't come with *any* guarantees. Being a parent may be the greatest risk we take in our lifetimes.

Ask those who've had a prodigal child come through their home. Ask us. We'll tell you.

But we can also tell you something else: God is sovereign. He is more than able to turn your children's lives around. As you release your children to make their own decisions, you may worry that their wounds will leave a permanent mark, disfiguring their lives forever. Yes, sin does have consequences. But as my friend Dan Jarrell says, "God delights in taking those wounds and turning them into holy scars that are useful for His purposes."

After all, the perfect Father, God, had a couple of children Himself who didn't fare too well in the Garden. He's had a lot of others along the way who've messed up pretty badly, as well. So don't lose heart. God can heal wounds and turn them into "holy scars" that declare God's grace, mercy and purposes.

Discuss
Think of a prodigal that God has rescued for His purposes. What can you learn from this person's story?

Pray
Pray for the prodigals you know . . . that God will restore them in His time. Pray, too, that your children will learn to trust God without having to become a prodigal.

Get Connected for More Information
http://www.familylife.com/moments/teens

SEXUAL HYPOCRISY

Among you there must not be even a hint of sexual immorality . . .
because these are improper for God's holy people.
EPHESIANS 5:3, *NIV*

When Stacey avoids fatty foods, she's being health conscious. When she stays away from alcohol, she's being responsible and resisting her impulses. For all these she is endorsed for keeping long-term goals in mind instead of giving in to peer pressure and immediate gratification.

But if she makes a conscious decision to delay sexual activity, she's described as being "not sexually active"—and given no praise or endorsement.

These startlingly honest words are from the author of *Unprotected: A Campus Psychiatrist Reveals How Political Correctness in Her Profession Endangers Every Student*, a book ascribed to an anonymous campus physician proclaiming truth in all its common-sense starkness. The author is simply asking why a medical world so concerned about bicycle safety and tanning-bed exposure and regular exercise has so little interest in discouraging a behavior whose participants are *three times* more likely to be depressed or attempt suicide than those who abstain. Not until sexual activity has resulted in a sexually transmitted disease or an unwanted pregnancy, the author writes, does the university medical establishment get involved—usually by scheduling an abortion or beginning an antibiotic regimen.

It's outrageous. It's absurd. But honest accounts like this are helpful in reminding us that our world is indeed sexually deceived. Satan has strung together one victory after another in creating a culture with the lowest standards of purity. By devaluing marriage and family, he is deadening the hearts of a generation, turning their attentions entirely on themselves . . . and away from God and His design.

It's past time for parents to reject passivity in this area and get actively involved in helping their preteens and teenagers stay as far away from danger as possible. The stakes are too high to sit quietly on the sidelines and say nothing. With prayer and God's guidance and grace, this is a winnable war.

DISCUSS
Sex education is more about character than human reproduction. How do you intend to teach your children about self-control and godly obedience?

PRAY
While sinking God's Word deep into the hearts of your children, pray hard for their protection.

Get Connected for More Information
http://www.familylife.com/moments/purity

QUIET DOWN

But Jesus Himself would often slip away to the wilderness to pray.
LUKE 5:16

Did you know there are cultures in the world that don't have a word for "minute" or "hour"? They simply have no need or desire to measure time in such short increments. Nor do they attempt to maximize every second of every day. Filling their lives to the brink would be unthinkable.

Sound too third-worldish to you? Isn't it easy to see how such words are not necessary in places where people grow their own food and rarely venture beyond their own village?

I'm not suggesting that we all move into the woods and live off the land. But I am encouraging you to consider the benefits of pulling the throttle back just a notch and embracing a more contemplative lifestyle. When you allow yourself time for creative solitude, you can see God at work and begin to rediscover life in all its richness. When you give yourself the necessary time and space to seek clarity, gain perspective and ponder decisions, you find more to savor, enjoy and appreciate.

As I reflect on these two different approaches to life—the rushed and the restful—I force myself to ask, How did Jesus live? Was He frantic or steady? Was He checking the sundial every few minutes, wishing He could cut some time off His commute to the next city? Or was He able to stop and tend to the needs around Him?

Jesus had more pressure on Him than any of us can fathom. His own disciples were always peppering Him with questions. The Pharisees wanted Him dead. The crowds wanted Him king. Many pressed against Him, wanting to be healed.

Yet He got alone to pray. To think. To be strengthened. He sought His Father and enjoyed Him in the quiet moments of life.

DISCUSS
What is one thing you could change in order to carve out more time to rest? Talk about how you use Sunday, the day of rest, as a couple.

PRAY
Ask the Lord to start you on a serious six-month quest toward a quieter heart. Let Him show you what could be eliminated to open up time with Him.

JUST SAY NO

BY BARBARA RAINEY

*Which one of you, when he wants to build a tower,
does not first sit down and calculate the cost?*
LUKE 14:28

One of the main causes of the pressure that invades our lives is our unwillingness to discard *optional responsibilities*—not because they're a waste of time, but simply because they distract us from the main goals for our family and marriage.

I remember being at my children's school one day, talking with other moms about plans for the coming year. The woman leading the discussion said, "We need some of you to sign up for substitute teaching, to help out on days when faculty members need to be out."

Normally I would have been quick to volunteer. Nothing comes much easier for me than taking on more than I can handle! But on that day, I did not raise my hand.

Every good reason for volunteering popped into my head: (1) I'd be helping the teacher; (2) I'd get to know some of the other students in the class; (3) I'd be supporting my school and could keep better tabs on what's going on.

But at that time, I knew my plate was already more than full. Just then, the woman next to me, whose hand had been one of the first to shoot up, looked over at me, laughed and said, "I just haven't learned to say no yet."

We feel such a pull to be involved in anything that sounds reasonably worthwhile or wins us outside approval. But when people have asked Dennis and me how we do it all—especially back when our home was full of six active children—we have responded, "We *don't* do it all."

"No" has been one of the most liberating words we've ever used.

DISCUSS
How often do you exercise the word "no"? Talk about how you can protect one another by discussing an opportunity *before* you respond. Being accountable to each other for decisions you make is not easy, but it builds oneness.

PRAY
Ask God for clarity in decisions—and the courage to know what to say yes to and what to say no to.

FOUR PLACES AT ONCE

There is a proper time and procedure for every delight.
ECCLESIASTES 8:6

If you were to point your car southwest of Cortez, Colorado, drive exactly 38 miles along Highway 160 and then hang a right on Four Corners Monument Road, in about a half mile you'd run into the only spot in America where you can be in four states at the same time: the intersection of Arizona, Colorado, New Mexico and Utah. It's out in the middle of an empty desert, surrounded by dust, rocks and boulders.

But that doesn't stop upwards of 2,000 people a day from visiting Four Corners and waiting in line just for the thrill of having their picture taken standing in four states at once. Truly the American way, huh—trying to be four places at one time!

Truth be told, it's a picture of the way many of us elect to live our lives. We are constantly pulled in several different directions. Our pressure-filled, rush-rush, hurried lifestyle has a way of leaving us winded, dazed and addicted to the next item on our activity list.

It leaves us little time for serious spiritual reflection. Little time for anything more than snap judgments. Little time to share our dreams with each other as a couple. Little sense of where we've been and where we're going.

What's more, I fear that by crowding out any room for meaningful communication, original thought or spiritual insight in our family schedules, we're fueling in our children a raw addiction to activity, constant motion, continuous noise and endless sensory stimulation.

I urge you to stop and check the speed limit on this road you're on. Imagine a life that allows for real living . . . the kind you'll never find at Four Corners.

DISCUSS
What cutbacks and other restrictions could you impose on yourselves that would make your lives dramatically more manageable three to six months from now? Start by finding one thing you'll say no to.

PRAY
Ask God to give you both the tenacity and the wisdom to build some margin into your lives and family.

UP, UP AND AWAY

From the end of the earth I call to You when my heart is faint.
PSALM 61:2

Ever since Larry Walters was a kid, he had a dream. It was not a strange dream to a young boy letting his imagination run wild, but it certainly seemed strange when, as a 33-year-old man, he actually took a shot at it.

His dream reached fulfillment one morning when he strapped an aluminum folding chair to 45 weather balloons he had inflated the night before. With a half dozen friends helping him stay tethered, he donned a parachute and strapped himself in for what he hoped would be a short ride.

Just him, his lawn chair and a clear blue sky. That was his dream.

As soon as his friends let go of their safety lines, however, the main tether securing his chair to the ground snapped. Minutes later, Larry and his floating chair had zoomed to 16,000 feet above sea level! The Los Angeles International airport tower started getting calls from jet pilots saying they had spotted a flying lawn chair!

Have you ever felt that way? One minute you are bobbing along, pretty sure you can handle all your various responsibilities and any possible contingencies. But suddenly, without warning, surprise interruptions and your fragmented schedule jerk you off the ground, sending you to great heights of stress and desperation.

Larry's story had a happy ending. Taking out his air pistol, he shot out several of the weather balloons in an attempt to get his out-of-control lawn chair headed back toward Earth. As he neared the ground, his ropes tangled in a power line and he ended up dangling only five feet off the earth.

Perhaps his actions provide one solution for us as we contemplate our busy schedules. What activities can we eliminate? What can we say no to?

DISCUSS
Are you in this kind of pressure pattern right now? What can you eliminate from your jam-packed schedule in the short term? Long term?

PRAY
Ask God for the wisdom to avoid heading knowingly into unnecessary stress. Or perhaps for the wisdom (and the courage) to see your way out.

Get Connected for More Information
http://www.familylife.com/moments/stress

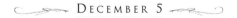

BALANCED THINKING

BY BARBARA RAINEY

Though your beginning was insignificant, yet your end will increase greatly.
JOB 8:7

A lot of moms, especially those with young children, ask me, "How can you balance making time to be with your kids when there are so many other tasks to do?" I think the answer lies in understanding the word "balance."

I think many mothers misunderstand what balance really looks like. I like to think of it like riding a bicycle. The only time a person on a bike can have it perfectly balanced is when the person is not riding at all but straddling the bicycle with both feet on the ground! When riding the bike, however, there are constant movements to the right and left, back and forth, dozens of muscles working in concert to stay upright and keep from crashing. Sometimes there are sudden swerves to miss a rock or a limb on the road.

Parenting is a lot like that.

I think moms (and dads) need to let themselves off the hook a little and realize that true balance can only be seen by looking at the overall ride. What matters is the sum total of what you've done over time, the choices you make for the important things that balance the mundane things of life.

For instance, your house may be a mess all week before you can take time on Saturday to re-create order. All week long you've berated yourself for letting the house get out of control. But look at things from a bigger perspective—did you accomplish something significant in your family because you used your time in a different way? Weigh the important choices with people against the more mundane choices with tasks, and you may see that you did in fact achieve overall balance.

DISCUSS

When do you feel the most out of balance? What kinds of choices encourage balance in your lives? Talk about how you can help each other daily and weekly.

PRAY

Pray for God's perspective regarding the truly important, because that always leads to balance.

ANTICIPATION

My beloved responded and said to me,
"Arise, my darling, my beautiful one, and come along."
SONG OF SOLOMON 2:10

We all know how easily boredom can slip into a marriage relationship. It can start soon after the honeymoon. All the emotion, passion, love and commitment between two people can steadily fade until they end up totally isolated from one another. Boredom and isolation are pandemic in marriages today.

One way to rebuild romantic energy is through the art of anticipation. This comes from taking a page out of Solomon's romantic songbook: Invest time in thinking about the things that fuel passion in your spouse and in making him or her eager to return your love. It's about injecting the element of surprise back into your relationship.

One of the most meaningful examples of this for me was the year Barbara gave me some very special gifts during the two weeks leading up to Christmas, each of them based on the familiar "Twelve Days of Christmas" song. She didn't give them to me in the day, however, but in the night. They were expressions of tenderness and affirmation toward me that communicated her love in a way only she could do as my wife.

I have never looked forward to going to bed each night like I did at that Christmas!

But, men, this works both ways. You need to take the time to think about what communicates love to your wife, to bust out of your ruts and pursue her in a way that surprises and delights her, as well. It doesn't have to be expensive or elaborate. It just needs to be you, thinking ahead, staying in tune with who she is as a woman—anticipating her anticipating you.

DISCUSS

What limits you from putting fun and energy into your relationship? Talk about the need to build anticipation into your marriage and how you will share that responsibility.

PRAY

Pray that no aspect of your life will become dull and cheerless, losing all the energy and spiritual spontaneity, which Christ enjoys adding to our relationships.

WORDS TO LIVE BY

Your word I have treasured in my heart, that I may not sin against You.
PSALM 119:11

At first, this may seem like just another story about the power of temptation, especially sexual temptation. In reality, however, it's a story about the power of God . . . especially the power of His Word.

Chuck Swindoll, the well-known pastor and Bible teacher, recalls a lonely night he spent in Canada years ago. He had been gone from home for more than a week, and his weariness was mounting. After finishing dinner alone, he went to the elevator to go to his room, and two young women got on with him. He pushed the sixth-floor button and then asked, "What floor for you, ladies?" They slyly answered, "Six is as good as any for us. Have any plans for tonight?"

Talking about this later, Chuck described what he felt at the moment: "We were all alone in an elevator. In Canada. I was flattered, to be honest, since most folks don't usually mistake me for Robert Redford. These women were available and I was lonely. I had a significant decision to make. The bait had been dropped."

But in those heart-pounding seconds as the elevator made its ascent, Chuck was surprised at the first things to flash through his mind. His wife and four children? His reputation? His risk of being seen? No, not at first.

His first thoughts were the words of Galatians 6:7: "Whatever a man sows, this he will also reap." And Ephesians 6:11: "Put on the full armor of God, so that you will be able to stand firm against the schemes of the devil." And Romans 6:11: "Consider yourselves to be dead to sin, but alive to God in Christ Jesus."

As Chuck recalled, "The memorized Word of God flew to my rescue, right on time."

You never know when temptation will strike. But when you know the Word of God, you don't really have to.

DISCUSS
Talk about the place of the Scriptures in your daily life. How could it be a bigger part? What's one verse you could memorize right now?

PRAY
Pray for one another to stand firm against the lures of the world, the flesh and the devil.

Get Connected for More Information
http://www.familylife.com/moments/remptation

BANK BREAKERS

Instruct them to do good, to be rich in good works, to be generous and ready to share.
1 TIMOTHY 6:18

If you could leave each of your children one million dollars as an inheritance, would you?

I imagine that for most of us, our first response to this question would be favorable. After all, the Bible says, "A good man leaves an inheritance to his children's children" (Proverbs 13:22). But there's more to blessing our kids than leaving behind large quantities of money for them. In fact, far too many adults who receive an inheritance windfall act like lottery winners, unable to handle the pressure and temptation of having too much all at once.

So perhaps this would be a good time to ensure that the financial priorities and perspectives you're handing down to your children are anchored in a biblical foundation. Teach them:

1. *God owns it all.* Some in the Christian community have taught their children that the tithe (10 percent) is the Lord's, but the other 90 percent is theirs to spend as they please. Our children need to learn that money is the EKG of our hearts—a track record of what we value.
2. *Giving is the privilege and the responsibility for every follower of Christ.* There's more than one way to instruct your children to give. My dad used to sit down at our dinner table and make out his check for the church every Sunday. He never said a word to me about giving, but he modeled how to give. Our children need to see us setting aside portions of our income to help Kingdom causes and needy people. Allowing them to participate in these decisions offers them hands-on, generational training in how good it feels to give.

Leaving your children an inheritance is more than just giving them money. Give and train them with the ultimate inheritance: God's perspective on money.

DISCUSS
How does your checkbook reflect your true values that you will pass on to your children? Talk about how well you are doing in passing on God's perspective on money, giving and wealth.

PRAY
Pray that you will never feel ownership, only *stewardship*, of the money that God entrusts to you.

 Get Connected for More Information
http://www.familylife.com/moments/giving

SHARED SACRIFICE

Sitting down, He called the twelve and said to them,
"If anyone wants to be first, he shall be last of all and servant of all."
MARK 9:35

Serving does not come naturally in the Rainey family DNA.

Selfishness does.

When our children were small, we gave them chores to teach them to serve one another. Chores included setting the table, loading the dishwasher, putting the silverware away, taking out the trash and helping sweep the floor.

Naturally, this led to some of our biggest battles with our children. Chores undone, half done, poorly done. Chores done with a crummy attitude. Chores done in anger. Children who disappeared during a chore. In fact, at one point all six disappeared at the same time! We thought the rapture had occurred! Teaching servanthood made us feel like a failure on many occasions.

I remember one specific occasion when I felt desperate to teach our children the importance of serving others. We seated our children in chairs outside on our deck, and I filled a big bowl full of warm water, donned a towel and knelt down and washed their feet. One by one I washed their feet, sharing how the God of the Universe, the Savior of the world, did the same thing with His disciples. We wanted them to have a visual picture of Jesus' words from today's Scripture: "If anyone wants to be first, he shall be last of all and servant of all."

Teaching servanthood in our families seems to be a lost art today. To revive it in your home, you may want to manufacture situations in which sharing and teamwork are required: family yard projects, helping each other clean rooms, sharing responsibility for household chores, and so on.

Also, designate certain items such as games or recreational equipment for multi-person use only. Obviously, these suggestions may end up creating additional conflict, but in the meantime all of this will help break down the fortresses of me-centered, arrogant selfishness in your home.

DISCUSS
How could you teach the importance of servanthood in your family?

PRAY
Pray that you both will be models of a Christlike servant spirit.

Get Connected for More Information
http://www.familylife.com/moments/charactertraining

DEFEATING SELF-DOUBT

We ourselves speak proudly of you.
2 THESSALONIANS 1:4

If there's anything that characterizes the teenage years, it's self-doubt.

Barbara and I had six teenagers progress through our house. At one point we had four at the same time. And it was frequently obvious that the origin for some of their behaviors—and for many of the words coming out of their mouths—was their doubts about themselves.

As difficult as they sometimes would be, we knew how imperative it was for us to look them in the eye and say, "I love you. I believe in you. I'm glad you're my son [or daughter]."

There's nothing like a mom and dad's love to soften their hearts and ease their doubts.

On our *FamilyLife Today* program, we interviewed Josh Weidmann, who has become a passionate Christian voice to teens and college students. He told us about once being at a youth camp and preaching on the biblical story of Esther. As he told about how beautiful the queen was in form and feature, he said, "You know, I want to stop here and tell you—every individual woman in this room—you are beautiful, and you are God's creation."

As soon as those words left his lips, he heard what he describes as the loudest gasp he'd ever heard in his life. Why? Because so few of these girls believed it. So few had been reassured at home that they had worth and value and were loved—just for who they were.

Even after my sons outgrew me, I would hug them and tell them I loved them. I never had the sense that I said it too much. When my girls had become beautiful young women and I wasn't always sure I should hold them too close, I would hug them and affirm them and tell them how lovely they were to me.

No matter how big they get and how adult-like they look, never stop expressing your belief in your children. They need it.

DISCUSS

Give yourself a grade on how well you do on expressing love and belief. Talk about how you can express it more.

PRAY

Pray that your children will never be starved for your love and affirmation.

Get Connected for More Information
http://www.familylife.com/moments/teens

LIFE ON THE HALF SHELL?

David, after he had served the purpose of God in his own generation, fell asleep, and was laid among his fathers.

ACTS 13:36

John Piper, a longtime pastor and author, was skimming *Reader's Digest* one day. He came across the story of a middle-aged couple who had been financially successful enough to retire early and pack their bags for Florida. Imagine the thrill, they said, to do nothing but relax. Just kick back and collect seashells.

John began wondering whether this should ever be the sum game of a Christian's earthly existence. "At the end of my life," John says, "I hope I'm mainly preparing to meet the Judge of the earth and give an account of my one little, vaporous life. And I'm pretty sure He's not going to ask to see my shell collection."

I'm not saying for one minute that there's anything wrong with play and recreation, perhaps even a seashell collection. God has designed these things for us to enjoy. But when you dream of your life in retirement, do you see yourself being content with lowering your golf handicap, bagging a bigger buck or traveling the world? Or do you see yourself pursuing a purpose that will outlive you?

As I look at the Scripture for today, I realize that in my latter years, I want to be fulfilling God's purpose for me in this generation. I want Barbara and me to be living smack-dab in the center of His will.

Do you have a heart that burns for building relationships and using your gifts, abilities and experience, even in the final chapter of your life? Or will you merely be a shell of what you could have been?

DISCUSS

When you think of retirement, how do you envision it? How do you think your vision of retirement compares with how God wants to use you? Where is God at work today? How could He use you as a couple?

PRAY

Ask God for nothing more than the desire to do His will all the way to the finish line. In fact, why not be so bold as to pray that you'll be miserable doing anything else?

THE SIGNATURE OF GOD

Therefore humble yourselves under the mighty hand of God, that He may exalt you at the proper time, casting all your anxiety on Him, because He cares for you.
1 PETER 5:6-7

They called my dad "Hook" because he was a left-handed pitcher who possessed a wicked curve ball. Hook also had great handwriting skills—his signature was absolutely magnificent. Unmistakable.

God has a signature that is unmistakable as well. He is at work in, around and through our lives. But I believe there are times when He does something very special to get our attention. My friend Joe Stowell, former president of Moody Bible Institute, calls these special acts "the signature of God."

Barbara and I have seen God's signature many times, usually when we were facing a major challenge and our faith was tested. One occurred shortly after we helped start FamilyLife in 1976. In our organization, we are responsible for raising our own financial support. It's simple: If the money doesn't come in, we don't get paid. At this particular time, challenges abounded everywhere— we had three young children, I was working long hours, and I was wounded by a decision made by my boss. Barbara and I felt like quitting.

But as we prayed, our thoughts kept returning to a letter we'd received a few weeks earlier. It contained a brief note and a check for our personal support: $5,000 from a couple we'd only met briefly, Ad and B. J. Coors. God didn't speak audibly, but He was saying, *I sent the money so that you won't quit.* It was "the signature of God."

Barbara and I came very close to missing a God-sized adventure of a lifetime—the privilege of seeing God use the FamilyLife staff team to touch millions of lives around the world.

What are you facing today where you *need* to see the signature of God?

DISCUSS

How have you seen God provide for you after you have cast your cares upon Him? What do you need to trust Him for today?

PRAY

Cast your cares, worries, doubts and struggles on Him. And thank Him that He does care and He does provide.

Get Connected for More Information

HOLY TERRORS

He said to them, "Follow Me, and I will make you fishers of men."
MATTHEW 4:19

Do you have a child with a strong will? When you look into his or her face and wonder where he or she is going in life, what do you envision?

Perhaps your child has instigated so many calls home from school that your number is on speed dial at the principal's office. Perhaps he or she has dared you to enforce so many different house rules and boundaries that your backbone has threatened to sue you for pain and suffering.

Perhaps you resonate with one of the chapter titles from Kendra Smiley's book *Aaron's Way: Prison or Presidency*: "Which Route Will They Take?" Kendra and her husband, John, can relate to the desperation you feel about your strong-willed child. But they would also tell you that they always knew God had a special plan in mind for their son, Aaron. They made it their plan and prayer that this boy, who caused them so much consternation throughout his childhood, would make good, godly, self-controlled decisions for himself by the time he reached high school. Like Jesus, who took one look at a handful of smelly anglers and saw in them "fishers of men," John and Kendra observed Aaron's maddening behavior and chose to see a bold, young leader—a real man in the making.

As a senior in high school, Aaron's Fellowship of Christian Athletes chapter was barred from advertising in the school newspaper. So he turned his strong will into action, phoning a Christian legal advocacy group to put legitimate constitutional pressure on his school's policies. They fought. He won. And Kendra and John knew their labors had not been in vain.

There's hope, Mom and Dad. Hang in there. Do your job. Pray for your child. And don't be surprised one day if your headstrong headache turns into a champion for Christ who melts your heart!

DISCUSS
What is your vision for your children? How can you pray and work at turning the negatives of their personalities into godly strengths?

PRAY
God knows what He's doing—both in your child and in you. Keep going, and keep trusting.

Get Connected for More Information
http://www.familylife.com/moments/biblicalparenting

ON GUARD

*If the head of the house had known at what time of the night
the thief was coming, he would have been on the alert.*
MATTHEW 24:43

As the verse above from Matthew states, if you knew when a burglar was coming, you'd double-bolt the doors, you'd secure your valuables off-site, and you'd call the police and have them positioned where they could make an immediate capture. You'd leave no possibility for the intruder to get inside.

But when it comes to keeping out the enemy of our souls, we're not always as diligent. We don't take quite the same pains to keep our hearts out of reach of harm's way. We don't check all the windows—the points that offer him the easiest point of entry into our lives. Things like the following:

- Isolation—Being alone should be an automatic signal to keep your guard up. Temptations seem particularly tempting when no one else is looking. The lures of laziness or mindless television or Internet pornography may be more enticing when you're alone or away from home.
- Bad company—If the enemy can't get you when you're alone, he may try to make his ways seem more appealing through the influence of someone who is already caught up in his web—a coworker, an old friend, a next-door neighbor.
- Fatigue—When you are unusually drained or under exceptional stress, it's much easier to compromise.
- Pride and arrogance—Sometimes when life is going well, you may not feel as much need to pray. You fool yourself into believing you can handle yourself just fine without God's help. But this is when Satan sets you in his sights.

There is never a time when you can't be on the alert, constantly watching and praying. Even the devil has a hard time defeating that kind of alarm system.

DISCUSS
How could you help each other steer clear of situations that make you more vulnerable to the enemy's schemes?

PRAY
Focus tomorrow on praying first thing when you wake up in the morning. Then practice prayer at every slightest nudge throughout the day.

Get Connected for More Information

http://www.familylife.com/moments/spiritualgrowth

POTTY MOUTHS

Let no unwholesome word proceed from your mouth,
but only such a word as is good for edification according to the need of the moment,
so that it will give grace to those who hear.
EPHESIANS 4:29

Fifty years ago, censors were allowed to delete crude terms from books before they were published. When James Jones, for example, included more than 250 vulgar words in his final manuscript of *From Here to Eternity*, censors eliminated 208 of them from the original hardcover edition. When the book came out in paperback, they deleted all the rest. They simply didn't want the masses reading profane words.

Things have changed a bit, haven't they?

Some R-rated movies today contain as many as 200 curse words—about 2 per minute. And we all know how pervasive cursing has become on television. We are being exposed to more and more verbal pollution in the flow of the average day—even from places like the church pulpit and the church softball league bench. Potty mouth pulpits! Who would have thought?

I think it's time to take a stand again, beginning with our own flippancy toward foul language. Here's why:

1. *It lowers the moral standards of our family.* Jesus said, "The mouth speaks out of that which fills the heart" (Matthew 12:34), which means that cursing exposes the condition of our inner person. It reveals that our hearts have grown sour and polluted with trashy words.
2. *It degrades interpersonal relationships.* It robs society of its civility. Used casually, cursing is just rude. When used on purpose, it's derogatory and demeaning. Certain curse words even devalue what God created—like the divinely designed act of intercourse.
3. *It sends a bad message to our children.* It tells them that cursing within moderation is acceptable behavior. But as Christians, our spiritual transformation—our desire to be more like Christ—should affect our words.

DISCUSS

Talk about your language and how you want your words to be remembered. Discuss where you stand in regard to swearing.

PRAY

Pray for bad habits to be broken and for pure hearts that show themselves in clean, redemptive speech.

Get Connected for More Information
http://www.familylife.com/moments/charactertraining

IT'LL BE GOOD FOR YOU

Obey your leaders and submit to them, for they keep watch over your souls.
HEBREWS 13:17

Every family has its own set of expectations that grow from a combination of core convictions and upbringing. Some of these can be little more than meaningless ritual, but many of them are healthy practices and preferences that we simply want as part of our family experience.

One example from our own family was our desire to sit together in church. I had no biblical mandate to do this. I just always liked all my family there with me. I liked catching their eyes during the service and sharing a wink or a smile. I liked putting an arm around their shoulders and giving them a hug as we worshiped. No matter how old they were or how many times they asked to sit with their friends, Barbara and I held firm on this one. Church. Us. Together.

And I'm glad I did. One day I was talking with an older teen, Katy, who remembered how in ninth grade she began doing more and more things with her friends. Every Friday night and Saturday. Even on Sunday morning at church, she'd hunt for her friends.

"But after a couple of years of that," she said, "I remember looking at other kids who sat with their parents and thinking, *I'm missing out.* I wish I had seen before how precious my time was with them and not tried to get away from it just because I could. Now that I sit with my parents in church, I can't believe I didn't want to."

Is it wrong to sit apart from your children during worship service? Absolutely not! But if you feel strongly enough about something like this, be the parent. Tell them the sun will still come up tomorrow. They might be glad someday that you did.

DISCUSS
What are some family rules or traditions you have been thinking about establishing? What can you do to implement them?

PRAY
Ask God for the courage you both need to lead and love your children.

SO RIGHT AND SO WRONG

*Why do you look at the speck that is in your brother's eye,
but do not notice the log that is in your own eye?*
MATTHEW 7:3

I'm sure you've had a disagreement (or more than one!) with each other that turned into a stalemate or brick wall. You didn't really care if it came to a conclusion. You just wanted a truce. You wanted this thing behind you. You were tired of fighting.

Maybe it started with an argument about the checkbook. Maybe it had something to do with the in-laws. Maybe it was a difference of opinion on a parenting issue. But somewhere along the way, the conflict turned into much more. It took on a life of its own. Now you can hardly stand to be in the same room together.

Well, are you prepared to let reconciliation start with you? Are you ready to give up the notion that you're mostly right? Deeper still, are you willing to strive to recapture the reality of what your marriage is all about—the transcendent beauty of reflecting God's love on Earth?

I know that you may be thinking, *When I'm hurt I don't care about God's glory. I just want to get even.*

Don't be ruled by your emotions. Instead, do it Jesus' way: Take the log out of your eye. No matter what your spouse has done, no matter how misguided you think he or she has been, the key to real resolution is to start removing your log. Accept full responsibility for your part in this, and place the value of your mate and your relationship above the value of your own pride and your need to be right.

God wants more for you than being able to tolerate each other. He wants you to show forth His glory in the way you honor, love and respect each other.

Remove the logjam. And shoot for something higher.

DISCUSS
Any log in your eye right now? What squabble of yours needs to end right now, with both of you saying, "It's me. I'm sorry"?

PRAY
Ask Almighty God to help you sacrifice pride for the grandeur of your marriage—so that it can reflect His love.

Get Connected for More Information
http://www.familylife.com/moments/conflict

CLOSED-DOOR MEETING

All those hearing him continued to be amazed, and were saying, "Is this not he who in Jerusalem destroyed those who called on this name?"
ACTS 9:21

Julie doesn't know how many hours she spent praying that God would show her husband the love of Jesus. But Gene wasn't your typical live-and-let-live non-believer. This was one hardened guy. Rigid. Stubborn. Extremely controlling.

Nothing had the power to crack that rough exterior. Not leukemia. He had weathered that crisis without noticeable cracking.

Not prostate cancer. If the door of his heart had opened any, it was barely recognizable.

But for some reason, when FamilyLife put on a marriage conference at the church Julie attended, Gene grudgingly agreed to attend. Not for the religious stuff. Certainly not for the cheap refreshments. Maybe he knew if he stayed home, he wouldn't have an excuse for not fixing the kitchen faucet. Who knows?

As they sat through the early sessions, he was bristling and arguing. He couldn't believe people actually believed in an actual devil who actually wreaked actual havoc in people's lives. *What a convenient excuse for one's failures,* he thought.

But in one of the last sessions, as the conference speaker was sharing about the wide chasm between God and man, the truth unexpectedly converged in Gene's heart. Even today, he's baffled by what happened at that moment.

While Julie was focusing on the message being delivered, Gene tapped her on the shoulder and directed her attention to three words he'd written in his notebook: "I GET IT." They were the three sweetest words she'd ever read.

They slipped out into a break room where they fell into each other's arms. He sobbed. She sobbed. He asked for forgiveness. She sobbed even more. And in another miracle of grace, God proved again that no one is beyond the reach of the gospel.

Not even a husband who wants nothing to do with it.

DISCUSS
Do you know a couple where only one is a Christian? Discuss how you could reach out and share the gospel with the non-believer.

PRAY
Pray for marriages in which you know that a relationship with Jesus Christ is a major sticking point. And ask God to break through.

Get Connected for More Information
http://www.familylife.com/moments/relationshipwithgod

HERE AND NOW

BY BARBARA RAINEY

My son, if your heart is wise, my own heart also will be glad.
PROVERBS 23:15

When Dennis and I began teaching the sixth-grade Sunday School class at our church, we decided to serve them some "meat," not just the "macaroni and cheese" curriculum we could have offered. But, my, were we ever surprised to find out just how hungry these kids were!

We asked our young students, "If you could ask your parents any question, knowing that I would ask it for you and then give you the answer later, what would it be?" Their responses, which amazed us, included:

- "If I became pregnant before marriage, what would your reaction be?"
- "Did you have sex before you were married? Who with?"
- "How old will I be before I can kiss?"

After seeing children respond this way year after year, we concluded that a lot was going on beneath the surface in these cute little boys and girls. They may not be able to connect all the dots yet, but their bodies and minds are changing and developing fast. Life is in full gear, and they are starting to make determinative choices.

Some parents thought it was too soon to discuss these issues with their sixth graders. But our "research" in the laboratory of sixth-grade Sunday School—as well as in many years of field testing in the Rainey home—has proven that these are "here and now" issues. In an age when many grade-school kids regularly view immoral media content, is it any wonder that they're thinking, talking and making decisions about subjects like dating, sex, pornography, alcohol and drugs?

Many of the most pivotal choices in life are being made between the ages of 11 and 15. And we as parents need to engage our young preteens and teens *now* and help them make wise choices.

DISCUSS

Have you considered talking about big issues with your 10- to 12-year-olds? Make a list of the issues they will face in adolescence and start now. How might you do it?

PRAY

Ask God to show you the real needs and thoughts of your children, no matter how young their age.

 Get Connected for More Information
http://www.familylife.com/moments/involvement

HIS NAME IS WONDERFUL

And His name will be called Wonderful Counselor, Mighty God,
Eternal Father, Prince of Peace.
ISAIAH 9:6

Certain verses of Scripture leap to our minds as we draw close to Christmas. In the majestic titles of Jesus found in the prophecy of Isaiah 9:6, we find Him to be everything we need. We find Him not only the "reason for the season" but the name that should be on our lips every day as God puts us in touch with others over the Christmas holidays.

Who doesn't need to know the Wonderful Counselor? Who doesn't need to know this One who can offer advice when they are facing a difficult situation? This One who has the answers for their marriage and family dilemmas?

Who doesn't need to know the Mighty God? You certainly know people who are dealing with a rebellious teenager or an aging parent or a sick child or an impossible job situation. When was the last time you told them how strong the arms of your God are? Perhaps you need to be reminded of how mighty God is by reading Isaiah 40.

Who doesn't need to know the Eternal Father? Who doesn't need the sense of hope that comes from knowing that—although we may suffer for a while—we have a God who dwells in eternity, which means that there is more to life than what we see around us?

Who doesn't need to know the Prince of Peace? In a culture of road rage and long lines and short fuses, with strained relationships and simmering discontentment, who isn't starving for deeper, more-lasting peace? Who doesn't need to know why even the most desirable possessions and experiences leave them feeling unsatisfied? Who doesn't need a peace that passes understanding? Who doesn't need more of the Prince of Peace and His peace in their home?

This Christmas, be watching for people who need to know Jesus for who He is.

DISCUSS
Which of the above names most needs to be celebrated this Christmas season in your marriage and family?

PRAY
Pray for more opportunities to share Christ's love with others while Christmas has them more open than usual.

Get Connected for More Information
http://www.familylife.com/moments/holidays

THE POWER OF YOUR ABSENCE

There is an appointed time for everything. A time to be silent and a time to speak.
ECCLESIASTES 3:1,7

The appointment had been on my calendar for more than a year. I was going to speak to the student body of Dallas Theological Seminary in their chapel service. But as the date neared, the flu bug that had kept Barbara in bed for a week showed no signs of letting up. A full week of suffering led to two.

And when the moment finally arrived for me to commit one way or the other, the choice seemed clear. Barbara couldn't take care of herself, and she needed me a lot more than the seminary students did. So I canceled.

Amazingly, though, God used me to give a message there. The proof arrived in an email I received a couple days later from a friend who told me of two people who remarked that "even though you weren't there, you taught them something. You showed them that family should be our main priority."

It's the first time I ever made such an impact by *not* speaking. Perhaps I need to start a *non*-speaking tour!

The experience reminded me that actions truly do speak louder than words. What you model matters. The lives you lead are being watched and measured much more carefully than you realize. And they're making an impact on others, from spouses to children, from coworkers to church friends, from neighbors to extended family members and beyond.

Never underestimate the power of your presence—or, in some cases, your absence!

DISCUSS
Think of some people who communicate Christian character without saying a word. What traits of theirs would you love to model?

PRAY
Thank the Lord for making our lives such powerful teachers and for the opportunity He gives each of us today to be a window of His heart and character.

Get Connected for More Information
http://www.familylife.com/moments/commitment

ME TOO

I know my transgressions, and my sin is ever before me.
PSALM 51:3

I remember listening one night to a woman who told Barbara and me that she had finally had enough. She was right—her husband had pretty much given her zero in the relationship department. Years of being taken for granted had finally reached a breaking point. She was angry—really angry. And she needed a place to vent.

As I sat there, I couldn't help hearing in her diatribe some of the same mistakes I've made in my own marriage. As I told Barbara in a note the next day:

It made me realize how hard I've been on you from time to time. Pressuring. Not appreciating your load and all that you've done for me. Not understanding your feelings.

To sit there and listen to a woman express her need for a husband to care for her, to dream with her, to think with her about her future and her soul, was like watching the last bit of light go out in her heart. It was more than just her anger. It was her whole countenance, her lack of radiance, her feeling of being "tired" of him. To think that a man could look into his wife's eyes and not find a companion, a friend, a person who *wants* to be there with him, is a scary feeling.

But I know I've been self-centered at points, too, just like this man. And it wasn't easy to hear again the hurt it can cause. I am sorry. Really.

When was the last time you came face to face with your own shortcomings? When you realized that in the pressure and practice of daily living, you'd forgotten the value of some very important things? If that's where you happen to be today—especially in your relationship with one another—it's time to own up. Say you're sorry. And maybe write your own letter.

DISCUSS
What do you most regret about the way you've treated each other—especially lately? Confess it now. And receive your best friend's forgiveness.

PRAY
Thank the Holy Spirit for His convicting work in your life and for keeping your conscience sharp and painful when necessary.

Get Connected for More Information
http://www.familylife.com/moments/repentance

CHANGING THEIR TUNE

Behold, how good and how pleasant it is for brothers to dwell together in unity!
PSALM 133:1

At one point, both our sons, Benjamin and Samuel, were students at the same university. One evening Samuel called home to talk, and he was interrupted by a young lady who came through the room and asked Samuel to let her talk to us. She said, "Did you hear what happened at the Campus Crusade meeting the other night?"

"No," we answered.

"Well," she started in, "first of all, Benjamin got up and shared how he was going to be taking a year off from school to go volunteer as a missionary in Estonia. Then, after he finished talking and sat down, Samuel stood up and told everyone what a phenomenal brother he had—how much he loved him and admired him, how much of a mentor he had been to him as a younger brother, how he had helped him make his way around as a freshman at college. Then Samuel sat down next to Benjamin, put his arms around him and just hugged him. It was so cool."

It was one of those moments when you sit back, take a deep breath and go, "Thank You, Lord! It has all been worth it."

These were the same sons who argued and fought each other so often that we often threatened to draw a line down the middle of their bedroom and declare each side a foreign country, off-limits to the other person. Barbara and I had our moments when they were teenagers when we wondered if they would ever get along.

If you find yourself in a similar situation—with children who fight like competitors in the World Federation of Wrestling—I want to encourage you that there is hope. Pray and ask God to knit their hearts together. God is able to do exceedingly, abundantly beyond all that you ask or think.

DISCUSS

Talk about your children's relationships with one another. Write down one developmental action step that you want to train each of your children with.

PRAY

Pray for perseverance and wisdom as you continue training and teaching your children.

Get Connected for More Information
http://www.familylife.com/moments/siblings

THANKS, DAD

Every one of you shall reverence his mother and his father.
LEVITICUS 19:3

Just about all of us know or remember what it's like for Christmas to roll around with little money for buying presents. Reminds me of the financially strapped college student who once wrote to tell me about a 99-cent gift he once gave his father . . . and how it became priceless in his family's Christmas lore.

The gift was a poem, a journey of memories that wound back through days he and his dad had spent in the woods and at the fishing hole, telling stories and swapping smiles. Pasted in a cheap store frame, it didn't have the look of a present that would still be talked about years after the event. But when his father began to read aloud the seven-stanza poem, he began to sob uncontrollably.

All gift giving stopped. Every eye turned to see, every ear to listen. Now others were crying. Soon everyone had gathered around him, embracing a family's love, warmed by the tribute of "this duckling, almost broke from the clutch, who wants to say to the father drake: 'Dad, I love you so much!'"

For years, I have been encouraging people to share these kinds of tributes with their parents. As wonderful as funeral eulogies can be, how many of them are delivered with the hope that loved ones can somehow hear these words never spoken during their lifetimes? We should bring out these verbal bouquets of blessing today, to honor parents who are still living. We owe it to them, and we owe it to God.

This young man's 99-cent Christmas tribute hung near his dad's easy chair for years, showering down honor and gratitude at every glance. And whenever guests came to their home, they were usually directed to the cheap frame and the college-age verse and asked to read it themselves. That's the power of a tribute.

DISCUSS

How could you show your honor and gratitude to your parents in some unforgettable way?

PRAY

Ask God to show you what to say and how to say it in such a way that your mother and father will truly feel honored.

CHRISTMAS PRAISE

He who was revealed in the flesh, was vindicated in the Spirit, seen by angels, proclaimed among the nations, believed on in the world, taken up in glory.
1 TIMOTHY 3:16

As I read the nativity stories in the Gospels of Matthew and Luke, one thing I note is that many of those who saw the first Noel up close responded in praise and worship:

Zechariah said, "Blessed be the Lord God of Israel, for He has visited us and accomplished redemption for His people, and has raised up a horn of salvation for us in the house of David His servant—as He spoke by the mouth of His holy prophets from of old—salvation from our enemies, and from the hand of all who hate us; to show mercy toward our fathers, and to remember His holy covenant, the oath which He swore to Abraham our father, to grant us that we, being rescued from the hand of our enemies, might serve Him without fear, in holiness and righteousness before Him all our days" (Luke 1:68-75).

Mary said, "My soul exalts the Lord, and my spirit has rejoiced in God my Savior. For He has had regard for the humble state of His bondslave; for behold, from this time on all generations will count me blessed. For the Mighty One has done great things for me; and holy is His name. And His mercy is upon generation after generation toward those who fear Him" (Luke 1:46-50).

Simeon said, "Now, Lord, You are releasing Your bond-servant to depart in peace, according to Your word; for my eyes have seen Your salvation, which You have prepared in the presence of all peoples, a light of revelation to the Gentiles, and the glory of Your people Israel" (Luke 2:29-32).

As you celebrate Christmas, may your response be the same—one of worship and praise to God our King.

DISCUSS
Have each member of your family write out their own words of Christmas praise and share them with one another.

PRAY
May Jesus Christ always have your attention the way He does today.

FOLLOW THE INSTRUCTIONS

The one who trusts in himself is a fool, but one who walks in wisdom will be safe.
PROVERBS 28:26, HCSB

A number of years ago while Christmas shopping, we came across one of those wooden swing sets on sale. Dirt cheap. The kids were outspoken in their desire to have one, and Barbara and I caved in. So later that day I returned to the store—without the kids—and picked one up.

In the box.

It was Christmas Eve before I finally got both arms into that "some assembly required" project. For someone like me who is not a real whizbang working with my hands, it took hours to put together. Barbara frequently stood alongside, calming me down, helping me read and interpret the instructions, encouraging me every step of the way.

And it was worth it. It was the hit of Christmas Day.

Marriage is a lot like that swing set. Most of us get married and try to put the thing together without ever consulting the printed instructions. Or if we do check the Scriptures, we tend to select only those portions that we want our spouse to follow. And we ignore what the instructions tell us about *our* responsibility.

Marriage is hard work. And many people are making it more difficult by overlooking the fundamental truth that marriage is a spiritual institution designed by God for two imperfect people to be joined together in their dependence upon Him and each other. If each of you wants to be "one who walks in wisdom" (Proverbs 28:26), you cannot ignore His instructions on how you build and maintain a spiritual union.

DISCUSS

Describe what it's like living outside the Bible's teaching and influence. What are the benefits of building a marriage according to the divine instruction manual?

PRAY

Pray that God will instill in you a renewed craving for His Word, a hunger to read it, retain it, rehearse it through the day and apply it, both in your marriage and in your family.

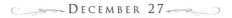

SKY HIGH

I said to myself, "Come now, I will test you with pleasure.
So enjoy yourself." And behold, it too was futility.
ECCLESIASTES 2:1

Perhaps you've seen one of those slingshot rides, like the one my friend Scott and I witnessed in Orlando, Florida. It's essentially two giant pipe-like towers arranged in a V shape. In between them, attached by steel cables, is an open-air capsule that's lowered to the ground and secured by hundreds of springs compressed with 40 tons of force. Smoke billows from underneath it like a volcano about to erupt. Then—ZOOM—the capsule is released at nearly 100 miles an hour, rocketing 35 stories into the air in a little more than a second.

And to make it even more fun, the passengers' faces are shown on a giant video screen. I'll never forget the first couple we watched. The man was in horror, wanting nothing but a chance to walk away alive. The woman, on the other hand, was totally absorbing the thrill, squealing and smiling with sheer adrenaline. She was an "all systems go" kind of a person.

She reminded me of many people in the world who are hooked on pleasure and excitement. When life doesn't deliver, they get disappointed. They keep searching for the next thrill to add a surge of adrenaline through their veins.

Is this a struggle for you? Do you often find yourself longing for the weekend or some other exciting diversion, unable to draw purpose and meaning from the midday, mundane moments of life? I believe that God wants us to learn to live contentedly within the usual and ordinary (see 1 Timothy 6:6).

To truly enjoy the life God has given you, you need to know how to be happy on the days when you're not at Disney World.

DISCUSS

How easily are you bored? What are your hobbies and passions? Talk about whether you are hooked on seeking the next experience or thrill.

PRAY

Thank Jesus Christ for the gift of each day, even when many days seem to be the same. Ask Him to help you see Him and the treasure that rests inside every moment.

Get Connected for More Information
http://www.familylife.com/moments/relationshipwithgod

THE GOODNESS OF GOD

What shall I render to the LORD for all His benefits toward me?
PSALM 116:12

We closed our first year-long devotional book with a letter written by a man named Obadiah Holmes to his nine children in the late 1600s. As we near the close of *this* book, we'd like to share another letter Obadiah wrote to his wife, tenderly exhorting her to remember a full lifetime of God's faithfulness. As you read it, notice what was important after nearly a half-century of marriage:

> My heart has cleaved to you ever since we came together, and is knit to you in death, which is the cause of these lines as a reminder of God's goodness to us in keeping us together almost fifty years. God has made all our conditions comfortable to us, whether in fullness or emptiness, lifted up or thrown down, in honor or disgrace, sickness or health, by giving us contentment and love for one another. We have every reason while we live to praise His holy name while we are together. And when death does separate us, may the one still breathing praise Him while breath remains.
>
> Therefore, having some thought that I may go away before you, having signs that my day is but short and it may be that I cannot speak to you at the last, I shall give you some considerations for your meditation—that they may speak when I cannot.
>
> Consider how the Lord carried you along ever since you came into this world. He has provided for you and preserved you in many dangers, and has given you food and raiment with contentment. He has increased our store, sometimes to our wonder, also continuing our health in very great measure. He has given us a great posterity, and has provided for them in a comfortable manner.

Like Obadiah did in this letter, make a point of frequently encouraging each other by reciting the great deeds of God, reflecting back on those spiritual milestones that prove His long-term faithfulness.

DISCUSS
How has God provided for you "sometimes to [your] wonder"? See if you can list 5 to 10 ways each.

PRAY
Give thanks for God's constant provision, care and attention to your needs.

ALL YOU REALLY NEED

The eternal God is a dwelling place, and underneath are the everlasting arms.
DEUTERONOMY 33:27

I want you to think for a moment of what you'd say to your spouse if you knew you were going to die. What words of comfort would you bring? Where would you point him or her for hope? What counsel would you give that would most certainly be true and not disappoint?

Think. What would you say? How would you pray?

Over 300 years ago, Obadiah Holmes must have grappled with questions like those. Evidently, Obadiah Holmes built his house upon the rock of Jesus Christ. And in a love letter he wrote to his wife before he died, it was only natural to gently remind her to trust Him:

> When I am removed, consider the Lord as your husband, as your father, as your Lord and Savior, who has said that whom He loves, He loves to the end. And He will not leave you nor forsake you, but will carry you through all until He brings you to glory. Therefore, lift up your head and be not discouraged. Say to your soul, "Why are you disquieted within me? Hope in God and trust in His name," and you shall not be disappointed.
>
> And now, my dear wife, whom I love as my own soul, I commit you to the Lord, who has been a gracious, merciful God to us all our days, not once doubting that He will be gracious to you in life—or death. He will carry you through the valley of tears with His own supporting hand. To Him I commit you for counsel, wisdom, and strength, and to keep you blameless till the coming of our Lord Jesus Christ, to whom be all glory, honor, and praise.

What would you say to your spouse if you knew your time was up?

DISCUSS
Talk about this love letter and what it means to you. How is this husband providing for his wife even in his death?

PRAY
Throw your trust on Him today, the same way you've been doing your whole life long.

CHEERING THEM ON

Comfort and strengthen your hearts in every good work and word.
2 THESSALONIANS 2:17

Evidently Obadiah Holmes, who lived in the 1600s, understood the power of a good word, as evidenced by the following words to his lifelong bride:

> Sorrow not at my departure, but rejoice in the Lord. In nothing be anxious, but make your request to Him who alone is able to supply your necessities and to help you in time of need. Let your love to me culminate in this: that it is better for me to be out of the body and to be with the Lord. Consider the fears you had concerning me every day, for the pains and weaknesses and dangers, now freed from sin and Satan and all enemies and doubts. At the resurrection, this weak, corrupt, mortal body shall be raised immortal and glorious.
>
> And now, my dear wife, it will be but a little while before your day will end and your time comes to sleep with me in rest. . . . Be cheerful and rejoice in God continually. Care not for the things of this world. Say not, "What shall I eat, and with what shall I be clothed," for your Father knows what you have need of. And He has given you much more of these things than you and I ever could expect or have deserved, and you have enough and to spare if His good pleasure be to let you enjoy the same. If not, He alone is a sufficient portion.
>
> Amen. Fare thee well.

Three hundred years later, Obadiah Holmes's words about how to love and live are still significant and relevant for us today.

DISCUSS

Talk about how you treat the Scriptures in your home. Do you read them regularly to one another? How can you make the truth of the Bible central to your marriage and family?

PRAY

Pray for an ever-deepening love and understanding of what the Bible says so that it will become for you a second language.

Get Connected for More Information

STRONG INTO THE NIGHT

He who trusts in the LORD will be exalted.
PROVERBS 29:25

In September 1939, Great Britain allied with France and several other alarmed countries in declaring war on Hitler's Germany, which had invaded Poland in its intended march toward global domination. By the end of the year, anxieties throughout England remained on high alert; everyone was fearful of bombing and invasion.

When King George VI sat down before two large microphones to make his Christmas Day speech to the nation, he was dressed in his official uniform as Admiral of the Fleet. With so many parts of the world facing an uncertain future, his goal was to reassure the people that their nation was prepared and able and their cause right and just.

"A new year is at hand," the king said. "We cannot tell what it will bring. If it brings peace, how thankful we shall all be. If it brings us continued struggle, we shall remain undaunted."

Then, turning to some lines of poetry his wife had recently shared with him, he concluded his speech with these words, which are a fitting close to our year together. They offer a word of encouragement that—we hope—will settle your hearts amid the troubles of our own era in history. These lines are from "The Gate of the Year," a poem written in 1908 by Minnie Louise Haskins:

I said to the man who stood at the gate of the year

"Give me a light that I may tread safely into the unknown."

And he replied, "Go into the darkness and put your hand into the hand of God

That shall be to you better than light and safer than a known way!"

DISCUSS

As you make the turn to a new year, what are you facing that needs you to sink your hand more deeply into God's hand?

PRAY

Pray for one another that as you embark upon a new year, God will grant you and your family His favor.

Get Connected for More Information

ENDNOTES

January 10: Dennis and Barbara Rainey, *Pressure Proof Your Marriage* (Sisters, OR: Multnomah, 2003), pp. 51-58.

January 16: Dennis and Barbara Rainey, *Growing a Spiritually Strong Family* (Sisters, OR: Multnomah, 2002), pp. 39-40.

January 17: Rainey, *Pressure Proof Your Marriage*, pp. 21-27.

January 22: Dennis and Barbara Rainey, *Staying Close* (Nashville, TN: Thomas Nelson, 2003), pp. 127-128.

January 24: Jennifer Carlile, "Jan. 24 Called Worst Day of the Year," MSNBC.com, Jan. 23, 2005. http://www.msnbc.msn.com/id/6847012/ (accessed May 2007).

February 4: Dennis and Barbara Rainey, *Rekindling the Romance* (Nashville, TN: Thomas Nelson, 2006), pp. 57-67.

February 5: Ibid., pp. 117-127.

February 6: Dennis and Barbara Rainey, *Parenting Today's Adolescent* (Nashville, TN: Thomas Nelson, 2002), pp. 305-306.

February 8: Rainey, *Pressure Proof Your Marriage*, pp. 43-44.

February 12: Mary Hance, "Couples Married 50-Plus Years Offer Advice on How to Live Happily Ever After," *The Tennessean*, February 18, 2007.

February 20: Rainey, *Pressure Proof Your Marriage*, pp. 75-78.

February 23: Rainey, *Staying Close*, pp. 205-206.

February 24: Dennis Rainey, *One Home at a Time* (Colorado Springs, CO: Focus on the Family Publishing, 1999), pp. 126-134.

February 28: Improbable Research, "The Ig Nobel Awards," at improb.com. http://www.improb.com/ig/ (accessed May 2007).

March 1: Rainey, *Starting Your Marriage off Right*, pp. 150-153.

March 3: Rainey, *Growing a Spiritually Strong Family*, pp. 34-36.

March 9: Rainey, *Rekindling the Romance*, pp. 240-242.

March 13: Rainey, *Pressure Proof Your Marriage*, p. 78.

March 17: Rainey, *Two Hearts Praying as One* (Sisters, OR: Multnomah, 2003), pp. 54-55.

March 28: Rainey, *Rekindling the Romance*, pp. 229-230.

March 29: Rainey, *Growing a Spiritually Strong Family*, pp. 62-69.

March 31: Barbara Rainey and Ashley Rainey Escue, comp., *A Mother's Legacy* (Nashville, TN: Thomas Nelson, 2000), pp. 65-67.

April 4: Dennis Rainey and Dave Boehi, *The Best Gift You Can Ever Give Your Parents* (Little Rock, AR: FamilyLife Publishing, 2004), pp. 59-63.

April 5: Rainey, *Rekindling the Romance*, pp. 42-44.

April 7: Rainey, *One Home at a Time*, pp. 123-125.

April 9: Rainey, *Starting Your Marriage off Right*, pp. 233-236.

April 16: Rainey, *One Home at a Time*, pp. 63-64.

April 17: Ibid., pp. 50-51.

April 23: Rainey, *Rekindling the Romance*, pp. 131-133.

April 26: Inspired by Rick Reilly, "Strongest Dad in the World," *Sports Illustrated*, June 15, 2005.

April 27: Dennis and Barbara Rainey with Bruce Nygren, *Parenting Today's Adolescent* (Nashville, TN: Thomas Nelson, 2002), pp. 161-162.

May 6: Rainey, *Growing a Spiritually Strong Family*, pp. 27-29.

May 11: Rainey, *Staying Close*, p. 262.

May 17: Dennis Rainey and David Boehi, *The Tribute and the Promise* (Nashville, TN: Thomas Nelson, 1997), p. 71.

May 19: Rainey, *Parenting Today's Adolescent*, p. 146.

May 22: Ibid., pp. 36-37.

May 24; Jen Abbas, *Generation EX: Adult Children of Divorce and the Healing of Our Pain* (Little Rock, AR: FamilyLife Publishing, 2007), pp. xvi-xvii. Used by permission.

May 29: Rainey, *Parenting Today's Adolescent*, pp. 65-66.

June 1: Ibid., pp. 117-118.

June 2: Dennis Rainey, *Interviewing Your Daughter's Dates* (Little Rock, AR: FamilyLife Publishing, 2007), pp. 7-8.

June 5: Ibid., pp. 69-70.

June 6: Ibid., pp. 52-54.

June 9: Rainey, *Rekindling the Romance*, pp. 96-97.

June 12: Rainey, *Two Hearts Praying as One*, pp. 46-47.

June 15: Inspired by Nahal Toosi, "Amid a Bitter Divorce, a Wall Goes Up in Brooklyn Couple's House," *Oakland Tribune*, January 20, 2007.

June 20: Rainey, *Growing a Spiritually Strong Family*, pp. 16-17. Newspaper quotes from *The Tennessean*, August 6, 2006, p. 4a.

June 22: Tim Ghianni, "Who'da Thought that Bubble Wrap Could Change Lives?" *The Tennessean*, February 4, 2007.

June 26: Rainey, *Rekindling the Romance*, pp. 39-42.

June 29: Rainey, *Two Hearts Praying as One*, pp. 24-26.

June 30: Rainey, *Parenting Today's Adolescent*, pp. 146, 153-155.

July 1: Rainey, *Starting Your Marriage off Right*, pp. 252-254.

July 2: Research numbers from Timothy Egan, "The Rise of Shrinking-Vacation Syndrome," *New York Times*, August 20, 2006, and Alan Fram, "Poll: A Fifth Vacation with Laptops," Fox News.com, June 3, 2007.

July 3: Rainey, *Starting Your Marriage off Right*, pp. 255-256.

July 7: Ibid., pp. 141-144.

July 8: Dennis Rainey, *One Home at a Time*, pp. 64-66.

July 9: Rainey and Rainey Escue, *A Mother's Legacy*, pp. 9-12.

July 12: Rainey, *Parenting Today's Adolescent*, pp. 77-79.

July 13: Ibid., pp. 53-54.

July 16: Rainey, *Two Hearts Praying as One*, pp. 35-37.

July 17: Rainey, *Starting Your Marriage off Right*, pp. 206-207.

July 18: Ibid., pp. 207-209.

July 20: Rainey, *Rekindling the Romance*, p. 61.

July 22: Dennis Rainey, *Ministering to Twenty-first Century Families* (Nashville, TN: Thomas Nelson, 2001), pp. 76-78.

July 24: Rainey, *Pressure Proof Your Marriage*, pp. 64-65.

July 26: Rainey, *Starting Your Marriage off Right*, pp. 45-46.

July 29: Rainey, *Parenting Today's Adolescent*, pp. 71-72.

July 31: Information taken from Lynn Vincent, "Full Circle," *World Magazine*, November 11, 2006.

August 4: Rainey, *Parenting Today's Adolescent*, p. 198.

August 5: Ibid., p. 170.

August 6: Ibid., pp. 256-257.

August 8: Rainey, *Pressure Proof Your Marriage*, pp. 48-49.

August 17: Rainey, *Parenting Today's Adolescent*, pp. 164-165.

August 25: Ibid., pp. 28-30.

August 26: Rainey, *Rekindling the Romance*, pp. 50-52.

August 27: Ibid., pp. 52-53.

September 1: Rainey, *Staying Close*, pp. 242-243.

September 2: Ibid., pp. 242-243.

September 3: Ibid., pp. 241.

September 7: Rainey, *Parenting Today's Adolescent*, pp. 271-272.

September 18: Rainey, *Rekindling the Romance*, pp. 117-128.

September 21: Information from www.sundayriver.com/summer/wifecarry.html.

September 27: Rainey, *Parenting Today's Adolescent*, pp. 51-53.

September 30: Ibid., pp. 87-88.

October 2: Rainey, *Two Hearts Praying as One*, pp. 32-34.

October 17: David Ginsburg, "Gibbons Calls Foul After Plunking Wife with Ball," *USA Today*, September 24, 2006.

October 21: Lucinda Secrest McDowell, *Quilts from Heaven* (Nashville, TN: B&H Publishing Group, 2007), pp. 75-76. Used by permission.

October 22: Rainey, *Parenting Today's Adolescent*, pp. 3-4.

October 23: Ibid., pp. 12-13.

October 25: Rainey, *Rekindling the Romance,* pp. 214-217.

November 3: Rainey, *Starting Your Marriage off Right*, pp. 196-199.

November 9: WGN Sports Baseball Blog, May 4, 2005. http://www.wgntv.trb.com/sports/custom/weblog/wgnsports/archives/2005/05/index.html.

November 14: Patrick Condon, "Fed Up Parents Turn Against Birthday Parties," *Topeka Capitol-Journal*, January 22, 2007.

November 18: Dennis and Barbara Rainey, *Building Your Mate's Self-Esteem* (Nashville, TN: Thomas Nelson, 1995), pp. 114-116.

November 19: Rainey, *Parenting Today's Adolescent*, pp. 66-68.

November 23: Barbara Rainey, *Thanksgiving: A Time to Remember* (Wheaton, IL: Crossway Books, 2003), p. 45.

November 28: Rainey, *Pressure Proof Your Marriage*, pp. 81-84.

November 30: Danielle Crittenden, "Bad for the Health, But No One Dare Say So," *Wall Street Journal*, Eastern Edition, December 14, 2006, p. D6.

December 1: Rainey, *Pressure Proof Your Marriage*, pp. 61-62.

December 3: Ibid., pp. 59-60.

December 14: Rainey, *Two Hearts Praying as One*, pp. 43-45.

December 19: Rainey, *Parenting Today's Adolescent*, pp. 16-19.

From simple beginnings ...

FamilyLife
has journeyed
more than 30 years
to provide hope and healing
to marriages and families alike.
It's been a journey of faith in God's
provision here and around the world,
marked with milestones that clarify
God's plan for FamilyLife.

◆ Over the years more than a million people have
  attended a Weekend to Remember.

◆ In 1992 *FamilyLife Today*™ extended reach into
  an entirely new medium—radio.

◆ In 1986 cofounders, Dennis and Barbara Rainey,
  published their first of many books, *Building Your
  Mate's Self-Esteem.*

◆ More than 2 1/2 million copies of HomeBuilders
  have been sold.

The journey continues,
with the best years still to come.

FAMILYLIFE™
www.familylife.com

Your marriage.

Our conference.

Discover biblical truths and practical tools to
nourish your marriage and keep it growing.
Weekend to Remember is an experience
you'll never forget.

An Experience You'll Never Forget.

FAMILYLIFE™
www.familylife.com/weekend

HomeBuilders

The HomeBuilders Couples Series® and the HomeBuilders Parenting Series® are the fastest growing small-group studies in the country. These series are designed to help your relationships build and grow on the solid biblical principles found in God's Word.

HomeBuilders Couples Series®

There is no better way to build marriages than in the fun and friendly environment of HomeBuilders.

Leaders Guide
Preparing for Marriage
Resolving Conflict in Your Marriage
Keeping Your Covenant
Making Your Remarriage Last
Overcoming Stress in Your Marriage
Mastering Money in Your Marriage
Growing Together in Christ
Defending the Military Marriage
Protecting Your First Responder Marriage
Building Your Marriage
Building Teamwork in Your Marriage
Improving Communication in Your Marriage
Building Your Mate's Self-Esteem

HomeBuilders Parenting Series®

Come together with other parents, improve parenting skills, and share in fellowship. Face the struggles and successes of parenting with others.

Leaders Guide
Establishing Effective Discipline For
Your Children
Helping Your Children Know God
Raising Children of Faith
Improving Your Parenting
Considering Adoption
Building Character in Your Children
Guiding Your Teenagers
Defending the Military Family

FAMILYLIFE™

www.familylife.com/homebuilders

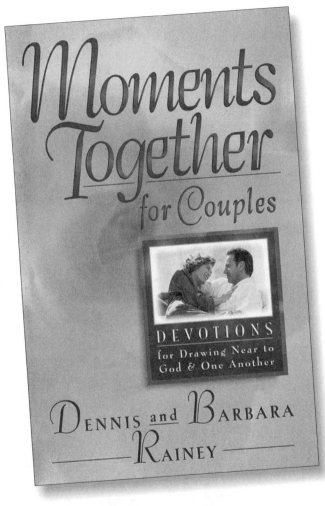

Also from Dennis and Barbara Rainey

More Devotions for Drawing Near to God and One Another

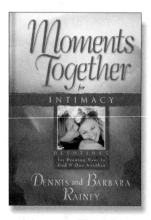
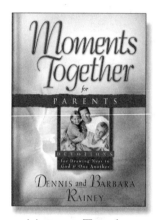
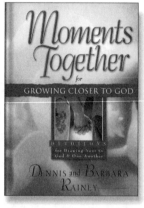

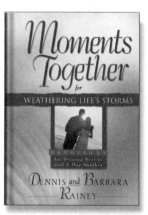
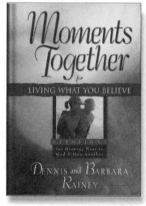